ADDITIONAL PRAISE FOR CROSS-BORDER MERGERS AND ACQUISITIONS

"Chinese companies are making record-high investments in overseas mergers and acquisitions (M&A), but most of them lack successful practices in those endeavors. This book describes the strategy formulation, transaction planning, execution, and post-merger integration. It provides practical and excellent guidance for cross-border M&A. This is an M&A reference tool worthy of in-depth and repeated reading. In particular, this book not only elaborates the impact of cultural differences in overseas M&A deal execution and post-merger integration, but also provides practical and effective measures to cope with them, which is worthy of special attention and learning by Chinese companies."

Lijun Liu, M&A Director of State Owned Asset,
China Minmetals Corporation

"The compilations of 10 contributors provide the holistic view of the art and science of integration with a continual focus on strategy alignment and drive for accretive value—remarkably overlooked and misunderstood by many IMO practitioners."

Jonathan E. Bunce, Senior Director, M&A Integration, Intel

"The reader will find many decades of hands-on cross-cultural leadership synthetized in practical concepts. The authors splendidly combine a holistic depiction with great depth on the critical topics. A must-read if you play any relevant role in a cross-border M&A or PMI."

Helio A. Castano, Vice President, Administration and
Integration, Bar-S Foods

"Most recent books about M&A focus on the need to ensure that the integration is based on the objectives and value drivers of the acquisition. In this book Whitaker takes this approach a step further by applying a cross-border lens. The result is both a good read and a great reference book for the M&A practitioner."

Pat Belotti, Director of Corporate Development Integration,
DocuSign

"A rich database for everyone involved in cross-border M&As; in many cases a 'must' in today's world with globally distributed value chains. The combination of both breadth and depth in one context will attract both professional managers and readers in search of knowledge in this area for the first time."

Arne Karlsson, Departing Chairman and Former CEO, Ratos

"Given my role at an M&A software company, I have read a library of M&A books. *Cross-Border Mergers and Acquisitions* easily rises to the must-read category for M&A practitioners at all levels. The material covers all topics comprehensively, makes complex situations easily understandable, and provides actionable advice to planning and executing global deals."

Ari J. Salonen, PhD, President, Midaxo

"Cross-border mergers and acquisitions are among the very few strategic moves that can change the competitive position of a company almost over-night. This book provides a unique and comprehensive perspective on how cross-border M&As must be prepared, executed, and managed over the long run. It is a must-read for executives, consultants, and students interested in the topic."

Bernard Garrette, Professor of Strategy and MBA Associate Dean, HEC Paris

"*Cross-Border Mergers and Acquisitions* provides the reader with practical, experience-based execution guidance in a complex area that is fraught with many value-destroying pitfalls. It's critical for M&A practitioners to understand the complexity and the cultural differences that are foundational to cross-border work. Without this understanding, value and synergy realization will be elusive."

Janet Phillips, Senior Director, M&A Integration, Symantec, Inc.

"China's cross-border M&A thrives in recent years as the result of great success in economic growth. Besides sustained enthusiasm of inbound investments, capital-rich Chinese investors are increasingly interested in overseas valuable assets, not only in order to acquire natural resources or market entry but also to fulfill the capability gaps in technologies, management, and so on. I find that this book provides comprehensive and practical knowledge in cross-border M&A and believe that it could be helpful for those emerging Chinese players and their global counterparts."

Yi Bao, CEO, Morgan Stanley Huaxin Securities, and Managing Director, Morgan Stanley

Cross-Border Mergers and Acquisitions

Cross-Border Mergers and Acquisitions

Edited by

SCOTT C. WHITAKER

WILEY

Library of Congress Cataloging-in-Publication Data:

Names: Whitaker, Scott C., 1963–
Title: Cross-border mergers and acquisitions / Scott C. Whitaker.
Description: Hoboken : Wiley, 2016. | Series: Wiley finance | Includes index.
Identifiers: LCCN 2016002841| ISBN 978-1-119-04223-5 (hardback) | ISBN
   978-1-119-22744-1 (ePDF) | ISBN 978-1-119-22745-8 (ePub) | ISBN
   978-1-119-26845-1 (obook)
Subjects: LCSH: Consolidation and merger of corporations. | BISAC: BUSINESS &
   ECONOMICS / Mergers & Acquisitions.
Classification: LCC HG4028.M4 W485 2016 | DDC 658.1/62—dc23
LC record available at http://lccn.loc.gov/2016002841

Printed in the United States of America

10 9 8 7 6 5 4 3 2 1

To our families, clients, and colleagues . . . and to Sheila
for keeping us all on task

Contents

PART FOUR

Unique Cross-Border M&A Transaction Scenarios

Preface

After *Mergers and Acquisitions Integration Handbook: Helping Companies Realize the Full Value of Acquisitions* (John Wiley & Sons, 2012) published, I realized that executives were looking for practical guides to handling the complex task of integration. They wanted books that were rooted in the realities of execution, not based on theory or outdated concepts.

Cross-Border Mergers and Acquisitions attempts to apply the same approach for handling global integrations. The book is a compilation from 10 mergers and acquisitions (M&A) professionals who together have experience handling hundreds of cross-border transactions across dozens of countries.

The authors bring perspectives on M&A from nine countries that represent the bulk of global M&A activity: the United States, the United Kingdom, France, Belgium, Germany, Sweden, Israel, Japan, and China.

Many mission-critical topics, including M&A strategy, integration, due diligence, and culture are covered in multiple chapters to allow the authors to share their respective experiences, and enable the reader to gain several different perspectives on many key subjects.

Note that several of the authors are writing in English as a second or even third language, which is quite impressive for such an intricate subject. While I have made efforts to mildly harmonize style differences across the book, I have tried to allow some of the country-specific nuances to show through to showcase the cultural point of view of the authors.

Cross-Border Mergers and Acquisitions is organized into four parts, each covering a wide range of M&A topics. Here's an at-a-glance summary of how the book is organized and what you will find in each section and chapter.

PART ONE: CROSS-BORDER STRATEGY AND DEAL PLANNING

This part provides some insights into the overall dynamics of the global M&A environment, along with some perspectives on region- and country-specific trends and nuances.

- Chapter 1, "Cross-Border Deal Evolution and Rationale," presents an overview of the evolution and rationale of cross-border deals, along with some general information on the overall M&A market—sizing of the current market, international development, existence of cycles, determinants of the M&A waves as an introduction to cross-border M&A evolution, and high-level specificities.
- Chapter 2, "Cross-Border M&A Strategy and Deal Planning Essentials," explores decision-making and strategic process approaches for managing cross-border integration activity.
- Chapter 3, "Legal, Financial, Social, and Political Interdependencies with Cross-Border Integration," introduces the key legal, financial, social, and political influences on, and implications of, cross-border mergers, acquisitions, and divestitures. It puts cross-border M&A programs in context within and between the jurisdictions and societies where the companies operate.
- Chapter 4, "Trends and Leading Practices in Global M&A," introduces important concepts related to strategic reasoning for doing the deal, along with the key phases and steps in the M&A life cycle. This chapter includes a step-by-step process that enables you to find and review potential targets for their fit, and introduces important issues related to cross-border due diligence, along with options and strategies for mitigating the execution risk in cross-border deals.
- Chapter 5, "Cross-Border M&A: Region- and Country-Specific Trends and Deal Planning Tips," delves into the countries and industries that dominate pre-deal M&A and what considerations are important when exploring cross-border opportunities.

PART TWO: CROSS-BORDER CULTURE AND LEADERSHIP ALIGNMENT

This part includes several chapters that explore how leadership and culture influence cross-border M&A.

- Chapter 6, "Leading during Cross-Border M&A," attempts to outline specific activities and practices leaders can take during an M&A event to help ensure transaction success and lay the foundation to make integration a core competency of their organizations.
- Chapter 7, "The Role of Culture in Cross-Border M&A," explains the importance of culture in a merger or integration environment,

and shows how to create awareness of cultural elements in both the deal teams and integration teams. The importance of company values in turning culture into a success driver for your deal is also explored.

■ Chapter 8, "Managing National Reactions and Sovereignty Issues," explores the "local" side of cross-border M&A and how region- and country-specific nuances such as regulatory constraints, sensitivities of local populations, unions, and many other areas can impact transactions.

PART THREE: CROSS-BORDER INTEGRATION, PLANNING, AND EXECUTION

This part includes an abundance of detail around the more tactical elements of cross-border integration, along with how country-specific nuances can impact planning and execution details.

■ Chapter 9, "Managing Pre-PMI Due Diligence," presents a methodical approach for cross-border due diligence based on lessons learned from hands-on project engagements, including a practical review of the due diligence process, and ingredients and tools to be applied in order to improve the quality of due diligence deliverables.

■ Chapter 10, "Ramping Up an Integration Management Office and Day One in Cross-Border Deals," provides a comprehensive understanding of the integration management office and describes activity to set up an IMO and to execute a successful Day One.

■ Chapter 11, "Integration Decision Making and Process Strategy in Cross-Border Deals," reviews the important factors that drive cross-border M&A success, including leadership styles and related decision-making and process development and change approaches.

■ Chapter 12, "Post-Merger Integration Process, Methodologies, and Tools," explores a multitude of integration planning and execution essentials across all phases of the M&A life cycle.

■ Chapter 13, "Managing Post-Merger Integration Globally," outlines various approaches for managing a PMI process in a cross-border scenario. This chapter also explores PMI governance concepts, managerial structure, roles and responsibilities, meeting management routines, and communications.

■ Chapter 14, "Country-Specific Trends and Tips for Integration Planning," outlines proven approaches for factoring cultures and work styles in cross-border integrations. The chapter also includes cultural tips and hints for the top three M&A countries along with key integration topics by region.

■ Chapter 15, "M&A and Post-Merger Integration Considerations for China and Japan," reviews the current trends and issues involving both inbound investment into China and Japan by foreign companies and outbound investment from China and Japan. It describes the motivations behind the inbound and outbound investments, and points out the critical issues that have significant impact on the success or failure of M&A projects in these countries.

■ Chapter 16, "Cross-Border Synergy Program Management," explores what to look for in cross-border deal synergies, and how to validate them during pre-deal planning. The chapter also explores how to structure a synergy program and track synergies until realized.

PART FOUR: UNIQUE CROSS-BORDER M&A TRANSACTION SCENARIOS

This brief part provides insight into some unique transaction scenarios and situations.

■ Chapter 17, "Managing Carve-Outs and Transition Service Agreements," describes what divestitures are, how they differ from integrations, and what the end state of a carve-out can look like. It goes on to describe the key contract associated with carve-outs, the transition service agreement, how it is structured, managed, and exited successfully.

■ Chapter 18, "Joint Ventures," explores some additional considerations on how to plan, structure, and execute joint venture agreements.

The topics chosen are intended to cover the most common planning- and execution-related elements of M&A transactions. I have also attempted to include a range of perspectives on region- and country-specific considerations to help readers appreciate the complexities associated with cross-border transactions.

About the Author

Scott Whitaker

https://www.linkedin.com/in/whitaker86

Scott has been involved in over two dozen mergers and acquisitions totaling nearly $100 billion in value. His industry experience includes health care, financial services, telecommunications, gaming, hospitality, chemicals, oil and gas, industrial manufacturing, retail, and consumer durables. Scott has worked in Canada, China, Europe, and Africa on a variety of assignments, and specializes in establishing integration management offices (IMOs) and helping companies develop integration playbooks. He holds a BA from the University of North Carolina at Chapel Hill and is the author of *Mergers and Acquisitions Integration Handbook: Helping Companies Realize the Full Value of Acquisitions.*

Scott resides in Atlanta, Georgia.

About the Contributors

Eitan Grosbard
https://il.linkedin.com/in/eitanbenizhak
Eitan has over 20 years of experience managing complex M&A life cycle management engagements (especially due diligence and post-merger integration projects). He's led dozens of M&A projects and programs for midcap global companies in a variety of industries but mainly in the high-tech arena (Internet, telecom, software, hardware, and more).

Eitan is a strategy expert working with blue chip companies, and is currently a project faculty member of the Global Consulting Program at the Wharton Business School (University of Pennsylvania). He holds an Executive MBA from Tel Aviv University and is fluent in English, Spanish, and Hebrew.

Eitan resides in Tel Aviv, Israel.

Stefan Hofmeyer
https://www.linkedin.com/in/hofmeyer
Stefan started his career at Accenture in the mid-1990s and is an established expert delivering management rigor to M&A integration settings across Europe, Asia, North America, and Middle East business environments. Stefan holds a BSE in industrial engineering from the University of Iowa and an MBA from Pepperdine University. He also has completed advanced management education at Harvard Business School and Stanford University and holds both Project Management Professional and Stanford Certified Project Manager certifications.

Stefan resides in San Francisco, California.

Michael Holm
https://se.linkedin.com/in/michaelholm2
Michael has 28 years of operative industry experience, including roles in M&A, post-merger integration, and strategy. He has project-managed nationwide telecommunication network installations and research and development projects; marketed and sold telecommunication networks; and managed large accounts and line units. He spent the remainder of his career in strategy, M&A, and post-merger integration at Ericsson.

Michael's expertise is in M&A strategy, M&A screening, integration pre-planning, integration lead, integration management office mobilization and execution, synergy management, divestiture planning, and transitional services management. He has led post-merger integrations in telecom, professional services, and fast-moving consumer goods industries. He has lived in Canada, Korea, Taiwan, the United States, and the United Kingdom, as well as worked on many M&A projects in the United States, Europe, and Asia.

Michael resides in Stockholm, Sweden.

Makoto Ideno

https://jp.linkedin.com/pub/makoto-ideno/62/b21/52/en

Makoto is an experienced M&A integration consultant located in Tokyo. He has many years of experience in integration management office, sales, and marketing process designs, communication planning and implementation, cultural convergence, and HR in industries such as health care/pharmaceuticals, system integration, advertising, and retail. Project highlights include the financial value analysis of a medical information company, negotiations with a telecom carrier on M&A, and the design and implementation of culture convergence in procurement. He holds an MBA from the Marshall School of Business at the University of Southern California.

Makoto resides in Tokyo, Japan.

Thomas Kessler

https://de.linkedin.com/in/thomashkessler

Thomas is a business executive with decades of U.S., European, and Asian experience in the field of merger integration and investment banking. He has a passion for M&A integration, supporting businesses in managing the integration of transactions and joint ventures. He has supported over 30 merger integrations from large to midsized and national to international as well as public, private, and family-owned businesses. Thomas is also a frequent keynote speaker and trainer on pre- and post-merger integration and has taught trainings around the world. He holds a BBA from Mannheim University, Germany, an MBA, summa cum laude, from Business School Lausanne, and a Master of Science from Frankfurt University.

Thomas resides in Bonn, Germany.

Gilles Ourvoie

https://fr.linkedin.com/in/gourvoie

Gilles has nearly 30 years of international experience in corporate strategy, organizational design, and mergers and acquisitions, with a growing focus on PMI in the past 15 years. He has led teams in all aspects of strategy and M&A, from strategy analysis, financial analysis to merger negotiation, post-acquisition design and execution, and optimization of M&A organizations and processes. He holds an MSc from HEC and an MSc from the University of Paris-Dauphine. He holds also a PhD certificate from the Conservatoire National des Arts & Metiers. He has lived in Mali, the United States, Italy, Lebanon, Morocco, and Russia.

Giles resides in Paris, France.

Andrew Scola

https://uk.linkedin.com/in/scola

Andrew is an experienced M&A integration and separation advisor, having worked within PwC and Deloitte for many years, as Head of Acquisition Integration for a global health care company and as the UK Partner for Global PMI Partners, which he co-founded in 2009. He has worked with clients across technology, financial services, health care, and consumer business. He holds an honors degree from the University of Nottingham, has worked with the Cass Business School mentoring students with M&A research projects, and is currently working with Sheffield Hallam University on a cross-border M&A research project.

Andrew resides in London, United Kingdom.

Christophe Van Gampelaere

https://be.linkedin.com/in/christophevangampelaere

Christophe is an M&A-oriented advisor, trainer, and practitioner. He combines his expertise in finance and investment management with people skills, and has worked internationally on iconic deals in the automotive, semiconductor, chemicals, telecom, media, and banking sectors. He is a certified coach, Lego® Serious Play® and Company Constellations facilitator. He is passionate about nature.

Christophe resides in Ghent, Belgium.

Masaki Yamamoto

https://jp.linkedin.com/pub/masaki-yamamoto/1/889/b17

Masaki has nearly 25 years of consulting experience in corporate strategy, R&D management, new business strategy, organization design, business process design, project management, and human resources development. His M&A expertise is in M&A strategy, integration management office, business process design, organization redesign back office integration, and sales channel integration. He has led many consulting projects in due diligence, organization redesign, overseas investment, business process redesign sales channel design, PMO, and human resources development. He teaches at the graduate school of Kyushu Institute of Technology. He holds an MA from the University of Tokyo and an MBA from the Marshall School of Business at the University of Southern California.

Masaki resides in Tokyo, Japan.

Robert Ping Yu (於平)

https://cn.linkedin.com/in/robertyu1

Robert has over 25 years of business strategy and operational experience in both consulting and Fortune 500 multinational companies such as Motorola and Pearson. He is a bilingual senior executive with a track record of driving corporate growth through successful development and execution of corporate strategy, especially in M&A, post-merger integration, and business performance improvement. His expertise includes corporate growth strategy, product marketing, strategic alliance, and M&A management. Born in Beijing, China, Robert lived in the United States for nearly 20 years before returning to China. Robert has not only a broad understanding of Western multinational corporate cultures and operations but also has deep insights into Chinese traditions and behaviors. He holds an Executive MBA from the Kellogg School of Management at Northwestern University.

Robert resides in Beijing, China.

Cross-Border Strategy and Deal Planning

Cross-Border Deal Evolution and Rationale

Gilles Ourvoie

CHAPTER LEARNING OBJECTIVES—IN THIS CHAPTER, YOU WILL LEARN:

➤ How cross-border deals have evolved over time and what key lessons we can draw from such analysis.

➤ At the firm level, what the main strategic motives are for cross-border deals and to what extent microeconomic factors influence the success of a deal.

➤ More generally, what the main factors influencing cross-border deals are, from global to micro levels, and how they can be correlated with cross-border deal success.

CHAPTER SUMMARY

Mergers and acquisitions (M&A) transactions in general, and decisions to engage in a deal, are connected to a wide number of internal and external factors that have been thoroughly analyzed over the past century. Even if the specific analysis of cross-border deals is more recent and therefore limited, any decision maker should have a view of the main economic forces at stake and how they might influence the M&A and PMI outcome. Building on this knowledge brings as well a better view of the potential determinants of any cross-border deal, and how these determinants may be part of the due diligence process. This chapter aims to provide this general background information, with a view of potentially improving the quality of the decision-making process and the end result of the transaction.

THE EVOLUTION OF M&A AND CROSS-BORDER DEALS

To understand the cross-border mergers and acquisitions (M&A) phenomenon, one has to look back to get some perspectives. The M&A market is historically a recent phenomenon, which has been linked to a certain form of economic development based in particular on fungible shares easily negotiable on markets.

The M&A market's evolution shows a globalization of this tool as a leading business transformation mechanism. However, this mechanism of ownership change and corporate value transformation has ups and downs. And there are still some major differences between countries in terms of how cross-border M&As are accepted and used.

Moreover, the analysis of these different M&A waves over a long period of time has yielded some details about the rationale for such transactions. A wide number of parameters have been connected to cross-border deals. We try here to provide an overview of the types of factors at play (both internally in the firm and externally), with the view that most of these factors play at different geographical levels (local, national, and global).

It is also important to note that cross-border deals are far more complex to achieve than purely domestic ones. The necessity to analyze business conditions abroad and gaps with domestic business conditions is a challenging intellectual process one should not underestimate.

The M&A market has been expanding globally to new territories and new sectors for more than a century. The number of countries in the world that are aware of such transactions is increasing, and the number of sectors concerned by cross-border deals is increasing as well.

However, this general expansion and commoditization of international M&A is far from linear; the market has had upward and downward movements, much like the financial stock market.

The M&A and cross-border market has its ups and downs, and executives must understand where they stand in terms of market situation to surf on the right waves. The timing aspect of a deal is an important element of success in order to pay at the right level of multiple and benefit from positive economic conditions to quickly finance the investment.

M&A: A Resilient Market[1]

The global M&A market is quite volatile. The year 2014 was a renaissance for the M&A market, and this growth has continued in 2015, surpassing the 10% expected growth.[2] This upswing comes after a prolonged financial and economic global crisis that began in the United States in 2007 with the mortgage crisis. This financial accident caused increased budget deficits all over the world (United States, United Kingdom, Spain, Portugal, Italy, France, and so on) when nations attempted to cope with the economic downturn and increased unemployment. This, in turn, generated more trading chaos, this time in sovereign debt and public and private bond rates, jeopardizing, in particular, the most vulnerable countries (Greece, Spain, and Italy). To cope with this phenomenon, public austerity measures were taken to limit budget deficits (Europe). This eventually hit the global economy and caused five to seven years of gross domestic product (GDP) negative to low growth. And all of these problems have not been entirely solved yet.

In parallel, new conflicts have grown from local ones (Libya, Egypt, Sub-Saharan Africa, Syria, Yemen, Ukraine) into new global risks (jihadist terrorism, cyber-war, migrating populations). The BRICS (Brazil, Russia, India, China, South Africa) nations seem headed into an era of lower growth, and their role as the economic engine of the world appears weaker—with lower oil and gas prices (Russia) and growing local reactions against corrupt elites and social inequalities (China, Brazil): How will they fund their investments in infrastructure, education, and technologies? This high-level picture shows to what extent the connection of M&A and the general economic and geopolitical context is a complex one, based on a wide range of factors and not strictly connected to financial market optimism or GDP accelerated growth perspectives.

In an upward cycle, the global value of the M&A market increases far quicker than the underlying GDP. In 2014, the M&A market reached its highest level since 2007 with $3.3t of announced deals in value. This climbed to $4.7t in 2015, after two years at about a 40% annual growth rate. Actually completed deals are a bit below in terms of growth: +15% in 2014 and +25% in 2015 to reach $2.5t. These growth rates are to be compared with global GDP growth of between 1% and 7% in the most important economies. There is no quicker way for a firm to reach critical size and competitiveness. Altice reflects this hypergrowth acquisitive strategy in the telecoms and cable sector, with four acquisitions achieved in 18 months: Suddenlink ($9b of deal value) and Cablevision ($15b) in the United States and Portugal Telecom ($7b) and SFR ($13b) in Europe—among other deals achieved by the group.

This M&A growth is based on an important but almost stable number of deals. There were 42,220 transactions announced worldwide in 2014, and 42,313 in 2015. This represents about 3,500 deals worldwide on a monthly basis compared to a low of 600–800 in the worst year (2009), or about 115 new deals every single day. This important number of deals has a direct impact on the entire M&A business: in a dynamic market, the number of commercial opportunities is high as well for investors, bankers, lawyers, accountants, and consultants. As a consequence, the number of players in the industry is high, as is the competition among them.

The average value of deals has grown more in 2015 than the number of deals. In each active M&A phase, it has been noted that the value of M&A deals (based on the firms' market capitalization) increases significantly.[3] In 2014, 95 deals closed with over $5b of value. In 2015, 71 announced deals have been over $10bn in value, the highest level ever. M&A players (banks, corporations, private equity firms) have been able to more easily fund such complex deals. Deal value is an important factor in terms of both profits for the M&A industry and technical innovation. Mega-mergers tend to be projects where the level of high complexity and the existence of important resources make it possible to make progress on methods. Service providers tend to learn and invest in mega-projects, and then leverage this experience on smaller projects. Logically, the more a firm or country experiments with mega-mergers, the more its teams or nationals innovate and benefit from a sort of comparative advantage.[4]

A Geographically Spreading Market

The international expansion of the M&A market is a major factor. All regions grew at a fast pace in 2014 (36%–56% year on year), except for the Middle East and Africa. In 2015, Europe was the least active region with only an 8% growth rate, while Japan and Asia-Pacific were the most active ones (+62%). This illustrates the pursuit of the globalization trend and the growing use of similar business strategies worldwide.

The Americas remain by far the most active M&A market worldwide. They accounted for 53% of the total value in 2015 ($2.5t of deals announced, $2.3t of which were in the United States). In the United States, large transformational deals in the health care, high-tech, and energy sectors have fueled the market. Buyers have been essentially strategic ones, benefiting from strong cash positions, high stock market levels, and low interest rates due to the "quantitative easing" monetary policy. In 2014, regulatory and tax aspects have also justified a number of "cash inversion" deals from European firms into the United States. About 50% of the deals have been equity based. The increasing role of activists has been a key element of change in 2014, although less so in 2015.

Europe at large is now the third-largest M&A market. It accounted, however, for only 36% of the value of the deals in the Americas in 2015, versus 50% in 2014. In terms of global market share, in 2015 Europe represented less than 20% of the global market ($907b). After having been the most active region in 2014 (+55% annual growth rate), the area has experienced a quasi-stagnation of 8% growth due mostly to the French downturn (–45%).

In Europe, investments from Chinese and other Asian countries have been pushing the market up, as have intra-European consolidation deals. The main sectors involved were consumer staples, energy, industrials, and pharma. In 2014, it was pharma, industrials, luxury goods, and financial services. Low economic growth rates, uncertainties about the European evolution (potential withdrawal of the United Kingdom, failing euro due to the implementation of a QE policy, lasting questions about a potential "Grexit," and conflict in Ukraine), and growing geopolitical difficulties have limited the 2014 rebound.

Asia-Pacific including Japan is now more active than Europe. It represented 26% of the market in 2015 versus 22% in 2014 ($1,242b). The main sectors are industrials, high tech, and financials as opposed to consumer, retail, and leisure in 2014. Asian outbound activity is still focused on the United States and Europe, but is becoming more and more global.

Middle East and Africa are still marginal markets. These regions accounted only for less than 2% of the 2015 market value ($80b versus $65b in 2014). Despite getting more and more private equity and financial attention, M&A transactions have been decreasing there due to political uncertainty, ongoing stumbling oil prices, and slow structural reforms.

Strong Lasting National Differences

The general M&A growth has virtuous consequences on future deals. As an M&A national market grows, it allows better access to competencies, a better circulation of information of the general public, better regulatory frameworks, and growing popular acceptance of M&A transactions as a managerial tool. Drilling into details, this also means better investor protection, better accounting standards, banking laws, financial and economic informational flows, corporate governance regulations, and compliance procedures, and increased market scrutiny by the financial press or activists. All these elements secure investment forecasts and multiply potential inward deals, even if valuation and transaction costs are a bit higher.

But in spite of the geographical expansion of M&A, there are still significant differences between countries. Deal-makers must pay attention to these differences, and not assume that what they see in their home country will be replicated in other contexts. This "principle of caution" will reduce considerably the causes of failure in a cross-border deal.

First and foremost, major differences exist between advanced and emerging countries. Country-specific differences are critical in explaining why funds go preferably to more advanced economies (the Lucas paradox[5]). These differences may cover a wide array of intertwined aspects: laws, national economic performance, as well as institutional quality.[6] Getting into more details, factors such as political instability, statewide corruption, weak or unimplemented laws, and inefficient administrations tend to limit transactions. Inbound investments are as a consequence higher in more advanced economies, where paradoxically the costs related to regulation, labor, or other institutional elements are higher.

But there are also significant gaps between advanced economies. Advanced economies, with comparable levels of institutional quality and high standards of administrative work, do vary a lot as to their M&A markets. This has to do with other more subtle differences, such as how banks relate to companies, how access to privileged information is channeled through, how tax, human resources (HR), or other rules monitor accepted business behaviors and corporate decisions, how the institutions and jurisprudence support or limit corporate growth strategies, how education and society design national cultural patterns, and so on. As a result of this bundling of multiple factors, whether they are solid facts or just perceptions, M&As do not play the same role in advanced economies.

Table 1.1 provides a simplified view of such national differences in terms of M&A activity. Based on 2014 figures, we can read this information in two different ways.

- The *M&A value/GDP* ratio shows to what extent the national economy is exposed to M&A transactions, and hence to what extent M&A is significant in terms of boosting economic change and business reorganizations.
- The reverse, the ratio *GDP/M&A value* ("Avg. control life span"), provides a measure of the time spent in a standard national firm between major control changes. A low ratio means a quick pace of change with a broad set of impacts on governance rules, job reallocations, geographical delocalization, investment priorities, and close-down of a number of sites. The more this ratio goes down, the more people and firms know about M&A consequences and tend to adjust their behaviors accordingly. A quick change in this ratio can also generate local resistance and difficulties.

We can distinguish four major types of national M&A markets. Based on these two ratios, we can distinguish countries according to their level of national M&A activity:

Type A—Balanced Markets. The main cluster is made of quite open economies (United Kingdom, France, Canada, Australia, South Korea). Deal values account for 5%–6% of the national GDP. Firms based locally have on average a capital control stability ratio ("control life span") of 15–20 years.

Type B—Outbound Markets. A very different cluster is made up of Germany and Japan. Deals here represent only about 1%–2% of the GDP. The ownership life-cycle ratio is far longer at 50–100 years on average. This slow motion in capital mobility is due to the structure of the firms, their capacity to finance their growth domestically and abroad, and their solid and long-term links with their ecosystems. This is close to what has been called the "Rhenish capitalistic model," as opposed to the Anglo-Saxon one. It does not mean German or Japanese firms are not active on the M&A market—they do have more outbound deals.

Type C—Very Active Markets. The United States shows a very high level of M&A volume, with an 8.8% rate in 2014. The capital control life span is far shorter than in other countries despite the global size of the economy, at about 11 years. This data, however, has to be partly discounted due to phenomena like "cash inversion" deals, which do not really represent major changes in the strategy of the firms.

Type D—Transition Markets. China is an interesting illustration of transition markets, as it is more active than Germany or Japan. China may well be using M&A deals and changes of control to foster corporate transformation, increase productivity and production, and create national champions before getting into the international M&A market.

TABLE 1.1 M&A National Gaps

Country	Number of Deals (target)	Value of Deals ($ b)	Average Value of Deals ($ m)	GDP ($ b)	M&A Volume/ GDP	Average Control Life Span
United States	9,802	1,531	156	17,419	8.79%	11.4
China	4,520	390	86	10,380	3.76%	26.6
United Kingdom	2,423	177	73	2,945	6.01%	16.6
France	2,040	165	81	2,847	5.80%	17.3
Canada	1,670	111	66	1,789	6.20%	16.1
Australia	1,229	81	66	1,444	5.61%	17.8
Germany	1,516	73	48	3,860	1.89%	52.9
South Korea	1,095	65	59	1,417	4.59%	21.8
Japan	2,115	65	31	4,616	1.41%	71.0

Sources: Thomson Reuters, International Monetary Fund.

Long-Term Evolution: The Concept of M&A Waves

One major aspect of the M&A market is that it is a cyclical one. Historical research—mostly focusing on the U.S. market first—has shown the existence of cycles in M&A activity almost since the mid-nineteenth century. The existence of such a synchronicity of M&A deals has been confirmed by more recent research covering several countries.[7] This extensive research brings powerful insights about the determinants and the strategic motives of cross-border deals. Table 1.2 provides a synthesis of these waves.

From a business standpoint, what does this wave concept entail? We may draw here a number of ideas aimed at M&A and PMI professionals:

- Timing has a direct consequence on negotiation possibilities and pricing. In our own survey on cross-border integration,[8] the company share price/valuation was considered by a sample of 115 M&A professionals as both the most important deal driver and the most successfully delivered, above sales growth, cost reduction, customer retention, and several other categories in both aspects.

- Good timing is not always short term. M&A markets are not stable over time. Volumes and values may increase and decrease significantly due to a number of factors. Too often, deals are driven by chance or individual contacts between C-level executives rather than by economic or strategic forecasts. The impact of this is all the more important as complex deals may be suffering major delays—for example, it took three years between 2011 and 2014 for RHJ International to obtain agreement from the Federal Financial Supervisory Authority (BaFin; Germany) and close the acquisition of BHF-Bank from Deutsche Bank.[9] Firms should ensure a long-term tracking of the M&A market situation and potential impacts on their growth strategy.

- **The management of M&A resources should be less short-term oriented to optimize countercyclical situations.** In a cyclical market, the general availability of M&A resources at large is very variable. In low M&A markets, firms tend to reduce their internal skills and this may hinder their decisions. Banks may also limit their staff and tighten their lending conditions. Benefiting more easily from an increased mobility of skills and assets is possible in growing M&A markets. When a group has sufficient resources and triggers long-term business portfolio growth, it should invest in its M&A resources as in a normal recurring process (such as purchasing or research and development [R&D]). It is too often not the case, with several negative side effects (lack of anticipation of issues, increased risks, suboptimization of the due diligence process, and poor post-merger integration planning and delivery).

▪ **Firms must have a competitive intelligence process in place to alert on any potential major market disruption.** We have seen that the M&A waves are influenced by many factors, not just financial ones. Regulation, technology, geopolitics, and many other elements may change a competitive situation and boost opportunities or freeze initiatives. This must be discussed internally and regularly and viewed with a three-to-five-year perspective so that there is sufficient time ahead to plan and implement an M&A deal.

▪ **Stakeholder management techniques should be applied in the M&A field to get a consistent view of M&A market trends and changes.** We have seen that banks and M&A advisors are key in the pace and intensity of the wave. It is thus critical to manage the interfaces with them, so that the insights they provide can be optimized. For instance, making sure there is a systematic feedback of the formal or informal contacts with bankers or lawyers on the market situation to the M&A and corporate development team is useful.

The Determinants of M&A Waves

Determinants versus strategic motives. It is useful to make a point on the difference between two types of elements supporting a deal. On the one hand, a firm may pursue specific strategic goals (i.e., economies of scale, access to new markets or skills). These goals will depend on its competitive position, its resources, and other factors that depend very much on the firm. On the other hand, at a statistical level, M&A deals appear to be quite well synchronized around cycles. The problem therefore is to understand why firms, pursuing very different strategic goals with different timing, may have an interest and an advantage in executing their deals according to a general cycle sequence, building on determinants that are located more at the country level or international level than at the firm level.

The concept of the M&A wave has been very productive in terms of identifying the determinants of these cycles. The historical analysis of these M&A waves has highlighted a wide range of M&A market drivers that evolve over time.[10] Figure 1.1 provides a synthetic view of the potential different types of drivers.

TABLE 1.2 U.S. M&A Waves

	1897–1904	1916–1929	1965–1969	1981–1989	1993–2000
Context	▪ Post-1883 depression ▪ Rail transport development	▪ Post-WWI growth period ▪ Car development, radio (advertisment) ▪ Easy access to funding—increasing role of investment banking	▪ Booming economy—weak role of investment bankers ▪ Development of the MBA ▪ Development of stock financing due to increasing PEs	▪ Deregulation trend: airlines, drugs, and medical equipment ▪ Financial innovation: new financing solutions (junk bonds) ▪ Role of investment bankers/lawyers in aggressive deals—increasing fees (Drexel Burnham Lambert) ▪ SEC position in favor of free market competition	▪ Extension of deregulation: banking, insurance, telecoms, high tech ▪ Internet ▪ Increased equity funding ▪ Increasing cross-border deals with the U.S.
End date	▪ 1904 depression	▪ 1929 financial crisis (Black Tuesday)	▪ Vietnam War and 1973 oil crisis	▪ 1990–1991 recession	▪ 2001 Internet speculative bubble crash and the high corporate debt level
Number of transactions	▪ 3,000	▪ 4,600	▪ 6,000	▪ 23,000	▪ 50,000
Impact	▪ Increased concentration ▪ Stricter anti-trust: Clayton Act (1914)	▪ Celler-Kefauver Act (1950)	▪ Tax Reform Act in 1969 against "paper gains" due to accounting mechanisms	▪ Development of anti-takeover techniques (golden parachutes, poison pills)	▪ First global M&A wave ▪ Development of oligopolistic situations ▪ Development of valuation techniques/due diligence

	1897–1904	1916–1929	1965–1969	1981–1989	1993–2000
Goals	▓ Economies of scale in production and distribution	▓ Merging for oligopoly ▓ Product extension, market extension	▓ Growth and profitability ▓ Functional optimization	▓ Shareholder value	▓ Globalization
Sectors impacted	▓ Mining, manufacturing, banking	▓ Metals, oil products, food products, chemicals, transport equipment		▓ Oil and gas, drugs and medical equipment	▓ Banking, telecoms
Type of deals	▓ 78% horizontal integration ▓ Large number of firms involved (75% over 5 firms) ▓ Some hostile bids—first takeover battle in 1868 (Erie Railroad by Vanderbilt)		▓ 80% conglomerate ▓ Small deals	▓ Mega-deals ▓ Hostile mergers—"corporate raiders" ▓ High debt leverage (LBOs/MBOs)	▓ Large deals but no significant impact on concentration ▓ More strategic deals—fewer sell-offs
Examples	▓ US Steel/Carnegie Steel, Dupont, Standard Oil, General Electric, Eastman Kodak, American Tobacco	▓ Conglomerates: Allied Chemical (GE, Solvay, Chemical) IBM, General Motors, Union Carbide	▓ ITT, Revlon	▓ KKR–RJR Nabisco (USD25bn)	▓ Daimler-Chrysler

Data from Patrick A. Gaughan, *Mergers, Acquisitions and Corporate Restructurings*, 2nd ed. (New York: John Wiley & Sons, 1999), 21–59.

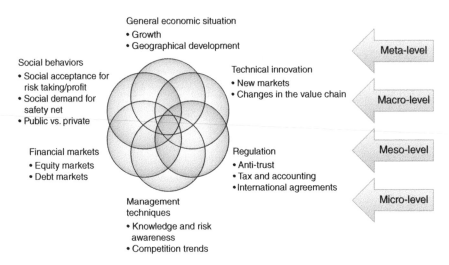

FIGURE 1.1   M&A Drivers

Each of these driving factors may have different levels of influence. We can distinguish between four major levels of forces interacting with M&A and PMI developments:

1. At the global level ("meta-level"), global forces are at stake, such as the launching of a QE program in several countries helping banks to develop credit lending, or the international development of public austerity measures to cut budget deficits.
2. At the national level ("macro-level"), national changes have an influence (e.g., a new government elected, with a new economic program, or a new anti-trust regulation). Research has shown that cross-border deals increase globally about one year before national elections, to cope with potential domestic law or regulatory changes.[11]
3. At the industry level ("meso-level"), industry-related factors may also favor or jeopardize M&A deals (e.g., a drastic change in the pricing of specific raw materials, or the introduction of a new technical application).
4. At the firm level ("micro-level"), there are also corporate-related forces that resonate with the global trends above (e.g., a new strategy following the arrival of a new chief executive officer [CEO]).

Each of these M&A driving factors may be viewed as a decisive competitive advantage at the firm level.[12] The situation of the bidder vis-à-vis each driving force has wide-ranging consequences in terms of securing an M&A deal. For instance, a firm benefiting from a good credit rating score and a low corporate bond rate has an edge over its competitors and may fund deals generating economies and further profits. To take another perspective, firms benefiting from a good headquarters (HQ) location may build on a fast access to information and skills, funnel their investments in a better way, and trigger more synergies. This is clearly what has happened in the past decade with the GAFA firms (Google, Amazon, Facebook, Apple). It is the job of corporate development to conduct such strategic analysis and business intelligence review in order to identify the most differentiating competitive factors and relate this information to the M&A strategy and plan.

Why should M&A strategy be directly connected to the anticipation of business disruptions? M&A waves tend to start with a major business disruption, that is, a phenomenon that has an impact on how executives can analyze and execute new M&A strategies. These disruptions may be of a different nature, but in the last few decades, technology (mass usage of PCs, Internet, mobile telecoms, connected objects) and regulatory or political changes have played a major role. This plays out at a global level, but also at the national level. Future trends, and potential global or local market disruptions, need therefore to be clearly identified and discussed within firms, with M&A-contingent strategies designed accordingly. Such disruptions are permanent if the perspective is global—countries need to reform past codes, to modernize their economy. Thus it should be considered as a normal part of the job of a CEO and of any executive to think about the next potential disruptions, not only to anticipate M&A deals but also to improve existing business. In reality, due to organizational inertia, management conformism, authoritarian management style, top-down myopia, management hubris, and other managerial mistakes, disruptions play into the Schumpeterian concept of inevitable economic destruction. To mitigate such risks, firms should pay particular attention to recruiting young people as well as strong independent personalities, proactively manage the creative potential of their staff, and maintain the anticonformist attitude of the start-ups that by definition bet on market disruptions.

If M&A waves build on business disruptions, deals need economic visibility to be rationalized and executed. M&A deals depend on positive economic anticipations: development of financial markets and new funding options, high stock valuations, increasing GDP growth rate and market demand, high level of corporate profits and in-excess cash, and so on. Such assumptions are key for buyers to secure the acquired assets. Volatile and uncertain markets increase the risk of actually delivering the stand-alone plan plus the synergies, and this in turn increases the related cost of capital and debt, as well as the need for efficiencies. Finding the right balance between business opportunism and deal rationalization is one of the most important success factors in the pre-deal phase.

M&A waves favor specific types of corporate strategies—not all of them. The historical analysis of M&A waves has shown that in each phase, firms have focused on specific high-level strategic goals. Three major axes of development have been identified—they are still very much applicable to current deal logic:

1. **Horizontal integration** and the consolidation of market shares. The corporate objective here is to benefit from excess profit due to improved negotiation power with clients or regulators (e.g., the case of AT&T in the early history of telecoms). Leading groups may emerge in this process ("national champions"), with sufficient resources and domestic margins to buy foreign competitors and grow abroad.
2. **Vertical integration** and control over the value chain. The development of production volumes increases the complexity of supply and logistics. This in turn forces firms to improve the reliability of the supplies. Insourcing part of the margins of the intermediates may also be profitable. This reintermediation strategy is, however, partly balanced by value-chain disintermediation strategic moves developed by growing specialized firms providing better costs and services ("core competencies"). The introduction of new distant quality control methods supported by better IT systems and methods regularly redefines the advantages and limits of outsourcing some aspects of the value chain.
3. **Product diversification** and the creation of conglomerates. Leading firms have very early focused on diminishing the volatility of cash flows and risks. The diversification of businesses enables them to benefit from different economic cycles and lessen the generation of cash (e.g., in the car industry with the acquisition of financial services assets). This strategy is regularly challenged by the need to focus resources to gain size.

Each M&A wave values specific funding strategies. M&A waves have shown varying funding preferences between cash, equity, and debt. This depends very much on the availability of innovative solutions, the risks induced, and the cost of funding to be paid. Any major change in such aspects has an impact on the potential deals. Low interest rates, as they are today, are in favor of M&A deals, as well as temporary high stock markets and the availability of cash for potential buyers. Chief financial officers must have a clear view of the potential options and market trends so that the M&A strategy may be more quickly supported by shareholders, bankers, or investment funds.

Each M&A wave may also favor some types of players against others. Buyers change over time with economic and regulatory conditions. Executive teams must have a proactive management of their potential stakeholders. To simplify, there are three major types of bidders, each with specific constraints and competitive edges:

1. *Strategic buyers* represent the bulk of the M&A markets. Their investment duration is linked to their strategy, but in principle they have no

exit deadline. Strategic buyers build on their knowledge of their industry to pursue long-term industrial synergies, increase their market share, and gain economies of scale and scope through internal optimization of processes, skills, and assets.

2. The development of financial investment tools and resources has increased the role of *financial investors* in the global M&A market. They account now for about a third of the deal values. They focus more on finance organization and reporting mechanisms, general governance, and the follow-up of transformation plans. Their investment duration is between 3 and 10 years.

3. A new type of player ("activists") is emerging as a sort of extension of this form of capitalist view of the firm. Activists promote quicker and focused actions. Their actions may be related to financial profits but not only, as they may promote some specific views of strategic priorities (e.g., the case of BP in the United Kingdom, with activists having forced the group to make progress on its climate change strategy).

Last, firms must also take the view that the M&A wave will end. Historically, M&A waves have ended with political crisis or even wars. Thanks to this historical experience, such crises have recently been managed with fewer dramatic consequences, but they have nevertheless ended with significant financial crises of global impact (the Internet bubble blowup in 2001 and mortgage-based securities in 2007). Very often, the beginning of the next phase has been linked to the evolution of the regulatory aspects that had led to the previous crisis—a mechanism that is very close to trial-and-error. The latest example of such an iterative process is the U.S. regulatory change to limit "cash-inversion" deals in 2014.

Cross-Border Deals and Evolution

Cross-border deals have been far less tracked and analyzed than M&A as a whole. Based on our own databases of research articles, we estimate that cross-border analysis represents only between 20% and 30% of the total number of publications. A 2015 comprehensive literature review[13] on determinants of cross-border mergers and acquisitions lists about 240 articles. Most publications have also focused on U.S. and Anglo-Saxon transactions: There is less research on the different European countries, and almost none on the transactions being done in emerging countries—inbound or outbound. This should progressively change both with the increasing internationalization of the M&A market, and the development of national education and research programs on finance and management.

Cross-border deals now represent a major and relatively stable segment of the M&A market. They accounted for 33% of the total M&A volume in

2015, against 37% in 2014 and 31% in 2013. They have represented $1.6t of value (+27% of growth year-on-year). This is the equivalent of the GDP of Mexico in 2014, the 15th richest economy in the world, or more than twice the GDP of Switzerland.

Cross-border deals have increased from 0.5% to about 2% of the worldwide GDP between 1980 and 2000.[14] In 2014, based on the previous figures, cross-border deals have accounted for about 1.7% of world GDP of 77.3t.[15] This figure represents what many economists now consider a "new normal" for world GDP growth. In other words, the cross-border M&A market represents about a year of GDP growth worldwide.

Major Specificities of Cross-Border Deals

Cross-border deals are more complex than domestic deals. The number of parameters to think about and anticipate at pre-deal level in an M&A deal is huge—and it is easy to understand that a cross-border deal increases that level of complexity. As an example, the Holcim-Lafarge Swiss and French transaction in the cement industry had to deal with 15 major competition and regulatory jurisdictions.[16] Cross-border deals must indeed cover such different areas of expertise as economy, regulation, finance, markets, competition, assets, people, technologies, and so on. Usually these elements are quite well known at the domestic level. In an international deal, when such driving elements and potential impacts must be analyzed for each of the countries at stake, this is a major issue that many firms do not correctly cope with.

Each cross-border deal is different from every other one. As a principle, each international acquirer should take as a basic assumption that most parameters change from one country to the next. By default, one should be more positively surprised by commonalities than by the local (peculiar) differences. How local economies perform, how they rely on infrastructure, how they optimize raw materials, how employees and clients consider the concept of proper social relations, work time versus leisure, duty, reporting, loyalty, and how all these apparently universal concepts are modeled is in fact very different from one country to the next. As an example, the French European leader of cosharing car transport (BlaBlaCar) has recently raised $200m to pursue its internationalization growth after the acquisition of the German second European firm in that segment. Because of currently very low gas prices, almost free highways, and a car-owner-dominant culture, the French "unicorn" (an unlisted start-up with an estimated market value of over $1b) might favor developments in Brazil, China, and India over U.S. acquisitions.

The buy-side strategies should be clearly based on international competitive gaps. In a cross-border deal, the local business context is important, but it should not be viewed in an isolated manner. In fact, the bidder benefits from his own preexisting business base. The gap between the local context and the context already known and mastered by the bidder is therefore a critical one to assess: GDP growth, customer demand, inflation rates, interest rates, forex rates, demographic trends, organization of retail networks, local goods or services produced versus imports, and so on. All these aspects must be known by the buying firm to ensure it has reliable expectations and a good leverage of potential synergies. The list of potential gaps is considerable—one way to tackle it is to list the key performance indicators of the target, and identify systematically how to modify the existing business model. Manufacturing or supply costs,[17] market growth rates, consumer spending, public subsidies, leverage of public infrastructure or educational resources, and tax rates are gaps that any international investor will compare and leverage in building its acquisition business plan. The bigger the gaps, the greater the opportunities.

Cross-border deals are a major way to implement new value chains and intermediate/disintermediate profits. Vertical integration strategies have been thoroughly explored for centuries by nations, empires, and entrepreneurs to gain access to gold, salt, or other needed resources. From a corporate strategy standpoint, firms may want to secure access to strategic resources (e.g., uranium in the nuclear industry, rare minerals in the chemical sector). This strategy is subject to geopolitical, economic, and technological contexts and the trade-offs that may be pursued by business executives. In a situation where the supply-side market is very competitive and increasingly reliable and homogeneous in terms of quality of delivery, there is limited need for vertical integration—outsourcing and supply chain management becomes a better option. Cross-border deals aiming at that strategy need to be assessed as an insourcing versus outsourcing strategy.

The target country characteristics should be viewed as a set of potential gaps to optimize. A large set of parameters may play a role in the importance and direction of cross-border transactions: stability and quality of the local laws and regulations, tax regimes, labor law simplicity and stability, financial markets' liquidity and sophistication, accessibility and reliability of local public institutions, availability of managerial skills and higher educational programs, and effective R&D organizations are among the national traits that help to develop foreign investments domestically as well as investments abroad.

In particular, the industry specialization is a major aspect to analyze and leverage. The relative development of an industry in a given country reflects a complex set of national advantages and constraints, built over a long period of time. It has also several impacts on cross-border deals: "Acquirers from more specialized industries in a country are more likely to buy foreign assets in countries that are less specialized in these same industries."[18] In other words, the higher the degree of specialization of a country in a given industry, the more a given firm in that country will be able to use available skills and assets to target and control foreign acquisitions. The more an industry is developed at the local level and represents an important chunk of the GDP, the more local firms in that industry may be on the buy side—this plays in favor of the general extension of the pharma industry out of Switzerland, the financial services out of the United Kingdom, the car industry out of Germany, or the consulting services out of the United States. The degree of specialization not only plays a role in the occurrence of the deals, it plays as well in the performance of the deals and the profits generated.

Successful deal execution comes with a focused and consistent corporate strategy. Cross-border deals are a way to pursue the generic strategies we have listed previously. But these strategies ask for particularly consistent approaches in order to be successful:

Horizontal Integration.   In this strategy, building international synergies is driven by the capacity to increase market share through a combination of both marketing and sales improvements together with an extension of the range of products and services delivered. By nature, the integration of sales and marketing organizations will be critical, as it will fix the integration strategy for the rest of the organization. Global branding, homogeneous marketing analysis and consistent strategies, Customer Relationship Management (CRM) approaches, global account management techniques, salesforce reporting, and incentive mechanisms are but some of the different levers that can be focused on. These commercial developments abroad will, as much as possible, build on comparative cost advantages[19] and product synergies.[20] Large firms with well-implemented economies of scale, as well as firms benefiting from high domestic industry specialization, can leverage such cost advantages in their foreign acquisitions.

Vertical Integration.   In this strategy, the coordination of information and decisions across the value chain is critical—from purchasing to client delivery. The quick integration of the purchasing organization and supplier management processes, the implementation of integrated information systems, quality management, manufacturing methods, and transport and logistics optimization are essential to executing this strategy.

Consistencies.   To be more precise, in both strategies above, there is a need to look at all the components of the value chain. Horizontal integration is not at all about a front-end-only action plan. Manufacturing improvements in terms of quality or product range extensions may be the key elements supporting the market share extension.

The role of intangible assets is increased in cross-border deals. Firms with a global presence have a high proportion of intangible assets,[21] and there is a connection between the foreign expansion strategy and the accumulation of such assets.[22] On the other hand, it is worthwhile to note that the more intangible assets a firm has, the easier it is to circulate those assets internationally and the greater are the potential synergies between countries and the value of being a multinational firm.[23]

The faster internationalization of firms generates a new type of cross-border deals and issues. Cross-border deals are expected to generate a number of outcomes, for example, limiting potential competition, enabling firms to insource local profits, to gain from incremental local marketing or manufacturing techniques, to benefit from different national economic cycles and extend the life cycles of and incremental profits from domestic products. The high degree of interconnection between national markets, the speed of information from and to these markets, and the growing role of technology as a critical industrial asset accelerate the need for firms to get global. The internationalization of firms needs to be almost instantaneous, so that the information gained from one competitor abroad cannot help him to adjust and react and build defensive strategies. The increasing globalization of markets thus accelerates not only the degree of internationalization of firms but also its pace. Cross-border deals historically were conducted by firms with well-established and profitable domestic markets. They are now more and more open to younger experts in their early stage of development, with home markets that are not yet even profitable. The risk is thus higher, and the well-accepted business principle "the first one takes all" can very quickly become "the first one risks all."

Funding is particularly important in cross-border deals, as it builds on international financial gaps. Buyers may benefit from many financial gaps in cross-border deals. As for funding, three elements are key:

Generation of Cash. Firms with well-established domestic positions can build on this generation of cash to accelerate their growth abroad. They may leverage their existing resources to accelerate foreign growth through aggressive product pricing or productivity investments. Once the acquisition is done, they may leverage their internal processes, systems, and assets for the benefit of their local firm, and boost innovation and growth at the local level.

Debt. Firms from advanced and important economies can benefit from low levels of national interest rates and lowered corporate bonds rates. They have access to large, sophisticated, and competing banking services that may optimize the debt strategy from a tax and risk perspective.

Equity. International acquirers may also count on a dynamic domestic stock market, with high valuation rates and a significant investment base.

Hostile cross-border deals are more difficult to handle than domestic ones. M&A transactions may be hostile or not. Hostile takeovers are not the dominant part of the market, but in some countries, the number of hostile transactions may be significant. This is a factor that plays a different role in cross-border deals:

- Hostile deals are less likely to happen on cross-border deals than on domestic ones.
- In many non-U.S. markets, hostile M&A transactions will not be considered likely to happen.
- On the contrary, friendly deals may be developed by local banks or other financial institutions or investment funds to protect national interests and create national champions. Such deals will benefit from the direct and indirect support of the local administrations or political bodies, and the public opinion and media.
- Differences exist between countries, but the more the bidder can demonstrate its understanding and care for local interests, the better.

Cross-border deals are often subject to geopolitical change—firms need to be ready on this. Any major international change affecting the economy, access to resources, foreign investment policies, or the creation of new markets may fuel or hinder the development of cross-border deals.

- The containment of risk at the local level is not a valid strategy anymore. Changes occurring at the local level will be instantaneously known at the global level. This means that any local subsidiary needs to be controlled as much as any component of the organization close to HQ.
- There are currently plenty of such geopolitical changes: Ukraine and the Russian border with Europe, Yemen and the Persian Gulf area with the risk of widespread destabilization, Iran versus Israel on nuclear developments, Libya and the North Sahel in the aftermath of the so-called Arab Spring, Nigeria and central Africa against the Boko Haram sect, Syria and Iraq against Daesh, and so on.
- All these geographical areas are not only generating risks within their own borders. They also have considerable domino effects on neighboring countries (the European Union, Egypt, Saudi Arabia, Mali, and Chad, or Lebanon, Jordan, and Israel). They create new terrorist risks that may develop in faraway places (the United States, the United Kingdom, France, Denmark) and influence public opinion, economies, and business contexts in their home territories.

- The globalization of the Internet is also generating a considerable set of new risks (e.g., cyber-security breaches).
- In return, firms tend to enlarge and deepen the due diligence process: assessment of country risks, analysis of operating risks, and mitigation plans.

STRATEGIC MOTIVES

We differentiate strategic motives for cross-border deals from external factors influencing their outcome. Strategic motives depend on the acquirer and its strategic vision. The definition of such strategic goals on the buy-side, and its clear communication with the target in the implementation phase, will be a critical success factor in any cross-border deal. It is therefore critical, in particular in SMEs considering their first international deal, to ensure that these motives have been sufficiently analyzed and challenged.

Agility (i.e., adaptability) is a business imperative. There is today a widespread consensus regarding the need for a firm to be agile. Being agile means to swiftly adjust the firm to the business context and enable the firm to make profit out of it. By nature, corporate strategy must be adaptive and react to external or internal stimuli. The decisions aimed at growing the revenues, improving the profits, monitoring the risks, improving the various aspects of competitiveness, and hiring more competencies are always context-based.

Agility must be actively monitored as corporate size increases. In reality, the bigger a firm is, the more structured and ambitious it should be in terms of portfolio review and asset trade-off. Being agile does not mean only accelerating the time-to-market routines and the innovation pace. From an organizational and patrimonial standpoint, it means also constantly challenging the boundaries of the firm. As firms grow, they need to be better at divesting. As they invest, they need to be better at targeting and executing.

Internationalization and cross-border deals ask for a strong decision-making process linking strategy, deal execution, and post-merger implementation. M&A and cross-border deals are a key solution to address fundamental strategic questions such as how to grow revenues, improve profitability, increase assets, and develop capabilities. Any executive looking for such goals will consider making deals. When markets become more mature, more concentrated, this same executive will not only look at domestic targets. He will also look at international ones. He will have to make his judgment call based on another dimension of the context—the international one. What are the specificities of the local country? How can it support the profitability and growth of the target firm? Will there be any regulatory issue or local law that will drastically impact the local business or its synergies with the global group? All these questions, which are already difficult to assess in a well-known domestic market, will have to build on an entirely new perspective of things. The more you get into an international deal, the more you grasp this complexity. So you had better be prepared for the type of questions and factors that will be linked to a cross-border deal. To be ready, any executive trying to assess a cross-border deal situation should develop a precise view of the business context. This is normally part of the strategic assessment of the early pre-deal analysis. We aim at providing here a general view of the major elements at stake that may justify and play a role in an international deal.

Internationalization of Firms: Strategic Goals Pursued

Firms may pursue multiple strategic goals through cross-border deals, and target multiple classes of assets, tangible or intangible ones. Depending on the specific nature of the deal, strong differences exist in the type of results targeted, the degree of integration required, and the duration of the integration process. We need to detail a few consequences of the strategic goals pursued on the integration approach itself.

Access to Natural Resources. Such a deal aims at controlling a particular resource that is produced locally: agricultural goods (sugar, coffee, wheat, wood, sheep) or other natural goods (mining, oil, uranium, rare metals). This type of deal requires attention to the contracts of ownership, exploitation, distribution, and any restrictions to produce, sell, and export. The evaluation of the inventories is a critical aspect (size, annual production capacities, incremental costs of production, evolution of market prices) as well as all the aspects related to the actual operations to produce (environmental obligations) and sell (transport issues, administrative authorizations to export). In many such deals, there may be considerations related to local political interferences and geopolitical risks.

Access to New Markets and Customers. The buyer's goal is to leverage the existing local customer base, develop it and increase the scope of products and services sold. By nature, this requires a solid assessment of the global market conditions and trends (segmentation, growth, product margins, competition) as well as a precise view of the assets bought (sales force organization and reporting mechanisms, customer databases, client concentration, client contracts). Revenue synergies are key, and are known to be quite difficult to assess and follow up.

Access to Production Assets. This strategy focuses on leveraging local conditions of production that are better than the existing ones. This may be on the purchasing and supply side (local suppliers, less transportation, limited supply risks). It may also focus on manufacturing costs (low labor costs and favorable legislation, high local subsidies, better transport and logistics).

Access to Research and Development Assets and Intellectual Property. Cross-border deals may also pursue the objective of increasing the control over interesting R&D teams. Elements such as easy access to engineers, math scientists, physicists, biologists, international universities or research organizations, public funding mechanisms, and so on, are critical in the due diligence process. Some countries have developed specific environments that play in favor of research and innovation. This is in particular linked to their educational system, their infrastructure, and their cost. Each firm must optimize the international development of the clusters active in their specific business scope. They may form the basis for the screening of the best environments where acquisitions can be made. We can list but a few such areas where global competition is developing: artificial intelligence (deep learning, virtual brain); drones (military or civil security, other business usage); enhanced reality (image recognition, man–machine interface) cyber-security (counterterrorism, network and data security, man recognition, hazard prevention); renewable energy (wind, solar, marine); energy piling (batteries); smart grids; air transport (light materials, electrical engines); aerospace transport; pharma generics and on-demand production; robotics (brain interface, exoskeletons); intelligent cars; distant medical care (surgery, prevention).

Cross-Border Deals versus Other Types of Transactions

Cross-border acquisition versus greenfield. Cross-border deals are often (and must be) evaluated against the greenfield option, that is, development from scratch. For a firm considering international growth, the greenfield option is to create a local subsidiary and manage its endogenous growth with the support of the rest of the group.

Such a market-entry strategy has a number of advantages:

- Better control on the level of local investments and growth pace
- No inertia in terms of organization, process, or skills
- Capacity to optimize the relations with HQ and the other subsidiaries (financial, governance, tax and legal, localization of assets)
- Absence of liabilities due to past business misconducts or mistakes

However, cross-border acquisitions very often represent a preferred market-entry option as opposed to greenfield investments:

- It goes faster (branding, customer and other stakeholders' relations are there already).
- It forces management at the HQ level to understand local constraints and adjust to local practices, which headquarters would otherwise have underestimated.
- It brings some potential opportunities of improvement on the buy side as well.

Cross-border acquisition versus joint venture (JV). Some countries—China, or Gulf Cooperation Countries (GCC), for instance—do force foreign investors to go for a shared approach with a local player. But JVs should not be viewed as purely defensive tools: they are indeed a true alternative to acquisitions in any domestic or international corporate strategy. JVs are well known for a number of advantages as compared to acquisitions:

- The co-owner may bring its local knowledge and assets to accelerate growth (e.g., Feng with Peugeot SA in the automotive sector).
- JVs may be a first step in developing a long-term market-entry strategy.
- The scope of what is shared may be very selective either from a product range perspective or from a functional or operational standpoint. The scoping is really customized.
- It is possible to negotiate the buy-back of the shares of the co-owner.

However, acquisitions are often preferred to JVs because of governance issues and lack of strategic alignment with the co-owner of the JV:

- The governance model in an acquisition is clearer; decision-making is simpler and decisions can be implemented at a faster pace.
- The risk of creating a potential competitor is more managed (e.g., Danone's problems in China).
- In a JV, there might be some costs and discussions regarding the pricing of the assets shared—this discussion may be very detailed, and endless. In an acquisition, the pricing issue is simplified.

Differences between Industries

Every industry is different in terms of M&A constraints and business context. Let's take some examples to illustrate the wide variety of topics to consider in a cross-border deal.

The Chemical Sector It is a business-to-business industry—it has a limited number of clients, which means that the contracts with such clients are key. These clients may themselves belong to major groups, so the degree of consolidation of the clients must also be analyzed carefully (CRM databases, key accounts' management organization). Volumes depend on the segment of the industry (specialty versus commodity). In many segments, products do have to move from one plant to the other before they are sold to the end-client. Transport and logistics are key, as well as transfer prices and tax impacts. Environmental constraints are critical, and there should be no deal without a thorough analysis of all such risks and potential costs. Revenue synergies will be more on client relations, cross-selling, and product range increase, and cost synergies more on support functions, engineering and R&D teams, industrial performance and utilization rates, maintenance, purchasing and logistics, quality, and EHS management.

Information and Communication Technologies This industry groups very different firms. If we take the telecommunication incumbents, cross-border deals will focus on the customer database, churn rate and market share, the coverage of the network, the roaming agreements, and the capacity to innovate and propose mobile or Internet services. Synergies with international groups will be focusing on joint product offerings, marketing costs, and management of the network backbone. In the electronic components segment, the R&D assets, the purchasing performance and contracts, the manufacturing and supply chain international optimization, and the forecasting and production planning systems and procedures will be key focal points.

Financial Services Financial services is a sector with very specific characteristics, in particular in the banking segment. It may have limited tangible fixed assets for some of its segments (financial advisory, research). On the retail and corporate banking side, it relies very much on the balance between its cost of resources (interbank rates, savings accounts) and the costs of its loans (corporate loans, mortgage loans, personal credit). On the asset management side, the quality of the portfolio of clients, the types of investment policies, and the capacity to deliver such investment strategies and to generate margins and fees are critical. The type of products and services definitions and regulatory constraints may vary quite significantly according to countries, and it is essential to understand the compliance and regulatory situation and potential changes. The distribution costs may vary a lot between banks in relation with social habits, or more technical elements such as the degree of local Internet usage, or the availability of e-banking services.

FACTORS INFLUENCING CROSS-BORDER DEALS

Many external factors may influence a cross-border deal—we identify four different clusters of factors that are intertwined. They cover, broadly speaking, finance, regulatory, sociopolitical, and cultural dimensions.

Before getting into some details about each of these clusters, it is important as well to highlight that there are different levels of influence. We identify four such levels: global, country, industry-wide, and firm-specific levels. Each factor and cluster of factors may be analyzed from a specific level perspective (for instance, corporate finance theories may give rise to the use of takeover techniques at a global level, and this may be different from one country to another, one industry to another, one firm to another).

Generally speaking, we view these entry points (types of factors, levels of influence) as an analytical grid helping business executives confronted with this general complexity to try and structure thoughts and ideas.

Global, Country-, Industry-, and Firm-Specific Factors

Firms have to permanently optimize their strategy, structures, processes, capabilities, and systems according to a number of external or internal change forces (e.g., the introduction of a new technology), based on inner assets or weaknesses (e.g., strong innovation skills but little cash).

A firm should never be viewed as a set of fixed long-lasting elements. It may appear solid and strong due, for instance, to a high level of physical assets, but the most solid element of a firm is its capacity to generate revenues, and this may change quite rapidly.

It is hence a basic duty for executive teams to spend intelligence and energy on what may be causing changes in the eco-environment of the firm and anticipate how those changes will impact revenue streams and profits. In a cross-border deal, there should be a 360-degree review of the forces at play.

Firm-Specific (Microeconomic) Forces   This definition is not that trivial—most financial or strategic decisions are in fact dependent on external factors. But let's assume that the financial situation of a firm, as opposed to another firm in the same sector and country, is linked to priorities, decisions, and efforts that are under the control of the firm itself. Its growth rate, its level of investments, its compensation and benefits policy, its manufacturing organization, and its acceptance of risk are elements that may differ from one firm to another.

- The decisions to invest abroad, to allocate a certain percentage of the cash flow on such investments, to choose between very similar locations, to acquire versus to build a joint venture or have a greenfield approach, all these elements are partly constrained by internal economic parameters and their perception within the firm. These financial elements that differ from one firm to another may justify or contradict the interest of a cross-border deal, and may ease or hinder its execution.

▪ These forces may vary significantly across firms, even in the same industry and country. And it is not only because of actual differences regarding hard facts and figures. Perceptions and corporate history are as important as the facts and figures themselves. Firms do not perceive hard facts the same way—this depends on the corporate history, the successes and war stories discussed among employees, the lessons learned over time and individual careers, the internal culture, and so on.

▪ Take for instance GM and Chrysler in the automotive sector in the United States. GM has implemented since 2008 a major U.S.-led change program, with the sell-off of major units to decrease its debt and improve its operating income. GM has exited the Chevrolet brand, closed a number of plants, transformed its dealers' network, and reimbursed the state funds provided in 2009. During that same period of time, Chrysler has been restructured under the leadership of Fiat and its CEO, Sergio Marchionne. The focus has been put on synergies in the design and production of new cars, growing international distribution, and improving the productivity of plants. To put it simply, GM has downsized its fully owned capacities to reengineer them, whereas Chrysler has been more integrated into Fiat to become more competitive. GM has been on the defensive side to retain customers, play loyalty, and regain past market shares, whereas Chrysler has focused on image, growth, and innovation. But there is another element to these differences, which illustrates the role of history in a firm. Chrysler had previously failed in a major merger process with Daimler—this failure is quite well known for a worst-case in terms of how to manage a cross-border deal. This very specific experience has helped Fiat to build with Chrysler a more synergetic organization.

Industry-Specific (Mesoeconomic) Forces   Industry-specific forces must have been identified in the strategic analysis and assumptions must be consistent with business forecasts. At the intermediate level there are also major differences from one industry to another in terms of economic forces at stake and their relation with M&A deals:

▪ Due to past managerial failure, banks and financial services have been put under growing public constraints, and this has had considerable consequences on how this industry may generate growth and profits. Executives find it more and more difficult to find growth in less regulated business segments or countries. Forced exits from tax haven–related services, banking secrecy, and other "optimization" services will force banks to reconsider their portfolio of activities and value more sustainable and acceptable business targets.

■ In some mature industries (pharma, banks, automotive), organizations have grown extensively, reaching sizes that generate diseconomies of scale, organizational inertia, and productivity problems. In these same sectors, new entrants are developing innovative services based on the extensive use of emerging technologies to break down structural costs and organizational inertia. Serial acquisitions of start-ups are a way to cope with the negative effects generated by the maturity of a sector.

■ On the contrary, other sectors are being deregulated with public approval, generating new sources of revenues and new M&A opportunities. For instance, a wide range of services emerged based on customer-to-customer concepts allowed by new IT platforms, such as in the transport sector, or the production of energy for individual energy providers.

Impact of the national degree of specialization. There is a connection between the degree of specialization of a country in a specific industry and the nature and role of the industry-specific forces. A strong industry in a country is generally linked to a set of favorable forces that are both a cause and a consequence of this development. Analyzing the target industry and its positioning in the target country should therefore be among the preliminary efforts of an international screening process. Based on the International Standard Industrial Classification (ISIC), it appears for instance that the United Kingdom was highly specialized during the years 1990–2010 in "legal, accounting, and auditing activities" and "advertising," whereas Russia specialized in "transport via pipeline" and "railway and tramway locomotives," France in "electric lamps and lighting equipment" and "tanning and dressing of leather," Germany in "retail trade not in stores" and "sales, maintenance, and repair of motor vehicles," Finland in "television and radio transmitters" and "paper products," and the United States in "renting of transport equipment" and "education."[24]

Country-Specific (Macroeconomic) Forces At the national level, one country may differ widely from another. One of the first tasks of a corporate development officer and his or her team is to gather information on the country's risk. This is evaluated constantly by international organizations, such as Compagnie Française d'Assurance pour le Commerce Extérieur in France. However, despite the seemingly converging trend on the level of institutions and industries, there are many examples of the lasting gaps between nations regarding collective priorities, regulations, investments, and public demand. Lobbies, media communication, industrial dependencies, and perception of risks do influence such sector-based changes. Transport, defense, health care, and public services are all indicative of major differences between nations as to what people expect from firms in terms of quality of service, productivity, costs, and so on.

Global Worldwide (Metaeconomic) Forces   There are a number of global forces that impact the business context as well as the rationale for launching a cross-border deal. Accessibility and cost of earning production resources or customer revenues is impacted by multiple forms of disruptions. Generally speaking, disruptions created by new regulations, new technologies, new energy sources, or new connected products or services can drastically impact the benefits of being located in one country or another.

Four Different Clusters of Factors

As mentioned above, a wide number of external factors may influence cross-border deals. The term "economy" is often used beyond its strict scope to cover all such external factors. This is partly true—one might say that everything related to M&A and cross-border deals must be related to economy. However, to be more specific in our analysis of cross-border deals, we need to differentiate between clusters of factors, with the view of being consistent between the different levels identified in the paragraphs above (firm, industry, country, global).

We suggest distinguishing between four major clusters of factors, which all interact together, evolve over time, and all have an influence on M&A strategies and cross-border deals.

Corporate Finance/Financial Markets/Economy.   This cluster covers all the aspects referring to the technical understanding, development, and actual use and optimization of funds—from the corporate finance allocation decisions in a firm or in an industry to the specifics of financial markets at a national or international level and, beyond this, to the key technical aspects of the national and global economy (growth rates, exchange rates, inflation rates).

Governance/Regulation/Institutions.   This cluster groups all the elements dealing with the formalization, tracking, and follow-up of decisions under a set of approved procedures, architecture of powers, compliance control aspects, and professional or regulatory constraints. This covers for instance the existence of strong corporate governance mechanisms, industry-based regulations and institutions, and state or nonstate agencies and their capacity to define, track, and sanction corporate misbehaviors.

Individuals and Unions/Industry Organization/Politics. This cluster of forces covers all the elements related to the representation and balancing process of individual and collective interests and viewpoints—starting from the individual level of each employee and the hierarchies to which they belong (e.g., employees versus managers), up to the unions and other professional organizations, to the representation of the sector as an industry, and ultimately to the social and political system as a whole.

Education/Corporate Culture/Culture. This fourth cluster covers all the elements that shape behaviors and influence and make sense of business performance. That covers the education of the local workforce from the shop floor to top executives, their access to and development of innovative knowledge, and the existence within firms of strong specific corporate identities, rituals, and beliefs. It covers as well such national cultural specificities as attitudes toward time and efficiency, authority and legitimacy, power and justice, and toward money and ambition.

It is worthwhile to add that we view this high-level clustering approach as purely instrumental—it serves our purpose to present all the different factors in a simple way. We acknowledge therefore the fact that this clustering may be somewhat challenged. Nevertheless, it is critical in our perspective that executives do understand that economic factors are only one among a list of other types of factors influencing cross-border deals.

Corporate Finance/Financial Markets/Economy

This cluster covers financial and economic aspects, from thoughts to statistics and results. There is a continuum of aspects there, from the understanding of corporate finance techniques within firms, to the leverage of these techniques in specific deals. These deals may build on a favorable development of financial instruments and markets. They may also benefit from specific economic conditions that will give decision makers information about the potential profits to be generated from a potential deal.

Use of Corporate Finance Techniques at Firm Level Cross-border deals ask for a certain degree of sophistication in finance terms. Valuing a firm requires the use of methods such as discounted cash flow analysis (DCF), concepts such as the weighted average cost of capital (WACC), and estimates of different types of risk-related rates (risk-free, country risk, firm risk, currency exchange risk). It requires the understanding of tangible versus intangible assets valuation, the analysis of the best funding strategy as well as tax and legal impacts and optimization options. These elements are not easy to understand, rationalize, and model. Cross-border deals cannot be successful without a sufficient level of such corporate finance and tax and legal skills to analyze, plan, and deliver. It requires as well good managerial leverage of such skills, and many deals are unsuccessful because of the CEOs' overcentralizing decisions without the right technical skills.

Size of the National Financial Industry The existence of listed firms in well-established and active stock exchanges is a positive factor for international transactions. It limits the risk of political interference in the deal process, provides a better stock valuation basis for negotiation, increases funding options and deal-structuring approaches, and may improve future exit strategies if needed. M&A waves are linked to the development of stock market volume, prices, and regulatory processes. And cross-border transactions (inbound and outbound) are linked to the general maturity of the M&A markets.

Stock Market Evaluation Price-earning, price-to-book, price-to-free-cash flows are all ratios that provide an evaluation of the value of a firm by financial analysts and investors and thus its capacity to buy or to be bought. The recent Nokia (Finland) versus Alcatel-Lucent (France-U.S.) deal is a good illustration of that. Pre-deal, the two groups were about the same size in sales and in number of employees, but showed a huge gap in terms of profits and market capitalization. Based on the pre-deal market values, the acquisition has been achieved on the basis of 55 Nokia shares for 100 Alcatel ones with a 28% premium. As a result, Nokia could represent about two-thirds of the combined value—by far not a merger of equals. This case poses also very clearly the question of timing—had Alcatel-Lucent been able to delay the merger and improve its profits, it would have modified the merger conditions and its capacity to decide on the future strategy.

Interest Rate Levels Interest rate levels have numerous impacts on international deal making. Major firms in well-rated countries have access to lower corporate bond rates than their counterparts in riskier places. This may help them fund their acquisition at a reduced cost and may also enable them later on to fund investments without having to pay for the local high rates. The positive spread between high foreign rates and low domestic interest rates favors international deals as well as future synergies. Corporate interest rates are interconnected with public debt rates—the higher the risk-free market, the higher the corporate bonds. National political decisions—such as the launching of a quantitative easing program or a sovereign debt default—may have major impacts on corporate interest rates. In a period of political uncertainty, the spread may be very volatile: In mid-2014, the 10-year government bond was at 18% for Greece versus less than 1% for Switzerland or Germany. Since that peak, international rates have significantly decreased in Europe, and spreads have shrunk. In general, most advanced economies benefit from lower public and corporate bond rates as compared to emerging countries, which favors geographical diversification and investments in these countries.

Inflation Rates   Cross-border deals have also to take into account international gaps in terms of inflation rates, especially in countries where inflation rates may be double-digit or more. In such conditions, it is useful to build the business case on deflated values as well as on nominal values. Generally speaking, a high inflation rate has a negative effect on the quality of business forecasts, as the capacity to model future sales and operating costs is altered. It is also important to notice that in some countries, cost elements such as infrastructure costs (transport, energy, public services), the minimum wage, or the pension system may be automatically adjusted to inflation.

Forex Rates   In the first months of 2015, the euro lost about 20% of its market value against the dollar. For any U.S. firm considering an acquisition in Europe, such a change may entail a number of consequences: lowered deal price in dollar value, and increased strategic capacity to target bigger acquisitions. In the same time, such a euro/dollar decrease cuts the level of potential dividends to be consolidated by the bidder, and the dollar value of the synergies achieved on the local market. The forex rate impact is a bit more complex if we view it over time: Whereas the deal value is calculated at one point of time, the consolidation of accounts, the debt payments, and the dividends paid will evolve over time according to the forex rates. A brutal forex rate variation may also impact significantly the sales forecasts at target level, or the supply of products and services between the group and the local target, thus impacting potential synergies. Generally speaking, the higher the forex rate volatility, the higher the profitability should be from the deal.

Gross Domestic Product Growth Rates   Local market demand is a major factor in deciding to invest abroad. In mature economies, and in the absence of any specific technological or other disruption, companies face declining market growth rates. At the national level, GDP growth rates tend to converge to 1%–3% per year. The lower the internal demand, the higher the need to look for foreign alternative sources of growth. Since the 1980s, advanced economies have progressively moved away from their 7%–10% GDP growth rates to lower rates closer to 1% to 3% per year. For the past decade, the BRICS have served as a global growth engine, with rates above 10 points. This is now changing, and economic slowdowns or even recessions in these countries are now occurring, generating increasing challenges on how to fuel growth and ensure political stability. Taking a helicopter view, the U.S. mortgage crisis of 2008 may end up being one of the most important macroeconomic and geopolitical events since 1989 and the breakdown of the Soviet Union. In this situation of slower and volatile GDP growth rates, other parameters such as country risk assessments become necessary inputs for M&A forecasts.

Governance/Regulations/Institutions

This second cluster is about laws, regulations, compliance, and procedures. It is about factors that influence the context of decisions, the possibilities of firms to develop their strategies, the obligations they have to face in terms of reporting to public or professional bodies. It covers the following.

Corporate Governance Cross-border deals depend very much on the quality of information and the traceability of decisions. Firms must respect a number of general principles shared at the international level since the mid-1990s:

Effective Board. People appointed at the board level must have sufficient relevant skills and information. Independence is needed, as well as a minimum level of commitment.

Integrity and Ethics. Firms should base their decisions on the existence of a formalized and agreed-upon code of conduct that promotes ethical and social and environmental responsibility. Corruption should be tracked and sanctioned.

Disclosure of Information. The roles and responsibilities of the board and management must be communicated externally. The integrity of the company's financial reporting should be audited independently. Procedures linked to financial information, major business risks, and mitigation actions should be clearly documented and assessed independently.

Equitable Treatment of Shareholders. This aspect requires providing open and honest information to all shareholders and organizing general meetings to explain and validate major business decisions.

Compliance vis-à-vis the Rights of the Other Stakeholders. Firms have to manage a fair balance of interests among employees, investors, creditors, suppliers, local communities, customers, and policy makers. The expression of such interests increases naturally with the development of the countries and with information. As a result, executive boards' goals are subject to a growing set of contractual or legal obligations.

Resistance to such collective trends and attempts to develop unethical or even unlawful corporate behaviors are increasingly risky and expensive.

Board of Directors versus Supervisory Board   Firms may implement different governance models according to their national contexts and regulations. Broadly speaking, two major models exist:

1. An Anglo-Saxon one with a board of directors that is normally dominated by nonexecutive directors elected by shareholders.
2. A continental European one (Germany, The Netherlands), with a difference being made between an executive board (company executives focusing on day-to-day business) and a supervisory board (nonexecutive directors elected by shareholders and employees focusing on the selection and compensation applicable at executive board level, and the evaluation of major business decisions).

Below this level, a managing board normally convenes all the executive directors every month or so. It focuses on all business operations. In a cross-border deal, the staffing of this board is key, as it reflects the degree of control the acquirer wants to impose on the target.

Such a hierarchy of instances may be simplified in smaller firms, with an executive committee only and the presence of executive directors and key shareholders focusing on all business operations. In any case, the meeting minutes are a critical piece of information in a cross-border deal.

CEO and Chairman of the Board   The two roles may be either split (often the case in the United Kingdom) or merged (often the case in the United States or in France). The split depends on the size of the firm and the situation (HQ level or subsidiary). The split between the two roles may be considered a positive element of stability in an acquisition, as it enables maintaining the CEO in place if that is of interest.

Committees   The existence of independent committees—the audit committee, the compensation committee—is another element of sound corporate governance, though it depends very much on the size and nature of the target. When these committees do exist, they may provide the bidder with more documented information and independent reviews.

The Human Resources Local Market   Countries may differ widely regarding the size and activity of the local market for executives. In emerging countries, it might be difficult to recruit new executives or individuals with critical skills.

In such cases, the staffing of expatriates may bring a temporary solution, but may also generate some negative effects (cultural ignorance, lack of local contacts, insufficient links with local employees, high costs). The absence of a very active local HR market may also give rise to a high level of local individual corruption, and informal business practices.

Investors' Rights   M&A research highlights the positive role of clear national laws and decisions about investors' rights on foreign direct investments and cross-border deals. The more the interests of foreign investors are protected, the more cross-border deals are likely to happen. On the other hand, political interference, corruption, lobbying against foreign investors, and the lack of legal enforcement of investors' rights are elements of risks that will normally be factored in when assessing the cross-border deal and the required rate of return.

Accounting Standards   This is another well-known element of influence on foreign investments and cross-border deals. The convergence of standards at the international level is a real trend (e.g., the rollout of International Financial Reporting Standards) but there are still huge national differences when considering small and medium firms operating in domestic markets only. The use of local correspondents of international audit firms is a common practice to track and model such accounting gaps.

Sector-Based Compliance Rules   The notion of risk and compliance is also a significant element supporting or jeopardizing M&A deals. This aspect has dramatically changed over the past 20 years, with a growing number of obligations in all countries (safety rules, environmental norms, labor laws, financial ratios, manufacturing and construction norms), which for most of them raise the operating costs. The number of people employed in internal control teams, audit, and compliance has risen. But gaps exist between countries—emerging countries do not impose the same rigor and level of compliance than do more mature economies. Local profits may be improved due to strong externalities: The collective costs of poverty, health problems, lack of education, and so on, are not financed by the firm itself. Corruption tends to delay the insourcing of such costs and maintain operating costs at low level. One must however anticipate that the incidence of business scandals (China, Kuwait, Pakistan, India) will not diminish. The development of the Internet and whistleblowers has tended to homogenize the international demand for norms and rules. At the other end of the value chain, customers from advanced economies are increasingly informed about production conditions, imposing their own needs and requirements (e.g., in the textile industry in Malaysia).

Institutional Quality   This parameter takes a broader perspective, as it qualifies the general national context in terms of lawmaking, regulatory constraints, and the functioning of the different public or private agencies enforcing such policies at the national level. Emerging countries face huge difficulties in setting up the required conditions to provide the level of institutional quality known in the advanced economies. Lack of financial resources leads to corruption, insufficient controls, and unknown corporate risks. Political instability, a weak state and administration, and lack of public sector independence are factors known to play against cross-border deals and foreign investments.

Sociopolitical Parameters

This third cluster is about how cross-border deals may be influenced by social and political factors, that is, existing collective structures. These structures play a highly differentiated role according to countries—they are built on different histories, convey different objectives, and show different operating modes of action. Because of their inertia, executives have to adjust to these factors at an industry or national level as much as they may want to change or modify them at the firm level. It is therefore key for executives to spend some intelligence and energy on catching the key specifics of the country, industry, and firm the transaction is focusing on. One must also have in mind that too often, the "one size fits all" approach on these factors is often a shortcut leading to integration misconceptions and failure. We will just list two of these factors here—we could extend that list to many other factors as well (professional organizations, political parties).

Unions   In many open economies, the existence of unions is conceived by managers as a burden. Unions are said to restrict economic choice, managerial creativity and freedom of action, and ultimately shareholders' rights. They are perceived to be essentially negative, conservative, against innovation, against corporate profits, and therefore against collective wealth. Investments abroad should therefore trigger places where there is limited employee representation and no or weak unions. This is not a universal standpoint, though its adherents make considerable efforts to present it as such. In other economies (e.g., Germany, or some other European countries) unions are perceived on the contrary as a means to achieve sustainable profits, helping firms to reach internal consensus with their workforce and helping therefore to mobilize people more effectively on well-understood and shared rational trade-offs. The impact of unions on the actual success of cross-border deals is not clear.

Our standpoint is that the impact of unions depends very much on the management approach itself, and on the corporate strategy triggered. In a strategy of profitability dependent on low production and HR costs and low standards of quality and poor work conditions, unions are an obstacle. It is less the case in a corporate strategy of long-term development based on non-instrumental relations with employees and cooperative management habits. Generally speaking, unions should not be viewed as an obstacle to progress, as long as progress is not limited to profits. The more firms communicate their values on ethics and human management styles, and the more they view human resources and capital as humans involved in a joint project, the more they learn how to manage unions in an efficient way. But this requires a real managerial education in local human resources laws, workforce practices and expectations, and a planned and structured communication with unions and workforce representatives.

Democracy This aspect is a tricky and highly sensitive one at the international level. Is there, and should there be, a connection between cross-border deals and democracy? Our standpoint is that this connection should not be viewed in a moral perspective—deals between firms cannot have as a corporate strategic objective to modify the political organization of a country. Cross-border deals may result in local changes and social patterns, but this is an indirect by-effect. More effectively, cross-border deals support the opening of an economy, and reflect the degree of social and political change that is implemented locally. They may support such changes, but are not decisive per se. On the other hand, in an open economy, by providing a high level of institutional quality (i.e., administrative strength, low level of corruption, strong legal framework, independent public agencies) cross-border deals are more likely to succeed. Profits therefore link cross-border deals with institutional quality rather than to democracy per se, but there are some links between the two.

Cultural/Geographical Parameters

The cultural aspect is a major topic—it is dealt with separately (Chapter 7). Broadly speaking, managers are often confused as to what the term *culture* means, and to what extent it refers to a complex set of knowledge, skills, beliefs, behaviors, or rituals. Chapter 7 provides a view of these aspects.

Social Fabric Advanced economies are the result of centuries of common educational processes, and historical events assembled in a collective process of sense-making. Individuals learn at schools a considerable number of elements that bundle their vision together and develop a sense of collective identity as well as a view of the different building blocks of the nation they live in. This social and educational process differs widely between nations. In many countries, school is still limited to a small elite, and this results in a social fragmentation that has major impacts on business practices. It is an advantage for a foreign entrant to understand those key dimensions and how they may evolve.

Languages and Dialects   In many countries, there is not one but several competing languages or dialects. In most African countries, there are many people knowing more than five different dialects. In the Democratic Republic of Congo, there are four national languages admitted, with French being the official and administrative one. This does not mean that all these dialects must be known, but any integration manager should take the view that language, and translation, may be a serious concern when managing workforces abroad, especially when dealing with large, populous countries.

Communities   The use of these different languages is linked to another aspect that any new investment abroad has to deal with, which is the type of cultural segmentations that may be built on from a business perspective. Any nation is made of multiple communities that are more or less assimilated and bundled. These communities exist both vertically (aristocracy versus the "untouchables") and geographically. They have their own representations, work patterns, educational specificities, consumption models, and financial archetypes. Particularly in business-to-consumer acquisitions, it is very important to understand early what are the social communities at play and to what extent this local configuration may play for or against the integration plans and financial forecasts. This view of social segments should be supported by local surveys and contacts with local faculties, and should result in well-designed marketing strategies. To take an example, a European bank providing services to high-net-worth customers had analyzed years ago a specific inconspicuous savings service focusing on women potentially facing repudiation.

Beliefs and Values   Among many evolutions, advanced economies are marked by the growing role of individuals, as opposed to local communities or extended families. This has huge impacts on the way employees value individual performance, reward individual efforts, and evaluate management decisions and loyalty. On the client side, it plays in favor of individual consumption, access to symbols of wealth and success, and a more challenging demand for service and quality. This trend is observed at the global level, but the status may be very significantly different from one country to another.

Firms have to deal with customers or employees who have social relations that are shaped differently. It is a success factor from an HR and a marketing perspective to take this eco-environment and set of beliefs and priorities into account and adjust accordingly internal services (e.g., analyze how to support the education of single-child employees or ease the commute of distant workers) or external ones (e.g., build a VIP-type approach).

Management Theories It is critical for an acquirer to share its vision on the long-term strategic goals and also legitimate the decisions the bidder takes. Of course, this legitimacy is easier to get when the concepts used are already shared per se. This is very true at a technical level—reaching a consensus in an integration work stream between engineers or technicians is normally quite easy. It is also true for managerial techniques and concepts. This is why training local executives to the key bidder's processes is so critical in a cross-border deal. Management consultants have also a significant role as they may provide an external and more neutral perspective and improve the legitimacy of the decisions taken.

Appetite for Innovation and Resistance to Change The way ideas and techniques circulate in a country and a firm is also a major element influencing M&A decisions. Countries may differ in terms of appetite for new ideas and concepts—this is linked to the education of people, the conservative aspects of a society, and its image of authority and legitimacy. Innovation is easier in a new country or region with a pioneer type of mind-set (Israel, Singapore, Taiwan, California). Development and mass success is easier in more organized societies with sophisticated chains of command (China, Germany, Ohio). But in a cross-border deal, resistance to innovation is not only about the countries at stake. It depends also on the direction of this innovation from an international standpoint. It will be more difficult for an emerging country firm to impose its innovative concepts in advanced economies than the other way around. The more a country perceives itself as advanced, the more difficult an integration may become for a foreign bidder.

"Soft" Psychological Patterns We can highlight this in a couple of ways:
- The "hubris hypothesis" is a theory that has been very much used to explain some irrational decisions made by well-informed management teams. Psychologically, executive teams may tend to underestimate potential risks in a context of collective bias for action. This psychological phenomenon may be diminished with the participation of several stakeholders in a deal, making sure that for instance post-deal implementation issues limit the sense of euphoria of the M&A team close to an agreement.

- The "herding" behavior is another major factor that has a general consequence on the nature of the business decisions and M&A deals. At the corporate level, in a world of uncertainty and lack of long-term entrepreneurial vision, mimetic strategies are developed by managers focusing on technicalities and short-term performance as an adaptive solution. The more there is information available, the more firms and individuals with available resources may engage in "me-too" behaviors and copy common patterns. The systematization of benchmarking surveys, competitive reviews, and equity research reviews strengthens this process of mimesis to a wider number of firms at a quicker pace. This mimetic process is one of the causes of M&A waves.

CHAPTER CHECKLIST

- **Consider the M&A market as a volatile market with ups and downs.** It has been a very active market in recent years, but it may also come down very quickly. These cycles have major consequences on the prices, the availability of resources, funding, and eventually risk. You must have a sense of the overall market situation before getting into a complex deal that will take long to close.
- **Consider a wider range of potential deal opportunities.** The M&A market is getting more important globally. The overall growth rate of the market is far above the GDP global growth. More countries are active, more sectors as well. Do not limit yourself in terms of regions or sectors. Restrictions may exist, but the general trend is in favor of cross-border deals. New frontiers arise.
- **Have a broad view of why M&A deals may develop or decrease.** Understanding the determinants of M&A waves is a positive factor in terms of strategy assessment and deal decision-making. The more you have a view of such determinants, the more you may catch the potential value out of a deal.
- **Consider cross-border deals as more complex to analyze and execute than domestic deals, then plan the work accordingly.** Take time to identify and assess all the gaps between the home business and the target business. These gaps may cover all the different components of the value chains. They may also be external to the firm targeted.
- **Make sure you have a clear and shared set of strategic motives for the deal.** Cross-border deals may pursue a wide range of strategic goals. You need to list them early and challenge them and the capacity to deliver before you close the deal.

▪ Working on the actual integration plan between signing and closing will secure success in many critical ways. You will have to get into the complexity of the implementation aspects, and challenge the early strategic assumptions through a better view of the local value drivers. The gaps between the target and the acquirer will be better understood, and the potential synergies and implementation costs and delays will be assessed more precisely.

▪ In this overall process, maintain a view that strategic factors of success and failure may exist at different levels. An organization evolves according to economic, regulatory, organizational, and cultural forces interacting between them and at different levels: individual, firm-wide, sector-wide, country-wide, or truly global. This framework is highly complex, but it provides a wide scope of potential areas of action and optimization as well. The broader your curiosity on local matters and empathy vis-à-vis them, not only at the technical level, the better your ability to make well-informed decisions that will accelerate and secure the integration process.

NOTES

1. All figures from Thomson Reuters, *Mergers and Acquisitions Review, Full Year 2015 and 2014*.
2. Bloomberg Business, *Global M&A Set for Record in 2015 as Companies Pursue Mega Deals*, July 29, 2015.
3. G. Andrade, M. Mitchell, and E. Stafford, "New Evidences and Perspectives on Mergers," *Journal of Economic Perspectives* 15, no. 2 (2001): 103–20.
4. S., Brakman, H. Garretsen, and C. Van Marrewijk, "Cross-Border Mergers and Acquisitions: On Revealed Comparative Advantage and Merger Waves," Tinbergen Institute Discussion Paper, No. 08–013/2 (2007).
5. R. E. Lucas, "Why Doesn't Capital Flow from Rich to Poor Countries?" *American Economic Review* 80, no. 2 (1990): 92–96.
6. L. Alfaro, S. Kalemli-Ozcan, and V. Volosovy, "Why Doesn't Capital Flow from Rich to Poor Countries? An Empirical Investigation," *Review of Economics and Statistics* 90 (2008): 347–68.
7. S. Brakman, H. Garretsen, and C. Van Marrewijk, "Cross-Border Mergers and Acquisitions: The Facts as a Guide for International Economics," CESifo Working Paper, No. 1823 (2006).
8. Global PMI Partners, 2015.
9. F. Mason and J. Dougherty, "Market Analysis: Current Trends in Cross-Border Public M&A," *Public Mergers and Acquisitions Multi-Jurisdictional Guide 2014/2015* (2014), global.practicallaw.com/6–586–3405.
10. Brakman et al., "Cross-Border Mergers and Acquisitions."

11. Chunfang Cao and Guilin Liu, "Political Uncertainty and Cross-Border Mergers and Acquisitions," Working Paper. http://zicklin.baruch.cuny .edu/faculty/accountancy/events-research-workshops/Downloads/SWUFE-Chunfang_Cao.pdf.
12. Michael Porter, *The Competitive Advantage of Nations* (New York: Free Press, 1990).
13. K. S. Reddy, "Determinants of Cross-Border Mergers and Acquisitions: A Comprehensive Review and Future Direction," Indian Institute of Technology, MPRA Paper, No. 63969 (2015). http://mpra.ub.uni-muenchen.de/63969.
14. UNCTAD, *World Investment Report: Cross-Border Mergers and Acquisitions and Development.* New York and Geneva: United Nations Publications (2000).
15. International Monetary Fund, "World Economic Outlook Database," April 2015.
16. Mason and Dougherty, "Market Analysis."
17. Stephen R. Yeaple, "The Role of Skill Endowments in the Structure of U.S. Outward Foreign Direct Investment," *Review of Economics and Statistics* 85 (2003): 726–34.
18. L. Frésard, U. Hege, and G. Phillips, "Extending Industry Specialization, Intangibles, and Cross-Border Acquisitions," Working Paper (2015). http://www-bcf .usc.edu/~gordonph/Papers/XborderAcquisitions.pdf.
19. P. J. Neary, "Cross-Border Mergers as Instruments of Comparative Advantage," *Review of Economics Studies* 74 (2007): 1229–57.
20. G. Hoberg and P. Gordon, "Product Market Synergies and Competition in Mergers and Acquisitions: A Text-Based Analysis," *Review of Financial Studies* (2012): 3773–811.
21. H. Robert and D. Ravenscraft, "The Role of Acquisitions in Foreign Direct Investment: Evidence from the U.S. Stock Market," *Journal of Finance* (1991): 825–44.
22. Yeaple, "The Role of Skill Endowments."
23. R. Morck and B. Yeung, "Why Investors Value Multinationality," *Journal of Business* 64 (1991): 167–87.
24. Frésard et al., "Extending Industry Specialization."

CHAPTER 2

Cross-Border M&A Strategy and Deal Planning Essentials

Michael Holm

CHAPTER LEARNING OBJECTIVES—IN THIS CHAPTER, YOU WILL LEARN:

➤ The components of a cross-border M&A strategy
➤ The responsibilities and accountabilities in the organization, to ensure the best decision possible
➤ What could be the target company criteria
➤ How to prepare and plan for a cross-border deal

CHAPTER SUMMARY

This chapter begins with a discussion of the inputs needed to formulate the components of an M&A strategy. Next is to set up the decision process with as much objectivity as possible. The chapter then goes into what could be the target company criteria and, finally, about how to prepare and plan a cross-border deal.

M&A STRATEGY OVERVIEW

When companies assess their growth plans (see Figure 2.1) the choices are to organically make, partner, or acquire an asset that will bring significant shareholder value. The M&A process is started when a company decides to buy an asset. The asset could be a whole company or parts of a company; for example, a factory and the rights to the products manufactured in the factory, which is called a carve-out. For simplification, "target" will be used in this chapter, which could be a complete company or a carved-out asset.

Maximizing return in growth with balance in time and risk

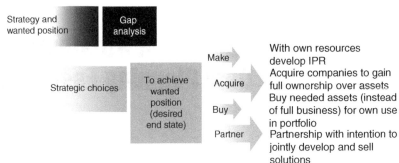

FIGURE 2.1 Growth Choices

Inputs to the Acquisition Analysis

The decision is made to start an M&A process, and this chapter's point of departure is to start exploring to acquire a target (see Figure 2.2). The acquisition integration framework (AIF) will be introduced in later chapters and this chapter covers the phases of M&A strategy and target selection within that framework.

The decision material from the "make, partner, or acquire" analysis should be used as input to the M&A project—that is, how much it will cost, the time it will take to organically develop the equivalent of the target, and what the revenues from that development will look like in a DCF (discounted cash flow) analysis. The choice needs to be revisited when the decision material on the acquire option is ready. Information will be learned during the M&A project that is not under a nondisclosure agreement (NDA) that could be used to update the make option. The same needs to be done for the partner option. This input will also give the M&A team part of the understanding needed to formulate the M&A strategy.

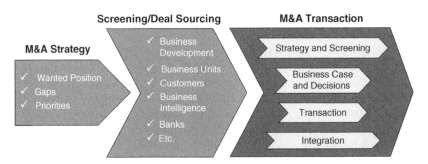

FIGURE 2.2 Strategy, Screening, and M&A Transaction

What questions could an M&A strategy answer?

- Is it one or many targets that are to be in the M&A strategy, be it competencies, products, market presence, or value chain control that is the driver behind the decision to acquire?
- Is the M&A strategy embarking on acquiring many targets and is there a sequence, triggers, timing, or other prioritization that sets what is optimal for the planned set of cross-border acquisitions? Figure 2.3 shows two possible sequences to buy companies A, B, and C. Which sequence is the most optimal for the acquiring company? Is it more optimal to buy the companies in sequence, A+B+C or C+A+B? If you look only at the targets individually, the sequence would be based on individual triggers per target rather than the full sequence. The considerations for choosing the most optimal sequence could be (1) resources to integrate or (2) to achieve optimal growth. For example, first, you buy a large distributor and then two service companies in a market.
- Are there many other initiatives within the company competing for funds or for management attention and energy?
- What is the current versus wanted competitive position?
- How much of the M&A project is cross-border—that is, how far away is it from the company's comfort zone and past experiences?
- What are the gaps and are there targets that perfectly fit those gaps?
- Will there be tens or hundreds or more targets that are to be tracked on long/short lists?

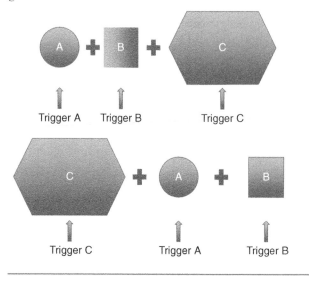

FIGURE 2.3 Illustration of Timing and Sequence of Acquisitions

M&A Strategy Components

The components of an M&A strategy can be quite complex and strategic, requiring a lot of resources to evaluate, or just opportunistic and case-by-case. The input and expectations on the ambition of the M&A strategy need to be clear and agreed upon.

To execute an M&A strategy there need to be cool objective heads as well as passionate champions who drive acquisitions. One question needing an answer is how the organization will support the M&A strategy and its execution. For a serial acquirer or a consolidator it is clear that M&A competence is a key capability. A consolidator is a company that acquires its competitors to achieve economies of scale or a value chain to control its market. A serial acquirer is a company that acquires a number of similar targets and gains efficiencies from repeating the M&A process. A serial acquirer uses one or two playbooks. A playbook is a variation of the corporate M&A process.

An example is a "sales acceleration playbook" where a serial acquirer buys a smaller company with a new unique product that has not been fully introduced to a global market. The acquirer has an effective global sales organization and new product introduction process that can quickly bring the new product to a global market, with recent examples being IBM and Oracle. The requirement on the acquirer is that newly acquired products can quickly be included in the necessary sales, delivery, and service support systems. Sales acceleration also occurs in the pharmaceutical industry where smaller companies perform initial drug research and development (R&D) and then are acquired by big pharma companies that then take the products through the final phases of trial and launch them on the global markets.

Another example is acquiring a company for the talent and product, meaning that the product may not have had enough sales to become established in the market. This could be called a "product redo playbook" because the target's developers are asked to develop the product again under the acquirer's world-class development management and process. Recent examples are Oracle and Google.

The answers to the following questions give an indication of how the M&A project will be run:

- Will all aspects of the M&A project be handled internally or will certain parts be outsourced to external advisors and consultants?
- Who will formally decide what—an already established decision committee or the management team?
- What is the degree of board involvement?
- Are peer reviews possible?

- Is it to be a broad team or a small team in the due diligence?
- What steps will be taken for internal alignment on M&A strategy and specific deals? There is a lot to be won by having everyone onboard early.
- Will staff be involved in a country where there is only a small team with not so much M&A experience in a cross-border deal?
- What kind of targets will be of interest?

M&A Screening Process

The next step, after formulating the M&A strategy and deciding on how the M&A project will be run, is to look at the M&A screening process (see Figure 2.4). A long list of potential targets is assembled where input could come from the acquirer's company management or business unit/division teams, the deal team's research, and outside advisors such as corporate finance advisors or analysts. How many targets should be on a long list? It all depends, but some serial acquirers track a long list of up to 300 companies as they look for the right timing and the best synergy possibility for an acquisition.

Short-list criteria need to be defined without looking at the available targets.

- What are the commercial, product life cycle/market window, and value added/synergy logic for the acquisition(s)?
- How will the softer side be evaluated, for example, quality of the target's management team, employees, corporate culture, operational effeciency, and quality of customer-facing activities?
- Are different criteria needed in different geographies?
- Will a tool or a subjective approach be used to evaluate targets and when will the team be allowed to be subjective?

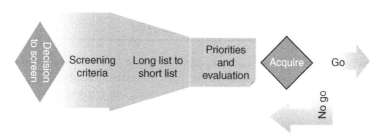

FIGURE 2.4 Screening Process

- Can in-house resources find the data necessary for the cross-border deal?
- Will a research agency make sense?

Accurate data and information on criteria is critical and every piece of data needs to be cross-checked from different sources, especially for a cross-border deal where there is a need to be extra diligent.

The more planning and preparation that is done, the less stress and pain will be felt by the organization and the smoother post-merger integration will be because internal alignment is in progress. Then the question is how much preparation and planning is to be done to prepare for the M&A strategy execution or for each case within that strategy and that is entirely dependent on current capabilities and the scope of the M&A project. Preparation will ensure that the value and synergies will be captured according to the business case for the acquisition. One thing that sometimes occurs when it is time to execute the post-merger integration project is that the key executives are exhausted and in bad shape due to lack of good preparation and resourcing pre-deal. Everybody needs to work hard to bring in a deal and the most important thing to decide up front is how much time the executives and M&A team will allocate pre- and post-deal. It is also time to think about how to use and develop contact networks in the region or country in question with, for example, customers, suppliers, or competitors.

In summary,

- Input to the M&A team needs to be complete and accurate.
- The evaluation and decision process needs to be defined and objective to the extent possible.
- Information and data gathered in a cross-border deal need to be challenged, cross-checked, and validated.
- Think through resource allocation carefully, both in-house and sourced.

COMPONENTS OF CROSS-BORDER M&A STRATEGY

Each company and its needs are unique depending on the operational model and employees. The components of the M&A strategy are also unique. Outside advisors can provide guidance and support, but a good strategy needs to be owned internally. The strategy components are the inside-out view of how to effectively capitalize on the opportunities that exist for the company going forward. Also look within to find a match between the company and the target. The acquiring company's ability to analyze the material received and created in the M&A process should be close to 100% if the staffing of

TABLE 2.1   Generic Components

Component	Example
Frequency of acquisition	Number of acquisitions/year
Timing of acquisition	Q1–Q3 preferred (Q4 is busy)
Synergies to look for	Sales-driven synergies
Value added	Sales and channel execution
Location	Northern Europe
Deal sourcing	80% internally generated
Ownership after closing	> 60%
Funding	Internal balance sheet
Risk	Risk of 1, 4, 8 in Anshoff diagram (lowest risk 1, highest 16)
Wanted position (or desired end-state)	Needs to be >6 on a scale from 1 to 10
Need for carve-out, product discontinuation, or significant redundancies	<5% of deal value
Revenues acquired	$100–$250m
Ownership	Privately held preferred
Value chain	Close to customers is preferred

the deal team is done right, thereby reducing the need for external advisors. That knowledge and a joint view on the market drives the components of the M&A strategy. If there has not been a discussion and a conclusion on how the company leadership views the market it is time to do so before selecting and setting values on the components of the M&A strategy.

The components of a cross-border M&A strategy can be divided into generic components (see Table 2.1), applicable to almost all strategies, and industry- or deal-specific components (see Table 2.2).

TABLE 2.2   Industry-/Deal-Specific Components

Component	Example
Trigger	EBITDA > 5% + Local market CAGR >5%
Management	Management will be retained to drive sales, business, and product development
Gap to close	X technology and IPRs
Talent risks	< 5% churn one year after closing, no stay-on bonuses
ERP system	SAP preferred

The main thing is not whether it is a generic or a deal-specific component, it is rather whether the team has an opinion and can set a value to it during the screening process.

Formulating an M&A strategy could be done in a few bullets that can be shared widely (see Figure 2.5). It can also be part of a detailed document that describes the reasons behind the strategy and the choices made. A more detailed document sometimes gets quickly out of date as the overall strategy of a company and its understanding of the industry dynamically change at a rapid pace:

- Deal rationale is to buy market shares
- Sales-driven synergies—target is selling to existing customers and match in distribution channels is preferred
- Targets where acquirer can add value, for example, strengthened product portfolio, efficient application support, commercial rigor, understanding of customer needs, enhancing the service portfolio
- Ideal location: Europe, North America
- 80% of target proposals to be internally generated
- Less than 10% of targets take a minority stake (with option for 100%) to keep entrepreneurial drive

FIGURE 2.5 M&A Strategy Example

RESPONSIBILITIES AND ACCOUNTABILITY IN THE ORGANIZATION

The key words to handle an M&A project in an organization are objectivity, passion, accountability, peer insight, and structure.

An M&A project is a big investment and a potential risk for a company. To abandon pursuing an acquisition just before signing can be compared to walking off 100 meters before a marathon finish line. The M&A team have committed physically and mentally for months to cross that finish line and to abort just at the end is difficult. The team has fallen in love with the deal logic, has invested a lot of personal energy and passion into the deal, has spent money with external advisors, and cannot always be rational. The deal champion is passionate about the value the acquisition can add and has committed a lot of credibility to the deal.

An objective decision process needs to be put in place for M&A projects that ensures that a rational decision can be made to abandon a deal just before signing if decision criteria are not met (see Figure 2.6).

There are two major decision points for the M&A team and mandates to be given:

1. To approach a target company and negotiate a deal
2. To sign the deal

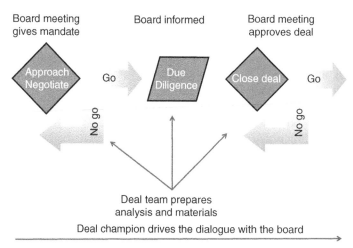

FIGURE 2.6 Decision Structure, Champions of a Deal, Contributors in Analysis

Minor checkpoints can be a decision to research a deal on the short list, to involve external advisors, and to set up a due diligence team.

A leading practice is establishing a deal champion who will stay with the M&A project from the start until two to three years into integration. It is to be preferred that the deal champion is not the CEO or chairman who needs to be an objective part of the decision process. The deal champion is there to ensure continuity and clear accountability. For cross-border deals this is even more important as the target's leadership and employees feel that the deal champion is their champion inside the acquiring company. If the champion moves on, there is a risk that the target will feel abandoned, betrayed, and lost. This is especially true for acquisitions of family-owned businesses where the family stays on in the business and is critical to its success. M&A projects can be complex and a large quantity of fragmented information is handled. One cause of risk and value erosion is handoffs between individuals during an M&A project. To mitigate the risk, handoffs need to be minimized, resources have to be kept on until the end of the project, and the handoffs performed should be carefully managed. There have been cases where intellectual property rights (IPR) or facts were not known to the integration project and value was lost in incomplete handoffs.

Resource Planning for the M&A Project

An M&A project can be very costly in terms of time, money, and resources or not so costly depending on the level of ambition and the targets. The major risks are pre-deal in strategy, valuation, revenue forecasting, and due diligence (not having the best people in the due diligence team) and post-closing in capturing the value from the deal and integration. Possible members in an M&A deal team could be, for example, project manager transaction, commercial, legal, operations, post-merger integration, portfolio/product management, HR, and financial members, or it can be just one, for example, a business development manager.

It is a leading practice to do a resource plan with named resources after the M&A strategy is ready, with the people who will be involved in screening, evaluation, due diligence, negotiation, closing, and post-merger integration. All needs in an M&A project cannot be foreseen, but a resource plan makes sure that the capabilities and internal agreement are there. In cross-border deals it is even more important to understand resource needs as local legal expertise, commercial and operational research pre-deal, and support for post-merger integration post-deal all need to be found. The resource plan is a base to select and control the cost of external advisors.

Target's Management Presentation

It is also important to think through who will attend the management presentation that the target company's management does presenting the business for sale. This is where trust and relationships are built, but also when weaknesses in leadership, business, and operations are discovered by the acquirer. The question and answer (Q&A) session after the management presentation is probing to validate the synergies without revealing what synergies are included in your business case for the acquisition. That takes some preparation and understanding as the price could go up if the seller understands what synergies the buyer sees.

Pressure can be applied to test individual leaders at the target and see how they react. In one such Q&A session the head of a loss-making business unit was so clearly exposed for being incompetent and not having an understanding of his unit's business that he pushed back his chair from the conference table, mentally left the room, and went into passive mode. In this case, the Q&A session alienated a C-level member and in a cross-border deal this could happen due to cultural, communication, or other reasons. It also happens in such meetings that opinions are formed if members of the target's management need to be replaced. In cross-border acquisitions there is a need to proceed with caution before key judgments or decisions are made because of the additional possibility of cultural and language misunderstandings.

There is always a competition for funds within a company and there might be a number of divisions pushing their pet M&A project forward at the same time. This competition could be reflected in the decision body where deals are compared and challenged. Post-deal it is the normal case that everybody has an interest that the post-merger integration is successful. If it drains the company's resources it might take a while until the next M&A project is possible. Peer reviews from the divisions that recently acquired can add value and ensure that knowledge is transferred and plans are complete. Such reviews can take place post-signing and pre-closing or just after closing. The value that peer reviews can bring is of course dependent on the corporate culture that supports them.

Always pick the best leaders, executives, analysts, and subject matter experts for the M&A project. For line managers allocate up to 50% of their time on a M&A project. Temporarily back-fill their line positions if needed with internal resources or with consultants. The line organization should have momentum and competence to move forward without 100% attention of a line manager.

Some poorly structured M&A projects are exposed as having the wrong resources when the perception is that there are large volumes of complex decisions to be made. It is actually the case that the wrong people are in charge of the project or the project is not well structured. If junior managers are involved, and they could be very bright, but without the mandate, then momentum could be lost, as the junior needs to clear everything with the senior line manager, thus slowing down the decision process.

TARGET COMPANY CRITERIA

One acquirer is said to have had as a prerequisite for being on the short list that the target's office environment, kitchen, lunchroom, coffee machine, and toilets were clean and in order when the M&A team visited. Whatever criteria selected for an M&A project there are benefits both from being objective and structured, and from being subjective and creative.

The balance depends on what is to be achieved and what is the ideal company that can be acquired. How good should it be? Ready for takeoff or an unpolished gem? All the targets on the short list will be evaluated toward the criteria as a way to get the feel for the dynamics in the different scenarios. For example, to capture the value in target 1 more resources are needed from the acquirer's organization, and for target 2 less resources are needed, but there is also less overall value.

Future value of a target is estimated in financial modeling, the DCF, and the cost of acquiring the target in the valuation. This value-added logic (see Figure 2.7) is part of the criteria for the deal and the comparison of different targets. It is suggested as a minimum to also look at the attractiveness and

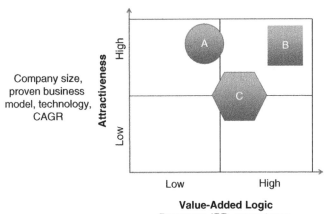

FIGURE 2.7   Attractiveness versus Value-Added Logic

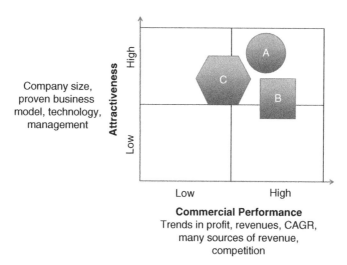

FIGURE 2.8 Attractiveness versus Commercial Performance

the commercial performance of the target to the present for all the targets on the shortlist (see Figure 2.8).

Target attractiveness criteria is where there is room for more subjective views, for example, how good the target's executive team and middle management are and whether they will be able to realize the value of the deal. How easy will it be to integrate and set in place governance of the target? It is essential in cross-border deals to formulate the most relevant criteria and an opinion on the attractiveness of a target.

Commercial performance criteria include looking at historical data and trends to understand, for example, if the target has been able to expand more than its competitors in its market. Are all the commercial trends positive? These criteria evaluate hard facts and the trends. The risk lies in trusting data that cannot be cross-checked. It is where targets' creativity in "dressing up the bride" can be found, but also misleading statements and pure falsifications of data. Things need to be picked apart, a thorough check done under the hood. Kick the tires and take it for a test ride.

Criteria can of course be added along the way as the team gains more knowledge and understanding. One important part is the understanding the team gets of the target by using and discussing the criteria. The other important part is that it makes it easier to compare different targets by plotting them out.

Certain team individuals or deal champions fall in love with a transaction and try to bend the analysis of the data to their advantage. They see it as a very good deal and they bend it a little bit so that it goes through the corporate red tape and hoops. The criteria could help catch that.

EXAMPLE OF CRITERIA

VALUE-ADDED LOGIC

- Product revenues
- Value of product IPRs
- Value of competence
- Market value

TARGET ATTRACTIVENESS

Prerequisites:

- Target company size: 10–50 employees
- Has proven business model and technology, meaning not only early adopters in customer base
- Highly advanced and are or has the capability of becoming number one or number two in its niche; this is ensured by, for example, patents, unique know-how, unique design, or unique customer relationships
- Target's market has a CAGR > x%

To be considered:

- The target's products are fully developed, have a proven concept, strong track record, and satisfied customers
- Buying company's existing R&D organization should ideally be able to take responsibility for target R&D if key staff leaves
- Quality of executive team
- Quality of middle management
- Alignment in market and industry future outlook and vision
- Ease of integration
- Ease of putting governance in place

TARGET'S COMMERCIAL PERFORMANCE

Prerequisites:

- Has had positive turnover and sales in the last three years, and trends are all positive
- Can be sold through the buying company's sales channels

To be considered:
- The target's products have expected organic growth of over 10% per year, driven by strong underlying market growth and the potential to increase installed base
- Is commercially accepted in the market
- Price of comparable offering on par with your company
- Will add to buyer's company results in year 2—that is, positive cash flow
- Has one main complex offering—that is, requiring advance sales, which ensures high margin
- Little competition in niche market
- Preferably a significant portion of recurring business

The criteria above should be used in the M&A screening phase to first create a long list of potential targets and then narrow this down to a short list. The long list is normally done with desktop research only and the short list might involve more hands-on research and potential contacts with the target's customers, users, suppliers, and competitors. Depending on the deal, this could be done prior to approaching the target, for example, when acquiring listed companies, or the understanding that the owners are willing to sell for privately held companies. The creation and contents of a long list can be outsourced to a market research company, but it is recommended that the buyer be more actively involved in the short list. Large and small buyers may follow hundreds of companies, defining triggers, priorities, or timing that will move a target onto the short list. A trigger could be that a barrier to entry is removed in a market; for example, when consumers are buying similar products in volume, government regulations are changed, a customer sets up operations, or a technology becomes available. A priority is perhaps to buy a regional distributor before buying local service companies. Timing could be related to when in an industry cycle or when in the calendar year to acquire.

PREPARE AND PLAN FOR A CROSS-BORDER DEAL

Once a company has decided that the business should grow by acquiring a cross-border target, the M&A deal team needs to prepare for it. Instinctively there is a view of the capabilities of colleagues and what needs to happen to put together the deal. Preparations are halfway there if the company has an M&A process and the tools that go with it. The other parts are people, leadership, and mind-set.

When planning for the M&A project it is wise to think things through before embarking. It is suggested that the team use the buyer's M&A process as the base to determine what approach will be taken in each step. There are workshop techniques that can help play out and plan for the different scenarios, such as storytelling. Write a simple resource plan that covers all phases of the M&A project as well as a time plan with key deliverables.

Previously in the chapter, the need to ensure good and accurate information was mentioned as a requirement for a high-quality M&A project, as well as the need in a cross-border situation to cross-check information and be critical of analyst reports (they may have been fed false data). This cannot be overstated as preparations are being made. If a person travels into unknown territory there is a need to pack for all possibilities. The task at hand is to, within reason, get to know the M&A deal territory through facts.

One way to avoid frustration and discussion in the target post-signing is for the acquiring company to up-front set up *M&A policies and directives* that can be just a slide or more detailed. Serial acquirers can be more detailed and develop a baseline or target operating model for acquisitions. The use of M&A policies and directives applies for most cross-border transactions where it is important to communicate and be clear on expectations prior to signing to avoid issues. It can be stated as absolutes, a baseline, or an operational model. It has been used successfully by many acquirers and presented to targets pre-signing to ensure ease of capturing synergies and managing the integration. It clearly defines what is up for discussion and what is not. The M&A policies and directives can be stated by all the various functions in the acquiring company.

Following are some examples of the contents that could be featured in M&A policies and directives documents:

- *Brand*, the company will have a multi-brand strategy and not change brand in the local market.
- *Remuneration* will not be harmonized or new employment agreements signed with all employees or benefits harmonized/integrated. Going forward a new compensation and benefit setup will be used for new hires.
- The company will have *one lean functional organization* with strong local presence according to market needs and a very lean administration.
- The company has very *conservative policies* on travel, company cars, office space, staff events, and extras.
- The company has a focus on *reducing working capital.*
- A joint *operational development plan* will be developed within six months.

- *One intranet*—the company will migrate to one intranet within x months. Consider that it might not be necessary to migrate all information and only focus on current and business-critical information.
- *One IS/IT (information systems/information technology) backbone and system*—the company will migrate to one backbone within x months.
- One IS/IT policy on *personal computers* and their usage.
- One group policy on *employee conditions and benefits* going forward within x months.
- All sales-related activities will use the *company (customer relationship management (CRM) system*.
- *Any deviations are to be approved by the CEO.*

The executive team cannot be in every M&A meeting and there is a need to set the mind-set of the team beyond revenues, profits, and synergies. The mind-set needs to be the same pre- and post-signing. This channels the energy of the team where it adds most value and provides guidance.

The M&A mind-set example below is specific for a transaction and is primarily used in the integration phases:

- Increased sales, growth, customers, staff efficiency, and hitting key performance indicators are all priorities above integration
- Create and keep momentum
- Do not forget that if nothing is broken, nothing needs to be fixed
- Focus on finding quick wins, leading practices, and improvements
- Focus on improving the full process or flow; for example, order to cash
- Qualify every day
- There will be changes

Staffing the M&A team can only benefit from an understanding of how the cross-border target will be governed after a successful acquisition. Which operational unit(s) will be working closely with the target post-acquisition? The M&A team needs a balance between subject matter experts and those who will be there for the long run. There are benefits of aligning key staff before the signing, which needs to be matched with the risk of a leak to the public pre-signing. Logbooks and personal NDAs with 100+ employees have resulted in M&A projects without leaks, but it all depends on corporate culture if that many employees can be involved pre-signing.

The acquirer's knowledge of the market or region where the cross-border acquisition might take place determines the scope and knowledge needed in the M&A team. What are products or services selling for? How does the value chain look? Channels? Customers? Suppliers? What are the barriers? What are the organic opportunities? There are of course market research agencies or government initiatives that can help buyers get a feeling for the new market, but nothing compares to a couple of field visits meeting people within the industry.

Companies sometimes acquire partners and see a partnership as a step to evaluate the business opportunities and get to know the people before acquiring. That could work out very well in many cases. For smaller family-owned companies, this could result in a 10%–20% lower purchase price in competitive bids if rapport has been established with the owners. The owners could then feel comfortable, and trust that the employees and the business they have created will be in good hands. That rapport can be difficult to achieve at arm's length, so a partnership or joint venture can help to get closer and understand the business. This tactic can be successfully used in cross-border situations, but there are some drawbacks.

A company cannot be too successful in terms of building up the partner's revenues. That is the revenue that will form the base for the price the seller wants for the target. There is a risk to end up buying a part of the acquiring company's own revenues if it is, for example, a supplier or a partner. The acquiring company's business case and strategy could have been to get rid of margin upon margin, but it ended up with a difficulty in agreeing on the purchase price. If the supplier/partner has products or components that have been embedded into the acquiring company's offering then there can be double the trouble because it is not possible to buy the partner and it is perhaps hard to switch them out of the offering. Success is now tied with the supplier/partner's success and how they handle the business. The partner may also sell the business to somebody else who is prepared to fully pay for the revenues. Some mitigation of the above could be a clause in the partner agreement, giving the other partner right of first refusal to acquire in case of an offer from a third party.

Some tools and template suggestions that can be useful:

- A DCF analysis template
- Presentation template for decision on negotiation mandate and signing mandate
- Portfolio mapping template
- Ansoff's growth matrix (see Figure 2.9)
- M&A screening templates for long and short lists

Developing a solid M&A strategy has many aspects, as discussed in this chapter. It cannot be fast-tracked, but needs to be agile to follow the market and the acquirer's business development. The alternative is an opportunistic approach and that increases the risk in spending energy and resources on

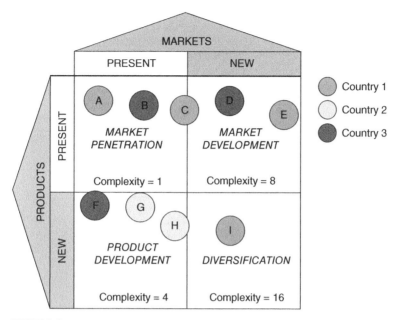

FIGURE 2.9 Ansoff's Growth Matrix

targets where there is potential, but not where there is the best value and fit with the acquirer.

CHAPTER CHECKLIST

- Components of a cross-border M&A strategy
- Responsibilities and accountabilities in the organization, to ensure the best decision possible
- What are the target company criteria
- How to prepare and plan for a cross-border deal

Legal, Financial, Social, and Political Interdependencies with Cross-Border Integration

Andrew Scola

CHAPTER LEARNING OBJECTIVES—IN THIS CHAPTER, YOU WILL LEARN:

➤ An introduction to the macroeconomic, legal, and social impacts on cross-border M&A and integration
➤ Recent regulatory, tax, and political concerns that are impacting cross-border carve-out and integration activity
➤ What integration teams should look out for to avoid some of the pitfalls, some of which can be very public and value destructive

CHAPTER SUMMARY

This chapter introduces the key legal, financial, social, and political influences on, and implications of, cross-border mergers, acquisitions, and divestitures. It puts cross-border M&A programs in context within and between the jurisdictions and societies where the companies operate.

INTRODUCTION

M&A is a complex world. From negotiation, valuation, and rationale, through to completion and integration, we are reminded with each transaction that every deal is different, and each integration will require specific skills and face different challenges. However unique the deal may be there are always numerous interjurisdiction, macroeconomic, and social variables surrounding transactions that affect not only the deal itself but also the success of the subsequent integration program.

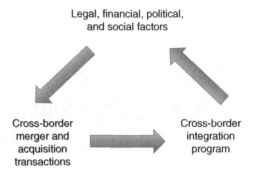

FIGURE 3.1   Cross-Border M&A Causal Triangle with Legal, Financial, Political, and Social Factors

Figure 3.1 illustrates that generically these factors impact the transaction, which of course will shape the objectives and specifics of the integration, which in turn will have legal, financial, social, and possibly political ramifications. This chapter provides an overview and introduction to some of these factors under the four groupings noted above; namely legal, financial, social, and political, and how they impact and influence M&A deals and integrations.

Well-prepared companies will have an understanding of this causal cycle in relation to the specific factors relevant to potential deals within target jurisdictions, plan accordingly, and be prepared to adapt the deal structure, deal objectives, or integration plans as necessary. Local factors are likely to be well understood, but where a company is acquiring or operating for the first time, or expanding or changing the nature or scale of its business in a foreign jurisdiction, extra attention is needed to ensure a comprehensive understanding of the potential requirements and pitfalls.

Companies headquartered in countries with well-developed legal and regulatory frameworks may find those of other countries ambiguous or worse—this should not preclude M&A activity in such markets, but a risk-based approach to the deal synergies and integration planning is advised, and allowance for the unknown is prudent. Global PMI Partners asked M&A professionals, with collective experience of cross-border integration across 36 different countries, which geographies had the highest and lowest levels of legal, regulatory, and political challenges.[1] The weighted average results are given in Figure 3.2, showing China and India with the most cross-border challenges and the United Kingdom and Australasia with the least.

In the rush to get deals signed, some of the influences and implications can be overlooked or bad assumptions made about them. Case studies on failed cross-border M&As are littered with examples of such failures to recognize and act upon what in retrospect are relatively simple oversights. These can cause risks and issues during integration, erode or destroy deal

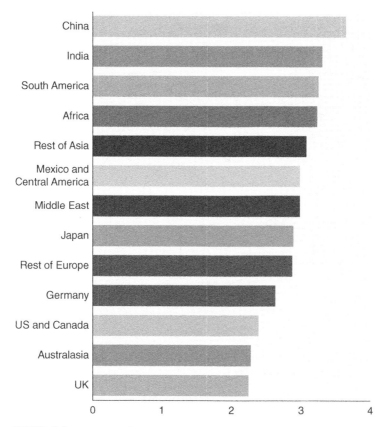

FIGURE 3.2 Degree of Legal, Regulatory, and Political Cross-Border Challenges Experienced by Global PMI Partners' Survey Respondents

synergies or, at worst, materially harm the reputation and the market position of the combined business. For this reason, professional advice and support should always be sought, for both the hard (legal and tax) and the softer (political and social) interdependencies referenced in this chapter.

In this chapter an attempt is made to describe the four factors and trends separately for simplicity; however, as Figure 3.3 illustrates, these should not be taken independently, nor should they be seen as exclusively one of these categories. Together they provide the context within which cross-border deals are done, the complexity that surrounds such deals, and some of the implications for integration. They highlight global trends that can precipitate international cooperation, change laws, form public opinion, topple politicians, and affect jobs and lives.

For example, taxation is a financial matter within a jurisdiction, yet the implications of tax differences between states, government incentives on the

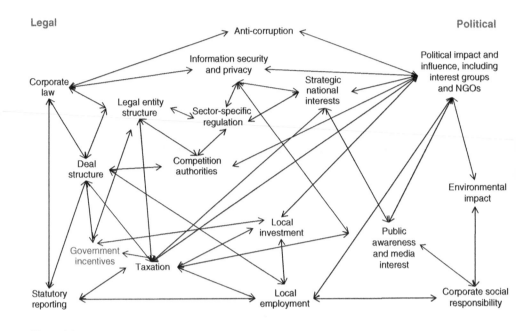

FIGURE 3.3   Web of Key Legal, Financial, Political, and Social Interdependencies Related to Cross-Border Integration

national or regional level, and tax departments' judgments and exemptions are the key determinants of deal structures and optimal legal entity structures. As the level of media coverage and subsequent legislation in America around "tax inversion" has shown, legitimate corporate M&A activity designed to optimize taxes can have huge public and political ramifications as well, putting M&A on the front pages of tabloid newspapers all around the world and putting taxes on the political and social agenda in many countries.

LEGAL IMPACT

When it comes to mergers and acquisitions, there are many basic legal and regulatory aspects that need to be considered, but the focus will be on these three:

- Deal structure and legal entities
- Competition
- Sector-specific regulation

In Global PMI Partners' 2015 survey on cross-border integration,[2] corporate law and sector-specific regulation were the top two areas impacting the integration of the respondents' cross-border deals.

Deal Structure and Legal Entities

Cross-border acquisitions can be structured in different ways according to the commercial objectives of the acquirer, and these can have major implications on the subsequent integration program. First, business deals can be structured as either asset deals, where specific assets and liabilities are purchased, or stock deals, where the owners' shares of the legal entity are traded.

Asset Deal. The seller retains the legal entity and the acquirer purchases specific tangible or intangible assets such as manufacturing facilities, offices, equipment, licenses, contracts, intellectual property, brand rights, or inventory. Asset sales can provide specific tax benefits and increase cash flow, while minimizing liabilities transferring with the sale.

Stock Deal. The acquirer purchases the stock directly, obtaining partial or full ownership of the seller's legal entity itself. All assets and liabilities, contracts, and permits held by the entity at the time of the sale are retained by it and come with the deal.

Buyers often prefer asset deals whereas sellers prefer stock deals reflecting the benefits and risks to the relative parties, but of course for a successful deal, both parties must agree. The majority of acquisitions are in fact stock deals, and the ratio increases with the size and complexity of the deal. For this reason, most cross-border transactions are stock (also called equity) deals rather than asset sales.

Set against this, though, are rules in some countries about foreign ownership, which will require an alternative structure or approach. Russia, for example, has a law on foreign investments restricting foreign ownership and control in business entities of strategic importance to national defense, national security, or over strategic companies.

Some of the high-level implications of stock and asset deals are compared in Table 3.1.

Whether the acquisition is a stock or an asset deal, the acquirer can, and may need to, restructure the legal entities at deal close, or during the integration. The most common path is to acquire a legal entity in a country where the multinational company already has a subsidiary of some kind.

If there already exists a full legal subsidiary, then the legal, tax, and finance work streams normally plan an appropriate integration path for these entities, taking into account all of the assets and liabilities, the sales

TABLE 3.1   Integration Implications of Stock versus Asset Business Sales

Stock Deals	Asset Deals
Simpler transaction structure and procedure, with one sales and purchase agreement.	Since contracts are with the selling company, not its assets, third-party consents are required for many contracts or other asset types, slowing down the integration, making it more complex, or requiring phased purchases.
More tax efficient for the seller.	Potential tax advantages for the buyer, but risk of double taxation for the seller.
All liabilities transfer with stock. Liabilities and risks need to be carefully analyzed during due diligence and mitigated during integration.	Since the deal has probably purchased assets but left liabilities, the risks for due diligence and integration are likely to be lower. Any transferring liabilities are usually time-limited.
The acquirer may choose to settle outstanding lawsuits or claims to avoid publicity and management distraction.	Asset preparation is required, including compliance with local requirements related to asset divestments.
Target company's operations continue to be performed irrespective of the change in ownership (unless change of ownership clauses apply).	Where the asset is a division or a business unit, it is likely to require a carving-out, which may require transition services.
Transfer of employment is usually permitted, allowing employees to continue under existing contracts.	A legal entity is required to transfer the assets into. This will normally be one or more of the buyer's existing entities, but could require setup of a new legal entity.
	New employment contracts will be required, effectively making transferees new employees of the buyer.
	Due diligence can be more onerous in an asset deal.

contracts, supplier contracts, tax credits or liabilities, and the assignability of all of these. Transfer of these may be in one go or phased, and eventually one of the entities can be closed.

If the acquisition is a geographical expansion and the acquirer has just a branch office, sometimes referred to as a *sales and marketing entity*, or no entity at all, then the target can become the legal subsidiary in that market relatively simply.

The emergence of rapidly growing technology, consumer, and gaming companies that may rely solely on the Internet to reach consumers and contributors, with no need for local brick and mortar operations, provides an interesting new dimension to the previous model. The debate over the tax optimization of these companies, where they do make profits, in recent years has highlighted to the public the operating models of such companies, and their tax status can rely upon having no local operations. Small bolt-on acquisitions of talented teams or specialized products anywhere in the world may require special planning and careful integration to avoid disproportionate tax implications to the acquirer.

Coming back to the implications of these various deal and legal entity structures upon cross-border integration, the integration needs to be very aware of, and plan around, the transfer dates of sales, supplier, and employment contracts between entities. Particularly in countries with stronger labor laws provisions, the operational restrictions around employee transfers can be surprisingly impactful. Where integrations have a major integration milestone, these are often largely determined by the legal transfers occurring on those dates.

Competition Authorities

A competition authority is a government agency that regulates competition laws and enforces them within a certain jurisdiction. There are a couple of multinational regulators that oversee antitrust issues across a trade bloc, most famously the European Commission's Directorate-General for Competition, but most are national regulators.

The number and scope of rules and regulators is changing and expanding rapidly at the moment, with major changes over the last few years in the United Kingdom, Brazil, China, Russia, the Common Market for Eastern and Southern Africa (COMESA), India, and Turkey. The most influential regulators tend to include those where M&A deal activity is high, consumer protection laws are more mature, or where national protectionist measures are in place, and we will focus more on these:

Brazil—Conselho Administrativo de Defesa Economica

China—Ministry of Commerce

European Union—European Commission (Directorate-General for Competition)

France—Autorité de la concurrence

Germany—Bundeskartellamt

India—Competition Commission of India

Israel—Israel Anti-Trust Authority

Japan—Japan Fair Trade Commission

Russia—Federal Antimonopoly Service of Russia

United Kingdom—Competition and Markets Authority

United States—Department of Justice Antitrust Division and the Federal Trade Commission

For a full list of national competition regulators, see Figure 3.4.

Objectives and Political Intervention of Competition Authorities The regulators' explicit aim is to protect the rights and interests of local consumers by identifying potentially monopolistic behaviors and to put in place rules, regulations, and measures necessary to prevent these. Authorities follow state laws, regulations, and merger guidelines that cover different types of integrations.

Competition direction, however, and sometimes specific judgments, can be subject to government or political intervention, and therefore can be used as a cover for protectionism. China, where anti-trust enforcement has increased significantly in the past few years, is frequently cited as using anti-monopoly legislation to penalize or prohibit foreign acquisitions, investment, and control in China, whether state-controlled or corporate, and protect indigenous Chinese businesses. Of course, China's competition laws differ from those of most Western governments because China is establishing "an aggressive antitrust policy that takes into account Confucian norms of ethics, morals, and fairness, and seeks to inspire increased corporate social responsibility"[3] within an explicitly socialist market economy, as opposed to Western authorities' "neutral and scientific neoclassical economic model,"[4] which separates law and politics. Even in the United States, the Committee on Foreign Investment can prohibit transactions involving either potential foreign control of sensitive American entities or critical infrastructure or technology assets (especially related to energy, import/export, and communications).

There has also been a growing concern from free-market and free-trade campaigners over the last few decades about the balance between competition enforcement and unproductive constraint of successful and legitimate businesses, and what is really in the interests of the consumer. In response to Western governments' anti-trust actions against such companies as Intel, Microsoft, Visa, and MasterCard, 240 economists wrote an infamous open letter to President Clinton in 1999,[5] stating that anti-trust protectionism means "open market competition is displaced by bureaucratic and political decisions. More of the energies of firms are directed to politics, less to production and innovation. Successful innovators are penalized, scale economies are lost, and competition is thwarted, not enhanced." The debate has

Flag	Country	Name
	Albania	Competition Authority of Albania
	Algeria	Algerian National Competition Council
	Argentina	Comision Nacional de Defensa de la Competencia
	Australia	Australian Competition and Consumer Commission and National Competition Council
	Austria	Wettbewerbsbehörde im BMwA
	Belgium	Raad voor de Mededinging/Conseil de la concurrence
	Brazil	Conselho Administrativo de Defesa Economica
	Bulgaria	Commission for Protection of Competition
	Canada	Competition Bureau/Bureau de la concurrence
	Chile	Tribunal de Defensa de la Libre Competencia–National Economic Prosecutor's Office
	China	Ministry of Commerce
	Colombia	Superintendency of Industry and Commerce
	Cyprus	Commission for the Protection of Competition
	Czech Republic	Office for the Protection of Competition
	Denmark	Konkurrencestyrelsen
	El Salvador	Superintendencia de Competencia
	Estonia	konkurentsiamet
	Finland	Finnish Competition Authority (Kilpailuvirasto)
	France	Autorité de la concurrence
	Germany	Bundeskartellamt
	Greece	Hellenic Competition Commission
	Hungary	Office of Economic Competition (Gazdasági Versenyhivatal)
	India	Competition Commission of India
	Indonesia	Commission for Supervision of Business Competition (Komisi Pengawas Persaingan Usaha)
	Ireland	The Competition Authority (TCA)
	Iceland	Icelandic Competition Authority
	Israel	Israel Anti-Trust Authority
	Italy	Autorità Garante della Concorrenza e del Mercato (AGCM)
	Japan	Japan Fair Trade Commission (JFTC)
	Jersey	Jersey Competition Regulatory Authority (JCRA)
	Jordan	Competition Directorate at the Ministry of Industry and Trade
	Kazakhstan	Agency of the Republic of Kazakhstan for Regulation of Natural Monopolies and Agency of the Republic of Kazakhstan for Competition Protection (Antimonopoly Agency)
	Kenya	Monopolies and Prices Commission of Kenya
	Kosovo	Kosovo Competition Commission
	Latvia	Competition Council
	Liechtenstein	Office of National Economy (Amt für Volkswirtschaft)
	Lithuania	Competition Council
	Luxembourg	Conseil de la Concurrence–Inspection de la Concurrence
	Macedonia	Commission for Protection of Competition
	Malaysia	Malaysia Competition Commission
	Mexico	Mexican Federal Competition Commission
	Republic of Moldova	Competition Council (Consiliul Concurentei)
	Netherlands	Autoriteit Consument & Markt
	New Zealand	Ministry of Commerce: Competition and Enterprise Branch and New Zealand Commerce Commission
	Norway	Konkurransetilsynet
	Pakistan	Competition Commission of Pakistan
	Peru	Free Competition Commission
	Poland	Office for Competition and Consumer Protection
	Portugal	Autoridade da Concorrência
	Romania	Competitionz Council (Consiliul Concurentei)
	Russia	Federal Antimonopoly Service of Russia
	Slovakia	Antimonopoly Office
	Slovenia	Competition Protection Office of the Republic of Slovenia
	South Africa	Competition Commission of South Africa, South African Competition Tribunal
	South Korea	Fair Trade Commission
	Spain	Tribunal de Defensa de la Competencia (TDC)
	Sweden	Konkurrensverket
	Switzerland	The Competition Council
	Taiwan	Fair Trade Commission (Republic of China)
	Turkey	Rekabet Kurumu
	Ukraine	Anti-Monopoly Committee (Ukraine)
	United Kingdom	Competition and Markets Authority
	United States	Federal Trade Commission and U.S. Department of Justice Antitrust Division
	Venezuela	Pro-Competencia

FIGURE 3.4   National Competition Regulators

only escalated since then on both sides of the Atlantic, most notably with the European Union's long-running argument with Google over anti-competitive practices employed by Google's search engine. While these competition investigations and legal cases don't directly relate to M&A practice, they generate negative publicity and distract management from other matters, including acquisition integration, which Google itself is busy with all the time. Google's acquisitions are also certainly scrutinized carefully for impact on competition.

The Process of Anti-Trust Approval   In terms of the anti-trust approval process, merging or acquiring parties now always need to identify required anti-trust filings, where there are regulatory bodies, the need for a pre-signing opinion from the competition authority and potential risks before signing any deals. The parties that may be obligated to notify include the selling shareholders in all cases, but also sometimes the target (in the United States) or even the nonselling shareholders if they continue to exercise control over the target (in the European Union). For this reason, while companies will only pursue cross-border M&A activity that they believe will be approved, the requirements for anti-trust filings and successful obtainment of anti-trust approvals are always inserted into sales purchase agreements now, in case competition clearance is not given.

Criteria set down by the relevant competition authority are used to determine the significance and potential impact of a specific transaction, and over specific thresholds, the parties may be obligated to notify the authority. Commonly used criteria include the parties' revenues, assets, market shares, and the transaction value. The concept of the "relevant market" within which to assess market share is a particularly contentious aspect of this calculation.

Competition lawyers can provide guidance and risk predictions, help prepare submissions, and provide transaction approval timetables, around which close dates and integration activities can be planned. They know that the European Commission and China have strict timelines for the review process, whereas the U.S. authorities have the ability to extend the timeline vastly. However, the variety of obligations between authorities, and indeed the differences between the jurisdictions a cross-border deal may straddle, cause the entire anti-trust process to be one of the biggest risks to integration planning, and a frequent cause of delay. The acquisition of Sauflon Pharmaceuticals by CooperVision is one example of this. The companies were unexpectedly issued an Initial Enforcement Order[6] by the newly combined UK Competition and Markets Authority in September 2014, after the deal had closed. This halted all integration activity and mandated the running of the businesses separately in the United Kingdom until clearance came through three months later.

This was because it is not mandatory to notify in the United Kingdom. In most jurisdictions, including the United States, India, and the European Union (EU), as Jay Modrall writes, "Notification is mandatory for transactions meeting the relevant thresholds. In some jurisdictions, including Australia, New Zealand, and the United Kingdom, however, notifications are voluntary. Merging parties may choose not to notify, bearing the risk that the authorities may later open an investigation on their own initiative. After a transaction becomes public, authorities in such voluntary filing jurisdictions may proactively request that a notification be filed."[7] Mandatory jurisdictions are usually suspensory, requiring notification in advance, but some such as in COMESA are mandatory but nonsuspensory, placing potentially unwinding burdens on the business post-close if not approved, and increasing the importance of good legal advice.

The European Commission cannot investigate mergers or acquisitions that it cannot argue put a company above the threshold for notification, but in the United States and China, the competition authorities reserve the right to investigate any transactions they wish, whether meeting the thresholds and notified to them or not. Again, this increases the potential for anti-trust implications post-close during integration.

Implications of Anti-Trust Rulings Risks to integration commencement and progress are referred to above, but the most impactful implication of competition authorities on M&A programs can come from the judgments and remedies of the regulators. Outright prohibitions of merger and acquisition transactions are rare given that competition guidance is quite transparent, precedents are usually established, and therefore lawyers have a good grasp of when clearance is unlikely. Far more common are contingent approvals upon some stated remedy, which may be negotiated or simply mandated by the authority. Frequently this requires "fixing" a competition problem generated by a merger, while at the same time preserving its economic rationale. Papandropoulos and Tajana believe that "divestiture commitments tend to be preferred by competition authorities because they are expected to restore competition without requiring constant monitoring,"[8] but intellectual property, licensing or other changes may also be possible.

The impact on the integration of such a remedy can be extensive, depending on the size of the deal relative to the carve-out, and the complexity and level of dependence of the carved-out business on other parts of the business. When Kraft acquired Danone in 2007, the European Commission agreed to the deal on the condition that Kraft divest a number of brands and a manufacturing facility, and to provide transition services to the divestment. A dedicated team was brought in to manage the divestiture at the same time as the acquisition, significantly increasing the complexity of the program.

In most cases, such divestments will not have been fully envisaged by the acquirer's deal team as necessary when the deal was agreed, and integration planning, synergies, resourcing, and timelines will all need to be reconsidered in light of the remedy. The parties are not obliged to accept the remedy and continue with the deal, subject to constraints within their purchase agreement, of course, and at this stage many deals, already in the public domain by this stage in the process, fall through.

Sector-Specific Regulation

The scope and mandate of sector authorities is another broad topic, but in regard to cross-border acquisition and integration, the relevant regulators to the buyer, seller, and the target may all need to be informed and often consulted before or after deals are signed. In heavily regulated industries such as financial services, health care, education, pharmaceuticals, and defense, they can also proactively put pressure on businesses to merge or divest if they judge there to be justification to do so.

In many jurisdictions, competition authorities work with sector regulators and share anti-trust powers with them, and regulators have separate legal authority over M&A transactions within their sector. In the United Kingdom, for example, the CMA works with Ofgem in energy, Ofcom in telecoms, ORR in rail, and Ofwat in water. In the European Union, both competition rules and those pertaining to sector regulation mandate the need for agencies to confer with each other, giving behavioral issues to the competition agency and structural issues to the sector regulator. There is a worldwide trend for regulators, themselves often growing and maturing, to take a much more active role in M&A.

Competition and merger guidelines tend to tell companies what they should not do, while sector regulation tells organizations what they have to do, and regulators have a much broader remit to question the parties, including sometimes aspects like management bandwidth, the identity of controllers, financial positions, and so on. Regulators are well placed to take such a broader view because of the depth of knowledge they have of the sector and history of the parties involved, who are likely to have been scrutinized by the regulator in the past through inspections, audits, and so on. When it comes to M&A approvals, "the best approach is one which involves cooperation between sector regulators and competition authorities,"[9] combining the expertise of both.

However, the involvement of regulators in transactions lengthens the transaction approval process, increasing the risks to the parties of proposed transactions being rejected or remedies proposed. In some cases, it can materially affect the willingness of executives to attempt M&A because of "concern[s] about 'hanging out there in the market' for prolonged periods of time due to difficulties in obtaining regulatory approvals,"[10] alluding to the commercial impact that public knowledge of proposed transactions can have.

Regulators also add complexity for M&A parties, as valuable company resources need to engage early with regulators to prepare information, answer questions and respond to them. In large transactions this can be hundreds of pages submitted through legal support under tight timelines, putting a strain on the acquirer's deal and management teams. Post-acquisition, companies may be required to provide further information to regulators as well, demonstrating that they are implementing certain recommendations. The post-notification submissions can also be requested and challenged by competitors as they are made public. Challenges include market definitions of an impacted market, as a wider definition might put the transaction below a threshold and a more narrow one above it.

Most acquirers turn to outside legal support for competition advice, which must be carefully chosen. All law firms specializing in anti-trust within a jurisdiction need to maintain good relationships with, and respect of, the relevant authorities, which could conflict at times with the interests of a client in a specific deal, for example, when it comes to remedies. The top law firms might come in at a high cost, but they are able to use their relationship and experience to negotiate and know when to stand firm.

The regulatory burden on transactions and during integration is particularly high in the financial services industry in the wake of the tighter controls put in place all over the world after the financial and regulatory crisis of the banking failures of 2007–2008. In this sector, regulatory reverse due diligence, where a seller performs due diligence on the regulatory standing of the buyer, has become common for identifying regulatory concerns in connection with a transaction.

In addition to their anti-trust roles, regulators have hundreds of other administrative legal functions that may impact the operations of the businesses during or after integration, and these should be considered during due diligence and integration planning. Because these vary between jurisdictions, and some of these may not be top of mind for executives and integration leads, companies need to ensure that the appropriate work stream leads are receiving advice and planning accordingly.

Examples of some of the regulations that can impact cross-border integrations include:

- Licenses to operate
- Professional accreditations and associations
- Local and international standards
- Health and safety certification

- Advertising regulation
- Food and drug licenses
- Banking regulation
- Environmental regulation
- Regulation and monitoring of pollution
- Regulation of acupuncture
- Sports and gaming regulation
- Telecommunication
- Vehicle licensing and regulation
- Wage regulation
- Cyber-security regulation

One note on the last point around information security and privacy to illustrate some of the potential impacts on integration. All organizations are now subject to complex regulation surrounding the protection of their own data, those of customers, suppliers, and employees, and especially those of the public. The numerous examples of information security flaws, leaks, hacks, and lost data make this important across all industries. Given the press and public interest in news of corporate failures in this area, there cannot be any complacency in this area. Management of data across borders is itself a complex area—Safe Harbor laws go some way toward enabling the free movement of data between countries that respect one another's data protection laws, notwithstanding the EU's striking down of U.S.-EU Safe Harbor laws in October 2015. However, acquirers must ensure that data security and data handling are sufficient immediately after taking control. Furthermore, integration plans can presume data integration without taking these laws into account.

FINANCIAL IMPACT

Naturally, the financial implications of cross-border integration are impactful, principally due to differences between the jurisdictions of the parties with regard to taxes and financial accounting and reporting. This section describes these in some detail.

Taxation

All mergers, acquisitions, and divestitures have tax implications to buyers and sellers, and the importance of these is hard to overstate. The previous section describes how a principal differentiator of stock and asset transactions is often their tax treatment, but the implications of taxation go well beyond deal structure, and thorough tax integration planning prior to close is still too often overlooked in the rush to get the deal done.

Because of the variations in corporate tax levels and rules across different countries, it is one of the most important contributors to acquisition synergy models, even though it is rarely stated in public. In fact, tax efficiencies not only make or break synergy targets, they can become in some cases the sole rationale for M&A transactions. In recent years, governments in higher tax countries have been focusing more and more on tax optimization techniques, and one in particular related to M&A has been widely reported in the press—tax inversion.

Tax inversion is a term that describes a company's restructuring or reorganization in order to reduce its tax obligations by legally moving to a lower tax country, often via acquiring a company headquartered there. This is done principally by moving a company's headquarters out of the United States, which has the highest corporate income tax rate that is imposed on profits collected worldwide, into a jurisdiction with a lower or zero tax rate and a territorial system of collection. This allows the company to legally avoid a potentially enormous amount of taxes collected outside the United States and avoid some domestic U.S. tax as well through loaning profits to subsidiaries abroad.

The United Kingdom was forced to move from a worldwide to a local corporate tax system to avoid corporate emigration, but the United States maintains such a system for the moment. Although inversion has been around since the 1980s, it is only in the last decade that it has really taken off, and has moved from a tax matter to a public and political one, as discussed in the next section. Tax regulations in the United States followed public opinion and political pressure and started to adapt in 2014 by inhibiting tax inversion behavior—it is likely that tax inversion will be prohibited in the near future.

It is not just levels of corporate tax that need to be considered, as there are other related factors such as stamp taxes, value added tax (VAT), incentives for new investment, subsidies and tax relief, transfer pricing mechanisms, and so on. As well as impacting deal structure, the implementation and reorganization to support tax efficiency may impact the integration program.

Withholding tax and VAT leakage are common issues that need to be addressed during cross-border integrations and carve-outs. If transition services are required as part of a divestiture, and these are provided across borders, care needs to be taken to ensure that there is no leakage caused by those payments.

Tax accounting and reporting requirements continue until the integration is complete and the legal entity exists and is not in liquidation, and therefore the accounting and tax information systems to support the tax function need to continue operationally until no longer required. If legal integration occurs prior to full IT integration, the additional complexity and inefficiency of reporting across multiple systems must be adequately resourced.

Another implication on taxation during integration, as in business-as-usual, are the decisions made by other areas of the business. Supply chain efficiencies are often tax-led, but operational decisions made about cross-border logistics, vendor consolidation, and importers of record have implications on tax and need to have oversight of integration plans in order to assess tax impact.

In summary, companies need to understand the economic conditions and applicable taxes wherever they operate, which are changing rapidly at the moment in all parts of the world. Multinational companies and those performing foreign acquisitions need to be especially aware, as the difference between jurisdictions provides an opportunity to maintain a tax advantage if well managed, and a serious threat to deal synergies and business profitability if not.

Financial Control and Reporting

International Financial Reporting Standards (IFRS) have been designed to provide consistent global rules for accounting and reporting on the financial positions and performance of companies. Although originating in the European Union, these are now widely used around the world, enabling convergence of local generally accepted accounting principles (GAAP).

For cross-border acquirers, these standards enable high-level due diligence of potential targets and reduce the complexity of financial integration, enabling reporting across the businesses immediately after close relatively easily as the elements defined by IFRS can be used to consolidate quickly.

However, the United States has not adopted IFRS, so U.S. companies may use standards set out by the U.S. Financial Accounting Standards Board, commonly referred to as U.S. GAAP, but not conform to IFRS, and non-U.S. companies are unlikely to conform to U.S. GAAP. While both U.S. GAAP and IFRS require reporting on an accrual basis (as opposed to cash basis), and share components such as balance sheets, income statements, and cash flow statements, there are still some significant differences between them, making cross-border reporting in and out of the United States more complex as the reporting has to be "translated" between one standard and the other. Chinese accounting standards are also somewhat different from IFRS and U.S. GAAP due to their origins under socialism, although they are converging with the former.

Acquiring companies need to be "bilingual" across these standards, and between close and full integration, translation is likely to be required in order to satisfy the acquirer's reporting obligations.

SOCIAL IMPACT

The social impacts on, and implications of, M&A can touch upon public interest and public policy, environment factors, pro bono and social contributions, local investment in infrastructure, and often most acutely upon local employment. The objectives of a cross-border deal need to be transparently presented to stakeholders, and if there are difficult decisions that impact local communities around the acquired business or the wider public, these should be well considered, well prepared, and well justified. Preparations need to include thorough risk assessment and risk mitigation.

Corporate social responsibility (CSR) is a term that can be used to broadly define those aspects of a business where it attempts to take ethical decisions to improve the quality of life of employees, stakeholders, and the wider communities within which it operates, and may include policy areas covering waste and the environment, education and social causes, employment practices, and governance. It is possible to measure some of these areas of CSR and compare acquiring organizations.

It is interesting to note that organizations that score highly when it comes to the governance aspects of CSR are somewhat less likely to engage in M&A activity in the first place[11] because deal-making is a centralized activity for CEOs and boards, often prone to personal bias and looking for personal reward over shareholder value. Therefore, companies with stronger corporate governance, and higher CSR scores, are less likely to sign M&A deals. This could lead to a somewhat cynical view of corporate M&A, but on the other hand, employee diversity, another key metric of CSR, makes a company more likely to pursue cross-border acquisitions, because the competitive advantage of this cultural diversity over competitors makes it more likely for the acquirer to make synergistic gains through the acquisition.

It is probably difficult to draw too much quantitatively about the impact of CSR and social factors on M&A, but the impact on integration is huge. Social concerns permeate the work streams of leadership, human resources (HR), communications, culture, operations, and research and development.

For example, an acquirer deciding to achieve synergies by radical changes to the target company's environmental policy and waste procedures, even if aligning to its own, is likely to find itself quickly criticized by employees, locals, environmentalists, the press, and politicians. A company can quickly be perceived as draconian if it chooses to close down social or charitable programs run by the acquired business, which are often as important to internal culture as to external and brand image.

Notable failures in cross-border integration have come when acquirers have ignored public sentiment or occasionally gone back on public commitments. Kraft's acquisition of Cadbury in 2009–2010 is a well-documented M&A case study now, and a prime example of this. The hostile takeover of Cadbury, a cherished national brand, by the U.S. conglomerate elicited a media and political outcry. The Cadbury board felt it necessary to make a public ethical commitment that its Green & Black's brand would be moving its entire range to Fairtrade days before signing the deal in order to force Kraft into this commitment. The acquisition itself became acrimonious, with the chairman of Cadbury stating that he would prefer any of the other potential industry buyers to Kraft, and the UK business secretary, Peter Mandelson, publicly warned Kraft not to try to "make a quick buck" from the acquisition of Cadbury.

To head off British public, union, and political pressure, Kraft's CEO committed to various integration principles, including the maintenance of the Somerdale factory with 400 jobs, a decision that was reversed later. On top of a difficult and expensive integration, not least because of the cultural and productivity dip associated with hostile takeovers, it is likely that consumer backlash in the United Kingdom contributed to the difficult financial position of Kraft that year. The high profile of this acquisition resulted in changes to the UK Takeover Code to protect and empower potential M&A targets.

In general, acquiring companies, particularly those involved in cross-border acquisitions, will tend to be cautious when it comes to integration planning in these areas with social implications, for fear of value destruction, making decisions without information, and bad publicity. Announcements of cross-border deals, besides their financial and strategic goals, often focus on the social consequences of the integration, with commitments or intentions to maintain current ethical policies, staffing levels, locations, and so on. Unless the deal rationale is dependent upon major changes during integration, it is prudent for companies to come back to any changes that may be required, when the implications will be better understood and association with the acquisition removed. It also leaves time for communication with key local stakeholders such as local government officials.

POLITICAL IMPLICATIONS

Like the social factors, the political interdependencies with cross-border integration can be hard to predict. Generally, politicians and influence groups such as unions, campaign groups, and other nongovernment organizations will be interested in cross-border M&A if the integration causes significant changes to causes that they are interested in, which will tend to be the legal, financial, or social factors listed earlier.

Stakeholder mapping is important here to identify all of the public and political organizations that may be interested in the M&A deal, at home and abroad, and to anticipate those aspects of the integration that will be of interest to them in advance. Political stakeholders will not be interested in synergies or corporate deal rationale, but rather with the public, social, environmental, and national implications of integration decisions. For this reason, a story is usually presented at announcement that addresses these wider social and political areas in a way that makes the deal positive or at least neutral to the wider stakeholder group.

It is usual for political intervention in cross-border M&A to focus on any negative impacts on the status quo, in response to announcements or integration activities. It was the announcement in July 2014 by AbbVie that it would acquire Shire for $55b so that it could move its tax base to Ireland and reduce its effective tax rate to 13% that precipitated U.S. government condemnation. President Obama called the move "unpatriotic" and the treasury secretary stated, "We should not be providing support for corporations that seek to shift their profits overseas to avoid paying their fair share of taxes." The U.S. government subsequently revised the rules on inversion deals making offshore cash immediately taxable by the United States, causing the abandonment of the deal at a cost of $1.635b to AbbVie. AbbVie was correct in asserting that the U.S. government had "reinterpreted longstanding tax principles in a uniquely selective manner designed specifically to destroy the financial benefits of these types of transactions."

The most common cause of political intervention, including unions, of course, is job losses. A foreign acquirer whose rationale entails cost synergies by making job cuts in the target market is a political and economic threat to the local country with little upside. While some back-office consolidation is understood and accepted politically, wholesale closure of offices or operating locations and movement of jobs offshore will be fiercely resisted unless it is obvious that there are no other options available, and those jobs would otherwise be under threat anyhow.

Another dimension, especially when doing business in emerging markets, is a consideration of the political links and dependencies of acquisition targets with politicians and political officials. Clifford Chance recommends performing "integrity due diligence" because "strong links with the government can be an asset but, if there is a change in political leadership, they can also become a liability."[12]

Political or special interest groups can and should be used to support and promote cross-border M&A where possible. Obtaining the support of nongovernment organizations, trade associations, and politicians is a legitimate means of boosting corporate public relations activity around an M&A deal, and throughout the integration. Social media can also be used for this purpose to positively influence public opinion.

MANAGING EXTERNAL RISKS AND ISSUES

Being alert to, and advised upon, the impacts and implications of all of these legal, financial, and social factors is essential to cross-border integration. Deal structure planning starts very early in the M&A transaction life cycle, but assessment of the impact of all of these factors may require buyers and sellers to be flexible.

By announcement, the impacts and the implications on the deal and the integration should be well understood, and reflected in the deal structure and terms, but the work of the integration teams has just begun. Integration leads and work stream leads share responsibility for mitigating, monitoring, and managing risks and issues arising from the deal and the subsequent integration. Investor relations, public relations, regulatory, government affairs, and HR work streams should be monitoring their relevant stakeholder groups and engaging with them actively throughout the integration.

Companies acquiring in countries where they do not have existing business teams, operations, stakeholder relationships, or local knowledge are obviously exposed to greater risks than those performing vertical or horizontal acquisitions to build out their existing markets. Local knowledge and experience of the harder legal and financial aspects is important, but so too of the softer political, social, and media implications. Where there are greater cultural differences between buyer and target, and language barriers that make assessment and feedback more difficult, there are more likely to be issues arising.

Western companies with free press buying in emerging markets are especially vulnerable to public and political pressures, and need to be especially vigilant to issues such as corruption and bribery, environmental impact, and human rights within target acquisitions as media stories on such subjects could destroy deal and corporate value very quickly.

Risk management for all integrations should start as soon as integration planning does, during due diligence. Integration teams should be engaging with the deal team and external advisors continuously to identify risks, plan accordingly, and monitor these on risk registers.

CHAPTER CHECKLIST

▪ Companies planning cross-border acquisitions need to consider both the impacts on, and implications of, the deal.
▪ Both the deal structure and integration program need to adapt to the specific context of the transaction, as competition and other regulators in any jurisdiction have the authority to block deals or mandate significant changes to them.
▪ Integration planning for cross-border deals needs to start during due diligence, with integration risk management taking a holistic view of the legal, financial, social, and political implications of the integration.
▪ Internal and external communication should follow the rule that the company communicates as much as it can as early as it can, engaging with government, union, nongovernmental organizations, media, and other stakeholders.

NOTES

1. Global PMI Partners, Cross-Border M&A Integration Survey, Question 12—"Based on your general experience, identify geographies where you have experienced the greatest degree of cross-border challenges (legal, regulatory, political, etc.)." 2015.
2. Global PMI Partners, Cross-Border M&A Integration Survey, Question 10—"Which of the following areas impacted the integration of your most recent cross-border deal?" 2015.
3. Thomas J. Horton, "Antitrust or Industrial Protectionism? Emerging International Issues in China's Anti-Monopoly Law (AML) Enforcement Efforts." *Santa Clara Journal of International Law* (2015). http://works.bepress.com/thomas_horton/21/.
4. Ibid.
5. Independent Institute, "An Open Letter to President Clinton from 240 Economists on Antitrust Protectionism," 1999. https://www.independent.org/pdf/open_letters/antitrust.pdf.
6. Initial Enforcement Order made by the Competition and Markets Authority pursuant to section 72(2) of the Enterprise Act 2002 (the Act) (19 September 2014). https://assets.digital.cabinet-office.gov.uk/media/541c3ad640f0b612d7000023/Cooper-Sauflon-_Initial_enforcement_order.pdf.
7. Jay Modrall, "Antitrust-Approval Risks: Issues and Pitfalls in International M&A Agreements," Norton Rose Fulbright, November 2013. http://www.nortonrosefulbright.com/files/antitrust-approval-risks-issues-and-pitfalls-in-international-m38a-agreements-108847.pdf.

8. Penelope Papandropoulos and Alessandro Tajana, "The Merger Remedies Study—In Divestiture We Trust?" *European Competition Law Review* 27, no. 8 (2006): 443–54. http://ec.europa.eu/dgs/competition/economist/divestiture .pdf.
9. Cornelius Dube, "Competition Authorities and Sector Regulators: What Is the Best Operational Framework?" ViewPoint Paper, CUTS Centre for Competition, Investment and Economic Regulation, 2008. http://www.cuts-international.org/ pdf/viewpointpaper-compauthoritiessecregulators.pdf.
10. David C. Ingles, Sven G. Mickisch, and Alex Blaszczuk, "Managing Regulatory Risk in Bank M&A," Skadden, 2015. https://www.skadden.com/insights/ managing-regulatory-risk-bank-ma.
11. Scott M. Morgan, "The Impact of Corporate Social Responsibility on Mergers and Acquisitions," University Honors College Thesis, 2009. https://ir.library .oregonstate.edu/xmlui/handle/1957/12180.
12. Clifford Chance, "Cross-Border M&A: Perspectives on a Changing World." http://www.cliffordchance.com/content/dam/cliffordchance/PDF/Feature_ topics/Cross_Border_Changing_World.pdf.

CHAPTER 4

Trends and Leading Practices in Global M&A

Thomas Kessler

CHAPTER LEARNING OBJECTIVES—IN THIS CHAPTER, YOU WILL LEARN:

➤ The key phases and steps in the M&A life cycle
➤ The importance of understanding the strategic reasoning for doing the deal, including the use of three tools that support developing this understanding
➤ Key reasons that drive cross-border transactions and financing strategies that may address cross-border concerns
➤ A step-by-step process that enables you to find and review potential targets for their fit
➤ Important issues to be mindful of during cross-border due diligence
➤ Options and strategies for mitigating the execution risk in cross-border deals

CHAPTER SUMMARY

This chapter describes trends and leading practices in cross-border global M&A. It stresses the importance of developing a clear set of strategic reasons how M&A and joint ventures will tie back to the corporate strategy. It goes on to discuss the concerns associated with transaction and financial strategies in a step-by-step process to find the right targets and what to consider in cross-border due diligence. It also highlights options and strategies to mitigate execution of cross-border deal risks.

GLOBAL TRANSACTION TRENDS IN THE POST–FINANCIAL CRISIS WORLD

The world post the latest financial crisis has driven a massive change in the financial services sector, causing a sizable build-up of government debt in many industrialized countries. The recession triggered restructurings, a push toward lean management, and a wave of M&A activities across a wide segment of industries.

Let's break down the events of the past seven years:

- Massive consolidation in the banking landscape of major economies
- Stabilization of the global banking systems backed by significant government aid
- Significantly reduced lending capacities and appetite, which intensified the recession across many economies
- Expansive government spending to kick-start economic growth caused spiraling government debts at levels never seen before and discussions on sovereign risks in the eurozone that has not been experienced before
- Many of the world's foremost currencies struggled, including the euro and the U.S. dollar
- Interest rates surged and triggered the necessity to cut spending significantly, which did not help struggling economies either

In the period post the financial crisis, central banks embarked on a quest to manage the recovering economies and currencies by keeping interest rates low. Improving profitability, growth, and low interest rates shifted capital toward the stock markets, driving valuations higher. Most recently, central banks engaged in buyback programs of government debt in an attempt to battle deflationary tendencies. While interest rates might rise somewhat through such programs, they most likely will remain still at historically low levels.

Let's shift perspective for a moment and look at the post–financial crisis from a business environment point of view. The post–financial crisis business environment had set the impetus to the next round of lean management. The recession created an even further urge to focus on core activities and capitalize from a differentiating position.

Many noncore activities have been sold or even closed down. Costs were slashed down to minimum levels and organizational restructuring activities included an increased focus on relocating industrial manufacturing activities to lower-labor-cost countries. Those activities that were retained in high-labor-cost countries saw improved efficiencies through further industrial automation and a significant push toward flexible use of the workforce.

Beyond cost, many corporates sought additional growth opportunities by exploring markets outside their difficult home turf economic environments.

Joint ventures, direct investments, and greenfields into emerging markets have been in vogue where it's possible to broaden the business base, eliminate dependencies, and generate much-needed growth.

Today's cash-laden balance sheets and limited alternatives for generating returns in other asset classes sparked even further the appetite for growth through M&A. Thus it is no surprise that M&A is a regular topic in boardrooms as companies seek to scale their differentiating position and technologies in an attempt to improve their competitive position.

It will be interesting to watch how far up the valuation and premium curve deal-makers move before transactions become prohibitively expensive to ensure value-generating integrations. Yet many board members perceive real assets as a safer investment given that they can forge their own destiny compared to retaining the excess cash in fixed income.

THE M&A LIFE CYCLE

The M&A life cycle (Figure 4.1) is an end-to-end process that spans five major phases and four major milestones. It incorporates every activity from defining your M&A strategy, to selecting the most appropriate target up to the operational integration of the same.

Description of the M&A Life Cycle Phases

Strategic selection: Cross-border M&A starts with the strategic selection phase and it is probably the most critical phase, although that is not often recognized. The fundamental decisions about the strategic fit, the *why* of the target, how its culture fits to the acquiring one, and what the acquisition will enable the buyer to achieve are defined here.

Some examples for the "why" could be:

- Access to new markets—topline growth
- Intellectual property—speed in innovations
- Closing a product portfolio gap—differentiating positioning
- Industrial automation/access to low-cost markets—improving the cost position
- Roll-up strategy

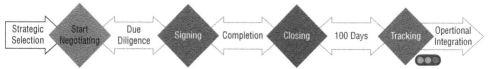

FIGURE 4.1   The M&A Life Cycle

The strategic definition of the search profile is followed by a phase of identifying suitable targets and approaching them. If an acquisition is an agreeable option to the target, *negotiation* is started.

If a true interest (strategically and financially) can be defined on both sides and the target/seller is selected to be on the short list, the next phase, the *due diligence,* is started. During due diligence, the buyer will gain a detailed understanding about the target company's solidity and commercial viability to engage in final price and transaction negotiations.

The negotiations will lead to *signing* a sale and purchase agreement (SPA) and announcing the transaction to the key stakeholders. As part of the announcement, all key executives and managers of the acquirer are to be briefed on the rationale for the transaction and its implications on the current business model and strategy.

During signing and closing a vitally important phase, the *completion* phase, is started. The early days of this phase are focused on gaining approval of the deal, if it is over the legal thresholds, from anti-trust organizations and other regulatory bodies that may need to approve it also, depending on the industry. In parallel both parties prepare for closing the transaction.

Vitally important during this phase is the planning of the integration. If the seller permits access to its premises and management, it is recommended to do a detailed revalidation of the synergy assumptions and evaluation. This is ideally followed with a *synergy working session* where senior executives from both parties are brought together for a two-day off-site review to prioritize the synergies according to impact and speed of implementation. Day One, the first day post-closing, needs to be planned by prioritizing vitally important administrative tasks that may not always have a significant value attached but require attention and prioritization to avoid overwhelming the target.

Post-*closing* the joint companies briefly revisit and move toward executing their integration plan during the *first 100 days*. This phase is typically started with a two-day off-site meeting, the *transition team kickoff.* Executives and managers of both companies meet to plan the details of implementing synergies and transition tasks, assembling a detailed integration plan. The huge benefit of this approach is that within two days, the joint company has a full understanding of the major milestones, where it needs to go, and is fully energized and focused on those tasks and activities. Asking a project management office (PMO) to establish a refined integration plan will typically take three to four weeks and stifle momentum. The kickoff approach provides quick and effective focus on what is important in the merger and permits time to stabilize the business and manage the day-to-day necessities while steering the companies toward their strategic goals.

Transaction Planning and Execution in the M&A Cycle

One of the most pertinent steps in transaction planning and execution for the C-level and board of directors is to align how a suggested transaction will link to the company's strategy and how it will generate value. If the *why* of a deal cannot be explained properly, utmost caution is required. Objectivity in assessing the *why* of the deal is essential. Deal-makers need to ensure that an in-depth due diligence is conducted and that any hurdles and risks identified are not pushed aside as management pressures the teams to get the deal done. Robustness of the target assessment, challenging the acquirer's assumptions on synergistic value creation and the joint business case particularly on customer retention and growth forecasts, is paramount. Often "forgotten" or mistreated as a nonessential is the cultural alignment of both companies; for example, how decisions are made and what behaviors are exemplified and incentivized. If a cultural assessment shows major discrepancies, it is a clear indication that major change initiatives need to be launched to align both cultures.

Another focal point is to ensure that a solid post-merger integration planning and execution process is in place. Clarity about, and repetitive communication of, the deal objectives and key performance indicators that will measure the success of the integration are important.

All discussed elements are part of a robust M&A process that leads the company from strategic selection, to valuation, financing, due diligence, synergy identification, and implementation through to closing and operational transformation in the transaction.

Securing a successful transaction requires therefore a fair amount of scrutiny and planning before the transaction can be approved. Post-signing, the planning intensifies. Post-closing, the integration planning continues as the execution of the various initiatives is executed.

Linking the M&A Life Cycle Phases to the Strategic Framework and Concepts Described in This Chapter

The M&A life cycle is a great primer for this chapter as it highlights the individual phases that take place from selecting a target up to completing its operational integration into the business.

It demonstrates that the "why" for any transaction is paramount. Developing this "why" requires that companies have a sound process to define their growth strategy. Research performed by the M&A Research Center at CAS University and Intralinks shows that firms of all ages that are extremely active perusing growth strategies through mergers, acquisitions, and joint ventures are generating significant total shareholder returns. Thus, the most successful strategies combine organic growth with transaction-driven growth. The next sections in this chapter offer a choice of strategic tools or, better said, a combination of tools that support the strategy process in identifying where, how, and why mergers and acquisitions may aid companies in their competitive positioning.

Following that is a look into a number of reasons that drive cross-border transactions, ranging from the need to drive growth to some very specific pointers that are associated more with cross-border transactions in developing countries such as deal structures, payment forms, relationships, and so on. The next section deals largely with financing instruments that are typically used in cross-border transactions. The choice of instrument depends largely on the type of acquirer—financial or strategic—the deal structure, the region, and the regulatory environment.

How to select the right candidate is also addressed in this chapter. It guides the reader through a process from finding targets to how to integrate the potential target.

The due diligence section addresses specific issues that companies need to focus on when involved in cross-border transactions. Finally the chapter closes with a number of options and strategies on how to mitigate risks in cross-border transactions.

DEVELOPING A SUCCINCT CROSS-BORDER TRANSACTION STRATEGY

M&A strategy has evolved over many decades. Numerous methodologies have been developed, with only a few creating stickiness in the boardrooms of highly acquisitive companies. The GE–McKinsey nine-box matrix focuses on identifying gaps and opportunities within a company's strategy. It allows companies to identify opportunities that require growth regardless of their immediate profit contribution. It also highlights selective investments for growth that will permit investments only if a minimal hurdle rate of return is met. Furthermore, it enables companies to identify when they should harvest the competitive position developed or even push actively to divest specific businesses. Focusing on growth through acquisitions, the Resource Pathways Framework taught at INSEAD provides a strategic framework that enables businesses to define the degree and strategic approach necessary for the acquisition of resources. Depending on the company's appetite for risk and control profile, it will define how and in what form it can internalize (build, borrow, buy) such strategically required resources. The cash value added methodology is the third concept and it enables businesses to identify which business activities add value beyond the required hurdle rates defined by their shareholders.

A Traditional Approach to Identify the Gaps Needed for Growth: The GE–McKinsey Nine-Box Matrix

General Electric and McKinsey initially developed the GE–McKinsey nine-box matrix in the 1970s. The intent was to structure and manage efficiently the key drivers for a business unit. Managing large conglomerates was a complex task and required very broad industry knowledge and deep management capabilities. An approach was needed that would focus management attention on the key drivers and facilitate the decision-making process on needed investments, including the necessary portfolio augmentations. Based on this initial impetus, the methodology developed and went beyond being used just for large multinationals. Today it is widely used irrespective of a company's size as its components have general application in business strategy.

Fundamentally, the GE–McKinsey nine-box matrix aligns industry attractiveness with business strength. Industry attractiveness is defined looking at the demand and supply side. The demand side is characterized by market growth rates and demand volatility. The supply side is defined by the firm's ability to set itself apart through product, service, and technology differentiation as well as its ability to manage effectively the degree of price pressure it experiences. The business strength of a company, subsidiary, or business unit is measured in terms of relative market strength, sales growth rates, cost position, and technology position, as well as market access. The required data points necessary to determine market attractiveness and competitive strength are not hard to collect as such intelligence from the market and internal information should be available for an effective budgeting and strategy process. Even smaller companies will easily be able to provide such data due to the need to think it through during financing rounds and to get a clear picture of their competitive position in the market.

Thus a company needs to define the benchmark criteria relevant in its industry for each parameter of the market attractiveness and business strength areas. The next step is to set the scale that makes a business or business unit attractive or unattractive, and the increments in between those two ends of the scale to complete the decision framework. The scale and associated decision parameters will typically be very different from industry to industry.

Once such a matrix is established for a business, business unit, or product group (see example in Figure 4.2) it also creates a strategic framework to identify gaps in the strategic position of the company. Those gaps may be closed through M&A. Logically this framework is applied for intelligence gathered about potential targets and their competition. Finally the framework also provides insights into the combined view and how the competitive and strategic positioning will change considering the impact of the M&A transaction.

Matrix of Determinants for Internal and External Comparison

Industry Attractiveness

	1 Unattractive	2 Moderately Unattractive	3 Moderate	4 Moderately Attractive	5 Attractive
Demand: Market growth rate	Very low growth rate	Low growth rate	Moderate growth rate	High growth rate	Very high growth rate
Demand: Volatility	High volatility of demand (= strong dependency on macroeconomic environment)	[Can be used if expert sees volatility between 1 and 3]	Moderate volatility of demand	[Can be used if expert sees volatility between 3 and 5]	Very low volatility of demand
Supply: Opportunity for product, service, and technology differentiation	Low potential for differentiation ("commodity-like")	[Can be used if expert judges opportunity for differentiation between 1 and 3]	Moderate potential for differentiation	[Can be used if expert judges opportunity for differentiation between 3 and 5]	High potential for differentiation
Supply: Price pressure	High price pressure	[Can be used if expert sees price pressure between 1 and 3]	Moderate price pressure	[Can be used if expert sees price pressure between 4 and 5]	Low price pressure

* Growth rates may vary by industry and region

Competitive Strength

	1 Low	2 Below Average	3 Average	4 Above Average	5 Leading
Relative market share (RMS) industry-dependent	Laggard (RMS < a%)	Follower (a ≤ RMS < b)	Average ("one of the pack") (b ≤ RMS < c)	Front runner (c ≤ RMS < d)	Leader or close #2 (RMS ≥ d)
Sales growth rate	Sales growth << market growth (Sales/Market CAGR < a)	Sales growth < market growth (a ≤ Sales/Market CAGR < b)	Sales growth = market growth (b ≤ Sales/Market CAGR < c)	Sales growth > market growth (c ≤ Sales/Market CAGR < d)	Sales growth >> market growth (Sales/Market CAGR ≥ d)
Cost position	Strong disadvantaged (only Company is "disadvantaged")	Disadvantaged (Company and others are "disadvantaged")	Average ("one of the pack")	Leading (Company and others are "leading")	Strong leading (only Company is "leading")
Technology position	Strong disadvantaged (only Company is "disadvantaged")	Disadvantaged (Company and others are "disadvantaged")	Average ("one of the pack")	Leading (Company and others are "leading")	Strong leading (only Company is "leading")
Market access	Strong disadvantaged (only Company is "disadvantaged")	Disadvantaged (Company and others are "disadvantaged")	Average ("one of the pack")	Leading (Company and others are "leading")	Strong leading (only Company is "leading")

FIGURE 4.2 The GE–McKinsey Nine-Box Matrix—What Is the Scale of an Attractive versus Unattractive Business?

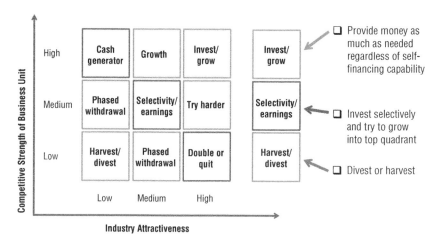

FIGURE 4.3 The GE–McKinsey Nine-Box Matrix—Where to Invest, When to Harvest or Divest

The framework enables companies to make critical investment decisions if set up for each of their major product groups and business units.

Figure 4.3 portrays a sample management decision framework that enables management to make investment decisions where they:

- Need to invest and grow regardless of initial capability to self-fund growth
- Need to invest selectively based on meeting defined return hurdle rates
- Need to monitor further investment carefully as it should only be permitted to a limited extent to continue to harvest cash flows before the competitive positioning deteriorates and leadership moves toward a phased withdrawal or straight divestiture

The GE–McKinsey nine-box matrix thus lends itself perfectly as a tool to manage portfolio augmentations effectively.

A Modern Approach to Link Strategic Growth and Resource Needs: The Resource Pathways Framework

The Resource Pathways Framework (Figure 4.4), developed by Laurence Capron and Will Mitchell, provides a framework for companies to effectively decide on how to manage growth based on resource availability, risk management, and process control requirements.

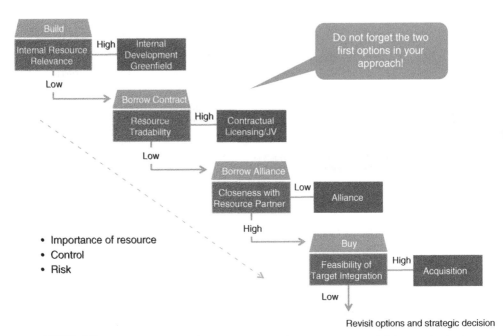

FIGURE 4.4   The Resource Pathways Framework—Resource Availability and Need of Resource Control as Decision Framework in Corporate Transactions

The framework analysis shows that greenfield operations, contractual growth solutions, joint ventures, strategic alliances, and mergers and acquisitions have different resource, risk, and process control profiles.

Greenfield operations are dominated by the need to internalize the potential and use or build up the required resources in-house. Simpler solutions like contractual joint ventures are chosen if resources are freely tradable and available in the market. If such resources are not readily available and more scarcely deployed, companies might choose to implement joint venture (JV) companies or strategic alliances. This preemptive strategy will permit mutual control among the JV partners. Mutually owned resources may not satisfy the need for a company to control the growth objective. If that is the case, it would inevitably lead a management team to decide to use mergers and acquisitions as the logical approach to drive growth.

The resource discussion is always accompanied by the understanding of the extent to which management can control the growth process and the associated risk appetite. Despite the fact that an acquisition might seem to be the best solution to drive growth, instead of a greenfield, it is also the most risky solution with respect to shareholder value generation.

Thus it is rather important that management weighs carefully its options to solve the strategic gap identified.

Cash Value Added, a Proven Concept to Ensure Acquisitions Are Value Accretive

Erik Ottosson and Fredrik Weissenrieder developed the cash value added concept in 1996. Conceptually it is focused on generating cash returns above the expected market rate. It is an integral part of the value-based management theory that has its inception with the 1991 publication of Bennett Stewart's book, *The Quest for Value: The EVA Management Guide*.

Cash value added (CVA) is defined as the difference between cash flow expressed as EBITDA plus and the minimum required cash flow. A very good example is provided in the annual report of Lufthansa AG, the German incumbent airline. The annual report of the company contains a section explaining CVA and demonstrating how they apply it in practice in their business.

EBITDA plus is an approximation of operating and financial cash flow. It contains all cash relevant items that are entirely influenced by management decisions. The operating result is adjusted for noncash items, such as depreciation and amortization; income from reversal of provisions; impairment losses on intangible assets; plant, property, and equipment; change in pension provisions before interests; and so on. The financial side of EBITDA plus includes among others pro rata pretax results of nonconsolidated equity investments, interest income, and results from the disposal of financial assets.

Minimum required cash flow is the sum of the required return on capital employed, the capital recovery rate, and the flat tax rate.

The capital base that is used to identify the minimum required cash flow is the sum of noncurrent assets plus current assets minus noninterest-bearing liabilities, in other words the capital employed in the business. The capital base is measured at historic cost.

The return on capital employed is based on the weighted average cost of capital (WACC). It is the cost of equity and the cost of debt multiplied by the respective weights of the debt and equity portion that the business is financed with.

The capital recovery rate is determined by defining the amount of investment needed each year and invested at the weighted average cost of capital to repurchase the asset at the end of its useful life. Expressing the absolute required capital recovery as a percentage of the capital base defines the capital recovery rate in percent that is used in calculating the minimum required cash flow.

The last element in calculating the minimum rate of return is the tax rate. The expected tax payment is also expressed as a percent of the capital base.

Finally the weighted average cost of capital, the capital recovery rate, and the tax rate are added and multiplied with the capital base to define the minimum cash flow required. Deducting minimum cash flow required from EBITDA plus results in the cash value added.

CVA is a general methodology that demonstrates if a business or business unit generates cash. However, it is also used to identify if a proposed acquisition will contribute positively to cash value added or not. In the case of Lufthansa, the 2012 annual report reflects that the sale of shares in Amadeus IT Holding S.A. resulted in significant cash value added. Using CVA as a key measurement for business success triggered on the other hand a number of portfolio augmentations such as the sale of the British airline BMI, as well as the sale of the loss-making equity investment Jade Cargo and other nonperforming, nonstrategic equity investments.

MATCHING M&A STRATEGY WITH TRANSACTION REALITY

Companies are well advised to understand some of the key drivers of cross-border M&A transactions in doing deals abroad while also considering various financing strategies.

The Key Reasons That Drive Cross-Border Deals

This section discusses the reasons that drive cross-border deals. It starts with finding information about the current trends in M&A. It continues with addressing strategic reasons why companies engage in M&A and joint ventures, highlighting the importance of relationships and hedging the risks associated with being a dominant force in one market but not in others, and discussing the reasons for current funding and deal-type trends.

In search of new investments: Many established companies have emerged from the financial crisis with strong balance sheets and deep cash reserves, which has triggered shareholders to request deploying such funds to either new investments to earn increased returns, or to return the cash to shareholders.

A number of global law firms, M&A software companies, and M&A information data services (e.g., Allen Overy, Latham Watkins, Baker McKenzie, Intralinks, Mergermarket) publish on a regular basis the trends in the market. Reviewing several of these sources, Europe shows a significant cross-border activity toward high-growth maturing markets such as India, China, and Brazil, while the United States is more focused on domestic investments and mature markets. Asia Pacific on the other hand focuses on its own region, China, and India. A growing portion of Asia Pacific investors is also focusing on Europe.

The "Why" for Engaging in Cross-Border Deals Companies have a wide variety of strategic reasons to engage in cross-border M&A activities. Among the most important reasons is a global expansion from a distribution and a capacity point of view. One factor that is less known, but should not be underestimated, is access to research and development (R&D) and software development talent. As companies shift more and more from using emerging markets purely as a sales channel toward a manufacturing base and on to creating intellectual property and know-how, acquiring skills and innovative software is largely an underestimated factor in cross-border deals. This factor will be increasingly important particularly due to the number of engineers, software developers, and pharmaceutical and medical students graduating in emerging markets.

Risk Sharing a Key Driver in Cross-Border Investments Cross-border transactions do not come without financial, cultural, and political risk, creating a reemerging trend toward joint ventures. The desire for risk sharing particularly from a financial and cultural point is the key driver for a significant number of cross-border transactions. The indigenous partner is typically well positioned to facilitate the necessary local registration processes while at the same time providing a learning environment for the foreign partner to assume a better understanding of the local cultural requirements to do business in that country. Furthermore there are still in some of the emerging countries' protective measures against full or majority-owned foreign direct investments, which leaves those with the desire to enter these markets with the only choice of setting up joint ventures.

Strong Relationships Drive Cross-Border Investments Prior to investing abroad, companies are well advised to build solid relationships in the markets they want to engage in. Typical are businesses building relationships to local distributors in an effort to test the market acceptance and need for their products. Once proof of concept exists the next step is normally direct investments in the form of greenfields, joint ventures, and strategic alliances or acquisitions. Acquisitions do not necessarily need to be 100% owned. They could also be minority stakes, depending on the strategic intent of such investments.

Long-Term Resilience Diversification of business risk is another key reason that drives companies toward cross-border and higher-growth markets. The world financial crisis has shown that companies with broader access to established markets and high-growth markets did well. This has triggered a review of strategic options for those missing the much-needed resilience to balance adverse regional economic development.

Beyond economic factors that can be hedged by a broader base, resilience itself is defined as the ability to manage any adverse situation. The world is converging and thus companies today need a broader multicultural personnel base to address business risks and opportunities alike. Cross-border M&A is driving this capability within organizations. It might be viewed as a side effect of doing business abroad, but building and developing the human skill base is an essential building block.

Cash Is King Cash has become the dominant form of payment in cross-border transactions in recent years.

The reasons are manifold. From a transaction point of view, one argument is the availability of cash on corporate balance sheets that is required to generate shareholder value or be returned to shareholders. Another argument is comparatively low interest rates, irrespective of the financial instrument. Companies therefore will carefully weigh the benefits of fixed income instruments versus financing a transaction via equity depending on the cost of debt or equity at the time of the transaction. Thus the use of equity may become less and less of interest as its cost might appear to be comparatively high, in low interest rate environments. This is particularly true as there is currently an abundance of fixed income financing available.

Taking a more operative view, chief finance officers are always interested in increasing the degree of natural hedges within the global operations they manage. A natural hedge is using the cash earned in local currency and reinvesting it by purchasing operating assets, financing acquisitions, or spending it for operations in the same local currency. Natural hedges eliminate the need to convert local cash earnings into the corporate currency, which triggers hedging cost, may incur foreign exchange losses, or may cause larger adverse tax effects associated with repatriating profits.

Asset Deals Dominate Cross-border M&A transactions are more often structured as asset deals. A key reason for this may be to target only specific assets while avoiding any hidden or understated liabilities that were not uncovered during due diligence. Most important is to understand the effect on tax burdens associated with the company you are targeting. Similarly, asset deals may prevent the acquirer from inheriting unlawful conduct issues if they shift the behavior once owning the assets. Conversely, acquirers need to weigh regulatory or third-party approvals that potentially need to be renewed if only assets and liabilities rather than the entire entity owning the approvals is sold. The discussion shows that there are many facets that companies need to consider when choosing either an asset deal or share deal structure for the transaction.

The current risk profile of cross-border transactions in emerging markets leads to a preference for asset deal structures while for established markets that follow global compliance and business ethics it leaves all choices open, from stock to asset deal structures and combinations thereof.

Key Financing Strategies for Cross-Border Transactions

Key financial strategies for cross-border transactions can vary significantly depending on the size and structure of the treasury organization of the acquirer. Most corporate acquirers manage their financial structure from a group treasury point of view for all business units, regardless whether the financing requirement covers internal investments or the purchase of a business.

Financial strategies may also be very different if the acquirer is a strategic or a financial buyer, depending on its industry, and they can vary depending on the degree of maturity of the market.

Cross-border financing strategies for established markets will typically include every conceivable financial instrument available in the market. This typically includes cash, any form of debt and equity, as well as hybrid financial instruments and various degrees of earn-out structures.

Equity financial strategies may include common stock. One of the most common deal structures where common stock is used is a merger of equals where each participating company exchanges its shares in a to-be-defined ratio into shares of the joint "new company." Common stock is also typically used for any other form of "nontaxable" acquisitions and mergers. ,

Leveraged buyout (LBO) funds, private equity, and venture capital firms typically use preferred stock instruments. They can incorporate above and beyond a preferential interest rate additional features such as participating preferred rights in the form of dividends and liquidation proceeds, or may feature conversion rights, antidilution rights, and multiple liquidation rights.

Loan stocks might be used to finance LBO structures as they convert to common stock only when a company defaults, thus ensuring that the equity provider next to the common equity–holding management also has "skin in the game."

Debt structures range from senior debt (loans with higher liquidation preference in case of a default), to subordinated debt (loans with a lower liquidation preference) up to bridge financing structures that are loans, debt, or bonds used as a preround financing enabling the acquirer to gain the time to put the final financial structure in place.

Hybrid financial structures combine equity and debt features into one financial instrument. This may include convertible debt (converting to common stock at a predetermined strike price and specific events) or mezzanine debt (subordinated debt that typically carries a warrant, i.e., the right to purchase shares or bonds at a predetermined price).

Earn-out structures are financial approaches to bridge the gap on price if acquirer and seller have differing views on the purchase price. They enable the acquirer to grant additional funds to the seller when certain key performance indicators are met. This typically requires the seller to stay on board at least for some time if not for good. Features can be that a portion of the purchase price is paid to the seller upon closing the transaction while other parts are paid upon reaching a predetermined performance. The final payout to the seller depends on achieving these metrics. If the seller over- or underachieves the predetermined metrics, the acquirer may pay more or less than the defined payout. Another feature can be that the acquirer pays the minimum price he was willing to pay for the acquisition in full at the closing date while the difference to seller valuation is paid upon reaching certain performance criteria. Furthermore, earn-outs can be capped or may feature no ceiling in their upper performance metric.

Publicly traded earn-out structures are contingent value rights. They act similarly to earn-out structures that upon reaching certain performance metrics, the seller of the common stock and holder of a contingent value right receives an additional predetermined cash payment.

In developing markets, we typically see cash and common equity structures used. Complex financial instruments are used to a much lesser degree.

The use of preference shares might be a good strategy for joint ventures in countries where the government prohibits a majority ownership by foreign investors. In such cases, common equity would be carried by the foreign investor up to the maximum level permitted by the government. Preference shares could be used to even out the ownership structure for a potentially planned or unplanned termination of the joint venture. Upon the sale or the liquidation of the joint venture, the preference shares would trigger the ownership to be equivalent to a 50-50 owned shareholding.

SELECTING THE RIGHT CANDIDATE

Selecting the right candidate is less a question of art than science. It is much more a series of logical steps that need to take place to identify the strategic fit with the companies' competitive position. The description of the strategic selection phase in the M&A life cycle started with the need to identify the *why* of doing the deal. How does it benefit the competitive position? The GE–McKinsey nine-box matrix is the tool described to identify those parts of the business where M&A is required to support the strategic position, while the Resource Pathways Framework provides insights into the decision process on transaction types. The cash value added methodology adds a tool that identifies if a chosen target may actually be value accretive. These are all critical elements in defining the DNA of the right acquisition candidate.

Managing Deal Sources

Where are ideas for potential candidates born? It is less important to name a list of sources, and more important to put them into the context of the annual strategic review of each business activity. The annual strategic review is a much better place as it puts equal opportunity at each business segment to think through how it is positioned today and how it will grow in the future. It requires all disciplines, from sales to procurement, from finance to HR, to participate in the process and as such to provide ideas where and why a potential target might benefit the growth strategy. Once that is identified, the question is where companies find such targets. The answer is obvious. Most targets, and typically the best targets, are identified from within the organization. Someone knows someone, has worked with a company, or has seen them at a trade fair and started a relationship. These types of targets make up the best candidates as they are reviewed in the context of the internal strategic process. However, there are also other sources that may generate interesting candidates that are then placed in the strategy review process or reviewed separately outside of the regular annual process.

External sources typically include investment banks, the corporate finance arms of accounting firms, trade associations, chambers of commerce, governmental trade agencies, and most recently M&A deal source platforms on the Internet. Other potentially important sources are the deal-lists of venture capitalists and private equity firms. These companies are not buying for the long term. They are interested in generating returns within a three- to seven-year time frame and as such will eventually divest of their assets at a certain time in the future. Building relationships to those that operate in the industry may prove to be extremely beneficial.

Building a Long List

The previously described approach of identifying potential targets that fit the strategic direction of a company is called building a long list. The long list may include companies that are not yet for sale, or have not been scrutinized for their specific value contribution, which is the process that starts once the long list has been assembled. The long list is simply a set of companies or business assets that may be of interest to the acquiring company, irrespective of timing. They are the candidates where it is vitally important to build long-term relationships as they may be on the short list in the future.

From Long List to Short List—Screening Targets for Strategic Fit

Once potential targets are identified as part of the annual or transaction-driven strategy review process, companies need to focus on building the merge case. This step requires companies to identify where they will find value post-deal. What are the sources and reasons to generate value? Is there value in driving geographic expansion, a better differentiated position, economies of scale, adding specialized resources and skills, or increaseing manufacturing excellence? Whatever the reason, it must fit the growth focus and core strategic understanding identified by the company.

The next step is to identify any potential issue or barrier that could threaten to erode the value that a company would expect to create from the acquisition. Hereby it is important to differentiate between hurdles and true risks. A barrier might be a hurdle, for example, an issue that can be overcome. It may however have the DNA of a risk in which case it is a management decision to either take or avoid that risk. As subtle as the difference between hurdle and risk may sound, it is important to pay close attention to the difference in nature as they may be the reason for the transaction to be value accretive or not.

Barriers may include geographic inconsistencies, differing sales force revenue recognition, technological and IT incompatibilities, widely varying management styles, cultural disparities, or underestimation of the financial investment needed to integrate the business. Last but not least, companies need to be sensitive to anti-trust investigations. Currently, we have over 100 merger regimes globally. This indicates that governments are intensely scrutinizing cross-border transactions.

All of these points make up good investigative questions for the due diligence phase and in particular the management discussions with the target's management during due diligence.

Finally companies need to develop their "M&A End-State Vision." How will the business be integrated from a geographical, functional, organizational, product, and customer point of view? Will processes, the IT landscape, and systems need to be adapted? How about facilities, human resource policies, the inherent culture? Addressing these points will force the company to focus not only on making a deal, it will also drive the leadership toward thinking of the acquisition as an integral value contributor. The highlighted areas become the first cornerstone in thinking about integration planning.

The previously mentioned steps are as true for national as well as cross-border deals. In cross-border transactions there is a need to be even more mindful of the geographical cultural and language differences that may be essential in turning the respective M&A deal into a long-term success story.

PLANNING CROSS-BORDER DUE DILIGENCE

Following the strategic selection phase, the acquirer enters into initial negotiations exploring the interest in the target to sell or merge their business with that of the acquirer's. If those conversations go well and interest is signaled by the target, the deal team typically moves quickly into exploring potential deal structures while initiating in parallel the due diligence phase.

Due diligence typically encompasses five core elements: financial, tax, legal, commercial, and HR due diligence. Depending on the industry, companies include other due diligence elements such as environmental due diligence for chemical and natural resources, deeper commercial due diligence for consumer goods, and operational due diligence for manufacturing type industries. It is key to understand the structure and capabilities of the target within a very short period of time. Information technologies and communication may also be a separate due diligence work stream if it is a vital component in the value chain of the company, such as in financial services.

Based on the work stream composition, it is essential to have the necessary skills on board while limiting the size of the due diligence team to avoid external information leaks and to more easily manage the work. Given the sensitive nature of M&A transactions, companies want to limit the involvement of the organization and manage the information flow proactively. Until signing occurs, the deal team is well advised to keep the fact that a deal is looked into very low key. Information leaking about the potential transaction can have a detrimental impact on the transaction management, including the purchase price that a deal team is willing to pay. All team members need therefore to sign personal nondisclosure agreements (NDAs) that prevent them from sharing any data they set their sight on outside of the core deal team and a log book is kept with the names of those who are on the team. The knowledge of a pending deal is considered insider information if the acquiring company is listed on a stock exchange.

Specifically important in cross-border transactions is local support. Whether the support is from within the company or external is not as important; speaking the language and understanding local customs is paramount for a full understanding of all the issues that need to be fully comprehended. Thus being able to translate subject matter information, whether it means literally translating documents or metaphorically conveying the meaning of a situation, behavior, or cultural differences, is essential for the appropriate decision-making process. Just applying a homegrown due diligence approach may be a risky way to conduct an investigation into a target. It may lead to wasted time, missed information, and overlooked key issues. Thus companies typically hire local advisors to assist with the due diligence as well as the legal requirements and possibilities to structure the transaction.

Additional critical success factors in managing an efficient due diligence project are the tools that are used. Virtual data rooms, an e-room, a Share-Point portal, and conference/video call capabilities are vital components, particularly if various work streams are managed across several geographical regions, time zones, and functional participation.

The seller typically manages virtual data rooms. They permit acquirers to review and analyze the data provided, ask questions, and receive answers. In some cases acquirers may be provided the opportunity to download or print certain documents; even so this is typically very limited. The data room requires the user to sign a nondisclosure agreement every time he or she signs in and each page is typically watermarked "confidential." Screenshot functions are regularly disabled on computers used to perform the due diligence to disallow copying data that are not intended for sharing with the acquirer. The acquirer benefits from virtual data rooms as they permit a segregation of duties regarding analyzing the data provided across regions. Specialists for each critical question can be engaged in the due diligence process enabling the acquirer to assess the risk and value associated with the potential transaction.

E-rooms or SharePoint portals serve an acquirer's deal team to exchange information within the team, perform data analysis, and create documents via a common project-based platform that enables only access to those who are supposed to have it. Given the highly confidential nature of M&A transactions, this is a prerequisite.

A similar critical role is associated with conference call and video call tools to enable an "all-hands meeting." This is a meeting of all work stream participants that usually occurs once a day to exchange the status and key issues each work stream is currently working on in the due diligence. It is most paramount for those work streams that are chartered to identify, evaluate, and develop synergies. They need to search across the entire data room and review more documents than subject or function-specific work streams. The all-hands meeting thus provides the synergy team with an opportunity to share what they are currently working on and receive tips from the various work streams on which documents to review in order to complete their tasks. In general, the meeting provides a platform to manage cross-functional Q&A as well as critical management presentation questions. Most important, it enables the due diligence manager to make quick decisions on whether to continue or stop the due diligence effort. Remember that once the due diligence starts the acquirer's transactions costs start to build quickly as it is regularly supported by external tax, legal, and financial experts who augment the internal skills within the various work streams.

Most important is to instill a clear responsibility to focus on assessing the risk and the value in the transaction. This is not about doing a deal "no matter what," this is about assessing a business and how it will generate value while mitigating the risks associated with the assets that are up for sale.

DEFINING SUCCESSFUL OPTIONS AND STRATEGIES FOR MITIGATING EXECUTION RISK IN CROSS-BORDER M&A TRANSACTIONS

This chapter focuses on mitigating execution risks in cross-border M&A. It therefore addresses three essential concerns companies need to address, the first being the political climate and legal environment the acquirer would get into when growing in a foreign market through M&A and joint ventures.

Second is the importance of understanding organizational culture differences and similarities that if understood and managed well are one of the key success factors.

Last is why integration does not start when the deal is signed or even worse closed but is to be addressed in each phase, starting with the strategic selection through due diligence, including the time between signing and closing and post-closing where specific integration activities will ensure value creation. Most important, each phase provides critical information to decide if the target is truly a good target and will successfully support the growth strategy.

Political Climate and Legal Environment

Starting out, the deal team needs to address any risks that may come from a politically motivated background such as anti-trust regulations, anti-corruption rules, rules that pertain to investments in certain sensitive industries (e.g., aerospace and defense, high-tech, and so on) as well as competition and foreign direct investment rules. By addressing questions around the political investment environment and climate first, companies ensure that too much time and effort is not spent on searching targets that may turn out to be unacceptable or where companies may be precluded from investing given the legal structure in the given country. Associated with these sets of questions are also political, country risk, and human development risk questions that need to be addressed. Companies typically check these issues as part of any foreign investment strategy that establishes the framework for the business or business units and defines where and by which means a company may be able to expand into foreign countries, be it with direct investments, distributor contracts, JVs and strategic alliances, or through M&A.

Cultural Differences

The next risk area that companies need to tackle early on is a solid understanding of the cultural implications and differences in a given country but more so with respect to a specific target. Culture can be defined in a simple but very precise way. Culture is a set of entrenched behaviors that define how companies get things done. If companies add an additional understanding about what behavior sets are incentivized, then they have everything that is needed to understand the culture of a company. Thus companies are well advised to start during strategic selection, initial negotiations, and while conducting due diligence a cultural assessment to seek out the differences in both parties and to highlight them.

Figure 4.5 illustrates a sample cultural assessment tool, which enables management to make assessments regarding cultural differences or similarities. The better companies understand the difference between their own behavior traits and those of the target the easier it will be to design change management activities that will bridge both behavior sets. Experience has shown that it is fairly reasonable to change behavior by changing incentives, one-on-one coaching, and demonstrating certain behavior traits top-down.

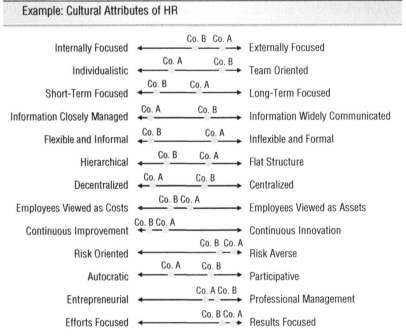

Example: Cultural Attributes of HR

	Co. B Co. A	
Internally Focused	←—•——•—→	Externally Focused
Individualistic	Co. A Co. B	Team Oriented
Short-Term Focused	Co. B Co. A	Long-Term Focused
Information Closely Managed	Co. A Co. B	Information Widely Communicated
Flexible and Informal	Co. B Co. A	Inflexible and Formal
Hierarchical	Co. B Co. A	Flat Structure
Decentralized	Co. A Co. B	Centralized
Employees Viewed as Costs	Co. B Co. A	Employees Viewed as Assets
Continuous Improvement	Co. B Co. A	Continuous Innovation
Risk Oriented	Co. B Co. A	Risk Averse
Autocratic	Co. A Co. B	Participative
Entrepreneurial	Co. A Co. B	Professional Management
Efforts Focused	Co. B Co. A	Results Focused

FIGURE 4.5   Cultural Assessment—Where Do Acquirer and Target Rate on the Scale of the Respective Cultural Traits?

Protective Employment and Labor Laws

One of the main findings in many transactions has been the absence of an understanding of key pillars in local labor laws. Receiving a short informational presentation about the key differences is very helpful for everyone involved in cross-border transactions. Whether the transaction will trigger the need to hire or to let go of local staff, both require an understanding of basic labor laws and customs. How fast can a person of interest change their jobs? What is the typical expectation toward compensation packages regarding pension, health care benefits, unemployment insurance, vacation days, and other fringe benefits? What are the prerequisites of letting employees go? What steps need to be adhered to, to do that? What are the basic rights that need to be granted to employees before a company can ask them to resign?

Asking for a simple presentation of the key issues may facilitate greatly the target selection and negotiations process and avoid critical mistakes and misunderstandings.

Pre- and Post-Merger Integration

Executives may be interested to learn that there are specific integration steps for each phase of the M&A life cycle, starting with the strategic selection all the way through to the post-closing operational integration work. During strategic selection and due diligence the focus is on developing and quantifying as much as possible an understanding of synergies while thinking through how best to integrate the target. Building an understanding of cultural differences is another vital step in the analysis of the target. Each of these steps will provide the acquirer with additional information if the target is well chosen and may provide vital information on the pricing of the transaction to ensure its success. Post-signing, companies start with the detailed integration planning. Typically this entails the "Day One" and "100 Day" planning and preparation, a more detailed dive into synergy evaluation and prioritization, as well as pulling the teams together that will execute the integration. How do companies handle this work during anti-trust investigation? The experience is that anti-trust regulation allows deal and integration teams to do some integration work and share some degree of data, while acting as two separate companies until closing. Data such as detailed customer and supplier data, and terms and conditions that would reveal information that may be subject to the anti-trust investigation, are off limits. It is also not allowed to plan already joint activities regarding customer activities and how to manage suppliers going forward. Sometimes seller and acquirer may decide to hold off on the integration planning until anti-trust is completed, and sometimes they even postpone it until post-closing.

However, acquirers need to know that there are also ways to press forward even during times when an anti-trust investigation is going on. This can be achieved through a clean team. A clean team is a team of external advisors who work with legal support from both sides and analyze information provided to the team to develop and plan integration activities. Important steps during signing and closing are also the executive alignment right after signing, as this will explain to a larger group of the companies' management teams why the deal was done, how it will unfold, and where acquirer and target see the value in the transaction. Another important event is the synergy working session done after closing. This is an important event at which the details about specific synergies are exchanged among the joint leadership team. Both parties develop a joint understanding of the priorities and can change the assumptions and results of the synergistic benefits. This is essentially another sanity check to ensure that once closing occurs the teams move at an accelerated pace in the right direction, capturing the value in the transaction. Post-closing the integration teams move toward executing "Day One" and the "Day 100 Plan," eventually handing over the integration from a project-based organization into the hands of the operational line management team.

CHAPTER CHECKLIST

- What are the key phases and steps in the M&A life cycle?
- Why is it important to understand the strategic reasoning for doing the deal?
- What are three key tools that support developing the strategic reasoning for doing the transaction?
- Which steps enable the reader to find and review potential targets for their fit?
- What issues should companies be mindful of during cross-border due diligence?
- What options and strategies exist to mitigate the execution risk in cross-border deals?

CHAPTER 5

Cross-Border M&A: Region- and Country-Specific Trends and Deal Planning Tips

Michael Holm

CHAPTER LEARNING OBJECTIVES—IN THIS CHAPTER, YOU WILL LEARN:

➤ Regional and country trends impacting M&A strategy and deal planning
➤ Some useful cross-border insights and tips
➤ Understanding corporate versus country cultures when doing deals
➤ Regional and country practices that influence post-merger integration

CHAPTER SUMMARY

This chapter starts with which countries and industries set the world trends in pre-deal M&A and where the trend is in looking for operational value. What are the considerations needed when choosing which country to establish in within a region is next. This is followed by a look at opportunities and competition clearance trends outside of the relatively stable economies of the European Union (EU) and United States. Some insights and tips for cross-border deals are shared and the chapter ends with local practices that influence post-merger integration.

INTRODUCTION

Competitive and deal-making advantage can be gained if trends or patterns can be extrapolated into the future and by that minimize the risks and maximize the results of M&A activities.

The majority of the deals done in the last few years originated or are tied to the United States, and that country's trends in deal making set the overall tone. Other countries at the top of the list of deal-generating countries are the United Kingdom, France, Germany, and China. China's deals have primarily been driven by access to raw materials for the Chinese industry and exploiting the valuation gap in stock price/equity between the Chinese and the western stock markets.

The industry sectors TMT (telecom, media, and technology), industrials and chemicals, consumer, financial services, business services, pharmaceuticals, and energy/mining/utilities are the top industries in M&A and the specific business and operational models in those industries set the trends (see Figure 5.1). So, the trends in those countries and industries are the primary focus in the beginning of this chapter.

On the other hand, there is not a deal that is identical to another deal. No share purchase agreement (SPA) is identical to another.

In cross-border deal planning there needs to be a decision pre-deal whether or not to allocate resources and analysis in the following areas:

- A *tax analysis* team that can look at country specifics to determine what is the best tax setup post-deal, for corporate tax, flows of products and services, pre-deal tax ruling, and what tax incentives could apply. This team can also look at how purchase price allocation can be done post-deal between entities in different countries.
- Local *legal assistance* for due diligence and share/asset purchasing agreement.

FIGURE 5.1 Trend-Setting Countries and Industries

- Local *pension and compensation and benefits* due diligence and agreements
- Financial due diligence, as accounting practices differ among countries
- IT due diligence
- EHS (environment, health, and safety) due diligence
- Post-merger integration due diligence

In this chapter, you will learn:

- World trends in M&A strategy and deal planning
- Cross-border insights and tips
- Corporate versus country culture
- Regional or country practices in post-merger integration
- Regional and country trends impacting pre-deal

The starting point for looking at trends must be the United States.

The *overall U.S. trend* in M&A is that the value creation has moved from financial leverage to operational improvements. What sets the pace of that trend is the maturity of the U.S. private equity sector. Private equity companies have analyzed companies across all U.S. industries for decades and reaped the value that can be found in the companies' balance sheets. They have explored various ways to leverage debt, sell out noncore assets, and slim down overhead.

The bigger private equity firms are now looking outside the United States and Europe in other markets trying to understand the trends, the market maturity, and repeat the exercise again and again on new soil. If the target is of a decent size there is a possibility that a private equity firm would be interested in bidding for it.

Operational and business improvements and deal synergies can be found in the following (see Figure 5.2):

- International expansion into new markets
- Supply chain
- People and talent management
- Production
- Marketing through digital media
- Moving up the value chain toward the customer
- Supplier management
- Portfolio optimization
- Customer base optimization
- Customer relationship management
- Service improvements
- Other efficiency gains and margin improvements

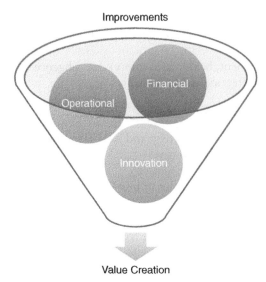

FIGURE 5.2   Sources of Value Creation

Another trend is the innovation of new tech and media companies (most of them coming out of Silicon Valley) who then go global and acquire local businesses to get into new markets if they need people on the ground (see Figure 5.3). The entry point into Europe has traditionally been the United Kingdom, specifically London, due to historical and language reasons. London is also a financial center and one of the centers for M&A in the EU. However, if one looks at where there is a match in business cultures, there is a better match between the United States and, for example, The Netherlands. If the rationale for an acquisition is to get into Europe or Asia, or a set of emerging markets, then it is best to set up the country selection criteria; following is a list of what those criteria could be:

- Match in business cultures
- Access to the industry's relevant talent
- Logistical concerns, that is, effectively cover the region or countries where the company has or will have activities
- Production and production process knowledge
- Universities that have focus or programs for your industries
- Multicultural environment

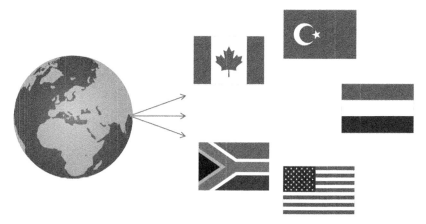

FIGURE 5.3   Geographical Expansion through Acquisitions

■ Ease of job rotation between the United States and target country, rules for expats
■ Tax pressure on business or the individual or on expats
■ Quality of life is attractive to employees
■ Available office or production or logistics space
■ Government incentives or local municipality incentives
■ Overall cost of establishment and acquisition plus cost of organic growth

Of course, some business models do work without their own local staff or international offices and hence there is no need for M&A to establish international marketing and sales presence. That trend is mostly in the TMT (telecom, media, technology) industry.

The foundation for success of an acquisition is leadership and people. The mind-set in acquiring and target companies has to be right. Sentiments between countries differ over time due to global politics, conflicts, sports events, individual leaders, and so on. This means that an acquirer might be met with cynicism and wariness in one country while in a neighboring country it could be a badge of honor to be acquired. For example, a U.S. company will be met differently in the United Kingdom than in one of the Baltic countries.

There is a small trend for companies coming from the EU acquiring U.S. companies to bring them into the EU, driven mostly by European private equity–owned companies. The rationale is that the EU-based portfolio company at the private equity firm can more quickly create value for the target company products in the EU than their U.S. peers.

The timing and sequencing of an acquisition can be impacted by country trends in:

- Private equity interest or absence of it
- Initial public offering window in the local stock market (multiples go higher when it is open)
- Government interventions or policies
- Local market or regional consumer or business patterns
- The speed with which the value chain can develop

Development of Regional/Country Business Environments

The U.S. and European economies are stable and very much in the public focus, but there are other developments that impact deals.

The *new ASEAN block* of 10 countries (Indonesia, Malaysia, the Philippines, Singapore, Thailand, Brunei, Vietnam, Laos, Myanmar, and Cambodia) setting up a market with almost all tariffs eliminated will result in more export and import business across borders between those countries. Next on the ASEAN agenda is free movement of people and capital flow. When that occurs, there will be deal opportunities for those in that bloc to establish a regional player. Those who are now outside could enter into that bloc through an acquisition. It is foreseen that Chinese companies will be very active in retaining a competitive advantage through the lower labor rates inside ASEAN and positioning their consumer brands.

China is moving toward a more consumer-driven economy as opposed to export driven. The lifestyle changes for the Chinese middle class and their consumption patterns will be a trend to follow. There are possibilities to establish foreign brands in China and also for Chinese brands in the near term to establish a presence in the region and in the ASEAN bloc. Logistics will be a sector that will expand following the consumer trends as online shopping and volumes increase. The products need to get quickly to the consumer. The Chinese travel industry has been doing well for some time. Next on the trend curve are the health care, wealth management, and insurance industries.

More foreign investments come into China via a wholly owned business model, that is, either starts an operation through greenfield development or via 100% M&A deal. This not only allows for better control of the new operations in China, but also helps protect the intellectual properties. Very recently, the Chinese government has begun tightening regulations limiting the use of foreign products in national defense–sensitive areas such as network and communication equipment, and this has led to several interesting "partial" asset divestitures, for example: Hewlett-Packard recently gave up a 51% share of its China server business to a local Chinese company, so it would be treated as more of a Chinese company rather than a U.S. company in China.

Due to the heavy investment in manufacturing sectors and the lack of proper environmental protection regulations in China during the "Made in China" boom in the last 30 years, many serious problems accumulated in air, water, and soil pollution. As a result, environmentally unfriendly product manufacturing investment in China will be limited or prohibited, and companies that bring better environmental results will be encouraged.

The change from a one-child policy to a two-child policy will create increased consumption over time and the market will grow.

The *U.S. competition clearance* starts quickly with limited information needed. The enforcement depends on whether it is a Democrat president who normally is more protective of the local market or a Republican who normally wants to expand abroad. Deals in the United States have recently been challenged also under the threshold for upsetting competition and thus creating confusion among deal-makers.

In *competition clearance* the EU commission has cleared 2,800 mergers and blocked only 5 in the last 10 years. This is due in part to the lengthy prenotification discussions with submissions of drafts and responses to information requests before filing. The EU commission has more and more defined the market to be European wide as opposed to national in merger clearances (60% in 2012–2013). Remedies are normally requested when there are national or EU-wide overlaps that disturb competition. There is currently a small debate over whether notification thresholds should also be triggered by large transaction value in addition to the turnover. There is a white paper out on updating EU merger regulation and the two main reasons for this reform drive are:

1. Improving the system where it is decided if a deal should be reviewed by the commission or by the national competition authorities in the EU countries. This comes with proposals to streamline, refine, and further simplify other procedural aspects.
2. Closing an enforcement gap related to minority shareholdings. There have been deals where a minority shareholder would have been able through that holding to impact competition negatively such as the Ryanair/Aer Lingus case where the UK competition authority required Ryanair to sell most of its stake.

In China, competition clearance has a lengthy prenotification and post-filing review period. There is a newly introduced faster procedure for simple cases that improves the time to clearance.

In large cross-border deals in multiple countries there is a challenge to coordinate these prenotification processes with the deal negotiation timetable pre-signing and then to get clearance between signing and closing. The biggest challenge is the effort it takes to create the information requested by the competition authorities. So, if a deal is over the threshold, the team has to make sure that resources in the deal team are set aside for coping with that demand.

In *Africa* there has been the recent formation of the Common Market for Eastern and South Africa (COMESA) with a requirement to file if the acquirer and/or target have operations in two or more member countries with a zero revenue threshold.

In *South Africa* acquirers have to be aware of the both the Narrow and the Broad-Based Black Economic Empowerment regulation and compliance needs to be worked into the M&A strategy and deal planning.

SOME USEFUL CROSS-BORDER INSIGHTS AND TIPS

Use the countries' "Invest in . . ." agencies to find advisors, facts, and all about how to qualify for government incentives. These agencies normally provide their initial services for free and can also provide specific market research at cost. Bigger cities and sometimes different parts of the country (e.g., in Germany) have their own agencies. They can also be a free resource for the deal team and tell about how your industry is doing on a macro level in the country. But these resources can only give so much knowledge.

Leave the office and go with the deal team to the region or country that is the focus of the cross-border deal. Get local insights from the lawyers, financial, tax, and other advisors on the ground and face-to-face. This can be a part of the local advisor selection processes. Utilize the resources that your government has in the country trade councils, chambers of commerce, and so on. Talk to the biggest real estate agents in the country who know the latest on which company has entered or wants to enter the country/city and where they are located. Visit trade shows and events.

Business and trust is between people:

- Meet often face-to-face to facilitate good communication.
- Arrange meetings with the full integration project team for the key items behind the rationale; for example, if the target has a great product that can be sold by the acquirer, present the product and its value to the whole integration team to make them internal ambassadors.
- Mix participants in cross-functional teams during the project.
- Seek many sources to validate significant facts for your acquisition business case or rationale or for understanding the stand-alone business.

In Asia and emerging markets there is a lot of prestige for the executives in having large offices, parking spaces, the latest devices, company cars, having an assistant, and so on. Such perks are mostly gone from a lot of areas and industries in the EU and the United States. How to deal with it post-merger? It adds marginal costs, but more important, it is not in accordance to the values and behaviors that are wanted across the combined company. In most cases the acquirer does nothing and mentally puts it down to local business culture. However, the rationale for the deal is perhaps built on changing and making the target more efficient. In planning for a cross-border deal these details cannot be left for after closing. There cannot be two, three, or more sets of policies on the other side of a border where there could have been one. Think of the employees rather than the executives and how to signal a change to them. The pre-deal team has to lower the threshold for change for the post-deal activities that will enable the synergies. Pick one or two of the perks that stand out and state pre-deal what will be changed directly after closing.

If two companies merge in a city and the plan is to have them share the same office space, the location of the senior manager's office could be hugely important. Perks or not, if two people were in charge before, and will now be in the same office it is "two tigers on one mountain."

The leadership in the target or in a country or in a city is sometimes in an unhealthy symbiosis with the local business community around them and the acquirer has an opportunity to disentangle that initially. These arrangements can be hidden in the due diligence and surface afterward. It could be office leases, logistics, cleaning service, lunch cantinas, and maintenance services that are not 100% competitive. It could be members of the family on payroll with little output. An acquirer needs to choose the right battles, and most are fought where the biggest spend is. For example, a remedy to avoid such symbiosis could be that negotiation of office and factory leases will be done by someone from headquarters or outside the country and signed centrally going forward. A tenant services consultant from a well-known real estate agent could be used instead.

Most countries have one set of laws and rules across the whole country. Watch out for *countries that are federations* as laws and regulations differ in between federal areas. For example, in Germany there is different taxation on company income depending on municipality, although it is not that significant. Other examples are Belgium and The Netherlands, where pre-deal tax ruling can be discussed and negotiated locally.

The use of *stay-on bonuses* and the rationale for using them differs across the world. Is the rhetoric for employment in the combined organization easy or is there a possibility of unrest when cost synergy programs such as redundancies are launched? There are many extremes, from

Japan, where employees traditionally have signed on for life, to Silicon Valley, where employees are more or less constantly looking for the best employment offer? The main factors in determining if a stay-on bonus is needed are:

- Is the local talent market hot in the industry and is there a risk of losing key talent due to this (competitors' headhunters will swoop in when the deal is announced)?
- What are the notice periods used at the target? What is stipulated in labor laws and what is the praxis for working during the notice period?
- What is the damage if talent leaves?
- Can talent lost from the organization easily be recruited from the local talent pool?

There could be a lot of maneuvering and disinformation that the target's leadership can communicate to get a stay-on bonus that is not really needed. In some deals there is an expectation that the top 4%–6% of the target's organization get a stay-on bonus based on local or similar deals. It is hard not to get judgmental by thinking "Do I have to give people a bonus just for showing up at work for 1–2 years?" The costs for stay-on bonuses are normally not significant considering all other costs. If the acquirer is too generous, the target leadership might feel that there is more gold to be found and start drilling more holes looking for gold pre- and post-closing and set a dangerous mind-set across the target.

UNDERSTANDING CORPORATE VERSUS COUNTRY CULTURES WHEN DOING CROSS-BORDER M&A DEALS

The world and business are becoming more and more global. Most businesses doing M&A are international and have international growth ambitions. All or most companies have at one point in time been start-ups where the starting leadership had set a corporate culture to guarantee initial business success. That corporate culture then evolved over time. It is primarily the consumers or the customers and the market that change a corporate culture over time. Leadership adopts the business and operations model to follow. Most international corporations also adapt to local customers and markets, leading to differences in the customer base of the organization between countries. Local differences can also impact products and services, as well as the supply chain. The term used often is that the corporation is "glocal," meaning both global and local. In corporations with many divisions or business units, there are subcultures and differences.

Country cultures are derived from history, natural resources, location, religion, wars and conflicts, politics, regulations, laws, migration patterns, and so on. It is a source of belonging and sharing of past and future that binds together families, friends, and citizens. Cultures differ inside countries depending on regions. For example, Italy has an industrial north and an agricultural south. Another example is Germany with a liberal north and a conservative south.

When doing and planning cross-border deals it is important to be open on how to manage the acquiring company and country culture and understand the target's company and country culture. If the acquirer understands these aspects, there is an advantage in communication, acceptance of the acquirer's arguments, and sharing of mind and vision for a successful deal negotiation. For family-owned targets, that benefit could be as much as a 20% bid premium—that is, the preferred buyer can bid less than other interested bidders. For public or professionally owned targets, an acquirer could gain an information advantage by asking the correct questions and understanding the answers.

There is a desktop analysis of the target and a people-based analysis. How to best prepare for the cultural challenge:

- When selecting the deal team members, who has insights into the target country and/or corporate culture?
- Put in place open discussions on what deal team members have picked up in communication with the target and how the target's deal team actions are perceived
- Step into the other side's shoes to understand their arguments
- When needed, do a cultural assessment of your own company and target if it is possible to get access

The desktop analysis of the target and a people-based analysis based on the interactions with the target are normally the two sources for the deal team. These could be complemented with surveys done with the target's customers or local competitors or with a cultural assessment (see Figure 5.4). Cultural assessment can, for example, be done by the acquirer's human resources organization or external advisors, or could be a part of the target's annual employee satisfaction measures. Assessment could be done through an employee survey and deep interviews with selected leaders and employees.

The deal teams' need to understand their counterparts is of course important in pre-deal communication and negotiation, but it also gives the integration objectives. A simple example is when the acquirer's customers love the after-sales department resulting in customer loyalty and add on

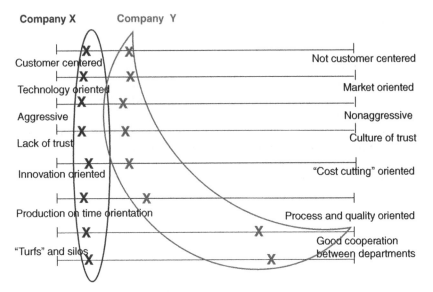

FIGURE 5.4   Culture Assessment Picture

sales while the target's customers do not like the target's after-sales department. The task for the deal team is then to understand to what extent it is
possible to transform the target's after-sales department and how to do it,
the cost, and potential revenues over time.

Regional and Country Practices That Influence
Post-Merger Integration

A factor or trend to look at is how well the professional service sector is
developed in the target's country when using external advisors or looking
for local advisors. For example, the use of advisors and consultants in domestic deals is very limited in China and India while external acquirers use
them frequently upon market entry into those countries. The seller might
have done local deals but is not used to working with intermediates for tax
or legal questions and in due diligence. Avoid the trap of choosing advisors
based on their command of the English language. It might be of comfort for
the deal team, but their local effectiveness might be limited if they are an
outsider in the local business community that is based on relationships. If
there is resistance pre-deal to advisors and consultants, there is even more
post-deal. A workaround could be to issue business cards with an internal
email address for those advisors to be involved post-deal.

The maturity of private equity, venture capital, and corporate finance banking in a country or region also follows the above reasoning on the professional service sector.

Some short examples of country specifics:

- In Sweden
  - Consensus needs to be formed pre-deal, which could be time-consuming.
  - The finance sector is well developed.
  - Most companies are very digitalized and it is recommended to do a IT due diligence.
- In the Nordic countries, the target could be unionized and there would then be a need for information to be groomed for the union.
- In Austria, consensus is formed post-agreement and the deal could be challenged internally, which could surprise an acquirer.
- In Norway, deals are handled pragmatically and the leadership always tries to challenge and boil down what needs to be done.
- In Denmark, it is more of an individualistic approach whether or not a deal is supported by the leadership.
- In the United States, there is a focus on the business numbers and how a product compares to the competition.

CHAPTER CHECKLIST

- Regional and country trends impacting M&A strategy and deal planning
- Some useful cross-border insights and tips
- Understanding corporate versus country cultures in deal planning
- Regional and country practices that influence post-merger integration

Cross-Border Culture
and Leadership
Alignment

CHAPTER 6

Leading during Cross-Border M&A

Scott Whitaker

CHAPTER LEARNING OBJECTIVES—IN THIS CHAPTER, YOU WILL LEARN:

- ➤ Importance of leadership during M&A
- ➤ Senior leadership responsibilities of acquiring companies
- ➤ Senior leadership responsibilities of target companies
- ➤ Leadership responsibilities for the integration management office
- ➤ Symptoms of leadership voids and how to address them
- ➤ Leadership leading practices

CHAPTER SUMMARY

An M&A transaction can be one of the most pivotal inflection points for any company. An acquisition of significant size can test the limits of a company's planning and execution capabilities. It is at this time that leadership can play a huge role and help both acquiring and target employees stay calm and focused on the integration activities.

This chapter does not attempt to outline general leadership qualities and attributes, as there are hundreds of books on the subject of leadership in business, civics, sports . . . most any discipline you can imagine.

Instead, this chapter attempts to outline specific activities and practices leaders can take during an M&A event to help ensure transaction success, and help lay the foundation to make integration a core competency of their organizations.

WHY LEADERSHIP IS SO CRITICAL DURING M&A

For many companies, an M&A event is one of the most intense and seemingly chaotic periods they will ever experience. Think of all of the things that are "in play" during a typical integration:

- The company's strategic direction and business focus
- Corporate leadership and governance structures
- Individual roles and responsibilities
- Policies, processes, and business practices
- Corporate office and facility locations
- Financial performance
- Reprioritization of business investment and capital allocations
- Product and service portfolios
- IT and operating infrastructures
- Suppliers and customer mix

These are just the most common examples, as virtually everything is in flux during a full integration. With all of the above comes a heightened level of anxiety for almost all employees. With so much unknown, people fear the worst and expect any change to be detrimental to their status quo.

But integration activities also can offer a tremendous amount of opportunity for growth, market and geographic expansion, product and service expansion, personal growth, and a host of other strategic drivers that have been discussed in the previous chapters of this book.

Leading during M&A is all about quelling the anxiety, and shining a bright light on the opportunity.

Without strong leadership, the anxiety caused by M&A activities can overwhelm both the acquiring and target companies, and erode productivity and employee engagement.

A leadership void during M&A events can negatively impact momentum and destroy value. And worse, it can permanently hobble a "newco" right out of the gate. Your leadership posture during an M&A event should be carefully planned and coordinated to avoid unexpected results and issues.

Leadership "failures" during integration can result in some significant pain points that can undermine an integration effort.

- **Conflicting goals and strategies:** Leaders fail to solidify company directions and the vision for newco.
- **Poor communication:** This unfortunately is a problem in most every transaction, and the primary reason is always that information and

decisions can be slow to develop, and people get anxious as a result. It is imperative that leaders proactively support communication planning, as senior executives will tend to be reactive when it comes to communications during integrations.

- **Conflict, conflict, conflict**: Conflict is unavoidable and many times a little conflict produces better results. When conflict results in paralysis and execution dysfunction, it can retard integration success significantly. At the end of the day, leaders need to resolve conflict that is detrimental to the integration and execution efforts.
- **Disparate cultures**: Sometimes culture clashes can become so distracting that they can grind integrations to a halt. Culture clashes also make most employees anxious and in many cases downright miserable. Leaders need to understand the culture of the target company, and appreciate where cultural attributes differ and why.

LEADERSHIP RESPONSIBILITIES OF ACQUIRING COMPANIES

Everyone, from the CEO to the functional leads who are part of an integration management office (IMO), have their own leadership-related roles and responsibilities when it comes to integration.

For the most senior leaders in an organization, leadership deliverables can manifest as outlined in Table 6.1. Note these responsibilities are primarily focused on integration-related topics, with the assumption that these leaders are already playing significant roles in regard to the transaction (i.e., getting the deal closed!). We have included leadership responsibilities for target company senior leaders as well.

As you can see, a big focus for senior leaders revolves around providing high-level integration planning direction, and removing obstacles.

Examples for each of these categories follow.

High-level integration planning direction examples

- Integration scope (what does and does not get integrated)
- Newco organizational structure and operating model
- Business planning assumptions
- Integration work stream prioritization
- Key message points and vision for the new company
- Stakeholder management guidance (e.g., investor community)
- Integration timing
- Cost savings and revenue enhancement synergy targets

TABLE 6.1   Senior Leadership Responsibilities during Integration

Position	Primary Leadership Responsibilities
Board of Directors	▪ Lay groundwork for productive interaction with target pre-close ▪ Manage minority ownership interests ▪ Articulate deal rationale, value drivers, and business priorities ▪ Reinforce importance of frequent and open communications ▪ Provide message points for external financial stakeholders
CEO and Senior Leadership Team	▪ Reinforce importance of integration as corporate priority ▪ Clarify integration planning scope, guidance, and assumptions ▪ Provide overall integration oversight and governance ▪ Develop organizational design and structure ▪ Establish goals and success factors ▪ Support proactive communications ▪ Manage timing and inclusion of target into pre-planning efforts ▪ Ensure proper integration resourcing and budgeting ▪ Communicate changes to investment thesis and/or deal structure that will impact integration planning
Target Company Senior Leadership	▪ Facilitate exchange of integration planning data ▪ Ensure proper resourcing for IMO when required ▪ Help ensure adherence to any guidelines established by legal regarding sensitive versus nonsensitive information restrictions ▪ Monitor target employee base to proactively address rumors regarding transaction

Removing obstacles examples

- ▪ Ensuring proper IMO resourcing so the IMO is not understaffed
- ▪ Making sure people engaged in integration work have the appropriate level of seniority and expertise
- ▪ Making sure IMO leaders and participants are trained in the basics of integration and are not thrown to the wolves
- ▪ Alleviating logjams relative to information exchange with the target company to ensure planning data is secured in a timely and consistent fashion
- ▪ Driving consensus on vision and key message points among the senior leadership team to avoid any mixed messages to the rank-and-file employee bases
- ▪ Being the last point of escalation to facilitate timely decision making

Another key responsibility of acquiring company leaders is to properly scope the integration challenge.

Leaders need to gain an understanding of what it takes to run a proper integration, and assign the right people to the job. Underestimating the task at hand is the first mistake leaders usually make.

Joseph Duffy, VP Integrated Planning & Control (retired),
Verso Corporation

If integration is an infrequent or perhaps completely new undertaking for an organization, leaders need to make sure the organization has a full understanding and appreciation for the amount of planning and execution work that is required to run a smooth integration.

LEADERSHIP RESPONSIBILITIES OF TARGET COMPANIES

Table 6.1 also includes some essential leadership responsibilities for target company leaders, who obviously can play a huge role in the overall success of any transaction.

Here is some additional detail as to what target company leaders should influence:

Facilitate exchange of integration planning data

- Most likely these leaders have been engaged in the exchange of due diligence data, but as integration planning becomes fully ramped up, the data requests and information needs increase in breadth and depth.
- Target leaders need to ensure that requested data is complete, up to date, and delivered in a timely fashion. Bottlenecks, delays, or plain old stonewalling can grind the data harvesting process for integration planning to a halt and frustrate everyone. Target company leads should make sure integration planning data is complete, well organized, and that the subject matter experts required to explain data are available and accessible.

Ensure proper resourcing for IMO when required

- Target company leaders need to ensure that experienced people are assigned to the IMO (integration management office). There is often a tendency to hold back deployment to the most suitable people until the deal is a sure thing. As we know, transactions are dynamic events with a lot of uncertainty. It is the responsibility of the IMO to plan for the deal as if it's going to happen, and to do this they need experienced and available resources to engage with from the target company.

■ Newbies or people with no available bandwidth will slow things down—acquiring company leads need access to the best from the target, and leaders to make sure they are available.

Help ensure adherence to any guidelines established by legal regarding sensitive versus nonsensitive information restrictions

■ Any transaction with anti-trust considerations will have strict rules of engagement for the exchange of data. Typical counsel from both organizations will weigh in on data requests to confirm the data being requested is nonsensitive and can be shared. There has to be some robust process around this that is adhered to by both organizations (acquiring and target) to ensure compliance. (There is an entire process around the exchange and review of sensitive information that is covered in other chapters.)

■ Target company leaders can help with this process by not arbitrarily deeming some data sensitive only because they are uncomfortable sharing it. Lawyers should decide what is sensitive versus nonsensitive, and this process should not be arbitrary. In almost all cases the acquiring company is simply looking for data to help plan and execute a smooth integration—denying them data may put some elements of the integration plan at risk.

Monitor target employee base to proactively address rumors regarding transaction

■ Target company leaders should be the first line of defense against the flurry of rumors and bad information that circulates pre-deal. They need to proactively address these issues and keep employees engaged and productive.

■ They can also help by not speculating themselves as to longer-term plans for newco, and simply reinforce when plans and information are still in development.

■ They can't do any of this unless they are walking around and talking to employees, as no one typically shares speculation and rumors with senior management. Get out and find out what people are worried about so you can address these issues head on.

Undermining the Integration Planning Effort

Unfortunately, there are times when target companies' leaders will be uncooperative and downright undermine the integration pre-planning efforts.

This typically happens when the target is a "reluctant bride" or in a hostile transaction. Whatever the reason, here are some of the typical side effects that occur when such a dynamic is in place.

- Skepticism that the transaction will be approved by shareholders and/ or regulators: If target leaders telegraph this sentiment to others it can impede cooperation and delay key planning deliverables
- Stymieing communication efforts: Leaders forbid any basic communication efforts relative to transaction updates, leaving a huge information void. This is most detrimental to target employees, the very people they think they are trying to protect.
- Under-resourcing planning efforts: Leaders who are stingy with allocating IMO resources can simply delay the pre-close planning efforts

LEADERSHIP RESPONSIBILITIES OF THE INTEGRATION MANAGEMENT OFFICE

When we speak of IMO leadership we are primarily talking about those individuals who have been tapped for leadership roles in the IMO and/or their functional area of responsibility.

These are people who are involved in the day-to-day planning and execution and who typically have visibility to most all integration work.

Along with the multitude of integration planning and execution functions they are already responsible for, these individuals have leadership responsibilities as well, as detailed in Table 6.2.

Here is some additional detail as to what IMO leaders should influence:

"Information Gathering" versus "Information Sharing"

As mentioned in Table 6.2, IMO leaders need to stick to "information gathering" in the pre-planning phase, and avoid excessive "information sharing" when plans are still in development.

IMO leaders will get bombarded with questions about "future state" (e.g., what will the organizational structure look like), and most of the time this information is not finalized. And by the way, these questions come both from the target company and the acquiring company.

Leaders need to avoid speculating on any future state plans, or if they indeed are in the know as to some future state details, avoid sharing them. This takes a certain level of maturity and self-control.

Leaders need to reinforce the "gathering versus sharing" concept to all members of the IMO consistently during the course of pre-planning prior to close.

TABLE 6.2 Leadership Responsibilities of the Integration Management Office

Position	Primary Leadership Responsibilities
IMO Lead Team Members	▪ Help establish tone for interactions with target company leadership team and integration leads ▪ Become subject matter experts on integration ▪ Reinforce importance of integration work and ensure it's being treated as a priority within the organization ▪ Make sure IMO lead team roles are clearly defined and not duplicative ▪ Ensure adequate resourcing for all IMO roles ▪ Ensure adherence to information sharing protocols
IMO Functional Leads (e.g., Human Resources, IT, Finance, etc.)	▪ Ensure each interaction with target is well planned and organized—set a great example of what's to come ▪ Keep senior functional leaders (e.g., SVP of finance) up to date on integration work ▪ Manage escalations within respective functions ▪ Stick to "information gathering" in pre-planning phase, avoid excessive "information sharing" when plans are still in development ▪ Ensure subteam leads and other participants receive a thorough grounding in the transaction details and are on-boarded properly ▪ Ensure IMO participants are "trained up" on all collaboration and data sharing logistics
Target Company IMO Leads and Functional Leads	▪ Set tone for cooperation and be supportive of pre-planning work requirements ▪ Ensure adherence to information-sharing protocols ▪ Escalate issues that may require resolution (official communication to address rumors)

When information is shared prematurely it only creates more work, as rumors and speculation will need to be addressed and dealt with at a time when most everyone is consumed with an increased amount of work already.

SYMPTOMS OF A LEADERSHIP VOID AND HOW TO ADDRESS THEM

Knowing when leadership voids are negatively affecting integration planning and execution work is critical so you can take the necessary steps to address the underlying issues.

Here are some typical situations and root cause issues that may point to some leadership deficiencies in the areas already outlined in this chapter:

Integration managers or IMO reporting into a single function like human resources or finance

- Unless the integration is narrowly scoped and confined to a functional area only (e.g., a tuck in), having the IMO reporting into a function is suboptimal and not recommended
- The function will likely be overburdened and resource constrained
- Integration planning may become myopic and overly focused on a single function
- Having an IMO report into a single function also sends a confusing message to the target (e.g., "Is that the only area they care about?")

Confusion at senior executive level as to who "owns" the integration work

- Integrations should have an established governance structure with a steering committee or some oversight authority in charge of the success of the integration
- If there is no steering committee–type governance, authority may be dispersed across one or two senior leaders, creating unneeded complications and complexity for IMO leaders
- This "dispersed liability" can also create a leadership void, as sometimes neither executive is fully engaged in the work
- Communication planning may also be negatively impacted because there is no clear ownership point for integration news and updates

No sense of urgency among integration leads

- Integration work should by nature have a "bias for urgency," so when there is none it is a pure reflection of a lack of leadership (i.e., leaders are not prioritizing the effort internally)
- Integration work may then be deprioritized among functional leads, resulting in lost momentum

Fluid post-close organization may mean senior executives are still "TBD"

- When the future state of the organization is still in flux and key leaders in limbo of their status and roles, this may create leadership voids when it comes to integration work
- Some leaders may avoid emphasizing integration work, as they are still uncertain of their status and want to avoid rocking the boat (the truth

is, integration work is an excellent way to stay visible during times of organizational change and uncertainty)

If the integration is experiencing some of these issues, some areas to explore for remediation may include:

- Establish (or recommunicate) IMO charter and governance structure
- "Relaunch" IMO effort to create urgency and a new sense of mission
- Accelerate post-close organizational planning to solidify leadership structure
- Create issue escalation and decision-making framework for the senior executive team to ensure high-priority issues get "moved up the chain" quickly

LEADERSHIP LEADING PRACTICES

This part of the chapter outlines some key areas where leaders can really shine, and make a difference in the overall management of an integration. The areas outlined below can also be instrumental in helping create a solid foundation for newco.

Engage in the definition of newco for newly acquired employees

- Often the creation of the Day One communication package falls to the communication lead, who must sometimes beg and plead for information to create an impactful orientation package for newly acquired employees. (This is sometimes called the "vision deck.") Leaders need to drive this activity and allow plenty of time for others to review and contribute.
- Inspire and avoid warmed-over corporate break room poster verbiage and uninspiring rhetoric. Leaders must "own" the creation of a communication package that inspires new employees and gives them a firm understanding as to the direction of the company.
- Share and be generous with information. One of the biggest gripes from newly acquired employees on Day One is "we didn't hear anything new or that we didn't already know."

Proactively communicate

- Sometimes getting leaders to sign off on communications is like pulling teeth. Many will simply avoid it altogether to delay having to be pinned down on any key messages and/or decisions.

■ Leaders need to embrace proactive communications, and support the development of messaging that is robust, accurate, and inspiring
■ Support robust and frequent communications throughout the integration period. Too often communications dwindle to a slow drip after Day One. This is when newly acquired employees crave the most information!

Respect legacy culture

■ The adoption of a common culture is easier said than done. It is virtually impossible to eradicate the vestiges of a legacy culture—even when it's in most everyone's best interests to do so.
■ Leaders can be realistic about this and embrace the fact that cultural assimilation takes time, and that newly acquired employees will cling to what they know and value long after the deal closes
■ Leaders should not ignore or disparage legacy culture, but work to drive and reinforce the culture they want to see in the organization

Be objective

■ Leaders can set the tone for the consistent and objective evaluation of people, processes, policies, and operation practices throughout the integration

CHAPTER CHECKLIST

■ Clearly define the leadership responsibilities for both acquiring and target company senior management.
■ Clearly define and communicate leadership responsibilities for the IMO team and functional leads.
■ Learn to recognize the most common symptoms of leadership voids.
■ Drive the adoption of integration leadership leading practices in the organization.

CHAPTER 7

The Role of Culture in Cross-Border M&A

Christophe Van Gampelaere

CHAPTER LEARNING OBJECTIVES—IN THIS CHAPTER, YOU WILL LEARN:

➤ The importance of culture in an M&A environment
➤ How cultural awareness will improve deal success
  ➤ Setting definitions
  ➤ Making distinctions between various kinds of culture: global, local, corporate, and innovative
  ➤ How to create cultural awareness in deal teams
➤ How to integrate cultural elements in the deal strategy
  ➤ Cultural dominance and leniency
  ➤ The importance of language in deals
➤ How to practically incorporate the culture dimension before signing, between signing and closing, and after closing

CHAPTER SUMMARY

This chapter describes the importance of culture in a merger or integration environment. It shows how to create awareness of cultural elements in both the deal teams and integration teams. The importance of company values and local language is highlighted before going into practical ways of turning culture into a success driver in a transaction.

UNDERSTANDING CULTURAL MANAGEMENT

The sentiment is that cultural considerations are essential in making cross-border deals (i.e., mergers, acquisitions, or divestments) succeed. This is certainly supported by countless studies. A Bain & Company survey found

139

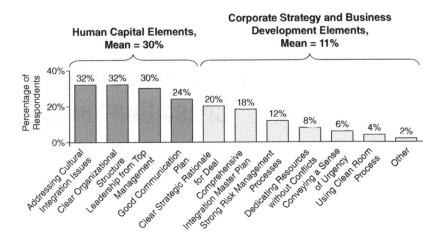

FIGURE 7.1 Top Integration Challenges

that cultural management is the single most important M&A success driver when it queried some 10,000 managers from 73 countries (see Figure 7.1). An Economist Intelligence Unit (EIU)/Accenture study shows that the top integration challenges are all related to human factors—and the most important one of these is culture.

Deal-makers are the persons skilled at bringing commercial deals to a satisfactory conclusion. The deal-makers who take practical actions to address cultural issues will hold an important key to success. Deal-makers who take practical actions to address cultural issues hold an important key to turning commercial deals into success. They take into account bottom-up cultural pressure from both buyer and target. They have a head start on individual decision makers who brush aside decades of evidence and any consideration to address the topic.

NOTE

A "buyer," or "acquirer," is any company buying another company, or assets of a company; a "target" is the company or assets of a company being bought by the buyer.

"Culture in cross-border M&A" is in itself worth a whole book. The purpose of this chapter, however, is to provide the reader with a practical manual and tips that allow him to identify culture pitfalls and transform these into opportunities.

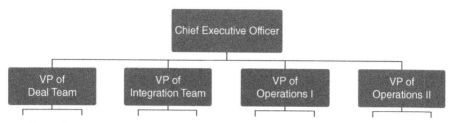

FIGURE 7.2   Organizational Chart Example

There is much at stake, and it is essential to recognize culture management as a distinct competency, spanning the transaction life cycle from pre-deal to post-closing.

Indeed, the M&A department is often not responsible for the operational integration of the acquisition. We often see an organizational disconnect between the deal team and the operational line managers. As a consequence, no funds are set aside and no energy is spent to assist the acquirer and the target with cultural integration (see Figure 7.2).

To get the ball rolling, a two-pronged approach is recommended: first, to create an awareness that by nature, most people are not conscious of the fact they are not equipped to deal with culture; second, a systematic and facts-based approach to manage cultural differences. It is surprisingly easy to quantify such an emotional topic, and to bring it into the fold with the larger integration management exercise.

CULTURAL AWARENESS

This section covers the general topic of "awareness," and then goes into a definition of culture, and the difference between global, local, and corporate cultures.

From a personal comfort zone it may appear that cultural differences are not really all that difficult to overcome. It is a false feeling of confidence fed by the fact that we are not exposed to the breadth and the depth of what cultural differences really are. There are so many cultural dimensions, and so many ways that people react and interact that it is a miracle to get along at all.

The Four Stages of Skillfulness

The EIU/Accenture study concludes that both deal and operational people (such as department heads and managers for finance, marketing, sales, IT, supply chain, operations, manufacturing, and so on) are aware of the importance of culture. However: they are not skilled in the matter. Psychological terminology describes these four steps toward becoming skilled (see Figure 7.3):

1. **Unconsciously unskilled:** The individual does not understand or know how to do something and does not necessarily recognize the deficit. He may deny the usefulness of the skill. For culture, this happens when managers are new to the M&A process, despite the fact that their company may have done many deals in the past. It is possible to be blinded by deal euphoria.
2. **Consciously unskilled:** Though the individual does not understand or know how to do something, the deficit is recognized, as well as the value of the new skill set needed to address the deficit. This is typically the case with seasoned deal professionals who know how to get internal or external support in the matter.
3. **Consciously skilled:** The individual knows how to do something. However, applying the skill or knowledge requires concentration. It may be broken down into steps, and there is heavy conscious involvement in executing the new skill. This may be the case for integration professionals who are actively acquiring cultural skills.
4. **Unconsciously skilled:** The individual has had so much practice with the skill that it has become "second nature" and can be performed easily.

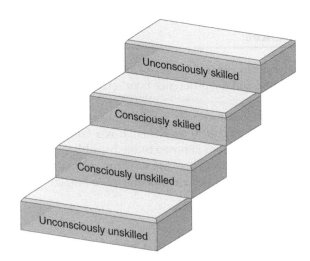

FIGURE 7.3   The Four Stages of Skillfulness

Definition of "Culture"

There are as many definitions of the word "culture" as there are focus areas and points of view. We will use a definition geared toward the needs of cross-border M&A. Culture in an M&A environment can be defined as

A combination of shared local and corporate norms, behavior, symbols, values, systems, and laws.

Cross-border cultural management is the systematic and facts-based management of differences between local and corporate attributes. The strength of an integration manager lies in the extent to which he can reinforce the positive elements and defuse any negative tendencies potentially leading to explosive situations.

Global, Local, and Corporate Culture

In an interconnected world, every country balances global culture with the local culture. Some cultural elements are changeable and flexible; others represent "no go" areas. Try to touch them and tensions may awaken and a culture clash erupts. Each region has its own way of coping with these tensions. It is up to the local teams to solve and digest this clash—the acquirer can facilitate, educate, and act in an informed manner.

Global Culture Every country in some way supports a global culture. People across the world share the same brands, watch the same movies, and hear the same news stories. The interpretations, however, might differ depending on the cultural glasses a country wears. In an economic sense, the concepts of generating profit and international expansion are evidence of shared cultural exponents. The very essence of globalization lies in the worldwide integration of economies, finance, trade, and communications.

However, the consequences of global culture diverge into opposite directions. In one sense, we move toward the homogenization described above, which crystallizes around Western patterns. In another sense, we move toward resistance against this homogenization and a polarization against Western norms symbolized by consumer capitalism. The resistance takes the form of global movements of the downtrodden such as "Occupy," the movement against social and economic inequality. It can result in extremism where ideologies in some parts of the world turn the clock back on education, gender equality, and science. The third direction is a hybrid of the two, where cultures blend by borrowing from each other. This hybrid differs from society to society, just like there are numerous varieties of capitalism, ranging from the United States' take on individual responsibility, over the more social variant in Europe, to the communist version of capitalism in China.

This contradiction makes it all the more difficult for international players to read cultural signals. Signals may look familiar, but have quite a different underlying meaning. For corporate managers, this global culture is a fact they have to deal with—it is not something they can change.

Globalization has so far had a limited impact on international law, even though law has a huge impact on corporate life. Time and again corporate management is surprised to learn that the legal framework they are familiar with at home does not apply in other territories. Just ask any U.S. company planning to lay off employees in Germany or France, where legal proceedings by unions can put plans on hold for months, even years. Even where the law is formally the same, the practical application may differ. Given that multinational acquirers by definition operate in many jurisdictions, they run the risk of litigation in any of those jurisdictions.

In addition to the formal legal restrictions, companies face certain cultural no-go areas. These tend to reside in the local taboo zone, so mentioning them may be controversial. Chapter 14 will discuss that.

Local Culture   The term "national culture" is avoided in preference to the adjective "local." As some citizens may acknowledge, there can be a difference between the culture in one city or region, and that of another in the same country. Nevertheless, some overarching and relevant generalizations can be made on a country level. Some of the classic sources of cultural values within the literature are the World Value Survey, Schwartz's cultural values, and Hofstede's cultural dimensions. Fresh perspectives on the subject are offered by Richard Barrett's Value Center and Erin Meyer's work, which we feature in Chapter 14.

Next are some reflections on Gerard Hendrik Hofstede's work. Hofstede is a Dutch psychologist who has studied national intercultural relationships extensively. We find his work particularly suited to creating a first-level understanding of how one country compares to another. Hofstede sets out five axes, called "dimensions." They are: (1) social orientation, (2) power distance, (3) gender roles, (4) uncertainty avoidance, and (5) time orientation (see Figure 7.4).

Social Orientation.   That is, individualism versus collectivism: Individualism can be defined as a preference for a loosely knit social framework in which individuals are expected to take care of only themselves and their immediate families. The opposite, collectivism, represents a preference for a tightly knit framework in society in which individuals can expect their relatives or members of a particular in-group to look after them in exchange for unquestioning loyalty. A society's position on this dimension is reflected in whether people's self-image is defined in terms of "I" or "we." For example, the United States scores the highest on individualism and China the highest on collectivism.

Power Distance. That is, respect versus tolerance: The degree to which the less powerful members of a society accept and expect that power is distributed unequally. The fundamental issue here is how a society handles inequalities among people. People in societies exhibiting a large degree of power distance accept a hierarchical order in which everybody has a place and which needs no further justification. In societies with low power distance, people strive to equalize the distribution of power and demand justification for inequalities of power. Hofstede demonstrates this with the reaction of Chinese authorities to the fact that Chinese author Liu Xiaobo was given the Nobel Peace Prize. According to people in the West, the writer advocates moderation; according to Chinese authorities, he advocates power sharing—and is imprisoned for political reasons.

Gender Roles. That is, masculinity versus femininity: The masculine side of this axis represents a preference for achievement, heroism, assertiveness, and material rewards for success. A male society at large is more competitive; see, for example, Japan. The opposite, the feminine society, stands for a preference for cooperation, modesty, caring for the weak, and quality of life (e.g., Sweden). The use of this gender-related terminology is becoming increasingly controversial.

Uncertainty Acceptance versus Uncertainty Avoidance. This dimension expresses the degree to which the members of a society feel comfortable with uncertainty and ambiguity. The issue here is how a society deals with the fact that the future can never be known: Should we try to control it or just let it happen? Countries exhibiting strong uncertainty avoidance maintain rigid codes of belief and behavior and are intolerant of unorthodox ideas. Societies accepting uncertainty maintain a more relaxed attitude in which practice counts more than principles.

Long-Term versus Short-Term Orientation. Every society has to maintain some links with its own past while dealing with the challenges of the present and the future. Societies prioritize these two existential goals differently. Some societies prefer to maintain time-honored traditions and norms while viewing societal change with suspicion. Those with a short-term orientation take a more pragmatic approach: They encourage thrift and pragmatism.

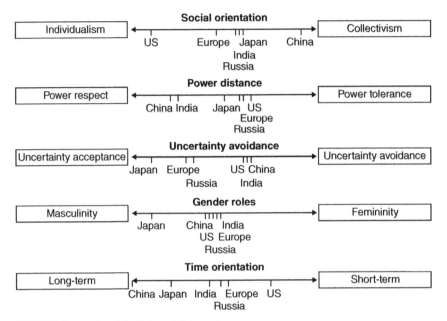

FIGURE 7.4 Hofstede's Cultural Dimensions

Visit the site and check out the country comparison tool on http://geert hofstede.com/countries.html. It provides one-page summaries per country, and is a great starting point to create a first level of awareness of cultural differences.

While the reader may not individually recognize his country's characteristics in the next example, the Daimler-Chrysler case illustrates how organizational cultures can be very much aligned with country cultures.

Country Culture Collision in the Daimler-Chrysler Merger

The attempted Daimler-Chrysler merger is an example of strong local cultures embedded into the corporate cultures. Seven years into the deal, when the author of this chapter worked on the break-up of Daimler and Chrysler in 2006, the cultural differences between the two firms were still very much alive.

Looking at the country background, the two countries score markedly different in their long- versus short-term orientation. According to the Hofstede dimensions, the United States is a country leaning toward one absolute truth, a concern for stability and a traditional approach to values. In line with that attitude, Chrysler management had "no lessons to learn" from Daimler, and was convinced of the absolute truth of the superiority of its products and production process. It did not want to uproot the stability of existing ways of working. In keeping with tradition, the Pentastar logo was resurrected on the very day Chrysler regained its independence from Daimler. Fireworks and fanfare accompanied the reinstatement of the old logo to the cheers of the employees.

Germany scores as a country with many truths and a pragmatic approach to problem solving, setting clear objectives, detailed assignments, formal control systems, and not accepting flexibility on quality. This clashed with a lower cultural acceptance of structured activities and written rules at Chrysler.

Similarly, German "Gründlichkeit" (thoroughness) was applied to the brand portfolio where Daimler had decided—for sound economic reasons—to terminate two Chrysler brands. One of them was a hallmark of blue-collar stability and tradition: Plymouth. Many years later, customers were still saying: "How dared they kill off the brand."

Corporate Culture   We do not necessarily see corporate culture as a subset of national or local culture, although we do notice that companies in the early stages of internationalization tend to be more centered on their own local culture. Corporate culture is very much influenced by a variety of factors, only one of which is local culture. Another important factor is the management style at the top. Harking back to our definition of culture:

A combination of shared local and corporate norms, behaviors, symbols, values, and systems

---

it is clear there is more to a company's culture than the country where it is based. Norms, behaviors, symbols, values, and systems can differ very much from one company to another. Following is a story of two vastly different cultures in the same country.

Corporate Culture Collision in France

Two €300m revenue companies; one, the patriarchal acquirer: a centrally led organization with multiple silos and no clear allocation of responsibilities (managers are not used to taking decisions); the other, the target: a lean management machine with a clear delegation of authorities.

The acquirer had obtained additional bank financing, based on achieving deal synergies. After closing, the patriarch decreed no effort was going to be put into aligning both companies. The systemic differences remained and escalated, prohibiting management from achieving the projected synergies. Two years later, external capital was needed to help the acquirer honor bank covenants.

The lesson learned here is that either the merger should have been called off, or the issue of the organizational differences should have been addressed head-on.

Corporate Brand Culture   Brand decisions are not taken lightly. Just like customers, employees develop a loyalty to their brands, and associate their culture and values with them. Slashing the brand is perceived at a minimum as a sign of disrespect and potentially as an attempt to wipe out the company culture, military style.

Deal-makers are familiar with applying financial goodwill to a brand portfolio. In accounting, goodwill is an intangible asset that arises when one company acquires another, but pays more than the fair market value of its net assets. However, employees do not apply accounting rules when they value their company's brand. Treat the target's brand with respect, and it will be of financial benefit, and:

- Create integration goodwill
- Alleviate employees' fears
- Tie stakeholders closer in
- Keep strong performers on board
- Remove distance
- Set a positive precedent

The right treatment of corporate brand culture is an ideal entry point to a successful integration. It deserves not only serious thought, but also a solid, fact-based approach, duly researched and documented in a brand evaluation analysis. Management can then decide in an informed manner, based on the merits of various scenarios, taking all pros and cons into account. That may mean that the acquirer keeps the target's brands, like Air France and KLM did. It's not about the ego of the acquirer; it's about creating value for the shareholder. And it saves a few bucks on the rebranding exercise.

Innovative Management Culture There are signs of very innovative management cultures. One such test ground is Brazil, where a company called Semco is challenging traditional ideas on management structure, growth, and remuneration. There are no job titles, people set their own salaries, and they decide for themselves whether or not to show up for work.

"It's all insane, except that is seems to work." This formula has allowed the company to grow consistently in a volatile economic environment. Since the article appeared, Semco has spawned a portfolio management company, helping foreign companies leverage business in Brazil.

STRATEGY AND CULTURE

When culture is made part of the acquisition strategy, it is possible to be a step ahead of the other acquirers. In the pre-signing phase, imagine your advantage over competitors who do not take culture seriously, and:

- Are hampered by misunderstandings
- Do not pick up and read negotiation signals
- Lack the tools to build trust and respect
- Fail to understand the fragile balance between giving and receiving
- Make target management feel uncomfortable, despite the ability to pay more

Linking the Deal with Cultural Factors: "Know Thyself"

It is good to map your organization's cultural traits, both from a local point of view and from a corporate point of view. It will help in putting a target's culture in perspective.

For each cultural element, map values and cultural elements in three categories: culturally dominant, culturally lenient, and culturally shared. Table 7.1 is an example.

TABLE 7.1   Acquirer and Target Cultural Mapping

	Culturally Dominant	Culturally Lenient	Culturally Shared
Acquirer	Hierarchical Higher power distance Silo structured organization Male dominated Centrally led Stability and tradition We do it better when we do it ourselves	Willing to learn Company cars Drinks on the work floor are paid	Individualistic Brand loyalty Passion for the work
Target	Flat organizational structure Clear allocation of responsibilities Continuous improvement, eager to learn We outsource noncore activities Company cars Free quality coffee	Short power distance Short-term orientation Female	Customer focus Individualistic Brand loyalty Passion for the work

Culturally Dominant   A culturally dominant trait is one that in size or influence towers over those of the target—unless the target shows the same trait. An acquirer will need to know where he wants his ideal target to be situated on that same cultural value axis. Being culturally dominant in a cultural dimension is a given fact; it is neither good nor bad. If both acquirer and target differ in how they are dominant in the same cultural dimension, it is advisable to tread carefully. In the example of the two €300m revenue companies, the issue was ignored, the owner did not take a decision on how the organization was to be run either way—and he paid for it by losing some of his ownership.

Culturally Lenient   An organization is culturally lenient on certain values if it is not too concerned about those elements being different between acquirer and target, or from one location to another. In Belgium, for example, most people in middle management and up have a company car, whereas in Japan, such a perk is highly exceptional. Take away the company car, and the acquirer risks losing target employees. If an organization can accept such a difference, it is culturally lenient on it. If the reasons behind this example are not clear, go to the facts. Company cars are popular in Belgium because the costs to the employer are lower than giving a similar advantage to the employee via regular salary.

Culturally Shared   A culturally shared trait is part of the DNA of your company, and it cannot be compromised. It is context-invariant and time-invariant. Infosys, a global corporation with Indian roots that provides business consulting services, defined five cultural attributes that need to be inherent to any target in order to be "Infosys-compatible."

- Openness
- Meritocracy
- Speed
- Imagination
- Excellence in execution

Values   In addition to the cultural traits, also examine the company's shared values. Infosys thought about this. The company summarized its value system in the acronym "C-LIFE," which stands for Customer delight, Leadership by example, Integrity and transparency, Fairness, and pursuit of Excellence.

The Infosys values are:

- The ability to accept deferred gratification
- An agreed protocol of do's and don'ts
- Subordinating individual egos and putting the interest of the organization ahead of individual interest
- Recognizing people's competency
- Accepting leadership of people in different areas
- Leadership by example—for example, the Infosys Leading Institute: "Our company is our campus, our business is our curriculum, and our leaders are our teachers"
- Start every transaction from a zero base
- Only an argument that has merit wins, nothing to do with hierarchy. Assertions need to be substantiated with examples
- Not using corporate resources for personal benefit

These values can be recognized as very close to your company's values, and you may feel quite alien to others—every company is different. A second example comes from the Netflix Culture Statement, with these nine values:

1. **Judgment:** You make wise decisions (people, technical, business, and creative) despite ambiguity, you identify root causes and get beyond treating symptoms; you think strategically, and can articulate what you are, and are not, trying to do; you smartly separate what must be done well now, and what can be improved later.

2. **Communication:** You listen well, instead of reacting fast, so you can better understand; you are concise and articulate in speech and writing; you treat people with respect independent of their status or disagreement with you; you maintain calm poise in stressful situations.

3. **Impact:** You accomplish amazing amounts of important work; you demonstrate consistently strong performance so colleagues can rely upon you; you focus on great results rather than on process; you exhibit bias-to-action, and avoid analysis-paralysis.

4. **Curiosity:** You learn rapidly and eagerly; you seek to understand our strategy, market, customers, and suppliers; you are broadly knowledgeable about business, technology, and entertainment; you contribute effectively outside of your specialty.

5. **Innovation:** You reconceptualize issues to discover practical solutions to hard problems; you challenge prevailing assumptions when warranted, and suggest better approaches; you create new ideas that prove useful; you keep us nimble by minimizing complexity and finding time to simplify.

6. **Courage:** You say what you think even if it is controversial; you make tough decisions without agonizing; you take smart risks; you question actions inconsistent with our values.

7. **Passion:** You inspire others with your thirst for excellence; you care intensely about Netflix's success; you celebrate wins; you are tenacious.

8. **Honesty:** You are known for candor and directness; you are nonpolitical when you disagree with others; you only say things about fellow employees you will say to their face; you are quick to admit mistakes.

9. **Selflessness:** You seek what is best for Netflix, rather than best for yourself or your group; you are ego-less when searching for the best ideas; you make time to help colleagues; you share information openly and proactively.

Systemically speaking, there are three universal values that any system needs in order to function well.

The Right Order of Positions. This is related to the goal of the organization. Whoever created the framework within which all others can function comes first. Those who create the framework for the next level down come second, and so on. This way, everyone has a stable position, in the right order.

A Fair Exchange between Giving and Receiving. Every employee gives something to the company, and gets something in return in an ever-continuing exchange.

Every Person's Right to His Place in the Organization Is Equal. Whether he is an inventory manager or a CEO, he needs to have earned the right to work in that position. This is true for the current employees, as well as for the people who were important in the past. They need to be "honored."

Company values are part of the organizational system in that they are part of the contract between the company and its employees. It would be highly coincidental if this contract in the acquirer mirrors the contract in the target company. The acquirer who unilaterally changes this agreement does so at his own peril.

In order to create a combined set of accepted values, the integration manager needs to know how to initiate and drive change. This is an ongoing process, where regular measurements of key value performance indicators are taken, and adjustments are based on the results, exactly like one would manage a company's accounts.

The elements to measure are the personal needs of the employees, the extent to which they feel aligned with the culture of the organization (values alignment), and the extent they feel the organization is on the right track (mission alignment).

Step by step, the values and behavior can thus be coached toward what is working for the combined organization.

Adjusting the Strategy to Optimally Leverage Differences in Values and Cultural Elements

The cultural differences and similarities described previously will need to be reflected in the integration strategy and in the day-to-day management of the integration. Mirvis and Marks have created a simple model of how these differences impact the type of deal (see Table 7.2).

The two variables they use are the degree of changes in the acquirer and the target. There are five resulting types: (1) "stand alone," where both acquirer and target have a low need for change, (2) "transformation," where both companies change significantly, (3) "absorption," where the target undergoes most of the change, (4) "reverse acquisition," where the target's ways of working eventually dominate, and (5) "best of both" mergers.

This typology is not only valid on a company level, it is also applicable to individual work stream and territorial dimensions. A well-prepared buyer will know beforehand how the acquisition fits the company's strategy and business model.

TABLE 7.2 Different Types of Mergers

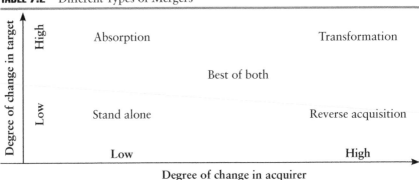

	Low	High
High	Absorption	Transformation
	Best of both	
Low	Stand alone	Reverse acquisition

Degree of change in target (vertical axis, High to Low)

Degree of change in acquirer (horizontal axis, Low to High)

Mirvis, P. H., and M. L. Marks, *Managing the Merger: Making It Work* (New York: Prentice Hall, 1992).

Language

Language reflects culture, not only in apparent but also in subtle ways. The undetected cultural differences have the potential to cause organizational problems. The use of English as a common language for business has a ramification for staff using English as a second language. There are tongue-in-cheek comparisons like the ones shown in Table 7.3.

The underlying reality is that mismatches in communications can decide if integrating is successful or not. Practical guidelines can be found in Chapter 14.

Digitization

The manners in which target and acquirer are digitized are equally part of their cultural DNA. A company's digital platform refers to its information and communication technology (ICT) and information systems (IS), such as its intranet, collaboration tools, enterprise resource planning (ERP) systems, human resource management systems, customer relationship management systems, blogs, and corporate social networking tools.

It includes the work structures built into that platform, for example, capabilities, process flows, guides, and the underlying financial, legal, and operational models, and employee feedback tools. The acquirer and the target can be on different levels of digitalization of the company.

In a brick and mortar business, culture may be:

- "Built into the walls"
- "The nail the picture is hung on"

TABLE 7.3	"What the British Say . . .": Communicators' versus Listeners' Perspective

What the British Say	What the British Mean	What Others Understand
I hear what you say	I disagree and do not want to discuss it further	He accepts my point of view
With the greatest respect	I think you are an idiot	He is listening to me
That's not bad	That's good	That's poor
That is a very brave proposal	You are insane	He thinks I'm courageous
Quite good	A bit disappointing	Quite good
I would suggest	Do it, or be prepared to justify yourself	Think about the idea, but do as you like
Oh, incidentally/by the way	The primary purpose of our discussion is . . .	That is not very important
I was a bit disappointed that	I am annoyed that	It doesn't really matter
Very interesting	That is clearly nonsense	They are impressed
I'll bear it in mind	I've forgotten it already	They will probably do it
I'm sure it's my fault	It's your fault	Why do they think it was their fault?
You must come for dinner	It's not an invitation, I'm just being polite	I will get an invitation soon
I almost agree	I don't agree at all	He's not far from agreement
I only have a few minor comments	Please rewrite completely	He has found a few typos
Could we consider other options?	I don't like your idea	They have not yet decided

In a digital corporation, the culture may be:

- "On the intranet"
- "Will send a link"
- "There is a webcast"
- "Have you taken the online tutorial?"
- "Have you seen the latest video?"
- "Just fill in the online form"
- "Have you not read the blog?"
- "It is all over the social network"

In most deals and integrations, the mere integration of the ICT and IS systems takes the longest to be implemented. Durations can range between four months up to two years and longer before both target and acquirer are on the same digital platform.

Consider If a brick and mortar target that is merging with a digital corporation, and the issues are amplified. There is a real risk that the target will never really belong and cannot merge into the acquirer's culture and information flow.

Resistance to change in the target and acquirer is at its lowest at the time just after deal announcement, and increases over time to a level where a crisis is needed before issues are tackled. The ICT and IS integration is typically ready by the time resistance to change is at its highest. Communication, involvement, and journey management of employees are therefore highly advised.

The mitigation is to build bridges and interim solutions to the digital platform. The target employees need to be involved in the integration to the digital platform. Training or introduction to the possibilities within the digital platform can help.

IMPLEMENTATION

This topic deals with the practical tools and actions to help implement the elements from the other topics in this chapter. It follows the chronology of the integration phases.

Phase 1: Before Any Deal Is on the Table

How to practically go about creating cultural awareness? There are several options that can be combined into a mix that is suitable for your company.

Management Training.   Some leading companies embody management training on culture as part of their annual strategic get-together. Typically such a training module would take from one hour to a full day. The topics covered would be very much aligned with the content of this chapter as well as Chapter 14.

Online Training.   Similar content can be delivered via online trainings. The advantages are that it allows the monitoring of who has completed the course, and that participants can complete it at a time that is suitable for them.

Manual on Culture.   A manual on culture serves as a reference document and is helpful both to complement trainings and as a stand-alone document. A separate manual on how to approach culture in an M&A situation can be handed out to anyone involved in an acquisition. These manuals are typically tailor made for a company, for obvious reasons.

A Culture and Values Statement. This is a very public way of stating the company's identity. The Netflix example earlier in this chapter comes from the firm's 124-page culture statement. Below are some snippets from that manual:

- The actual company values, as opposed to the nice-sounding values, are shown by who gets rewarded, promoted, or let go
- Our culture focuses on helping us achieve excellence
- You challenge prevailing assumptions when warranted, and suggest better approaches
- You keep us nimble by minimizing complexity and finding time to simplify
- You say what you think even if it is controversial
- You care intensely about Netflix's success
- You only say things about fellow employees you will say to their face
- You share information openly and proactively
- Adequate performance gets a generous severance package
- You question actions inconsistent with our values

Company Culture Expert. Invest in an independent, external culture expert who coaches the leadership on culture issues. The expert would be in a trusted coaching position and needs to be an external advisor in order to maintain his independence. He can advise an internal team to act as the Cultural Competence Center, in order to implement culture and value alignment.

Cultural Competence Center. Some serial acquirers have embedded the cultural work stream as an actual Center of Excellence within their business development team. This is not done out of charity, but from hard-earned experience, having to pull out of a country or a deal after it backfired for cultural reasons.

Those who don't know history are destined to repeat it.

—George Santayana

The remit of the Culture Competence Center includes:

- Creating cultural awareness within the team
- Promoting cultural competency

- Creating and delivering culture workshops aimed toward understanding and integration of companies. These workshops are tailor made, depending on the local and management cultures involved.
- Gathering on-the-ground feedback from current and past acquisitions
- Researching cultural competency within the organization's management team
- Creating guidance on how to deal with linguistic sensitivities
- Developing the elements of a culture due diligence
- Overseeing the cultural dimension throughout the M&A life cycle: integration structure, team creation, mixing teams, handling global teams
- Frequent reinforcement of culture and values

Phase 2: When a Deal Is Being Considered

As soon as reasonable, do a cultural due diligence and fact gathering. A due diligence is an investigation into certain aspects of an organization, conducted with all due care and diligence. A due diligence can focus on many different areas, and is traditionally limited to such areas as financial, legal, and tax.

A cultural due diligence does not necessarily have to be as substantial as a financial due diligence. It is an iterative process, starting with first impressions, and gradually working into more granularity while moving along the M&A timeline.

Start with taking stock of what is known about the target's country and local cultures. What is the acquirer's experience there? Maybe suppliers, customers, or employees can tell more about the country. What can be found on the Internet? A comparison between country cultures can be done by using Hofstede's Cultural Compass, or by flipping to Chapter 14 in this book, which focuses more on Erin Meyer's work. That will give the acquirer easy one-on-one comparisons, and will already provide some great insights.

Continue with the facts of the acquirer—the "know thyself" part. Some examples of facts that shape an organization's culture are:

Behavior
- Statements and practices
- Decisions of senior leaders and key influencers
- Organizational design
- The way employees and managers interact on a daily basis
- Messages to peers, customers, and suppliers
- Forms of remuneration
- Overtime tracking and payment
- Informal rewards and recognition

- Corporate social responsibility
- Meetings and mail protocols (e.g., punctuality, keeping to agenda)
- Communication and employee feedback
- Consensus seeking versus top-down directives
- Freedom and responsibility versus restrictive
- Masculine versus feminine
- Chaotic versus systematic and organized
- Pragmatic versus rules based
- Social events, team parties, informal get-togethers
- Getting things done versus taking forever to finish a project
- Proactive compensation versus remedy compensation
- "Striving for excellence" versus "good enough"
- Value statement
- Extent to which the official value statement is aligned with what is really valued at the company
- Rewarding innovation

Symbols

- Logos
- Brands
- Office layout
- Availability, price, and quality of coffee, food, snacks, and so on
- Location
- Dress code
- Company pay level versus market pay level
- Language, terminology, and jargon used for formal and informal communication
- Awareness of company vision and mission
- How to promote and develop within the company

Systems

- Reporting and measuring
- Goal setting and budgeting
- Human resource policies and practices
- Time tracking and badging
- Learning and improvement

Values

- Examples: accountability, achievement, adaptability, ambition, balance home/work, being liked, being the best, caring, caution, clarity, coaching/

mentoring, commitment, community involvement, compassion, competence, conflict resolution, continuous learning, control, courage, creativity, dialogue, ease with uncertainty, efficiency, enthusiasm/positive attitude, entrepreneurial, environmental awareness, ethics, excellence, fairness, family, financial stability, forgiveness, friendship, future generations, generosity, health, humility, humor, independence, initiative, integrity, job security, leadership, listening, making a difference, openness, patience, perseverance, personal fulfillment, personal growth, recognition, reliability, respect, reward, risk taking, safety, self-discipline, teamwork, trust, vision, wealth, well-being, wisdom

After having listed these, determine which ones are most significant to the organization. Some of the items above can be positioned on an axis with two extremes. That will help to define the essence of the company's culture. More on this in Chapter 14.

Then, start to compare those facts with the target's facts. Much may be available via public sources. The way the data room and its documents are organized and the interaction with the target's management will gradually provide clues. If there are significant gaps, specific clarification can be asked in writing or during Q&A sessions with the target's management.

Approaches to the Cultural Due Diligence Outcome   Based on the comparison, define the approach. Depending on whether the result was culturally dominant or lenient on any given issue, it is possible to:

- Implement the acquirer's culture and take no prisoners
- Adjust to local culture for essential elements and build consensus
- Adopt a "pace and lead" approach and give the process of integrating ample time
- Go for the opportunistic, profit-driven approach and keep the target as a stand-alone entity
- Abandon the deal. If the acquirer has a very strong culture with very explicit values like Netflix's, which are opposite to those in the target, consider exiting the process and stop any further due diligence.

The findings from the cultural due diligence need to be embedded in the execution plan for the integration strategy and the individual work stream actions.

Communication   One of the first public signs of cultural understanding that an acquirer can make will be in the communication: what is said and what is not said, how is it said, what jargon and terminology is used.

Cultural understanding will manifest itself in the target audience addressed by the acquirer: who is being addressed, and who is not. Will suppliers be notified? Customers? Workers? Will that be done in a person-to-person chat, via a call, or by mail?

It will be apparent in the consistency of the message across various target audiences: Will the same message be given to top management as to employees, unions, the community, and investors? It will be in who makes the announcement: a representative of the acquirer or the target, the CEO, or business unit management.

The preparatory work done on culture can be implemented immediately by tailoring the communication on the signing of the deal to some specifically sensitive issues.

Phase 3: Between Signing and Closing

After signing, there is often an opportunity for more dialogue between buyer and target. That window can be used to dive a bit deeper into mutual cultural understanding.

Solicit feedback on the signing communication. Check with the work stream heads what specific sensitivities may be, and refine the communication in time for the closing of the deal.

Prepare a question and answer list, as a guide for senior and middle management, to help them bring the right message across. Consider the creation of a company web page with the same questions and answers, and provide a feedback forum.

Welcome Pack Preparation   It is customary in some cultures that the acquirer distributes a welcome pack to the various target stakeholders. Examine the suitability of the welcome pack: Is it aligned with the culture implementation plan? Whatever the approach to culture—dominance, lenience, pragmatism—the message can be sent in the welcome pack.

Workshop   Prepare a culture workshop to be implemented soon after closing, and directed toward the outcome of the pre-signing information gathering. Elements to include in such a workshop can be:

- Stimulating face-to-face contact
- Use of serious gaming techniques
- Working around the combined business model and the deal rationale
- Mutual inclusiveness

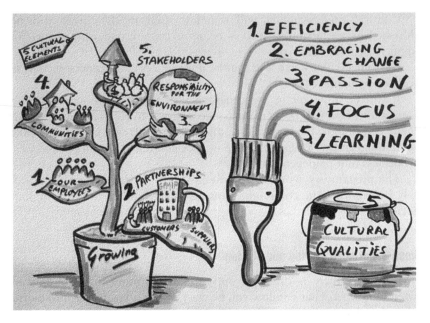

FIGURE 7.5   Visual Mapping of Culture Workshop

- Laying the foundation for the creation of international buddy teams
- Working on the "know thyself" elements mentioned above, but then with a view from both sides.

Figure 7.5 shows a snippet from a visual mapping of a culture workshop at a global fertilizer company, focusing on the company's five cultural elements and five cultural qualities.

Preparation of Management and Integration Team

- **Terminology:** Create a common project terminology, with actual definitions and examples; if the integration managers are aligned, you will be off to a great start
- **Business model:** Ensure mutual understanding of the deal rationale, and where the acquisition fits in; the Business Model Canvas® is recommended as a simple and effective tool
- **Techniques:** Use inclusive techniques to foster a common approach and team alignment; an example of a technique is the Lego® Serious Play® methodology: This is a process designed to bring out the best business performance in new teams.

Phase 4: After Closing

If it was not possible to prepare the cultural integration prior to closing, it can still start after closing—even months later. The acquirer is now free of the pre-closing restrictions, it is the right time to start implementing and refining all the actions prepared so far. This is best done in an iterative way, gathering feedback and incorporating that in the actions. Cultural enablers help to achieve that goal.

Cultural Enablers Once cultural differences have been identified, a plan can be developed to address hindering differences. Table 7.4 is a list of cultural enablers.

TABLE 7.4 Cultural Enablers

Category	Enabler	Expected Result
Leadership	Senior leadership embraces cultural awareness	Cultural issues are part of the M&A fabric
Training	Senior leaders and managers are trained on culture integration techniques	Leading by example Mandate and endorsement from the top
	Employees be trained on one set of standard forms, systems, and procedures	Efficiency through alignment and sharing of leading practices Professionalization of the company
Respect	Leaders show respect for employees and peers in other cultures	Development of a shared frame of reference
Involvement	Leaders disseminate a values and culture manual via informal chats and formal, uniform presentations	Dissemination of values and cultures through all levels of the organization
	Feedback system for all employees to provide feedback and improvement suggestions	Involvement of everyone in the integration effort
Humility	Solicit input from clients, employees, suppliers, and other constituents	Credibility, persuasion, consensus, buy-in
Repetition	Creates a "command and control" setting	Effective where employees are expected to do as they're told
	Go for the long term	Development of trust and bonds

Value Alignment   A company's values are what keep it on track to realize its mission. Vibrant cultures display high levels of values alignment. Richard Barrett has developed a widely utilized framework around values-based leadership, with books, trainings, web-based tools, and practitioners who support companies worldwide. Organizational values tell you how you need to be, individually and collectively, to achieve the organization's mission and vision. At the start of an integration process, the combined company needs to move from the current state of mixed values to a desired state of shared values.

When the values of the organization are in alignment with the personal and desired culture values of employees, you will experience high levels of employee engagement. People will bring their discretionary energy to their work and go the extra mile to get the job done.

The value alignment envisaged is that between the employee, the target, and the acquirer. Imagine that the desired state for all three is to share values like "making a difference," "goal orientation," "open communication," and "trust." At the time of the acquisition, any discrepancies in alignment are measured: there may be some on "trust" and "open communication." To measure is to know, and the sheer fact of measuring and sharing common goals is a step in the right direction.

Dissemination   Last, disseminate values and culture to all levels of the organization in a uniform manner. This can be achieved via a values and culture manual, through local opinion leaders and change agents, and with informal chats and formal presentations. A frequent reinforcement of values and culture tops things off.

CHAPTER CHECKLIST

- Cultural considerations are essential in making cross-border deals succeed
- There is local, national, global, and organizational culture
- Hofstede sets out five cultural dimensions: social orientation, power distance, gender roles, uncertainty avoidance, and time orientation
- On any aspect of culture: determine cultural dominance or lenience
- Cultural elements have interdependencies with all other integration work streams
- Preparations on culture start before any deal is under consideration, and continue throughout the complete deal life cycle

BIBLIOGRAPHY

Accenture/Economist Intelligence Unit. *Top Integration Challenges* (New York: Economist, 2006).

Barrett, Richard. *The New Leadership Paradigm* (Raleigh, NC: Lulu, 2011).

Coisne, Christine. *La gestion des différences culturelles dans les fusions-acquisitions internationales: Une compétence distinctive?* (Roubaix, France: Edhec Business School, 2012).

Hernandez, Daniel Guardiola. *Cross-Border M&A and the Impact of Cultural Differences* (Roubaix, France: Edhec Business School, 2012).

Hofstede, Geert. *Culture's Consequences: Comparing Values, Behaviors, Institutions, and Organizations across Nations*, 2nd ed. (Thousand Oaks, CA: Sage, 2011).

Laneve, Marc, and Thomas Stüllein. *The Influence of National Culture on Cross-Border M&A* (Sweden, Linnaeus University, 2010).

Pollan, Michael. *The Omnivore's Dilemma: A Natural History of Four Meals* (New York: Penguin, 2006), 99–100.

Renison, Daniel R., Byan Adkins, and Ashley M. Guidroz, *Managing Cultural Integration in Cross-Border Mergers and Acquisition: Advances in Global Leadership 6* (Bingley, UK: Emerald Group Publishing, 2011), 95–115.

Stam, Jan-Jacob. *Het Verbindende Veld* (Avonhorn, The Netherlands: Het Noorderlicht, 2004).

Vaara, Eero. *Constructions of Cultural Differences in Post-Merger Change Processes: A Sensemaking Perspective on Finnish-Swedish Cases*. M@n@gement 3, no. 3 (Helsinki: School of Economics and Business Administration, Department of International Business, 2000), 81–110.

Valentini, Todd, "Cultural Enablers," *Thoughts from Taddeo* blog, 2016, http://thoughtsfromtaddeo.blogspot.be/2016/02/shingo-dimensions.html.

CHAPTER 8

Managing National Reactions and Sovereignty Issues

Gilles Ourvoie

CHAPTER LEARNING OBJECTIVES—IN THIS CHAPTER, YOU WILL LEARN:

➤ The background factors that have an impact on foreign direct investment (FDI) policies
➤ The main elements of FDI restrictions
➤ The types of sectors considered to be sensitive and how this list evolves according to countries and history
➤ Potential approaches implemented from strategy to post-deal execution to comply with FDI restrictions or national sensitivity issues

CHAPTER SUMMARY

Nations are facing historic challenges in our current period of economic globalization, technological and scientific unification, and cultural homogenization. Political regimes, state organizations, and all the constituents of most countries on earth are struggling with the best way to preserve local equilibria and gain from the global movement of capital, ideas, and people. In most countries, conservative forces and extremists use nationalism as the political utopia of last resort, opposing the boundaries of the known to the risks of the distant and uncontrolled unknown. Cross-border deals are particularly sensitive to this mind-set, and it is essential for countries to ensure to their constituents that foreign direct investments do not jeopardize national security or stability. This chapter provides some details about how FDI restrictions are defined and what are the types of issues a potential acquirer has to anticipate.

THE AMBIVALENT RELATION BETWEEN CROSS-BORDER M&A AND NATIONAL INTEREST

Cross-border deals are a major component of the economic globalization process. As such, they are to be viewed in a global perspective of changes occurring both in the nature of firms and nations, and in the way they interrelate together.

International trade has always been considered a great accelerator for economic growth and potential social, cultural, and political convergence as well as a source of political risk, foreign influence, strategic dependence, and wealth inequality.

From a political standpoint, nations are struggling with major issues that have an impact on the proper concept of nation and the acceptance of foreign investments:

- International human migration is growing and destabilizing advanced countries throughout the world. Europe may have, for instance, to receive up to 3 million migrants over the next few years. This comes on top of the existing 21 million citizens from non–European Union countries (28 countries) living in the EU. This is generating significant social and political reactions to limit migration and increase controls over foreign activities.
- Many communities are pushing ahead to redefine the existing national boundaries inherited from the past. Kurds in Iraq and Turkey, as well as Russians in Crimea and other Eastern European countries, are examples of such a process.
- In the Middle East and Africa, a wide variety of civil conflicts and wars is destabilizing populations (Shiites versus Sunnis, against minorities). This has consequences on many Middle East and African countries (Yemen, Lebanon, Saudi Arabia, Egypt, Mali), but also on faraway countries (the United States, Australia, Indonesia, Russia), which are confronted by the need to have a modified military and defense doctrine of risk and national security.
- In parallel, unemployment, poverty, and inequality are still endemic ills in most countries. National preference is used as a political defensive barrier against job cuts and social regression in advanced countries. Increased protectionism and state regulation is asked for by a growing part of the population while promarket contenders are still asking for fewer barriers and rules to maximize corporate freedom and profits.

This general tension, between increased globalization and tighter national protection, has direct impacts on cross-border deals. As a consequence, cross-border deals generate reactions, and reactions have progressively led to regulations and controls over foreign investments. In this chapter, we will try to provide a global perspective on these aspects. A list of acronyms is provided at the end of the chapter.

Acquiring Abroad—Outbound Foreign Direct Investments

Different Types of Foreign Direct Investments. Foreign direct investments (FDIs) are traditionally separated into two different categories. One is the development from scratch of foreign businesses ("greenfield"), the other being the acquisition of an existing local business ("brownfield"). These two forms of investments have pros and cons in terms of business strategies, and they also partly face different regulatory constraints.

Greenfield Investments. Starting a business from scratch is historically considered to be long term and requires a lot of energy to understand local specificities, to build relations with the relevant stakeholders, and to develop route-to-market adjusted processes. This is somewhat changing in an environment where IT technology and knowledge are the key capital aspects to transfer to the new entity. As a result, we can observe the quick development of international start-ups building on greenfield strategies leveraging domestic IT investments (Uber, AirBnB). Such investments are in general perceived quite positively at the local level as they bring locally foreign skills and assets (e.g., the Peugeot plant development in Morocco). On the other hand, greenfield investments are an alternative to exports, and therefore may be managed as a way to reduce not only transport costs but also labor costs, generating job cuts or lowered employment in the home country.

Brownfield Investments. These are cross-border deals enabling the acquisition of existing assets and businesses. This saves time but may be subject to specific FDI restrictions on ownership limits.

Outbound Foreign Direct Investments and Corporate Strength. The acquisition and development of assets abroad strengthen corporate wealth and enable to expand its influence. But there might be a wide gap between the initial strategic intent and the actual implementation. Foreign transactions may generate more risks than domestic deals, and mitigation actions may be late to launch and difficult to execute. Does the end result always play in favor of the foreign bidder? Absolutely not.

Corporate Foreign Direct Investments and National Strength. Let's take now a broader national perspective. Does the accumulation of outward FDIs from firms of a specific country generate a national advantage? Yes, without a doubt, nations with outward FDIs are improving their relative economic positions over nations with predominantly inward FDIs. But this net positive impact has both potential benefits and potential pitfalls. On the positive side, the more a country acquires foreign assets, the more it may benefit from geographical diversification of trade flows, access to clients with different macroeconomic cycles and situations, and multiple sourcing options. The more its workforce understands the details of the local situations, the more it may develop new products, new sales strategies, new legal structures, new financial optimization, and new intellectual property.

Inward Foreign Direct Investments and Industrial Policy. Inward FDI restrictions have been widely analyzed as a major potential instrument of industrial policy, together with other tools such as trade import and export restrictions, custom taxes, and EHS policies. The case of the automotive sector in China illustrates very well this potential positive role for an industry latecomer:[1] Through restrictions to foreign (and private domestic) investments and obligations to create JVs with a limited number of local firms and with a minority foreign ownership, China boosted its car manufacturing skills and capacities in the mid-1980s. These initial JVs have enabled the achievement of knowledge and technology transfers, leading to increased domestic production (from 5,000 cars produced in 1958 up to 5 million per year in the late 1990s) and skills (copying first, then developing original national models), and eased the emergence of national firms. In a second phase, building on the existence of these independent national champions, restrictions were reduced at the end of the 1990s to boost national competitiveness, thus preparing probably a third phase to come focusing more on international outward investments and exports, in line with the Korean and Japanese industry benchmarks.

Outward Foreign Direct Investments and Industrial Policy. In a free market economy, monitoring outward FDI with an industrial policy objective is a much more difficult process. Favorable conditions may be developed to support investment decisions and cross-border deals (tax regulations on foreign investments, administrative and financial support to investors acquiring abroad, banking policy). Governments may also use the sales to public organizations to influence private firms in their development path and investments abroad. But the lead time and the effectiveness of such an approach depend very much on the decision making at corporate level, and this may be blocked by minority shareholders or general public reactions. It is much easier, quicker, and more effective for nations to monitor outward FDIs through state-owned enterprises (SOEs). The understanding of such potential strategies has forced most nations to develop FDI inward restrictions specifically targeted at foreign investments of SOEs or government-related firms. One case example of that has been the passing of the Byrd Amendment in the early 1990s to extend the Exon-Florio provisions to the acquisitions of U.S. companies by foreign-government-owned or controlled firms.[2]

Foreign Direct Investments and Delocalization of Work. Foreign acquisitions improve the ability of firms to build on the relative advantages of nations, and modify their value chain accordingly. In this approach, multinational firms' interests may diverge significantly from the initial national interest, as the international flexibility acquired through cross-border deals may lead to job cuts at a national level. They may maintain research and development (R&D) at home level, develop their manufacturing sites in low-cost countries, locate their supply chain entities in low-tax countries to benefit from advantageous transfer prices, and locate their sales or group entities in low-profit-tax countries. In making such trade-offs between international sites, headquarters (HQ) do it focuses on corporate goals and with a limited list of stakeholders. The general consequence must not be underestimated on the image of cross-border deals in the general public, not only on the target side, but also on the buy side.

Inbound Foreign Direct Investments

FDI restrictions do not cover outbound investments, because these investments are broadly considered to be positive from a national standpoint. Exceptions may exist, though, to prevent money transfers against tax rules or financing of illegal activities. The focus of FDI restrictions is on inbound investment, for a number of reasons that need to be stressed.

Bringing in a Foreign Shareholder Raises Uncertainty on the Ultimate Strategic Goals Pursued. Most stakeholders (public administrations, political bodies, unions, employees, clients, suppliers) are wellinformed about the potential consequences of transferring a part or all of the shares to foreign investors. There are positive and negative potential consequences to that, the net being a potential profit with a higher level of uncertainty. Why should there be an increased uncertainty? Because the factors influencing the decision will change in nature, and include parameters that are linked to the domestic situation of the acquirer or to other countries. In other words, it exposes the target firm to a more complex set of influencing factors. The perception resulting from that, at least in the general public, is that there must be a political action to limit uncertainty and risk.

Commitment Required vis-à-vis Local Growth. One of the perceived FDI risks is a potential loss of jobs at the national level. Every target firm in a cross-border deal expects an increased capacity to develop the local business, based on an extended international sales force, a potentially wider portfolio of products and services or easier access to funding to invest and increase productivity, and so on. But this may not materialize, and negative consequences may then be harsher than with a domestic shareholder. Taking into account that particular sensitivity regarding job cuts, bidders have to understand and manage proactively these sell-side expectations, because these positive elements will play a major role in the local loyalty to the new brand, and enable the company to retain key talents and limit value erosion. Integration is very much about trust and a cooperative mind-set—not implementing what has been communicated is a violent breach of trust with potentially lasting results. With this in mind, it may be very useful for a bidder to reconsider potential synergies in a bottom-up process, and check to what extent initial downturn plans can be reassessed based on a more precise local information. More broadly speaking, it is critical to challenge the integration plan from the different stakeholders' perspectives. Focusing too much on some elements may prove to be highly counterproductive.

High Expectations on Communication. Bidders rarely communicate on what their view is of the potential synergies, which may actually include the closing or exit of some noncore assets, the centralization of some activities by their own existing teams, and workforce reduction or wage reductions. However, the development of M&A and cross-border deals tends to increase the capacity of the different local stakeholders to anticipate future decisions. This is why a growing number of local reactions is observed when a deal is announced. We tend to think that this increasing maturity of the stakeholders must be leveraged by the buyers in terms of communication and planning of the post-merger phase. Synergy estimates may be communicated early as long as they reflect a shared burden on the acquirer and target side. Synergies per se do not pose problems as they are perceived to be normal goals in an M&A deal. Fairness is instead the major issue executives must trigger in their integration strategy design and execution.

Dealing with the Governance Aspect. One perceived risk is about decisional uncertainty. The decision-making process will be significantly changed, and the parameters of the decision will be less determined at the local level. In this context, the risk becomes more important to be dependent on distant decisions, focusing more on figure-related analysis than on human-related elements.

Economic Globalization and National Interest

The development of FDI restrictions, the increased potential variety of the transactions covered, the growing inclusion of economic as well as military risks to be looked at, all these phenomena are linked to the general globalization of our economies, and the growing interdependencies between nations in their cultural and social dimensions. Let's detail here a bit more the different issues at stake.

Economic Globalization and National Well-Being. Since the 1980s, hundreds of millions of people in China, Brazil, India, and other emerging countries have moved from under-poverty levels to being part of the middle class. This is a major historical achievement by any account. At a lower level, the Eastern and Central European countries are making significant progress in reaching the standard EU conditions of living. All this is mostly linked to the international expansion of the free market economy, and the development of local jobs and more competitive firms. FDIs and cross-border deals have been major parts of this overall globalization process.

Globalization, Inequality, and Public Opinion. This overall economic and social progress has not eliminated inequality. In fact, the concentration of wealth and revenues has increased in the past 50 years in both emerging and developed countries. Does this mean that the economic international integration is negative per se and should be restrained or even stopped? There is no evidence of this. On the contrary, inequality is the result of the optimization of regulatory competition between nations, and fragmented information leveraged only by the already richer individuals. As has been viewed on the tax aspects, it is because of national egoism that tax evasion is made possible. When international political agreements are passed such as the one with Swiss authorities on the automatic transfer of banking information, demonstrating a shared and single view of issues, the "free-rider" behaviors have to adjust, and they do so very quickly. But in many advanced economies, there is a popular confusion between economic globalization and cost and tax optimization, leading to the banalization of free-riding, short-minded, and greedy behaviors.

Systemic Risks and National Security. The specific evolution of FDI regulation on foreign investments is an illustration of the balance between the perception of potential risks and the need to look for foreign investments. The United States' evolution of FDI restrictions, for instance (see later), shows to what extent the types of risks covered have evolved over time, extending the possibility to terminate a deal. However, the number of deals actually blocked by FDI official decisions globally appears to have been very limited—the actual numbers are not known.

Economic Interdependencies and Peace. However, in spite of this historical knowledge, the choice has been made to establish peace in Europe through increased economic interdependencies and the creation of the European Coal and Steel Community (1951) and later on the European Economic Community (1958), which was transformed into the current EU with the Lisbon Treaty (2007).

Political Scrutiny over Interstate Relations. There is today a huge sensitivity regarding globalization as a vector of inequality and social and political injustice. Political actions are facing disbelief and skepticism in most advanced nations. In this context, it is absolutely normal to see cross-border deals face increasing public scrutiny and political reactions. This in turn demands better deals and better management plans.

INWARD CROSS-BORDER DEALS: KEY RESTRICTIONS

Based on the previous elements, nations have progressively defined a set of procedures tackling precisely the FDI in order to limit the potential risks on national security and stability. These FDI restrictions are built on a number of pivotal concepts that need to be detailed here. We will see in particular that these concepts may have evolved over time based on the perception of the potential threats. The increased sophistication of these procedures has not always led to a greater precision of the definitions. It is also interesting to note that the concept of critical industries may be significantly different from one country to another. But, broadly speaking, there is a general consensus on the importance of having FDI restrictions and regulations in place.

Most Countries Have Set Up Rules Limiting Foreign Acquisitions. These rules are basically related to restrictions imposed on foreign FDIs (greenfield and brownfield), specific rules related to foreign M&A's, industrial policies as to foreign ownership or trade rules, anticoncentration policies, and core national security rules related to defense and homeland security issues. All these elements contribute to the overall policy vis-à-vis foreign investments.

The Major Role of United States' Regulation. Because of the importance of the United States' M&A market both domestically and cross-border (outbound and inbound), its regulatory framework has been used by other countries as a key source for benchmarking. Below is a list of key historical milestones.

- In the United States, restrictions have been imposed on German investments with the Trading with the Enemy Act (TWEA) signed in October 1917. This has been strengthened by other regulations triggering investments in specific industries: the Merchant Marine Act and Mineral Lands Leasing Act in 1920, and the Air Commercial Act in 1926.
- In the 1970s, the rise of foreign investments from the OPEC countries led to the Foreign Investment Study Act in 1974. Following the OPEC oil embargo against the United States, President Ford signed in 1975 an executive order to create the Committee on Foreign Investment in the United States (CFIUS). According to Executive Order 11858, it has a "primary continuing responsibility within the Executive Branch for monitoring the impact of foreign investment in the United States, both direct and portfolio, and for coordinating the implementation of United States policy on such investment."
- In the 1980s, Japanese investments in the United States increased, targeting technological assets. The attempt in 1986 by Fujitsu Co. to acquire Fairchild Semiconductor Co. raised important political and public reactions about the potential national security threat. It led to the 1988 Exon-Florio Amendment, which added to the CFIUS monitoring role the possibility for the president to review any deal potentially impacting national security and to terminate any such deal. The 1991 regulations passed by President Reagan gave the CFIUS—under the leadership of the secretary of the treasury—this presidential authority to review and terminate any deal potentially threatening national security.
- In 1992, the attempt by the French defense group Thomson-CSF to acquire the missile and aerospace division of the United States LTV group failed following actions initiated by the competitors Martin Marietta and Lockheed on the alleged ground that Thomson-CSF had a history of weapon transactions with Iraq. Thomson was a state-owned firm, and France had an old presence in the region. It was also against the intervention of the United Nations in Iraq. But France as a whole could not be viewed as a national enemy of the United States. This situation led therefore to passage of a new set of rules (Byrne Amendment) to restrict foreign investments made by state-owned organizations supporting foreign state policies potentially threatening

United States national security. This regulation covering state-owned or state-related foreign investments played a major role later on.

- A new adjustment of the regulation occurred in 2007 with the implementation of the Foreign Investment and National Security Act (FINSA). This followed the 9/11 terrorist attack, and the "war on terror" launched by President Bush. The acquisition of the British group P&O by DPW (Dubai Port World) is an illustration of this evolution. Though not a U.S. group, P&O managed six ports on the U.S. East Coast. Because of this, and because DPW was a United Arab Emirates group at a time when the UAE was considered to be supporting terrorism, the acquisition of the six U.S. ports was blocked. This happened despite a unanimous positive vote of the CFIUS. As a reaction, the new FINSA framework detailed the role of the CFIUS and confirmed its role in terms of national security reviews on foreign M&A. It increased the number of members of the CFIUS committee to 16 representatives to include more expertise. It detailed as well the three major goals of the CFIUS: (1) check if the transaction is achieved by or with any foreign person and could result in a foreign control of a U.S. business, (2) check if there is credible evidence that such a control might lead to actions threatening the national security of the United States, and (3) check that there are adequate legal safeguards to protect the national security of the United States. One other major added feature of FINSA relates to the creation of a prenotice consultation phase, which favors information sharing and negotiations between potential acquirers and the CFIUS.

These Rules Build on Terms That Are Not That Easy to Define.   These different types of restrictions are based on a number of elements that pose in general a problem of definition. The following ones are the most important:

- What is a foreign person or firm?
- What do we mean by "control" over the domestic businesses?
- What do we put under the "national security" or "general interests" concepts?

Enterprise Nationality—a More and More Difficult Issue.   The proper concept of an enterprise nationality is more complex than it seems, in a world of rapid circulation of people, interlinked economies, and increasing cultural interdependencies:

- Is the HQ location defining the nationality of the firm? What about the firms that have transferred their HQ location abroad for tax reasons and remain significantly staffed in their historical countries? One might argue as well that the nationality of a group resides where major strategic decisions are taken—but this as well might be highly mobile.

- Is the ownership of the firm defining its nationality? What about the actual nationality of listed international groups with a majority of foreign shareholders? Is it linked to where the listing is done? To where the CEO is based?

- Are the actual operational assets and human resources defining the nationality of a firm? What about the firms that have massively delocalized their productions in low-cost countries? Is it more a question of R&D and innovation location? Is it linked to where the most important investments are being achieved?

- Is the nationality of a firm more a cultural issue? What about the groups that have CEOs coming from abroad—does this reflect a change in their nationality? In another perspective, could we say that a group's nationality depends on its most used internal language (after English)?

Different Countries, Diverse Definitions.   As we see, the reality that national regulators have to deal with is complex—there is no clear-cut situation or one-for-all solutions. At the international level, it is not a surprise to find a diversity of approaches, such as:

- Differences exist between countries due to political priorities, military or homeland security context, and economic situations

- In each country, changes may occur over time, based on new cases, governmental changes, new economic context, and jurisprudence

- In each country as well, there might be different approaches due to the different layers of stakeholders and their focus point (central versus local state, defense versus economic ministers)

- There is a difference between texts and actual practice. Terms that are not well defined in the texts are more explicitly defined through jurisprudence.

- Many decisions are not formalized, either because the official process is opaque, but also because informal discussions may happen before the launch of the deal, resulting for instance in no-go decisions that are not documented.

The Nature of the Acquirer

FDI restrictions are triggering foreign investments. What is a foreign investment? The answer is indeed not trivial, and in particular it asks for details as to the nature at large of the acquirer. Regulations have had to come up with a number of principles in order to both limit the scope of deals covered, and adjust the regulation to the nature of potential threats. Some such elements are detailed next.

Foreign versus National. As we can imagine, regulators are confronted with questions as to how to define the type of acquirer to analyze and filter out. Defining the nationality of the acquirer has been among the first questions. Answers vary according to countries, and there have been iterative evolutions over time, as regulations have had to adjust to more and more complex international ownership structures. Now what is a foreign acquirer in our complex world? Is a domestic subsidiary owned by a foreign group listed on an international stock market with international shareholders a foreign acquirer? Is a Chinese investor financing an investment in the United States of a United States citizen of Chinese origin modifying the nationality of the acquirer?

- In China, there is no specific definition of a "foreign investor" in the 2006 Provisions on Mergers and Acquisitions of Domestic Enterprises by Foreign Investors. The term "investors" covers both enterprises and individuals and the foreign aspect is tested on the basis of their nationality. But the 2006 Provisions apply as well to foreign invested enterprises in China, when 25% or more of their equity is held by foreign investors. They apply as well to special purpose investment vehicles, that is, overseas companies directly or indirectly controlled by a domestic company or a natural person.[3]
- In the United States, the Exon-Florio Amendment developed a wider approach. A foreign person is "any foreign national or any entity over which control is exercised or exercisable by foreign interest." Acquisitions achieved by domestic firms under the control of a foreign national individual or entity should therefore be reviewed, regardless of the percentage owned. The focus is put on the existence of influence, be it via shareholdership or any other mode.

Military Enemies: Direct War Enemies, Coalition Opponents, Countries Supporting Terrorism. Investment restrictions are directly linked to national diplomatic and military positions. As such, the concept of military enemy has evolved over time, generating iterative adjustments in the regulation against foreign investments. Logically, restrictions have initially been applied to national military enemies. This view that foreign investments coming from nations considered to be national enemies must be identified, controlled, and if required stopped is still the core basis for FDI regulations. But the proper notion of national military enemies has in a certain way been transformed under several trends—there are fewer wars opposing countries front-to-front, and more situations with civil wars and international interventions. With the development of such multilateral military interventions (Iraq, Afghanistan, Libya, Ukraine, Syria), restrictions have been imposed to countries or firms conflicting specifically with such interventions. This evolution has later on backed actions against firms not supporting the Iran embargo. Another step has been linked to the 9/11 terror attack and the "war on terror" launched in the United States and in other countries.

Economic Competition. With the United States' regulation restricting investments for acquirers from OPEC countries after the first oil crisis in 1974, it is clear that restrictive FDI policies do not only apply to direct or indirect enemies, but also to economic competitors. In fact, many negative consequences that regulations FDI want to limit are purely economic ones: aggressive job cuts, abnormal transfers of profits and tax, development of competitive positions based on knowledge takeovers and transfers. In this context, the FDI regulations of the different countries have growingly extended restrictions to cover "national interest"–related aspects rather than only military ones.

State-owned Enterprises versus Independent Firms. There are major differences between countries in terms of relations between states and corporations, but in general, state intervention is always there, be it in the form of direct ownership and golden shares, attribution of contracts and sales, direct or indirect subsidies, accounting, legal, or tax policies, trade regulations, and so on. For instance, the German model is one where Länder (a state or a region) are very strong and autonomous and have shares in major groups (e.g., Bavaria in Volkswagen); the French model is a more centralized model where the Agence des Participations de l'Etat (APE) has direct shareholderships and golden shares in major groups. In China, complex relations unite state central administration, local government bodies, and firms. In the United States, the federal government and the different states have also considerable influence on the development of firms, based on contracts and sales, United States preference principles, or other restrictive regulations rather than on state direct ownership. Because of this variety of links, and the recognition that state influence may be so important that companies become a way to deploy national policy, FDI regulation has progressively reinforced the analysis of the relations between the acquirer involved and the related foreign states. In the United States, the CNOOC case in 2005 has led with the P&O case to the FINSA regulation enacted in 2007.

The Nature of the Target

What is a domestic firm? There again, the definition and the leverage of this concept varies according to countries. In some countries, the existence of local activities involved is sufficient to intervene (as long as their change of control may impact national security) and therefore enable to review and potentially block M&A transactions, even if these deals involve both an acquirer and a target of foreign nationality.

- In China, the definition of a Chinese firm is not 100% clear. Though the 2006 provisions seem to define a domestic entity as an entity with absolutely no foreign investments, some academics consider that it is an entity with less than 25% foreign ordinary shares ownership.[4]
- In the United States, there is no special focus on the nationality of the target per se. The Exon-Florio Amendment covers in fact any person (individual or entity) "engaged in interstate commerce." This approach has enabled the United States to leverage procedures in deals involving foreign firms because of their local activities in the United States (e.g., the P&O case). There seems to be no limit in terms of relative weight of the business actually achieved in the United States as opposed to the total business of the target—the focus is put on the notion of national security as it is assessed under the CFIUS review process.

Assets versus Firms.   FDI regulations also address the diversity of the legal nature of the acquisitions. M&A cross-border deals may not only trigger existing legal entities—they may also deal with assets that are carved out of one or several legal entities. In most countries, inward M&A restrictions do trigger assets as well as legal entities.

The Type of Transaction

Acquisitions versus Joint Ventures.   FDI restrictions cover in general acquisitions as well as other forms of relations with foreign partners. In many emerging countries around the world, foreign investors are obliged to share ownership and control with local entities and persons. This enables boosting of national economic skills and preserving the long-term national independence of key industries. When there are no existing or limited capabilities, the creation of JVs is a way for nations to import knowledge and technology. It is interesting to see to what extent national strategies over JVs and acquisitions are interrelated, vary across countries, and change over time.

▪ The development of the Chinese automotive industry is a superb illustration of this development path. There was a local centralized production—mainly focusing on executive official cars and trucks—long before the Chinese reforms of 1978. This production was based on Russian methods and technology. China started to look for foreign cooperation at the end of 1978 with a limited number of international firms (GM, Ford, Nissan, Toyota, VW, Citroen, Peugeot, Renault, and Fiat). The first JVs with foreign firms were signed in the mid-1980s (VW and Peugeot being the first ones to be signed). The domestic content rate of the production was progressively forced up (60% in 1990, 90% in 1997 for the SVW [JV with VW] production) so that subcontractors could develop their local skills and investments. The development of the industry was supported by other measures: a limited number of new car manufacturers, high protectionism and entry restrictions, restrictions over domestic greenfield investments, or acquisitions to grow a short list of well-identified national champions. Tariffs on auto parts imports were calculated on the basis of the importance of local production. To adjust to the entry of China into the World Trade Organization (WTO), foreign investments were eased in 1997 with a focus on technology transfers. As a result of this overall industrial policy, competition increased domestically, and the significant progress achieved in local production enabled China to quickly lift off the domestic content requirements and ease foreign investments. Passenger car production boomed from 6,211 vehicles in 1983 to 81,055 in 1991 to 435,615 in 1997 and 1,657,259 in 2006. Import substitution was successfully reached in 1997. The Chinese auto industry is now entering another phase, the long-term goal of the Chinese industry probably being to develop exports and try to replicate the South Korean auto industry development model (successful entry into the United States market only 10 years after its kick-off).

▪ In that same industry, Brazil opened the door to foreign investments in the 1950s—with the obligation of a high local content ratio (around 90%). But because of competition, local producers were either terminated or acquired by foreign firms. As of now, foreign firms dominate the Brazilian market.

Minority versus Majority Ownership. In general, there has been an evolution regarding how the percentage owned is perceived. The initial simplified view that corporate control could be tracked through majority ownership has been challenged over time. FDI restrictions are now increasingly focusing on the concept of influence rather than on simple majority shareholder criteria. Effective influence on corporate strategy and decisions may come indeed from a broad range of factors and may occur even with a minority shareholdership. As it is possible to influence a firm for instance through its dependency on specific sources of revenues and contracts, on financial and banking arrangements and links, its top management profiles, and on R&D and technology transfers, regulations now pay more attention to this broad (and somewhat voluntarily vague) notion of "influence" than to the single notion of capital control. As a consequence, in a growing number of countries, potential FDI restrictions may be implemented regardless of the percentage owned by a foreign person (enterprise or individual).

The Definition of National Security

Defense integrity versus national security. Though the two concepts are close, there is a significant difference between them.

- Defense integrity focuses on munitions, armament, and dual civil-defense technology industries (electronic equipment, aircraft and satellite production, telecommunications). It is often monitored directly by specific military national ministers, administrations or agencies, congressional groups, or external think-tanks, conducting specific reviews and assessments, in connection with, or embedded into, general FDI processes and committees. In most countries, military forces as well as public opinions and local manufacturers are very sensitive about the potential impact of investments on the national capacity to maintain an independent and reliable armed force.
- The national security concept is broader as it includes critical industries (water, steel) or infrastructure (energy, airports, and aircraft). It may as well cover the notion of economic security (strategic supplies) or social stability (media). Progressively, this concept of national security has gained attention in the policies applicable to inward FDIs.

Differences between countries. There are differences between countries as to the notion itself:

- In China, the development of a legal framework covering foreign investments that could potentially impact national security has been initiated via Article 12 of the 2006 Provisions, which state that a review is compulsory when a deal made by a foreign investor (1) involves any critical industry, (2) affects or may affect the security of the national economy, or (3) causes the transfer of actual control over the domestic enterprise that possesses a well-established trademark or a time-honored brand. Article 31 of the Anti-Trust Law issued in 2008 has reinforced the principle of a compulsory review when national security is involved. But the organization of a national security review system has been established only in 2011.

■ In the United States, the Exon-Florio Amendment authorizes the president's intervention only when "the foreign interest exercising control might take action that threatens to impair the national security"—with the view that no other laws provide the adequate and appropriate authority to protect national security. To be more specific, 12 factors have been identified to consider blocking a foreign acquisition. They are in a way a definition of what national security is about. But it is interesting to note that there is no explicit reference to the concept of a "critical industry" as it is used in the Chinese or in the French regulation.

The Definition of Critical Industries

Critical industry. The concept of "critical" or "strategic" industry is a pivotal one regarding FDI restrictions. Most regulations tend to limit foreign control over such industrial capabilities to preserve national independence and sovereignty. However, countries cover this goal through different approaches, with either very explicit or more indirect descriptions.

■ In the United States, the Exon-Florio Amendment has enabled extension of FDI review to nondefense-related sectors and economic issues, with the use of the critical infrastructure term. This covers aircraft, telecommunications, financial services, water, and transportation. With time, a greater emphasis has been put on high-tech industries. However, we may note that in 2005 the oil independence issue was a strong argument used against the bid proposed by the Chinese National Offshore Oil Corporation (CNOOC) for Union Oil Corporation of California (Unocal) with public reactions leading to the failure of the deal. The Department of Homeland Security has widened this scope, with a list of 17 sensitive sectors. This list shows to what extent the proper concept of a critical asset may be large.

■ In China, the definition of "critical industry" has been established by the SASAC in 2006. It listed armaments, power generation and distribution, oil and petrochemicals, telecommunications, coal, and aviation and shipping industries. This definition reflected the situation of the

Chinese economy and strategic priorities at the time, and in particular the need to provide a high level of production of raw materials and manufactured goods to fuel the national growth.

■ In France, a list has been established of such "strategic industries" requiring state review and approval.

Natural resources. Access to key natural sources of wealth is in general under FDI coverage. The list of such sensitive natural resources varies according to countries based on both national supply and national and international demand. Potential restrictions exist when considering cross-border acquisitions of:

■ **Land.** For instance, such restrictions are important in Australia (despite its huge national surface). Local restrictions may also exist due to the proximity of defense-related or other sensitive activities.

■ **Oil and gas reserves.** In most oil and gas–producing countries, there are restrictions vis-à-vis foreign investments. Policies have been enforced to improve higher national levels of control over such resources (nationalizations, JV obligations, foreign ownership limitations) and ensure the long-term leverage of such resources. In Europe (France, the United Kingdom), as opposed to the United States, environmental pressures have limited foreign investments to analyze and exploit potential schist oil reserves.

■ **Mines** producing industrial minerals (coal, steel, copper, bauxite, zinc, phosphate) are also covered by potential FDI restrictions. The rise of China and India has increased the pressure on the production of steel and aluminum, generating competition on steel and bauxite mines across the globe. The objective of such restrictions is not only to preserve access, but to limit potential threatening price policies.

■ **Precious metals** (diamonds, gold). Such mines are also subject to restrictions in most countries because they may still represent a huge proportion of the national wealth and have a strong popular symbolic significance.

■ **Uranium.** Uranium is used as a raw material in the nuclear energy sector. The development of nuclear energy at the global level (in China in particular) has put a particular pressure on the importance of access to uranium. Investments in uranium mines are hence often subject to diplomatic and state relations. Investments in such mines are also monitored by international agreements triggering the nonproliferation of nuclear military capabilities, in order to limit banned exports or fraudulent activities.

- **Rare earth mines.** The growing use of high-tech products in most economic sectors has here again considerably increased the global competition for such resources. As a reaction, they have been included within the scope of critical resources subject to national reviews.

Defense and Aerospace

- **Munitions.** Though it is a traditional core defense capability under high national surveillance, there are however some cross-border deals in that sector—for example, the deal announced in 2015 between Nexter (France) and KMW (Germany) to create a group of 6,000 employees and €1.7bn in sales. In the missiles sector, the creation of the MBDA group— the third largest group in the world in this industry—has been established through several cross-border transactions between France, the United Kingdom, Italy, Germany, and the United States.
- **Equipment manufacturing.** A huge number of suppliers provide equipment or parts to military forces. This may cover a wide range of solutions and services related to transport (land, naval, airspace), battlefield man equipment (protection and mobility devices, training solutions), or any form of equipment supporting troops. Because of their technological edge and innovative character, some of this equipment may be restricted to military purpose. In this case, FDI restrictions may limit change of control.
- **Defense-related dual technologies.** A considerable set of technologies are applicable to both defense and civil usage (e.g., radar, calculators, imaging systems, shipbuilding, space launching devices, satellite design and production, telecommunication devices and networks, virtual reality systems). Firms may build on such technological skills to provide solutions to both military forces and civil clients. It is the case in many major groups in telecommunications, electronics and IT equipment, aircraft manufacturing, nuclear energy, training and simulation, or to a lesser degree in the car and truck construction sector, in health care, chemicals, energy, and so on. Such firms may be subject to national security reviews in order to ensure the separation between civil and military assets and governance.
- **Military terrains and lands.** Specific areas are dedicated to, or close to, military operations (airports, training compounds, ports).

Information and Communication

- **Electronic components.** Some electronic components may have a particular national security importance, as they may have a dual civil and military/intelligence purpose or usage. Based on the technologies developed, limitations may exist as to foreign ownership.

▪ **Telecommunications.** The history of telecommunications is a military one, from the telegraph to satellites and to the Internet. It is no wonder most countries have supported the creation of national champions in this sector. As a result, foreign ownership of such telecommunications incumbent in more mature markets is highly complex and subject to strong resistance. The deregulation of the sector has opened M&A options in fixed and mobile lines by multiplying the number of players and potential targets and is also facilitated by the concentration of cable companies. The concentration process is not ended, though, because of the infrastructure costs and scale effects. At the global level, the skyrocketing development of telecommunications firms in emerging countries will probably be a major component in cross-border M&A activity.

▪ **Media.** Media and the production and distribution of content are, since Montesquieu and the theory of "balance of powers and counterpowers," an important building block in national political systems. In most democracies, regulations exist to secure the degree of independence of the media, in particular vis-à-vis the consequences of an excessive ownership concentration. In state-controlled countries, strong links between the government and the media limit the type of content provided and the influence of political opposition. In general, media is a sensitive and visible industry, with a high degree of political interference and multiple levels of actions (technical diffusion authorizations, use of public infrastructure, compliance with media regulation, investment in local production of content, and so on).

Other Sensitive Sectors

It is not the goal of this chapter to detail all of the sensitive sectors. However, it is important to have a view of their broad variety:

▪ **Infrastructure.** Most states consider infrastructure as highly strategic assets. This covers rail transport networks and equipment manufacturing, airport operations and lands, air transport services and equipment manufacturing, civil or defense naval port operations and lands, and postal services.

▪ **R&D and technology.** As mentioned earlier, most innovative technologies may have a national strategic interest. This may be due to either their direct military usage, or to the competitive edge gained on civil markets. The list of potential technologies at stake may differ from one country to another, depending on national industry priorities.

▪ **Energy and water utilities.** The entire sector of energy and water is, for obvious reasons of national attention, of critical strategic importance.

This covers oil and gas energy production (reserves, production facilities) in many emerging countries; one of the first marks of independence has been to nationalize such assets. Energy diffusion and distribution may also have a strategic importance, enabling the secure delivery of energy in all conditions. It is important to note that the transport of energy is a critical geopolitical asset (Suez Canal, Russian gas in Ukraine, gas between Russia and Turkey).

- **Nuclear energy.** Nuclear energy is highly sensitive, and there is a limited number of nations with civil nuclear capacity and a division between civil and military nuclear capabilities. JVs and foreign investments exist in the production of nuclear energy (e.g., in China or in the United Kingdom), but within very strict constraints. Dams and river equipment are also very often critical infrastructures, as they may be sources of catastrophic incidents and have an effect on large populations and territories. Another type of utility may be considered critical from a national standpoint: the consumption of water, as it may have tremendous impact on populations. Foreign investments in water purification plants or water distribution networks may also be subject to FDI review.

- **Additional sectors.** As we can see, the list of potentially critical sectors is very much context-dependent. Investors must for instance consider that some elements of the agriculture and food industry, chemicals industry, pharmaceuticals industry, and automotive industry may also be considered critical industries, due to either their technologies, their products, the population involved, or their political significance.

Other Restrictions

FDI restrictions are not the only regulations that have an influence on cross-border deals. Other regulatory constraints may impact the interest of conducting such deals. It is not the objective of this book to provide a detailed view of such elements. However, it is important for an executive considering a potential deal to make sure, with the support of his in-house or external legal advisors, that he has a 360-degree view of all the potential obligations and constraints. We list here a few of them.

Industry Regulations. Countries have a huge number of potential levers to monitor the development of foreign-controlled entities at a national level. Acquirers must anticipate all such regulations as they may alter their operating conditions:

- Import restrictions (quotas, tariffs) bundled with requirements over local content weight and local ownership role (e.g., China or South Korea in the car industry)

- Public tender offers supporting national preference clauses
- Compliance rules (product/service specificities, production constraints, administrative declarative obligations, employment conditions, investment requirements) that are specific and potentially too expensive for foreign firms
- Consumer information having a potential impact on consumer behaviors (preferences for national brands)

National Defense Laws and Rules. Each country has its own definition of the core defense scope that needs to be well understood by a foreign acquirer. In some countries (Algeria, China, Russia, Turkey) the traditional importance of the army is such that most economic sectors may depend on its budget and procedures. The same applies all the more in countries actually engaged in conflict (Egypt, Nigeria, Iraq, Israel, South Korea). In such environments, the definition of the defense-related scope may be very broad and include civil activities. But generally speaking, the notion of the military scope depends very much on the situation of the country and the nature of risks it has to mitigate. Where water is rare, the management of water resources may rely on defense rules. Where territories are unstable, all civil activities may be potentially under military surveillance. But it must be noted that in most advanced and stable countries an important set of laws and regulations may be related to military ruling. In France, the management of the radio wave frequencies is subject to defense rules, as is the use of airspace above nuclear or any other sensitive sites. In the United States, a small deal has been blocked due to the vicinity of the assets involved near armed forces terrains. This military scope may change over time. In some advanced countries, the need to decrease defense budgets has led to the acceptance of a bigger area of competition between suppliers, thus easing the potential entry of foreign firms. In less advanced countries, the lack of resources limits military sovereignty to a core set of competencies focused on the payroll of human forces, also facilitating the entry of foreign firms.

International Trade Agreements. We have seen earlier the impact of China's entry into the WTO on its auto industry. The development of bilateral or multilateral free trade (EU, Mercosur, NAFTA, TAFTA) entities has had an impact on FDI restrictions. Generally speaking, the development of zones of free circulation of capital tends to reduce FDI restrictions to more specific national security concerns, as such zones are intended to develop foreign investments. The EU is a good example of this trend, showing that most economic areas have been able to develop cross-border M&A transactions, even in the core defense sector.

International Political Agreements. Each country is nested into a set of diplomatic and economic relations, which vary from very negative to very symbiotic ones and may evolve at any time. Such relations have an impact on the assessment of foreign-related investments. As an example, the United States' "Five Eyes" agreement on electronic surveillance is by nature a vivid proof of a high degree of connections between the five countries involved (Australia, Canada, New Zealand, United Kingdom, United States) that may support cross-border deals. The strategic agreement existing between the United States and Israel may also ease cross-border deals in sensitive firms. More generally speaking, defense-related cooperation agreements as well as other interstate cooperation efforts (e.g., China in African countries) have a role in the capacity of firms to develop cross-border deals. On the other hand, diplomatic clashes may threaten some cross-border deals when it comes to passing FDI approval decisions.

Anti-Trust Ruling. As mentioned previously, most FDI regulations target the potential negative impacts that may be generated on national security and economic stability. Anti-trust rules cover specifically the aspects of a change of market share, and the consequences in terms of market supply, prices evolution, or other elements of influence the acquirer may impose on the clients. Anti-trust procedures must be carefully planned and worked on during the due diligence phase, so that all elements required are ready for circulation to the relevant administrative bodies, ministers, local authorities, or dedicated national or international (EU) agencies. Specialized lawyers or consulting firms may support this preparation process that may lead to carve-out and sell-off decisions, or even block some deals. It is critical to note that the time frame of the entire deal, together with its strategic outcome, may vary according to this work. In general, the integration preparation should be very well connected to this anti-trust documentation and negotiation process, so that actual integration implementation is fully consistent with the negotiation options and trade-offs.

INTERNATIONAL DIFFERENCES AND SIMILARITIES

As observed earlier, a wide range of parameters may have a role in a country's view of its strategic assets and risks and therefore on its FDI restrictions. We highlight in Table 8.1 a number of such parameters. But there are

TABLE 8.1   High-Level Differences and Similarities in FDI Restrictions

International Differences	Global Similarities
Underlying socioeconomic national contexts and histories	The multilayer administrative and regulatory approach
The definition of strategic industries	An M&A specific review system for foreign investments
The link with a national industrial policy	The core objective of military and strategic independence
The role of central versus local state	The need to attract FDIs as well as limit their risk
The role of democratic institutions (associations, parliament, president)	The role of the international organizations to grow FDI (OECD, WTO)
The influence of unions and other stakeholders	The growing role of public opinion and labor laws
The role of the informal negotiation process in the FDI review process	

similarities between countries that every potential acquirer must have in mind to be prepared on such issues.

HOW TO DEAL WITH SENSITIVE CROSS-BORDER TRANSACTIONS

Investments in sensitive industries are possible, but they need to be carefully planned and executed. We provide below some lessons learned on how to succeed in such deals, with a focus on the smooth execution of the integration phase. More details are available in Chapters 2, 3, and 9 of this book.

Deal Strategy

Firms dealing with dual technologies and producing key assets of the target country must be highly sensitive to potential FDI restrictions and procedures.

They must, as soon as they get into the strategic analysis phase, identify the capacity they will have to conduct a cross-border transaction building on informal contacts at the local level.

Such contacts with local advisors, administrations, or the relevant ministers or agencies should be centrally monitored by the acquirer, so that they do not jeopardize a potential deal due to a breach of confidentiality.

As a general rule, this assessment should take the assumption that the more people are involved at this stage, the bigger the risk of generating negative reactions, communication to the general public, or anti-deal procedures organized by local competitors. This risk must therefore be analyzed early by the acquirer and its advisors (bank, strategic consultant, lawyer, industry expert) and the list of contacts established in this early assessment phase must be well challenged and carefully processed.

Stakeholder Management

In order to monitor this process, it is also, as we have described above, highly critical to map the different stakeholders early on, so that there is a broad view of the potential reactions and mitigation actions to discuss.

The list of potential stakeholders is quite large, as reactions may come from the entire value chain: clients, employees and unions, suppliers, regional and central administrations or political representatives, ministers, professional associations, and so on.

The objective of this mapping should not be to organize direct contacts with them all, but to ensure there is a strong understanding of the logics at play, and a capacity to structure a consistent vision and integration strategy that will address the potential concerns. Stakeholders' mapping, Q&As, and active risk mitigation plans are simple and efficient tools.

In many cases, risks are linked to an underestimation of the capacity to block a deal even with a minor or irrelevant rationale. Investors must be aware that, once the case is negatively positioned, it is quite difficult to rebuild the level of trust that is necessary to back a fluid and quick positive agreement. The more the general public is mobilized against the transaction, the more the official decision will be difficult to take in favor of the foreign investor. As a consequence, the number of cases where deals have had to be terminated even before the end of the official FDI procedure is huge—it shows to what extent procedures themselves should not be viewed as a way to justify a given transaction against all stakeholders, but as a way to validate a smooth and cautious process that carefully manages the positions of the different stakeholders.

Due Diligence Process

The due diligence process in such a context should not only tackle the target per se, but also enable a check and review of the feasibility of the deal. This means that a number of informal contacts should be planned and managed during the due diligence process, so that there is a clear link between the review process and the normal negotiation path, with the target triggering financial, tax and legal, human resources, or other standard business issues.

Ideally, there should be no closing without the assurance that the deal will not be stopped later because of a parallel procedure.

This may have a strong influence on the overall planning of the pre-closing phase, depending on the nature of the discussions with the relevant public stakeholders involved. It is up to the M&A team and its advisors to ensure the right level of coordination of these parallel initiatives, so that there is consistent work being done, with a well-adjusted set of legal and operational agreements and action plans well fitted in a global master plan.

Deal Structure

The local sensitivity vis-à-vis a foreign acquisition may generate particular constraints on the overall deal structure, such as the enactment of local majority shareholders, the creation of state-owned golden shares, or the implementation of specific rules regarding the share voting rights.

Some other aspects must be anticipated within that approach, for instance, as to the use at international level of the profits generated, the need to reinvest locally a certain percentage of the cash flows, to fuel local agencies or funds with specific taxes, the need to leverage local suppliers, to commit to a certain level of local jobs, and so on.

It is critical for firms investing abroad to be advised as early as possible on all these deal structure constraints, so that it is possible to build the right business case, and analyze carefully all the pros and cons of the potential financial, legal, and operational structure design.

Anti-Trust Compliance

One of the most frequently recurring aspects to impact a cross-border acquisition is the application of anti-trust policies. Based on the will to preserve the possibility for customers to benefit from different supply options and a fair price based on a sufficient degree of competition between suppliers, it is often a major element of the overall investment process.

The potential exposure to national or regional (EU, for instance) anti-trust rules must here again be analyzed early, and it must be carefully processed in parallel with the rest of the standard M&A work.

As such, it may have major consequences on the complexity of the deal, and of the post-merger work to be executed. Separations may have to be organized for sell-offs of specific assets, and initial public offerings may have to be organized.

Because of these widespread consequences on the potential post-merger integration (PMI) program, there should be a permanent coordination and dialogue organized between the anti-trust legal and operational team, and the integration manager and his organization planning the Day One actions and the post-closing work streams.

National Security Review and Other Compliance

In fact, working on the national security review and other nationally sensitive issues is very similar to the general approach conducted on anti-trust issues.

On the one hand, a specific set analysis and work process should be conducted by a specific group of individuals, so that there is a limited circulation of information. Informal contacts should be planned and organized as early as possible, in order to detail the risks and build the potential options and select the preferred solutions.

In parallel, because this work has a very important set of consequences on a wide range of strategic and tactical business aspects, it is necessary to ensure that at the acquirer level, there is a strong coordination with or by the M&A and with the PMI team. The objective is that operational clauses impacting the integration strategy and process should be anticipated before closing, and executed seamlessly.

Governance and Legal Design

Some of the most sensitive issues will be about the choice of the new CEO, the selection of the executive team, and the designation of the main bodies governing the new organization.

In a sensitive foreign deal, this aspect will have to be dealt with extreme care. It is important to preserve access to local relations, build trust with the local eco-environment, and ensure there is a possibility to develop a sustainable local business.

However, it also is very important for the acquirer to ensure that there is a certain degree of control and harmonization with group-wide practices and expectations. Critical roles such as the chief finance officer's role or the tax and legal role may be considered to be international by nature in order to limit risk. Operations, R&D, and human resources may be more sensitive to fill with foreign profiles.

One of the most common approaches in very sensitive deals is to ensure that only nationals, with due authorizations, will be in a position to manage the local entity. In this case, it is critical to engage early on in an informal discussion with the national relevant bodies to detail the operating model of that "proxy" entity, which will enable containment of sensitive information and assets at a national level only. The scoping of the entity is important. The reporting mechanisms and the degree of autonomy provided to the entity in terms of financials, investments, recruitments, and business strategy (exports, clients, contracting) is also to be discussed and agreed on.

The functioning of a proxy entity from an integration perspective entails a number of limits—for instance, some synergies may not be possible due to national considerations. On the other hand, some internal competition between service offerings may have to be maintained beyond group rationale. The consequences of this governance and legal separation must therefore be challenged from an economic model standpoint as early as possible.

Integration Strategy Design

Building a clear integration strategy design has a huge positive impact on implementing a cross-border deal. It is even more important in sensitive industries or transactions, as the most important topic is about what will be absorbed, what will be merged, and what will remain locally unchanged.

The design of this integration strategy may build on tools such as the Haspeslagh matrix, applying such tools either with a functional view or a process view of the combined organization. It should provide a detailed operational view of the degree of integration for all the building blocks of the organization, matched in a quick process with the view of the IT systems (applications and infrastructures) and of the legal and financial structures supporting the targeted organizational design.

Why is such an integration design so useful when it comes to sensitive deals? Because in such deals the notion of what remains local and what is embedded at international level, therefore depending somehow on distant decisions, is the key one.

In a normal deal, there may be resistance to change and a willingness to preserve a brand, a sales network, or an R&D team to avoid value destruction. In a sensitive deal, the preservation aspect may be linked to national sovereignty aspects and the need to maintain a local autonomy of decisions.

It may be worthwhile to add that, in most cases, what is really of national security is very often a limited set of tangible or intangible assets in a global value chain. Working on the integration strategy mapping in a structured way may enable clustering of specific elements that need to be preserved, and planning the implementation and synergies for the rest.

Employees

In a sensitive deal, the buy-in of the local employees is critical, as it will help the foreign acquirer in convincing local stakeholders that the deal is positive.

One recent example is the acquisition by General Electric of some assets of the former Alstom group. Generally speaking, this deal, involving a group providing high-tech equipment goods such as turbines to the nuclear industry or trains and tramways exported around the world, was first considered as a less interesting deal than a pan-European solution (with Siemens). However, the positive links established for decades between GE and Alstom, as well as the commitment of GE to leverage France as its international center of excellence in the turbine activity, have played very much in favor of a good image of long-term investment in France, of sound and subtle human resources management, and of a capacity to internalize French public opinion concerns. The deal closed without any major demonstration or employee reaction, in total contradiction with the violent reactions generated by the approach of the group Titan in the Continental France deal.

More generally speaking, one of the main concerns in a sensitive industry or transaction is to maintain a national set of skills, and grow it as much as possible. Conditions are often discussed in such deals on the evolution of jobs, and of the types of jobs to be cut at local levels.

It is essential to capture the fact that the media coverage transmits globally a negative image of job cuts done by distant investors biased in favor of low-cost and high-margin business conditions. In the old advanced economies, public opinion is very much aware of the financial trade-off that has often been made by predatory investors. Defensive reactions are a consequence of the education of people, and their capacity to anticipate the job cuts often associated with foreign investments.

Based on this simple fact, it is all the more important for foreign investors to adjust integration strategies to the different markets in order to limit the negative externalities created by lack of long-term commitment. The repetition of destructive buys, with quasi-automatic short-term trading financial considerations, chasing local subsidies, and wage gaps, is indeed mechanically growing FDI restrictions and public demand for more regulation and more labor protection.

As a professional, I can only state that in most cases, the first obstacle to a successful integration in a country like France is the reaction of employees who see mergers and acquisitions less as an opportunity than as a problem.

Communication

In a sensitive deal, pulling together the right communication messages and process is critical. It must start by listing all the potential concerns linked to a deal, through informal contacts or any sort of specific local survey.

The leverage of a well-established public relations firm may be useful. Connections with well-known personalities who may promote the deal vis-à-vis local authorities, political heads, or even the general public, may be remarkably efficient in the deal-making phase at least (e.g., the Pinault support provided to the Mittal acquisition of Arcelor, which resulted later in major political confrontations when Mittal decided to close down sites in Belgium and France).

Communication is often not sufficiently precise, not sufficiently honest, not sufficiently reliable. This has dreadful consequences in sensitive deals and transactions due to the number of potential stakeholders, and the strong positions they may defend. In that context, it is very important to ensure that all the messages are backed with quick actions that will demonstrate a high level of consistency and reliability.

Vis-à-vis employees, it may be a safe bet for executives to anticipate a high level of stress on the employee front, and to prepare to address direct questions. In a sensitive deal, it is important to ensure that there is no possible misinterpretation of things, and that the different stakeholders are really communicated to with specific messages.

There is another specific aspect of sensitive transactions. In a way, their visibility and high media coverage has lasting consequences on the business decisions and the corporate image. This "retina impact" may last beyond the normal integration phase. Subsequent events will also be reconnected to the deal communication messages and promises. If, for instance, the Nokia group announces in 2019 or beyond that it has to cut jobs by more than it has announced during the Alcatel-Lucent deal communication process, this will inevitably be viewed in the general public opinion as proof of built-in insincere communication.

This raises another particular communication difficulty in a sensitive deal, which is the difficult trade-off between communicating and explaining. Communicating short messages on promises rather than explaining the uncertainties and the difficulties of a merger and integration situation often creates expectation gaps, which may lead to negative backlashes. It is therefore essential to back as much as possible, at least with key stakeholders, the communication process, with a strong effort of pedagogy and even training. This effort will not be perceived as an attempt to take advantage of information biases—especially at a historical time where education in the world is booming.

CONCLUSION

Most countries, facing the development of cross-border investments, have developed a consistent and quite complex set of procedures and regulations to limit the potential conflicts between foreign investments and control and national security and stability. These regulations have evolved over time, and are executed by multiple layers of administrative bodies. They complete other forms of regulations or restrictions that apply to any domestic firm in terms of anti-trust or compliance. Because these regulations are complex, and evolve over time, it is critical for executives not to underestimate the analysis and planning of this work, so that very early in the process, all mitigation actions and solutions may be discussed with the key face-offs in the relevant ministries or agencies, in an informal and pre-deal phase when it is possible.

List of Acronyms

AML	Anti-Monopoly Law (U.S.)
APE	Agence des Participations de l'Etat (France)
CFIUS	Committee on Foreign Investments in the United States
DHS	Department of Homeland Security (U.S.)
FDI	Foreign Direct Investment
ICT	Information and Communication Technology
KORUS FTA	Korea-U.S. Free Trade Agreement
MOFCOM	Ministry of Commerce (China)
EU	European Union
FINSA	Foreign Investment and National Security Act (US)
JV	Joint Venture
MNC	Multinational Corporation
NAFTA	North American Free Trade Agreement
NDRC	National Development and Reform Commission (China)
OECD	Organization for Economic Cooperation and Development
OPEC	Organization of Petroleum Exporting Countries
SASAC	State-Owned Assets Supervision and Administration (China)
SOE	State-Owned Enterprise
TMAFT	Trade-Market-Access-For-Technology (China)
TRIPS	Trade-Related Aspects of Intellectual Property Rights (WTO)
UNCTAD	United Nations Conference on Trade and Development
WTO	World Trade Organization

CHAPTER CHECKLIST

- Take the view that firms evolve (also) in national markets. Do not underestimate the force of national boundaries vis-à-vis employees, clients, suppliers, and regulations. If the cross-border deal benefits from differences between countries, it is primarily because these differences exist and have a certain degree of rationale and substance. You should pay attention to them before embarking on your own vision of the world.
- Assess what you will bring as much as what you will benefit from. Develop your "multi-domestic" understanding of the constraints and potential strategies. Enrich your existing view of your business with a dose of what is expected from local champions. If your strategy is a long-term strategy, you must be a local champion as well as a global one. This approach will help you optimize all your local contacts, and create the level of trust that is needed to build sustainable growth.
- Take the view that national reactions change according to context. Any economic slowdown and employment change will generate more scrutiny and public demand for more regulation vis-à-vis potentially predatory foreign investments. Be prepared to engage discussions on how your decision-making process will not discriminate against local jobs and local development.
- Consider that the enterprise nationality will be a sensitive issue to manage both on the buy side (underestimation of local assets) and on the target side (lack of buy-in, resistance to change). Anticipate that an organization is a delicate balance between processes, structures, culture, and systems. In a different environment, your organization may lack efficiency or even be at risk. Pay attention to the right fit between the different building blocks of your organization.
- Take the assumption that resistance to foreign investments is a multi-factor and universal human pattern. FDI regulations show that all rational definitions partly fail to describe the complexity of the reality. What is at stake very often is the sense that a foreign investor will have a different decision-making process that is potentially not optimizing the local interests. In order to limit such cases, regulations evolve based on actual cases and international mimetism. All countries have FDI regulations in place.
- FDI restrictions may cover almost all industries or situations, depending on local context and priorities. Take the view that national sensitivity and FDI restrictions is a political and thus partly emotional topic. It is based on the local perception of risk and national sovereignty situation and needs. Past history and sociopolitical trends are key. You must be aware that no nation is exactly the same as to its level of independence and sovereignty. We are not focusing here only on raw materials

or sourcing issues in technologies or products manufactured. National sensitivity may also result from induced changes in the way of life, the social manners, the vision of things. Be prepared to deal with such potential reactions.

■ **The more you anticipate such potential reactions, the better off you'll be.** Assess the potential FDI or regulatory risks as early as possible. Conduct this process in parallel with the due diligence process in a coordinated way, which provides the integration manager with all the information required to optimize the implementation path. Solicit local expertise to identify and challenge risks. Contact local agencies and ministries as early as possible and engage in informal discussions and negotiations. Anticipate potential delays, list actions, and secure consistency of objectives and delivery.

■ **Build trust with local stakeholders.** Any investment in a new country should be viewed in the long term as a way to ease further strategic moves. To maximize the option cost, building trust and an image of local loyalty and transparency is critical. International investors who chase local subsidies, dismantle production assets, and create massive job cuts play against international investments.

NOTES

1. Wan-Wen Chu, "How the Chinese Government Promoted a Global Automobile Industry," *Industrial and Corporate Change* (2011): 1235–76.
2. C. Zhao, "Redefining Critical Industry: A Comparative Study of Inward FDI Restrictions in China and the United States." Master of Arts Thesis, Department of Political Sciences, University of Victoria, 2015.
3. Kenneth Y. Hui, "National Security Review of Foreign Mergers and Acquisitions of Domestic Companies in China and the United States," Cornell Law School Inter-University Graduate Student Conference Papers, 2009.
4. Ministry of Foreign Trade and Economic Cooperation, the State Administration of Taxation, the State Administration for Industry and Commerce, and the State Administration of Foreign Exchange, "Provisions on Mergers and Acquisitions of Domestic Enterprises by Foreign Investors," 2006, Article 2.

Cross-Border Integration, Planning, and Execution

Managing Pre–PMI Due Diligence

Eitan Grosbard

CHAPTER LEARNING OBJECTIVES—IN THIS CHAPTER, YOU WILL LEARN:

➤ How to describe the entire due diligence phase and its purpose in the overall M&A process
➤ How to describe which stakeholders, functional areas, and roles should be involved in the due diligence activity
➤ The importance of a good governance framework during due diligence and how to describe what this means
➤ How to describe the transition from the due diligence phase to the negotiation and integration planning phases
➤ The critical elements within the due diligence process and the complexities of conducting due diligence across borders
➤ How to define key tasks that should be taken care of in this phase in light of the post-merger integration phase; thus actions that are PMI-oriented must be taken care of while in due diligence (key employees and retention planning, Day One planning, and so on)

CHAPTER SUMMARY

This chapter describes the overall due diligence process, including types of due diligence, areas of inquiry within each type, and management of the due diligence process including routines, structure, and use of tools.

The chapter starts with an introduction to due diligence, followed by a review of due diligence and its common elements including legal due diligence (commercial, intellectual property, labor, anti-trust), financial due diligence (including tax), and commercial due diligence.

The chapter moves on to integrated due diligence, or 360-degree due diligence, which focuses on a variety of additional areas and is the basis for later post-merger integration planning. It then provides a practical review of the due diligence process, ingredients, and tools to be applied in order to improve the overall process.

INTRODUCTION

The M&A life cycle consists of different phases. In each, the M&A practitioner needs to apply a different set of skills. Due diligence is a crucial phase in this life cycle as it is an introductory and investigative milestone preceding the post-merger integration (PMI) planning activities.

This phase includes elements of project management and synergetic data-driven analysis. Alongside these, areas that should be addressed include risk management and mitigation planning (this is crucial looking forward) and the go/no-go decision-making process. Last but not least, during this phase, the integration team will start to focus on PMI preparations, analyze and define gaps, and create a high-level integration plan to address these gaps.

There are several different ways in which the due diligence process is described. It makes one wonder which statements are correct and which are not.

"Due diligence is the process of systematically researching and verifying the accuracy of a statement."

"Due diligence refers to the full investigation of a transaction, before the transaction takes place."

"Due diligence is a legal standard of care that determines the legitimacy of a transaction."

All statements are correct!

Due diligence, in the context of M&A, refers to an end-to-end investigation of a potential acquisition, before the deal is signed or the transaction takes place. This process confirms that all details are correct, and no important information is left out. It is the buyer's responsibility to conduct a thorough investigation to ensure it is receiving the value of the deal. The company's officers should do everything within their control to ensure any decision made will maximize value for existing shareholders.

In addition, due diligence is a way of preventing unnecessary harm or risk to either party involved in a transaction. Inadequate due diligence will hinder a company's legal position if something is later found incorrect with the transaction, because there will be an aspect of negligence.

The due diligence phase of *any acquisition* can make the difference between success and failure.

The focus of due diligence is on identifying unknown risks and undisclosed concerns, identifying the real state of issues, reducing uncertainties, and validating initial findings.

A few years ago, traditional due diligence was required to validate financial statements. The goal was to ensure that all stakeholders associated with a *financial transaction* have the information they need to assess risk accurately. Other than financial statements, the traditional due diligence dealt with legal practices, and in some cases, tax as well.

Nowadays, the new evolved practice known as 360-degree due diligence or *integrated due diligence* holds much more than financial and legal examinations. Acquirers pull together all competencies of the acquiring firm around the transaction and investigate an array of areas such as commercial and strategic rationale, financial and tax issues, operational and technological issues, synergies, culture, regulations, anti-trust, legal, human resources, and more.

Effective due diligence is a combination of *art* and *science*.[1] The *art* is the style and experience to know what questions to ask and how and when to ask them. It's the ability to create an atmosphere where the seller is fully engaged and complete disclosure is taken. The *science* of due diligence is in the preparation of comprehensive and customized checklists to be presented to the seller, in maintaining a methodical system for organizing and analyzing the documents and data provided by the seller, and in quantitatively assessing the risks raised by those problems discovered in the process.

Due diligence also refers to the investigation a seller does on a buyer, but usually there are lesser due diligence processes of this type.

The purpose of this chapter is to present the due diligence process and components and identify considerations that must be taken into account. These considerations and their impact on the different steps of the M&A processes will be presented with a special emphasis on the PMI phase.

The details one discovers in the due diligence phase will suggest how to integrate the acquired entity with the acquiring company. If due diligence is the gathering of information, integration is the implementation of what you discover. The two parts of the process go hand in hand.

TRADITIONAL DUE DILIGENCE

Traditional due diligence has been standard practice for many years predominantly to validate financial statements, legal practices, and taxation as well. Many companies continue using the traditional due diligence merely as a decision-making tool and disregard any of the other areas of due diligence. The problem with adopting this approach is that a narrow focus on financial performance, forecasting, and legal harmonization will overlook many of the acute issues that tend to surface later in the PMI process. Funny enough, while the M&A paradox is that approximately 50% to 80% of M&A processes end up not fulfilling their targets and partial due diligence is part of the problem stated, companies continue acquiring and the annual number and size of acquisitions continue to grow (see Figure 9.1). Checking too quickly and focusing too narrowly is often a recipe for disaster.

This point will be further addressed in the section on 360-degree due diligence or integrated due diligence.

Traditional due diligence is mainly focused on the target company's past. Legal aspects are the only ones analyzed looking forward. It means that this process usually analyzes past performance and does not emphasize future opportunities and trends. It doesn't predict the organization's future, but it does relate to the legal risks that may arise. The motivation of such due diligence is to assess if the deal can be executed as opposite to what the future merged company will look like and whether the integration would be successful. This approach aims to close the deal and nothing but that.

Areas of inquiry in traditional due diligence are financial, legal, commercial, and also "unpleasant surprises" that usually come up. In order to execute, participants are usually economists, accountants, or lawyers. Participants are usually a combination of internal resources, contractors, and service providers. The information sources are mainly past and present contracts, agreements, past financial statements, management background, and some interviews with key managers and employees. See Table 9.1.

At a minimum, this type of due diligence effort should include:

- Financial statements review (to confirm the existence of assets, liabilities, and equity in the balance sheet and to determine the financial health of the company based on the income statement and cash flow statement)
- Legal compliance review (to check for potential future legal problems stemming from the candidate company's past)
- Management and operations review (to determine the quality and reliability of the financial statements based on an assessment of internal controls and to gain a sense of contingencies beyond the financial statements)

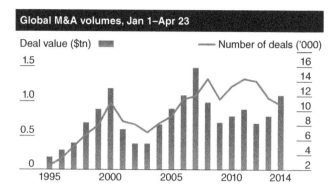

Worldwide M&A Ranking

2014 (year to date)

	2013 Standing	Financial Adviser	Value $bn
1	1	Goldman Sachs	776.7
2	4	Morgan Stanley	688.7
3	9	Citi	629.8
4	2	JPMorgan	534.0
5	3	Bank of America Merrill Lynch	529.9
6	5	Barclays	490.3
7	10	Lazard	407.4
8	7	Deutsche Bank	371.5
9	8	Credit Suisse	345.9
10	13	Centerview Partners	208.3

Global M&A Volumes

$tn

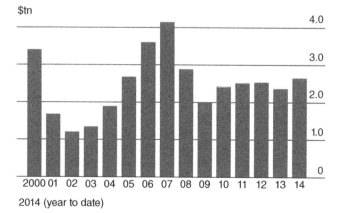

2014 (year to date)

FIGURE 9.1   M&A Deals in 2014 Eclipse Levels in Past Five Years
Source: Financial Times. www.ft.com/cms/s/0/e0c9cbae-45be-11e4-9b71-00144feabdc0.html#axzz3x10E3g7v.

TABLE 9.1 Different Approaches: Traditional Due Diligence Differs from Integrated Due Diligence in a Number of Areas

	Traditional Due Diligence	Integrated Due Diligence
Focus	Target company's past	Combined companies' future
Key question	Can the deal be done?	Will the acquisition succeed?
Areas of inquiry	Financial, legal, unpleasant surprises	Traditional concerns, as well as validation of key operational and strategic assumptions
Participants	Accountants, lawyers	Traditional participants, plus operations, information technology, human resources, and other key players, as needed
Information sources	Limited, mostly documents, in addition to checking management background	A wide array of sources, including customers, competitors, suppliers, and former and current employees

Source: Michael May, Patricia Anslinger, and Justin Jenk, "Avoiding the Perils of Traditional Due Diligence," Accenture, *Outlook 2002*, no. 2.

■ Document and transaction review (to ensure that the paperwork of the deal is in order and that the structure of the transaction is appropriate)

The due diligence process often starts with a kick-off meeting with all parties involved (acquiring company: officers and key managers, accountants, lawyers, tax experts, and others). The kick-off meeting is set to define the scope of due diligence, the length of the process and timeline, and the boundaries between functional areas and scope as well.

Legal Due Diligence

Legal due diligence[2] consists of an examination of all or specific parts of the legal affairs of the target company with a view toward uncovering any legal risks and providing the buyer with an extensive insight into the company's legal matters. There is a variety of areas that are being checked under the legal due diligence, such as commercial law, labor law, anti-trust, capital markets, intellectual property, environment, litigation, and so on.

Professional legal areas that are being explored include: legal structure pre- and post-transaction, contracts, loans, property, employment, pending litigation, and so on.

The legal examination in M&A due diligence is usually managed and integrated by the legal function leading the commercial aspects of the deal. All other legal professionals participating in due diligence efforts (intellectual property, labor, and so on) are peripheral in the way that they support the commercial leader by handing over their legal representations and other findings and the inputs deriving from them.

Once the M&A process is started and the acquiring company is on the edge of due diligence, the legal commercial "leader" will work closely with the acquirer to confirm which legal areas should be covered in the due diligence process. The legal areas are one factor and the other is the depth of the due diligence report requested. The report presented to the client may vary between two ends. One end would be an in-depth report covering all associated legal areas, the risks deriving from them, and a mitigation plan, actions that should be taken throughout the process as well as after closing (PMI era). The other end would be a risk assessment combined with a "red flags" report. This type of report is presented when the acquirer is short of time or alternatively knows the industry and type of business very well and therefore does not need to go into all the details.

The legal "leader" is usually an external lawyer—an experienced partner at a top legal firm. That individual should define as a first step what type of findings or issues he's looking for. It will be defined based on the specific deal he's encountering as well other elements such as the industry he's encountering, the depth of the due diligence, the time restrictions and workforce he may have, and so on.

On the one hand, there are "technical" legal aspects that should be reviewed such as agreements with customers or suppliers, third party agreements, partnerships, and so on. On the other hand, there are material drivers that must be inquired into as well, such as geographical spread, intellectual property, knowledge, distribution, branding, and structure, including workers and departments.

There are several sources of information that will be applied in such a process. The *first* one would be the annual reports or statements, which hold a lot of information that may be of high value to the legal team. There are trends "hiding between the lines" with legal implications such as long debt that indicates a long-term leasing commitment, debt to a supplier that might indicate a dispute, and so on. The *second* would be meetings with key stakeholders such as customers, suppliers, workers, and others. These meetings might be straightforward meetings, but some of them are discreet and some may be taking place under a "cover story"—not indicating directly that there's a deal happening. The *third* is a thorough review of all legal documentation.

Cross-border processes are more complex. The local legal "leader" might be experienced in local laws and sometimes in international law as well but has absolutely no knowledge of the local laws in other countries around the globe. In that case, a leading practice is to hire, as part of due diligence, a local legal firm that will contribute with all legal issues, cultural issues, as well as language barriers in some cases. In case of using local legal representation, the legal "leader" holds the responsibility for integrating their inputs.

Central principles to apply in legal due diligence:

- Focus on the core business and implications, not on peripheral small issues
- Understand the business and transaction, don't just follow a checklist blindly
- Flexibility: Be able to alter the scope of due diligence as findings are analyzed
- Coordinate tightly the legal work and efforts with the financial due diligence team's findings
- Be aware of nonlegal elements such as culture, globalization, and human resources

There are several areas of practice when it comes to legal due diligence. The following sections cover most of the legal due diligence domains and their importance for the overall process.

Anti-Trust Due Diligence　The anti-trust due diligence process is conducted prior to a transaction. In a situation where the potential transaction is between competitors, the process involves two conflicting interests: On the one hand, the acquirer should receive extensive commercial data on the acquired company in order to make the right decision. On the other hand, the transaction may not be completed for various reasons (among others, if the anti-trust authority does not approve it). If a transaction is not completed, then the two competitors will compete with each other again after the purchaser may already have been exposed to competitively sensitive information regarding the acquired company.

The due diligence is a legitimate and important tool in the process of formulating merger transactions and providing a complete picture of the object of sale. In parallel, the due diligence involves transmission of secrets and commercially sensitive information. As such, when talking about parties that are competitors, due diligence also carries the risk of reduced competition and the creation of a restrictive arrangement. The fear of reduced competition exists both in the mid-term (between disclosure of the information and closing of the transaction), as well as in the long term.

The anti-trust regulations provide to the parties involved in a merger transaction guidelines for identifying competitively sensitive information, and for managing its disclosure to the competitor in a way that minimizes the risk of injury to competition while keeping them clear of the perimeter of a restrictive arrangement.

The rules are not exhaustive: The more sensitive the disclosed information in terms of competition, or the more the transaction itself raises a genuine concern of reduced competition (which in turn would also decrease its chances of approval), the more the level of care required by the parties intensifies. Among other precautions, the parties should make sure that:

- Disclosure of the information is essential to the due diligence investigation;
- The volume of information transmitted is minimized; and
- In disclosing the information, they take all necessary measures to minimize the concern of reduced competition.

In a cross-border transaction, the challenge is greater:

- The acquirer needs to check anti-trust implications across all jurisdictions involved in the transaction. This type of complexity usually occurs in the case of a merger of global "blue chip" companies where the process might cover possibly dozens of companies that file for an approval. In order to get this approval, the acquirer's legal representatives who manage the anti-trust stream will approach a local anti-trust lawyer in every country and jurisdiction where an approval should be granted.
- The process should be centrally managed and executed across the globe.
- Costs associated with anti-trust diligence are higher as lawyers in each participating country are remunerated for their services.

Intellectual Property Due Diligence Nowadays, companies are increasingly becoming aware of the importance of intellectual property (IP) assets. When discussing IP issues, the following domains of practice emerge:

Patent Assets. The most obvious component of any IP due diligence process is a review of existing patent assets. This should include a review of issued patents and also an assessment of any accompanying documentation including applications, prosecution materials, prior art reviews, assignments, and ongoing continuations along with similar documentation for pending applications.

Invention disclosure policies and practice: Review of existing effective invention disclosure policies and procedures provides insight into whether a company is adequately capturing potential IP. Reviewing existing disclosures will indicate what current inventive flow looks like along with whether ideas are being effectively pushed into the patent pipeline.

Trademarks. Trademarks drive significant value for companies' establishment. In an era where countless competitors have the resources and means to copy a successful model, it becomes essential for a company to corner the market by making its brand equal with their product offering. Failing to obtain broad trademark protection may expose the company to liability in case of confusingly similar names that steal market share.

Confidentiality Agreements. A trade secret is only valuable if it is a secret. If a company shares its proprietary information without the benefit of nondisclosure agreements, that information may not only be protectable by trade secret law, it may later prevent obtaining patent protection for the technology. Confirming the existence of necessary confidentiality agreements is therefore critical.

Licenses and Joint Ventures Documentation. Joint development efforts may expedite research and development. However, if the agreements are not structured correctly, the resulting IP can be substantially devalued. Therefore, reviewing joint venture and collaboration agreements is an important component to understanding potential risks to IP protection.

Capital Markets Due Diligence Capital markets due diligence is mostly applied in M&A transactions where a public listed company[3] is either involved as the acquirer or acquired side. There are many restrictions and requirements that derive from regulations, which is why extra focus should be allocated in this area. In parallel, the nature of this type of deal involves underwriters and underwriting, which requires a knowledge that the commercial lawyer isn't always aware of.

Regulations. In parallel to the common commercial work, the capital markets practice must check the corporate history in the areas of corporate law and securities law. The acquirer may find that a past fine that was assessed on the acquired company was never paid, and thus could expose a lawsuit or alternatively could be of high impact financially.

Professional Checks. In terms of areas of practice that are being examined, the capital markets due diligence will focus on taxes, regulations, employees, legal procedures, and market structure assessment. The capital markets lawyer will review annual statements from past years, financial statements, tax assessments, and ruling decisions. The work is conducted with the help of the legal and financial functions within the company.

Global Capital Markets Implications. There are several implications that must be carefully checked. Review of historical timelines and timetables is acute. Authorities check if public companies meet the requisites they're supposed to meet, such as submitting financial reports a number of times per year or specific annual timetables that are applied.

Tax is always a major issue in the capital markets due diligence. All related tax processes are being checked and must be aligned to the compliance level needed in this area.

Labor Laws Due Diligence Regardless the type or structure of a deal, virtually all corporate transactions involve the transfer of employees. Even in the simplest share purchase, the purchaser will need to address retention issues, define benefit programs and make sure that they are put into place, take the risk of constructive dismissal actions post-closing, and analyze the financial implications that may derive from compensation, benefits, pensions, and so on. In more complex transactions, the due diligence process for labor, but specifically pension issues, may take a fair amount of time and involve the expertise of actuaries and benefits consultants.

The basic starting point is that it is not open to an employer simply to transfer employees to another employer. There are formal methods to transfer employees. But transferring the employees is not the only focus in this type of due diligence. Review of the compensation and benefits granted as well as the terms and conditions is central. Reviewing the contractual agreements and learning about the work environment including incorporation of employees is acutely important.

Different countries have different labor laws. Some countries hold strict labor laws that are in favor of the employee (France, The Netherlands, and others) while others favor the corporation rather than the employee (the United States, for example).

Within the labor laws' due diligence, points that should be taken into consideration while conducting the due diligence are as follows:

Labor Relations Issues. Labor relations issues should start by understanding the nature of the transaction. There are two common sale situations—asset sales and share sales. Which type of transaction is applied: asset sales or share sales? What are the implications on the employees? Are the employees incorporated in a union? Are there contractors?

Employment Standards. What terms and conditions do employees currently hold? Do these terms and conditions align with market standards? Do the employment contracts clearly and legally cover the employment of all employees? This area includes a variety of topics, including salary, period of notice, base salary, bonuses, grant of options, minimum wage, and so on.

Another point relevant to employees' standards are employees with special needs or special status such as pregnant women, people with disabilities, employees in fertility treatments, and so on.

Privacy Issues.   Privacy is an area of law that relates to personal employee information, and whether it is protected by existing legislation. While some countries have privacy legislation, some don't. This point should be checked on a global scale as, while in the acquiring country there aren't strict privacy laws, in the acquired company's country there may be.

Key employees.   After defining who the key employees are, a defined personal agreement is crafted for these key people to sign. The agreement is utilized for locking this group in for a certain number of years to continue working in the acquiring company.

Other contractual agreements with employees (not labor contracts) that are being reviewed are in the areas of vacations, illness, absence from work, use of digital communication, and so on.

Outcomes from the labor laws due diligence:

- Description of the labor current status and implication on the day after the closing
- Risk mapping and mitigation plan. In that sense, a clear understanding of the potential legal exposure.
- Mapping of all employees in the acquired organization and classifiation in terms of contribution to the acquiring company and future potential

Environmental Due Diligence   Environmental due diligence is a combination of legal and technical practices that are performed to uncover liabilities that may arise under environmental laws. Environmental due diligence is also utilized to develop information about environmental conditions and compliance with local regulatory requirements.

The environmental due diligence involves looking systematically into the areas of air emissions, water management, waste management, chemicals, and hazardous substances, as well as transportation and permits. These elements are being checked on two different levels:

- A physical test, where the acquirer will check the business license, air quality and odor nuisances, dangerous substances, toxins and waste permits, wastewater, sewage, prevention of soil contamination, and more.

■ Legal proceedings and environmental insurance: review of existing procedures (indictments, civil lawsuits), pre-administrative or legal proceedings (hearings, warning letters, requirements for water corporation), fines, and collection insurance.

In the last couple of years, as public opinion has become more sensitive to environmental concerns and regulation in the area of environment has progressed, more and more companies conduct this type of due diligence.

Key environmental issues in due diligence:

■ On-site conditions and releases
■ Compliance
■ Permits and licenses
■ Potential liability for off-site conditions
■ Records
■ Communications with regulatory agencies
■ Environmental management system
■ History of prior ownership or operators
■ Insurance coverage

Financial Due Diligence

Financial due diligence focuses on verifying the financial information provided to the acquirer. It analyzes the target company's books, records, and other internal reports and documents of a financial and business nature as well, including areas such as: revenues, assets, liabilities, cash flow, debt, and so on. The financial due diligence exercise explores previous financial performance and it is a "go/no-go" point to determine whether it can reasonably be expected to continue the M&A process toward signing a sales and purchase agreement and closing the deal.

Important to add: Conducting a financial due diligence is not only related to acquisitions or mergers, it can also be directed against joint ventures, financing, or other deals and transactions. In parallel with the financial checking, the financial due diligence assesses the business's performance. This type of due diligence provides additional clarity that may not come to light in a typical negotiation. Going beyond the numbers assists in understanding the larger context of the business, and identifying potential problems or areas that may impact the acquisition rationale.

Due to the differing characteristics applied in financial due diligence of various industries, the knowledge and understanding of a certain industry on the side of an acquiring party might also differ from one acquisition to the other. Therefore, financial due diligence processes should be modified or adjusted to meet the acquiring party's specific needs and expectations.

The most important use of financial due diligence is as follows: *First*, reveal the financial and tax risks, for example, to verify that there aren't any irregular tax assessments that should be paid or irregularities in the annual reports that may lead to additional tax payments, and so on. *Second*, analyze the acquired company's past profitability and cash flow, and according to these parameters, forecast the firm's future performance. *Third*, understand the target's assets and liabilities in a way that will enhance better negotiations, strategic investment and acquisition decisions, and the formulation of a post-acquisition business plan and integration plan as well. Last but not least, the *fourth* is to determine whether the item of acquisition in question is in line with the acquirer's strategic targets and acquisition principles. This is compiled with other due diligence results such as legal and tax and other complementary due diligence.

The financial due diligence focuses its analysis efforts in the following areas:

- **Notes to financial statements:** The notes to the financial statements should be reviewed with care as they provide the reader information that is not always apparent from the statements. There may be a note on economic dependence; that is, the business may be greatly dependent upon one large customer. The loss of this customer would, obviously, impact substantially upon the value of the business.
- **Income statement:** The idea at this point would be to look for trends in sales or income generated by the business. Is the percentage of gross profit reasonable considering the nature of the business? One may find that certain expenses are low due to different reasons.
- **Balance sheet:** This document relates to the company's assets and liabilities. Certain asset values included on the balance sheet may not reflect actual value. There may be no recognition on the balance sheet of any upward changes in the value of an asset. Transactions that involve related parties should be closely watched.
- **Deal financing:** In the majority of cases, the ability to purchase a business depends on financing from a bank or other lending institution. It is extremely important that models are prepared to show the benefits of integrating the two businesses together, thus potential "synergies" that should lead to improved financial results.
- **Valuation:** Valuation is the process of defining the acquired company's value. This process is separate from, but usually takes place close enough/in parallel to, the financial due diligence. The valuation process reveals issues that impact the financial due diligence as well, such as

reporting quality, costs and revenues that are "one timers" versus recurring, budgeting versus realization of the budget, and so on.
- Other issues that drive this analysis:

- Understanding of the financial and accounting state in the day after
- Defining future reporting methods (International Financial Reporting Standards, U.S. GAAP, other local GAAP, and so on)
- Authenticity and accuracy of the information provided

Tax Due Diligence

Tax due diligence is the investigation of the current and future tax liabilities of a company. The tax due diligence is usually associated with both financial and legal due diligence and is part of the traditional due diligence approach.

In M&A transactions, when one company plans to acquire another, the process requires a close review of tax documents in all deal-related jurisdictions.[4]

For many years, tax practitioners did not consult with respect to the tax-sensitive aspects of the transaction until the final stages of closing. In the last several years, this trend slightly changed and now taxation experts analyze the acquisition documents and provide suggestions as to next steps and deal structure. The growing *complexity* of global, federal, state, and local tax laws, as well as the *numerous* taxes imposed on corporations worldwide, become a risk in the context of acquisition and should be therefore mitigated. See Chapter 4 for further information on tax inversion and other implications of tax on cross-border integration.

As tax issues are mainly being taken care of by the buy side of a transaction, the goal of tax due diligence is to uncover significant potential tax exposures. Tax due diligence is less concerned with relatively small missed items or miscalculations (as opposed to an annual audit). A significant tax liability would affect a buyer's negotiation and decision on whether to proceed with the deal.

Tax due diligence covers income taxes, but also sales and use taxes, payroll and employment taxes, property taxes, unclaimed property, and independent contractor versus employee classification. Where target companies have either foreign subsidiaries or foreign parents, tax due diligence may include a review of transfer pricing and foreign tax credit issues. The process includes reading tax returns (for all types of taxes) and nontax documents, and making inquiries of management and the target's tax advisors.

Reading nontax documents, such as minutes of corporate board meetings, financial statements and related footnotes, or equity compensation plans and employment contracts, can lead to the discovery of a variety of potential tax issues, including prior ownership changes that affect a corporation's ability to utilize net operating loss carry forwards against future income, aggressive or uncertain tax positions taken, and deferred compensation and golden parachute issues.

Commercial Due Diligence

Commercial due diligence analyzes all commercial aspects related to the acquired company's business. The broader approach considers the market in which the business acts, the business potential, and assessment of the competition. A fuller analysis will refer to the assumptions that lie behind the business plan, including: acquired company overview, market environment, customer priorities, competitive landscape, business design analysis, business plan review (top line), and commercial risks.

All of this is intended to determine whether the business plan stands up to the realities of the market.

The depth of the commercial due diligence depends on the acquirer's knowledge and familiarity of the acquired business. An acquirer entering into a new industry, with no prior experience, should conduct a detailed due diligence covering both the acquired company's strategy and business as well as the impact on the acquiring company itself. It should consider the potential revenues synergies as well as industry-related trends that might affect the deal.

An acquirer buying a business in its own industry will approach commercial due diligence differently. This acquirer will probably need to conduct a minimal due diligence and focus on other elements such as legal and financial due diligence (in some cases, tax as well), with partial commercial due diligence.

In conducting the due diligence from a commercial perspective, the acquirer usually encounters a variety of legal and financial problems as well as risk areas when analyzing the target. These typically include the following areas: undervaluation of inventory, overdue tax liabilities, inadequate management information systems, an unhealthy reliance on a few key customers or suppliers, aging accounts receivable, unrecorded liabilities (e.g., warranty claims, vacation pay, claims, sales returns, and allowances); or an immediate need for significant expenditures (people, inventory, IT systems). Each of these problems poses different risks and costs for the acquiring company, and these risks must be weighed against the benefits to be gained from the transaction.

Strategic commercial due diligence provides the acquirer with a factual analysis of the strategic-business-commercial-related issues to be handled. The outcome of this analysis is a report on the following areas:

- Market structure, size, and drivers,
- Key competitors, market share, basis of competition and barriers to entry,
- Customer and supplier feedback, and
- Business plan achievability, key risks, and areas for improvement.

INTEGRATED DUE DILIGENCE—360-DEGREE DUE DILIGENCE

As previously described, acquirers perform due diligence, yet most conduct only the scope of traditional due diligence. Of those who conduct this type of due diligence, a significant number of companies operate a quick and narrow due diligence process. They mainly focus on understanding historical financial reports, uncovering possible legal liabilities, and hunting for other unpleasant surprises. In other words, most acquirers concentrate on the past and not on the future of the merged companies.

In the last couple of years, a new due diligence movement has arisen. Some refer to it as "360-degree due diligence," others call it "integrated due diligence." The main innovation is that the methodical investigation doesn't only reflect the past but also looks toward the future and takes into account the possible synergies as well as the likelihood that they will be implemented and the integration process as well.

This new approach simply states that conducting a financial and legal due diligence is not enough; the major problems that will emerge in the PMI phase are in every area but financial and legal. The main conclusion deriving out of this statement is that the due diligence phase should be broader, looking toward the future and being a basis for the PMI phase.

This is the extension of the traditional due diligence!

Integrated due diligence is characterized by several factors:

- The due diligence scope goes beyond financial and legal due diligence and all other functional areas are being checked as well. Areas such as operations, sales and marketing, human resources, research and development (R&D), and others are checked as well.
- The due diligence is not performed to solely check the different functional areas but is also analyzed in comparison to state where the merged company should be after the merger. This indicates that following the due diligence, an *initial* PMI plan should be assembled.
- The acquirer perceives the due diligence process as something strategic. As such, at this point in time, the acquirer sets the strategic vision and the integration approach.
- A disciplined due diligence process is not enough; companies should reflect on questions such as: "industry impact," "customer reaction,"

"competitor response," and more. This will improve acquirer outcomes from the M&A process.

This type of due diligence is usually a lot of work, much more than the traditional one. But this type of process contributes to M&A success. In order to improve the M&A success rate, other than using this approach, the acquirer should start with defining the deal's rationale and PMI implications. Once the rationale is clear, the acquirer can verify that all areas are aligned with this rationale. For example, verifying that the human capital in the acquired company is on par with the quality level of the acquirer, and that distribution, manufacturing, sales, IT, and other areas are compatible with the acquirer.

In order to achieve success in this type of process:

- **Information should be gathered by several sources:** Information should be gathered both internally—interviewing management, key employees, middle management, and veteran employees—as well as externally. On the external level, suppliers, customers, past executive team members, and others should be interviewed as well.
- **Involve key professionals:** These professionals could be internal resources such as vice presidents or midlevel managers or could be external professionals, such as consultants relevant for the upcoming deal's needs. These professionals (it doesn't matter if they are internal or external) should have the capabilities to analyze their domain of inquiry and present the key findings and implications deriving from this analysis. If possible, nominate professionals who could continue to accompany the company with its PMI efforts.
- **Train the due diligence team:** In order to utilize these professional resources in the most effective way, the due diligence program manager should train the due diligence team, align expectations, set a clear timeline, present vision and goals, and kick off the due diligence process.
- **Translate the due diligence findings** (especially issues and risks deriving from the due diligence) *into an initial PMI plan.* If possible, get the due diligence professional to craft this initial PMI plan and utilize their assistance and experience for the PMI phase as well.

Different Types of Functional Areas Conducted in Integrated Due Diligence

As previously described, integrated due diligence is comprised of a number of domains. These domains will be presented in the following pages.

Human Resources Due Diligence   Acquiring companies entering into an acquisition look to identify human resource risks early in the due diligence process. "Human resources" (HR) refers to the target company's management team and broader employee talent pool, as well as the programs and infrastructure that help the company to attract, retain, and motivate that talent. Those leading the HR due diligence process will need to ensure that any HR risks are appropriately captured in the valuation model.

Acquirers focus their HR due diligence efforts around the following four areas:

Employee Demographics and Key Terms of Employment.   At a minimum, buyers will want to understand the following: How many employees does the target have and where are they located? Are any employees covered by collective bargaining agreements? Acquirers will also use these demographics to assess whether there is an opportunity to reduce the number of staff, to measure the savings achieved and the associated one-time cost, and to reflect this in their financial model.

Other points for review: Knowing where the target company's employees work or reside can help the buyer to anticipate potential labor issues. Acquirers will want to understand how a target company's turnover compares to industry norms and whether a material percentage of turnover is focused on one employee group or department. Agreements require careful review to ensure that financial implications and any change in control triggers for payment are fully understood.

Material Compensation and Benefit Programs.   Employee benefits represent a significant percentage of overall employee cost, typically between 15% and 30% of total salaries in the United States. Outside the United States, benefit provision is more statutory in nature—benefits often comprise a lower percentage of overall costs, but are often more than compensated for by higher social costs.

Retirement plans generally come in two flavors: (1) a defined-benefit plan that will guarantee a specified payout at retirement according to a fixed formula (generally tied to the employee's salary and years of service); (2) a defined-contribution plan that will provide a payout at retirement that is dependent on the amount of money contributed by the employee and company. Health care costs continue to be one of the fastest growing areas of employee costs.

Management Talent Assessment.   The approach to management assessment will very much depend on the nature of the deal. Where the acquisition is an add-on purchase to an existing portfolio company, there may be a need for a selection process to ensure that the acquiring company takes advantage of the opportunity to improve the talent in the existing portfolio company together with selected members of the target's management team. The importance of a fully functional executive team cannot be overstated as any delay in achieving an exit due to a lack of cohesion among the management team has a serious financial consequence.

Human Resource Transition Challenges. A key question to consider is: How might the target company's HR-related costs change following the transaction? In stand-alone situations, there may be operational synergies to be achieved by benchmarking human resource effectiveness across an array of metrics and by identifying opportunities for improvement.

Key focal points of the HR due diligence are: (1) identifying human resource management risks, (2) determining the availability of fitting interventions for mitigating identified human resource management risks, (3) determining employment costs of the prospective business, (4) assessing organizational leadership models, and (5) assessing the human resource management process of the deal.

Cultural Due Diligence   Cultural due diligence is the process of analyzing a culture with the purpose to identify and outline the cultural strengths and weaknesses of each party, compare the culture of the acquired company with the acquiring one to identify the gaps in between the two companies, and prepare a cultural plan.

Nowadays, cultural due diligence addresses the following needs:

- A framework describing, assessing, and comparing human behavior in an organization
- A way to identify and evaluate cultural risks and opportunities in an organization
- A leadership tool that can facilitate an acceleration in organizational performance
- A valuable tool when prioritizing the tasks in a change process

More information on culture can be found in Chapter 6.

Operational and Supply Chain Due Diligence   This due diligence intends to check not only operational and supply chain aspects but also for potential additional value to be brought out of the target company by improving its operational function. This type of due diligence focuses on operations and internal data rather than strategic and commercial aspects, and aims to find "quick win" opportunities to improve performance.

In parallel, operational due diligence searches for opportunities that might affect the deal's value. Elements such as the value of inventory, the utilization of the machinery (or lack thereof), and more are addressed.

Operational due diligence is mainly conducted in the industrial sector, and reviews the main operations of the target company and attempts to confirm if there is compatibility between the business plan that has been provided with the existing operational facilities plus the capital expenditure that is outlined in the business plan.

The operational due diligence conducts sample site audits and external comparisons to look for relocation and consolidation opportunities in the overall manufacturing network. It also examines all the operational processes, such as manufacturing, procurement, delivery (logistics), returns (from customers or to suppliers), planning, and so on. The main focus is on those that are poorly aligned, underutilized assets, and redundancies with an intention to improve operations while leading to savings through increased asset effectiveness, improved efficiency, and automation.

Operational due diligence focuses on the following areas (among others):

- **Inventory analysis:** In-transit inventories, international sourcing and procurement, intracompany transfers, and customer sales
- **Outsourcing:** How providers perform, overall and individually
- **Cycle time:** The time from when the purchase order is issued through to payment received from the customer for his purchase. This is a critical measure for profitability and for cash flow. Supply chain management is central to the time.
- **Customer service:** What percent of customer orders are shipped complete, accurate, and on time; lost sales from multiple shipments for each customer order
- **Supplier performance:** How well suppliers perform—delivery on time, accurately, completely, and at expected quality
- **Forecasting accuracy:** Lead time for replenishing inventory, longer stocking/restocking, product life cycles, and inventory levels
- **Risks:** All related risks defined and proper mitigation steps taken
- **In addition:** Review of supply chain management, Lean and Six Sigma, critical operational processes, plant assessments, productivity analysis, industry benchmarking, operations team assessment

Information Technology Due Diligence Information technology is the use of any computers, storage, networking and other physical devices, infrastructure and processes to create, process, store, secure, and exchange all forms of electronic data. Typically, IT is used in the context of enterprise operations.

IT architectures have evolved to include virtualization and cloud computing, where physical resources are abstracted and pooled in different configurations to meet application requirements. Clouds may be distributed across locations and shared with other IT users, or contained within a corporate data center, or some combination of both deployments.

Performing IT due diligence usually involves checking the IT ecosystems in both companies, analyzing what types of systems exist, life span, level of implementation, and the level of integration of business and operational processes in between the company/corporate and subsidiaries, as well as cross-company. This test is followed by a gap analysis in between the current *processes* versus actual needs (e.g., procurement processes, purchasing, and so on), and *systems* and *infrastructure* as well.

The IT due diligence includes several areas of examination as follows:

- Layers of *physical equipment* (hardware)
- *Virtualization* and management or automation tools
- Operating systems and *applications* (software) used to perform essential functions. *Business applications* include databases, transactional systems, email servers, web servers, customer relationship management, and enterprise resource planning systems.
- *User devices* such as laptops, smartphones, and so on
- Architectures, methodologies, and regulations governing the use and storage of data
- Computer *servers* that run business applications
- *Storage*, as a technology that holds information as data
- *Additional areas* that are being examined include: technology in place, stability, support methods, IT organization, contracts, software ownership and licensure, costs, ongoing support costs, key investments planned and capital investments needed, planned initiatives, risks, internal client satisfaction and needs related to technology, and more.

CONDUCTING THE DUE DILIGENCE PROCESS

So far, this chapter has described the different domains that are being taken care of in the due diligence process. The upcoming sections will focus on techniques and ideas to better implement the due diligence phase.

Steps of Due Diligence

While the length of time necessary for effective due diligence varies with every project, it is wise to build into every transaction a clear and methodical approach. The typical steps we use at GPMIP with our Acquisition Integration Framework™ (AIF) include:

1. Understand the essence of the potential transaction, including the investment thesis and key value drivers for the potential investor.
2. Understand the specific risk areas that require focus, and tailor procedures to be performed.
3. Manage all requests for information, and work with management to establish an appropriate work plan.
4. Perform detailed procedures including financial analysis, detailed discussions with management, and site visits, when applicable.
5. Provide real-time updates and present draft findings and reports to ensure that the purchaser is aware of all issues, and to be confident that the final report will meet stakeholder needs.

Methods of Due Diligence

During the investigative process, the due diligence team usually will employ the following fundamental methods:

Review. Through review of due diligence materials, identify critical and material factors that may impact own functional stream of review as well as the impact on other streams.

Analytical Procedures. Includes procedures such as performance analysis, trend analysis, structural analysis, analysis of materials acquired through all channels, then through collating the results of this analysis, discovering abnormalities and important issues.

Interview. Sufficient communication with every level of the internal hierarchy, employees of different positions and roles, as well as intermediary institutions.

Internal Communication and Routines. Due to investigative group personnel coming from different backgrounds and specializations, mutual communication and timely sharing of work results creates an effective method of accomplishing investigative targets (to be further discussed in the "Managing the Due Diligence Process" section next).

Global Work. To manage a global due diligence, usually a defined period of time is allocated for work on the target's premises. Thus the due diligence team must fly over. After a period of "on-the-ground" work, the additional work is done virtually, utilizing tools to support the process such as virtual data rooms (presented later).

Managing the Due Diligence Process

Defining the due diligence domains is very important, because it defines how the process should be conducted. One cannot just jump into the due diligence process and start working. The main difference between a successful process and an average one relates to the following guidelines: defining deal rationale, setting up governance (structure and routines), and managing a project (timetables, deliverables, key performance indicators, and so on).

1. **Set up the deal rationale and due diligence initial parameters.** The deal rationale should be defined and clear to participants as the basis for the due diligence examinations. There's a huge difference between a strategic acquisition, where a massive integration will be following and thus the future perspective is highly important, versus a financial investment where the acquirer is usually focused on past performance and is looking to avoid legal barriers.
2. **Set up the due diligence structural governance and teams selection.** The due diligence organizational chart is similar to other project management assignments and usually consists of three layers: (1) the due diligence steering board, (2) the due diligence management team, and (3) the different functional work streams.
3. **Kick off the due diligence process, define routines, and set a timeline.** To properly initiate the due diligence process, a kick-off session should be held. This session is intended to align all participants, provide the needed working guidelines, and define the scope and depth of the process.
   In case of a quick due diligence process (7–14 days) the daily routine starts with a morning debrief where the due diligence team as a whole receives directions and areas of focus. The team disperses and starts working stream by stream, and each day ends with a round table where each representative presents the main findings and impact on other streams.
   In case of a longer due diligence process, the basic rules remain the same but the intensity goes down, so instead of a daily meeting, it is a weekly encounter.
4. **Open a VDR (virtual data room).** A virtual data room is an online repository of information that is used for the storing and distribution of documents. The virtual data room assists facilitating the due diligence process during an M&A transaction. The due diligence process

traditionally uses a physical data room to accomplish the disclosure of documents. For reasons of cost, efficiency, and security, virtual data rooms have widely replaced the traditional physical data room.

5. **Perform detailed due diligence, close the process, and translate outputs to an initial PMI plan.** The due diligence team is working on a stream-by-stream basis collecting data, analyzing and extracting out of this analysis several outputs: (1) the risks they will phase after the closing, (2) the opportunities or synergies they may exploit as well as potential quick wins, and (3) action items that must be taken care of following the deal closing. Other than that and most important, a "go/no-go" recommendation should be applied.

   Assuming it's a "go," all of these findings may and should be directly translated into an initial PMI (post-merger integration) plan.

6. **Hand-over to the PMI team.** There might be two situations: one, where the due diligence team is also the team that will be performing the PMI. In this scenario, the PMI team will further review and analyze, but it would be a great starting point to manage as opposed to a situation where the PMI team starts its work with no reference and needs to review all materials (or most of them) from scratch and then start planning.

   The second situation is when there are two teams, one dedicated to the due diligence and the second to the PMI. In this case a proper hand-over should be managed. Both functional area teams (due diligence and PMI) must get together. The due diligence team should present the outcomes of the process, provide recommendations for next steps, and hand over all materials collected and analysis done.

Common Mistakes in Due Diligence

After reviewing all elements that should be taken into account to excel in the due diligence efforts, the last point that should be taken into account is the awareness of the common mistakes in this process. Taking care of these areas beforehand will improve the due diligence execution. Major points are as follows:

- Lack of planning and focus in the due diligence preparation. The focus must be on defining the right scope, asking the right questions, and getting the needed decision-making information.
- Poor communication leading to unnecessary misunderstandings. The communications between the due diligence functional teams as well as between the acquirer and the acquired companies must be open and flowing. The process must be managed, including routines, structure, and decision making.

- Incompatibility between the skills needed to manage and execute the due diligence and the acquirer's due diligence team.
- Focusing on traditional due diligence and disregarding the additional areas that may be impacted in the PMI phase. Inadequate time devoted to legal, tax, and financial aspects only.
- Lack of proper working environment and hostile attitude toward the acquirer due diligence team. Not only does this impact people personally, it also affects the outputs in terms of time and quality.
- Misinterpretation of the data provided to the acquirer's due diligence team.

CHAPTER CHECKLIST

- Understand the due diligence phase as part in the overall M&A process.
- Understand the evolution of due diligence over the year (traditional due diligence, integrated due diligence) and the different components that are being applied in these processes.
- The type of due diligence categories applied (legal, financial, tax, human resources, and so on).
- The due diligence process stakeholders and the functional areas and roles involved in due diligence activities.
- How to set up a due diligence governance framework and manage it.
- How to utilize due diligence findings in negotiations and in the integration planning phases.
- The critical elements within the due diligence process and the complexities of conducting due diligence across borders.

NOTES

1. Andrew J. Sherman and Milledge A. Hart, *Mergers & Acquisitions from A to Z*, 2nd ed. (New York: AMACOM), 2010.
2. My appreciation to the Israeli law firm SHIBOLET that assisted throughout the writing of the "Legal Due Diligence" section. Special thanks to Gadi Graus, Partner, and Omri Sarid, Associate.
3. As opposed to a privately owned company.
4. Dependent on the deal itself and the countries or geographies involved.

CHAPTER 10

Ramping Up an Integration Management Office and Day One in Cross-Border Deals

Stefan Hofmeyer

CHAPTER LEARNING OBJECTIVES—IN THIS CHAPTER, YOU WILL LEARN:

- ➤ End-to-end understanding of integration management office (IMO) setup and initiation
- ➤ Key concepts of the IMO charter and plan
- ➤ Resourcing the right team in an international setting
- ➤ Effective rollout and use of IMO tools and methodology
- ➤ Cultural considerations of IMO team dynamics
- ➤ Understanding of Day One activities

CHAPTER SUMMARY

The IMO is used as an effective tool for complex cross-border M&A integration success. This chapter provides comprehensive understanding of the IMO and describes activity to set up an IMO and to execute a successful Day One.

THE IMPACT OF AN INTEGRATION MANAGEMENT OFFICE ON CROSS-BORDER INTEGRATION

The integration management office (IMO) plays a valuable role in complex cross-border integrations, but can also be seen as too bureaucratic by executives looking for speed of execution. Why is this? Managers sometimes follow a standard IMO process very closely—too closely, without tailoring the process for their needs. In this chapter we address how to establish an IMO that combines both efficiency and structure for overall success.

Depending on how large and how acquisitive your company is, the IMO may or may not own integration plans and other deliverables for the integration. In the case of a larger, high-frequency acquirer where multiple international integrations are ongoing at any one time, the IMO may act as a reviewer of plans, playbooks, and dependencies, with individual integration project teams developing and submitting plan and playbook updates to the IMO. In the case of a smaller company or lower frequency acquirer, which is more often the case, the IMO develops plans and playbooks directly, requiring input from functional leads that directly report into the IMO. For our discussion, we focus on the IMO driving integration activity directly. If the IMO provides oversight to multiple projects in your company that in turn drive integration efforts, the leading practices found in this chapter then apply to your integration management *projects* that report into the IMO.

Purpose of an Integration Management Office

The IMO has a very significant purpose during a complex integration. Based on a recent survey by Global PMI Partners of 143 M&A executives,[1] 67% of respondents incorporate IMOs during an acquisition on at least half of their initiatives in a cross-border setting. IMOs are engaged to manage the complexities of the integration. In smaller events or events such as an acquihire (an act or instance of buying out a company primarily for the skills and expertise of its staff with little integration), the IMO is of less importance and may not be needed.

In a 2013 survey of 50 executives with M&A integration experience,[2] the following feedback was provided by respondents and then grouped by common themes. Results highlighted typical M&A integration challenges. The role of the IMO is critical in mitigating these challenges in a cross-border setting:

Survey Feedback—Planning

- "The scope, schedule, and budgets of most transactions are incorrectly defined by the Corporate Development team in the pre-close pro forma."
- "I am based in India where timelines are rarely met and almost impossible to enforce. That needs a special far less legalistic approach."
- "Plan early. Sign-off of plan by vendor and buyer prior to close for rapid and efficient implementation."

- "Establish responsibility for provided assumptions, and execute the integration as quick as possible without losing the acquired institutionalized value."
- "It is all about cross-functional collaboration and effective program management. If your business functions don't collaborate well, then your integration will suffer."
- "Don't undercook the planning."
- "These integration programs always display three characteristics, they will be: *complex, emotional,* and *political.* These cannot be avoided but they must be prepared for, recognized, and managed proactively."
- "Importance of integration cannot be overstated. If too much is paid for a deal then the future is bleak but securing a good price without a plan forward comes at price."

Survey Feedback—Speed

- "Speed is of essence."
- "Beware it does not turn into a technical exercise."
- "Do it fast. Like ripping off a Band-Aid. Be quick, decisive, and don't allow naysayers to drag their feet and delay necessary integration tasks in order to placate existing political or social structures."

Survey Feedback—Communication and Focus

- "Constant communication and reducing anxiety of the company being acquired."
- "Loss of management focus on the core business eats into profitability and impacts morale."
- "Communication is important to guarantee the integration, both at target and buyers."
- "Open and often communication is key to success."
- "It can be a place of pure creativity that brings out the best from all participants, or it can be a partisan hell that alienates employees from whom you need creativity and passion. It is dangerous to set up expectations that cannot be met of 'how good it is going to be.' Mergers are a slog, but do not have to be ugly. There is a lot of detail, and clear communication and a realistic timeline are critical. It can be a lot of fun, as something new is being created that properly framed can be better than either original participant."

In addition to developing the IMO process, integration practitioners are advised to look at the above listed comments to ensure that, above all else, the IMO stays effective in addressing planning, speed, and communication challenges.

UNDERSTANDING THE INTEGRATION MANAGEMENT OFFICE

The integration management office is key to the success of a complex integration effort, especially in the context of a cross-border integration.

What Is an Integration Management Office, and How Is It Different from a Project Management Office?

What is the difference between an IMO and project management office (PMO)? To refer to the Project Management Institute's *Project Management Body of Knowledge*, 5th ed., "A Project Management Office (PMO) is a management structure that standardizes the project-related governance processes and facilitates the sharing of resources, methodologies, tools, and techniques. The responsibilities of a PMO can range from providing project management support functions to being responsible for the direct management of one or more projects."[3]

A PMO is usually continuous, managing multiple projects through their life cycle. An integration management office is a specialized form of PMO focused on M&A integration. IMOs can be ongoing and supportive in the case of highly acquisitive companies. Unlike a typical PMO, IMOs can also ramp up and ramp down as part of the integration process and can be responsible for the direct execution of the integration effort—our focus in this chapter.

Functions of an Integration Management Office

The IMO manages core functions of the integration effort and provides structure for efficient integration delivery.

Typical Integration Management Office Organizational Structure We develop the IMO organization to address each specific integration. A common structure is identified in Figure 10.1.

An IMO typically reports up into an executive steering committee and manages across each functional team of the acquisition; these functional teams can be referred to as work streams. It is important to note that there are integrated business processes that *cross* work streams and must also be overseen by the IMO in an integrated fashion. Table 10.1 identifies general functions of an IMO.

Work stream scope and level of effort vary based on the level of integration required for the acquisition. However, even in the case of an acquisition that is considered stand-alone (no integration), there are critical interface

FIGURE 10.1 Typical IMO Organization Structure

points between the acquiring and acquired companies that need to be addressed.

Charter Development As described in the *Mergers and Acquisitions Integration Handbook*, a charter is "a simple document designed to clearly outline the who, what, and how elements of the integration and to gain commitments from resources owners in advance."[4] A charter is an initial document, approved by the leadership team, that establishes the purpose and authority of the IMO, and establishes foundational expectations of the integration.

It is important in cross-border deals for IMO leadership to establish a concise integration charter working with executive sponsors. The charter establishes the authority to start planning for the integration and the

TABLE 10.1 Functions of an Integration Management Office

Governance	Planning	Execution and Control	Leading Practices
Charter Development	Plan Development	Resource Management	Methodology Management
Synergy Alignment	Playbook Development	Work Stream Management and Communication	Technical and Process Support
		Transition Service Agreement Management	Post-Mortem Analysis
			Center of Excellence

authority to set up the IMO. Charter development must be accomplished quickly and effectively, as there is pressure to bypass the charter completely and move right into planning. The charter establishes clarity of purpose for the integration. If the integration is complex in nature, each work stream itself may be its own project and require a charter as well. The use of the word "charter" can sometimes be associated with slow-moving bureaucracy. Don't use the word if that helps, but take forward the charter's content in documents that are delivered.

Synergy Alignment   As a merger or acquisition transitions from deal-makers to the integration team, there is risk that pro forma expectations, including estimated synergies, are lost as integration team members focus on executing. The IMO plays a critical role in the transition from deal-makers to the integration team to fully understand expectations and govern activities that are aligned with synergies and overall corporate strategy. In tightly executed PMO activities, each major integration activity can be assessed for both cost and contributions to synergy goals, tracked for the life of the integration project and beyond. This assessment can be transitioned to the operations team of the newly integrated organization for continued measurement.

Plan Development   A key responsibility of the IMO is to establish integration plans based on specific requirements of the integration effort. Plans take a comprehensive view and are aligned with Knowledge Areas from the Project Management Institute's *Project Management Body of Knowledge*.[5] IMO planning areas to consider include: integration management (how the related management activities come together), scope, time, cost, quality, human resources, communications, risk management, procurement management, and stakeholder management. Each of these areas does not have to have its own stand-alone plan or even be formally developed, but each plan's content should be addressed to an appropriate level and be reflected in the use of a playbook. As an example, procurement planning may be very concise or embedded in other documents, whereas human resources, communications, and risk management plans typically go quite in-depth for a cross-border acquisition and are independent, stand-alone plans.

Playbook Development   Plans provide input to a playbook: a packaged set of activities and tools that the integration team uses to execute their integration engagement. As described in the *Mergers and Acquisitions Integration Handbook*,[6] playbook content includes:

> **Purpose and Scope.**   These parts of the playbook help you to establish what the official role of your playbook will be to support your

organization's integration activity and how the playbook elements all fit together. Consider these sections a "Playbook 101" overview (topics: playbook scope, relationship between playbook elements).

Integration Management Plan. These sections detail how to set up an IMO and some suggestions on integration governance (topics: organization, governance).

Integration Planning Processes. These sections detail the primary integration phases (e.g., preplanning, execution) and repositories for due diligence checklists and formats for initial integration plans (topics: integration phases overview, collecting planning inputs such as due diligence checklists, initial integration plan).

Executing and Monitoring Processes. Consist of all work stream execution activities and how they are monitored (topics: integration program management, program management processes).

Resource Management Most often the IMO must rely upon resources loaned from business units and external consultants. In international deals, complexity compounds resource needs and obligations. As part of a planning effort, resources must be planned both from a financial budgeting perspective and most importantly from a commitment level perspective. In most cases internal resources take on responsibilities *above* the operational commitments that they still need to maintain. Planning for and balancing resource commitments is one of the major challenges and responsibilities of a cross-border IMO.

Work Stream Management and Communication After plans are in place, the IMO and each work stream must be managed—this is the monitoring and controlling responsibility of the project. Special emphasis is placed on risk mitigation, communication, and integration management to address cross-border challenges. These items are tracked and managed during concise, recurring IMO meetings with work stream leads who provide updates on delivery performance, recent activities, upcoming activities, active issues, dependencies or "Help Needed From," emerging risks and related mitigation, current and planned budget, and resource status.

It is the IMO's responsibility to coordinate, manage, and take action on all of this information efficiently by utilizing tracking tools that range from Microsoft Excel and Google Spreadsheets to more elaborate management tools like eknow and Midaxo that have been developed specifically for M&A integration management purposes.

Transition Service Agreement Management   In cases where an acquisition is a carve-out of a company, a key function of the IMO is to designate a team member responsible for the management of a transition service agreement (TSA). This primary function is for the buyer to ensure that the selling company adheres to the terms of the deal, that all dependencies are planned for and managed between the seller and buyer, and that the required activities of both the acquiring and acquired company are on target. For the seller, preparing a clear TSA menu during the pre-signing phase allows them to provide clarity to potential buyers, remove post-closing uncertainty, and eventually to obtain a higher selling price. In addition, transfer of information between the two companies is managed through the TSA with alignment to the legal terms of the agreement.

Methodology Management   Key functions of the IMO are also to ensure that methodology is implemented consistently and owned and improved by the integration team as a whole. Ensuring that work streams follow the playbook methodology and make contributions for improvement is a priority. This may be difficult as integration teams are made up of senior team members who most often drive their own approach and can do so under the cover of a distributed international team. Individuals not following the defined process can be disruptive. Encourage leaders throughout the organization to set examples to follow and contribute to standardized practices that all team members can use.

Technical and Process Support   During the integration, the IMO will continuously monitor for delivery gaps and areas of needed support. This includes providing technical resource expertise, connecting the integration team with other experts in the acquiring or acquired company, and ensuring via processes and value streams that cross-functional areas are addressed in a holistic manner. In general, the IMO is responsible to ensure all appropriate integration areas are covered and integrated.

Post-Mortem Analysis   As an integration project wraps up, the IMO works with team members in a nonthreatening manner to capture what worked well, what didn't work well, and areas of improvement. This typically runs smoothly with significant information capture—the challenge and often forgotten part of a post-mortem analysis is to follow up and take actions on the lessons learned, and to assess past lessons learned at the start of the next integration effort.

The Integration Management Office as a Center of Excellence   In cases where an IMO manages multiple projects on an ongoing basis or when the

IMO stays active in preparation for future acquisitions, the IMO can take the role of a center of excellence. This includes utilizing plans, playbooks, tools, and lessons learned to (1) provide guidance to future integrations, advising the deal team early on to take into consideration integration aspects of the deal, (2) to complete research on industry and internally developed leading practices, and (3) to ensure integration team members are trained and prepared to support an integration prior to planning and Day One activities.

ESTABLISHING AND EXECUTING THE INTEGRATION MANAGEMENT OFFICE

In the previous section we discussed the core functions of an IMO— functions that are typical for any complex integration. Now we discuss how to implement these functions for lasting value within a cross-border integration effort to achieve optimal results. The following is a standard M&A integration life cycle, the *Acquisition Integration Framework™* (AIF), developed by Global PMI Partners (see Figure 10.2).[7]

Relate Phase (Pre-Close)

The relate phase provides specific steps with the related cross-border considerations.

Establish the Charter   Top priority during the relate phase is to establish the charter and socialize it with the executive team and deal-makers and the integration team members as they ramp up the project. In addition to providing clear guidance to all team members involved, the charter establishes the baseline expectations of the IMO and overall integration. Second, it

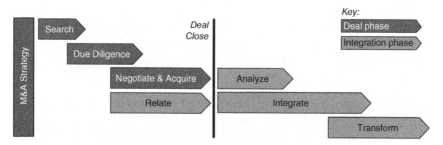

FIGURE 10.2   GPMIP Acquisition Integration Framework™

establishes IMO and integration team authority to ramp up teams, make purchases, and build governance.

The IMO charter also lays the foundation and template for the IMO (see Table 10.2). To emphasize, *charters and plans can be overdone and get too complex to be managed.* It is important to focus on aspects that are needed for your specific integration and to move quickly within a cross-border setting.

The following is an example of a simple charter template. Note that more sensitive items can be added to charters, such as budget and quantifiable synergies. However, this needs to be balanced with the desire to communicate the charter out to all personnel participating in the acquisition. To address this, a full charter can be developed for the executive team, while a "public" charter can be created with a redaction of sensitive information.

The charter and other documents, especially in a global setting, should not be relegated to a printed document or buried in an electronic folder structure. The charter should be communicated via a variety of channels, including: being referenced in presentations, incorporated into M&A integration tools, handed out as a reference card to team members, placed on intranets, and where appropriate, printed and placed on the IMO's working room ("war room") walls. As an example, placing content prominently on an intranet should always be considered for both exposure and availability to a global team. Limit the addition of confidential topics as part of the public charter to ensure the documentation can be distributed and communicated as broadly as possible.

TABLE 10.2 Integration Charter

Integration Name	\<Name\>
Scope	\<Describe Scope of Effort\>
Sponsor	\<Name of Executive Sponsor\>
Lead	\<Integration Lead\>
Team Members	\<Committed Team Members and Roles\>
External Support	\<Third Parties Engaged\>
Goals and Objectives	\<Business Drivers of the Integration\>
Critical Success Factors	\<Description of Critical Success Factors\>
Interdependencies	\<Interdependencies between Work Streams and External Impacts\>
Major Milestones	\<Listing of Categorized Milestones, Their Description, and Completion Criteria\>

Cross-Border Considerations: In a global setting there are often many interpretations and a skepticism regarding the real purpose of an acquisition. The charter defines the clear purpose and follow-on integration activities. If done right, execution will track to the charter, providing confidence and clarity to the newly integrated team and employees globally. Integration team role definition and allocation of authority are also very important. Especially within a cross-border acquisition, executives look to position themselves in the best possible light and in a considerable number of cases will look to take responsibilities during the integration to control their own destiny. Role definitions in the charter identify specific definitions of authority and help mitigate risk of a global power play between impacted executives—an important consideration.

Set Up the Integration Management Office and Take Initial Action Utilizing the charter as a guide, IMO resources are identified early on and activated preferably 120 days before close. If internal resources are engaged, part of their existing operations activities will need to be backfilled. The IMO is then officially kicked off with the participation of deal team members to confirm deal rationale and approach. The governance and reporting framework is also solidified at this stage.

Once a charter is established, planning can be started in earnest with a kick-off meeting to crystallize a common vision with all members involved. The meeting can be via webinar to support an international setting—the more real-time integration participants, globally, the better. All key stakeholders should attend along with the assigned integration team. Representatives from the deal team should also attend. This acquiring company kick-off simply presents material related to the charter and answers any questions as input for the planning effort. This also allows for clear communication between the deal team and the integration team to validate business drivers.

After kick-off, IMO leaders work closely with the deal team to capture as much information as possible to prepare for the integration. This is difficult as the first priority for deal-makers is to finalize due diligence, negotiate, and take action to acquire the company. Participation with the integration oftentimes is an afterthought. An additional challenge for a cross-border acquisition is that deal-makers are often spread geographically in different time zones and can be very difficult to track down for a conversation. IMO leaders must be relentless in their pursuit of information. Additionally, since much of the target's information is off limits prior to close, an option that may be considered is to have a clean team and clean room if information needs to be exchanged prior to close. This allows access to sensitive information to support the integration, but it must be understood that if the deal falls through, clean team members may be restricted to returning to work at the target and acquiring company for some time.

In tandem with information gathering, actions also need to take place that include analyzing key staff, negotiating retention, developing job offers, and making initial leadership announcements. Corporate security, communications, branding, facilities, human resources (HR), and product preparations for legal close must be addressed. Key customer and supplier meetings also need to be executed in addition to regulatory filings as needed.

Cross-Border Considerations: IMO setup is by nature a chaotic stage as plans have not been fully developed and avenues of information gathering have not been defined, yet action needs to be taken. This is compounded by cultural differences, globally distributed work environments, and individuals looking to make their mark in a new environment. To mitigate these challenges, travel may be required for alignment meetings. Use of collaboration tools and video conferencing is recommended to facilitate as much communication as possible. The acquiring company kick-off meeting is critical and should include all key IMO participants and resources transitioning from the deal team—this is one of the few opportunities to establish a standard view of the integration, driven from the integration charter.

Establish the Plans Many managers confuse plans with a Microsoft Project plan (a Gantt chart), which is only one component of an overall plan. In our case, we are talking about communication plans, risk mitigation plans, resource management plans, and so on. In large deals, plans should be very detailed. However, for smaller deals, plans can be documented concisely, even as line items in a spreadsheet or in an integration management portal—the key is that plan content and needs are effectively addressed—function over form should be stressed. A costly trap that brings down IMO effectiveness is to fall in love with a deep level of documentation that will likely not be utilized—the integration team will see the IMO as having less tangible value and individuals will blaze ahead in a manner that fulfills their work stream or their personal goals, resulting in a less than optimal overall integration. Keep it simple and effective to encourage ongoing alignment and maintenance of plans.

Four of the more important planning areas impacting cross-border planning are human resources, communications, risk, and integration. These planning areas are further described below.

Human Resources Planning and Resourcing the Right Team There is significant depth in HR work stream planning, specific to each integration. The following are applicable considerations:

Project versus Operations Experts. Senior resources, typically at a director level, should be identified to lead integration work streams. A challenge exists as these individuals may be operationally focused versus project focused in their skill set and may not be prepared to address tight timelines and task execution needed for an integration project. Be aware of this to ensure project management fundamentals are evaluated and understood by experts prior to IMO execution. The socialization of project management fundamentals across the enterprise is important, especially in an international setting where project management fundamentals have a greater chance of not being followed. If there is a deficit of project management capability, consider other project-based support staff to augment assigned experts.

In-House Resources versus Consultants. All things being equal, skilled in-house integration resources are preferred over consultants as they have deep internal knowledge and directly benefit from a successful integration. However, consultants may still be necessary to instill M&A integration leading practices and drive integrations to completion. Consultants are more accustomed to short project sprints, overtime, and travel that will be necessary in an international setting.

Time Commitment. When considering internal resources, also understand that they will most likely be used in a matrix capacity, reporting to their existing line of business being loaned to the integration team. Since their incentives most likely are driven by their permanent role, when unexpected operational events occur or when work estimates change, these resources will complete operational duties first. During the HR planning process, ensure that time estimates are considered and commitments are in place. If there is an opportunity to tie financial benefit to integration success, this should be considered to mitigate bias toward operational execution.

Centralized versus Local Resources. When cross-border acquisitions occur, location consideration is essential. Local integration resources are important to obtain a first-hand view of integration actions and to leverage local experience and culture wherever possible. Two areas to consider include: (1) face-to-face meetings for collaboration and planning, and (2) periodic check-ins to ensure that local resources maintain dedicated time for integration activities. This is augmented by the use of video conferencing versus phone calls for meetings to take into consideration nonverbal communication.

Utilization of Acquiring Company versus Target Resources. Pre-close target resources are often off the table due to confidentiality; however, the resource plan should consider the participation of target resources in post-close, as these resources help set the example for collaboration and international cultural integration. These resources can also provide insight into the acquired company for cultural integration.

Communications Planning   When not planned methodically, communication will be spotty at best. Employees assume the worst, freeze in their roles, and are at greater risk to leave. At minimum, the communication plan, with use of a communication matrix, should identify all audiences and define when and how communication occurs, what is being communicated, and who owns the communication. Planning efforts must take into consideration consistent talking points both to internal and external audiences. In a cross-border setting, compliance issues must also be considered, such as time of announcement related to stock market announcements (if a public company) and timing of communications to offices in different time zones. Be sensitive to one-off employees who may be out of touch given their time zone and define a plan to engage each of these members accordingly.

The IMO should plan the primary communication points of the deal announcement and Day One. For this communication activity, on-site participation by executive management is strongly encouraged. When the acquisition spans many locations across the globe, live video conferencing is also a suitable option, with representatives on-site to take questions and address reaction points. Planning should include activities and tone that is culturally sensitive. Table 10.3 shows a simple communication matrix to support and manage these efforts.

TABLE 10.3   Simple Communication Matrix—Example Columns

Communication	Purpose	Vehicle	Audience	Owner	Approver	Frequency
Name of communication	Why the communication exists	Newsletter, email, webinar, and so on	Suppliers, Customers, Internal teams, and others	Person responsible for development and delivery	Who will review prior to distribution	Weekly, quarterly, ad hoc, and so on

Risk and Risk Mitigation Planning   Risk and risk mitigation planning takes into consideration input from key leaders who represent all geographies and functions involved in the acquisition. Items to capture include the risk, likelihood of occurrence, impact, how to monitor, and what actions to take for prevention or to mitigate if the risk is realized. Information in the risk matrix is realized in a risk plan detailing how risks will be tracked and reported and who will be responsible for addressing risk prevention and mitigation (see Table 10.4).

Risk and risk mitigation planning is a risk in itself. In the risk plan, risk metrics and related tracking activity can be established and implemented as part of IMO meetings. The goal is to track risks and address them prior to problems occurring. A measurable and actionable plan is a key result.

TABLE 10.4 Simple Risk Matrix—Example Columns

Risk	Impact	Probability	Priority	Mitigation	Metrics	Owner
Name of risk	What is impacted, level of severity	Likelihood of risk realization	Importance: relates to Impact X Probability	How to avoid or resolve if risk is realized	How to monitor potential for risk realization	Responsible person for owning and monitoring risk

Integrated Planning Integrated planning is a key purpose of the IMO and is the least tangible of our activities from a tools and templates perspective. A simple method to start integrated planning is to hold a workshop session to identify on a whiteboard all the core functions of your specific integration area and identify all dependencies and timing between these functions. As a second level of effort, draw a circle around this entire integrated function set and identify other external corporate functions, people, and systems requiring interaction, globally. Once completed, results can be incorporated into the overall integration playbook, in Gantt charts, in dependency matrices, and in standing meetings with internal and external teams. It is less important to have stand-alone integrated planning documents—it is more important to incorporate integrated results in all other plans, in IMO meetings, and in actions. Integrated planning really is about awareness to think outside of silos, and to ensure that plans take into consideration and track the whole of the integration.

Cross-Border Considerations: When planning for a cross-border integration, communication is of great importance as in-country teams may "black box" their planning efforts to maintain autonomy, not allowing proper oversight and working unilaterally with little coordination. It is important to empower local in-country teams to participate in overall planning. During engagement with centralized teams, transparency and ongoing communication expectations can be set. Cultural aspects are also important. Some cultures may say "Yes" to plan acceptance but will not follow through, while other cultures will push back as a first protocol, slowing plan development and delivery. In these cases, establishing IMO governance and process is a first step. The process should not be burdensome. It should take the mantra of "work the process." What does "work the process" mean? Let's take two examples:

1. Some cultures may say "Yes" to plan acceptance. In these cases, planning runs smoothly but critical feedback is not delivered. When plans are executed they do not flow well and unforeseen challenges occur. In the worst case, responses are "we are working on it" with no results. Identify this situation early on and engage participants in troubleshooting to bring out plan considerations. Set the expectation that critical analysis, even to the level of pushback, is desired and part of the process. Challenge situations where critical feedback during planning is not received. When executing plans, follow up with measuring metrics that are quantifiable. "We are working on it" will not cut it. Get down to activities that are completed, ongoing, and planned. Do not tolerate vague answers, which can derail the integration.

2. In cultures where pushback is the first response, clear communication also needs to be established. A key approach is to engage participants who are pushing back with a challenge to resolve what they see as problems. This is a simple approach that leads to collaboration. As we require quick movement, lock-in meetings may be necessary to systematically identify and address all concerns. It is important not to postpone any discussion of resolutions as this can freeze IMO activity—time is of the essence.

Ensure Plan Consistency   Contingencies and aggressiveness in plans should be deeply assessed in a cross-border setting for consistency. Some regions never meet their schedule as a standard, other regions are hyperaggressive, and others are too conservative—consider the international regions and corporate culture you are working in. Establish a plan baseline and adjust it accordingly on an ongoing basis. Integrations must move quickly and teams will not have all the answers before moving forward. Due to this, appropriate contingency should be put in place in addition to incorporating strong risk management. While planning, if there is a choice between a more complex solution and a simple one, choose the simple one when all else being considered is equal. Establish your plans and contingency to adjust and meet end goals.

Establish the Playbook   The playbook is a living document that is maintained over time and utilized as the framework for integration activities. The playbook provides organization and activities that are easily understood by the integration team. The IMO's responsibility is to ensure that integration team members follow standardized processes within the playbook, and when processes are improved, ensures that these updates are reflected within the playbook. Involvement of international team members in the maintenance of the playbook is key to their ownership, execution, and repeatability success. This continuous process improvement effort both helps the existing integration project and provides a foundation for future M&A integration success.

Table 10.5 lists typical artifacts of a playbook, with notes related to cross-border integration.

TABLE 10.5 Playbook Artifacts

Playbook Section	Typical Section Components	Cross-Border Considerations
Purpose and Scope	Integration Strategy and Objectives Playbook Scope/Usage Guiding Principles Pre-Close Legal Guidelines IMO and Team Charters IMO Kick-Off Agendas Strategic Frameworks	Given geographic and culture differences, each integration participant will have a different view of the purpose and scope of the integration. It is important to assess the viewpoints of each distributed region and establish concise, clear, and simple terms clarifying how the integration should be viewed.
Integration Management Plan	Governance Model(s) and Process IMO Roles and Responsibilities IMO Infrastructure Functional Organizational Models Phasing Constructs Integration Leader Requirements Integration Resourcing Model(s) Functional Work Plans Day One Framework Planning Communication Plan/Matrices Cross-Functional Dependency Mapping Input from All Other Developed Plans	A clear understanding of the management plan should be defined down to the regional level and not relegated just to a central IMO. Any void in the management plan at the regional level has a great likelihood of being filled by the regions, creating runaway activities uncontrolled by the IMO. Engage regions in comprehensive centralized planning versus risking rogue regional activities.

(Continued)

TABLE 10.5   (*Continued*)

Playbook Section	Typical Section Components	Cross-Border Considerations
Integration Planning Processes	Discovery Process and Checklists Due Diligence to Integration Process Flows Data Harvesting Process/Templates Talent Assessment Worksheets Cultural and Change Assessments On-Boarding Process/Materials Talent Assessment Process First 30/90 Templates Retention Planning Worksheets Transaction Scenario Matrix Training and Orientation Tool Evaluation Criteria Tool Usage Guidelines Escalation Protocols Employee Communication Plans Divestiture/TSA Planning Templates Work Stream Prioritization Matrices	Planning efforts will be ongoing. The integrated international team will not be aware of how to consistently update plans and engage on an ongoing basis. The best approach is to develop simple processes and checklists to telegraph how planning should occur. This should be combined with training—both live and on demand (documents, video, etc.) and easily accessible. As a reminder, keep it simple.
Executing and Monitoring Processes	IMO Weekly Meeting Structure/Agendas Integration Dashboard Functional Status Reporting Templates IMO Calendar Synergy Identification and Tracking IMO Budgeting Scorecards and Measurements End-State Process Tracking Issues/Risk Logs Day One/Week One Planners Day One Checklists After Action Reviews (Lessons Learned) Employee Surveys Scope Change Requests Risk Assessment	Roll-up of integration status is daunting on the two fronts of obtaining status and consolidating status in similar formats. Make monitoring simple, nonduplicative, automatic, and as closed-loop as possible. Any friction or reason not to complete status will be used, especially in an international setting—ensure this is an easy process for the team. Similarly for execution, any additional effort for the team to decipher activity for execution will add friction and misunderstanding. Use checklists whenever possible.

Utilize Technology Tools during Startup and Planning Technology tools can be both a help and a hindrance. There are some great tools on the market that support full M&A life cycle and M&A integration. Companies such as Midaxo, eknow, Deven Software, and IBM have established M&A integration tools. These tools help establish consistent process and clarity and should be considered when serial acquisitions are planned. However, it is not recommended that tools be investigated while in the midst of IMO setup and planning—they should be considered well before this time so there are no additional change management and learning curve burdens on the integration team.

Manual, stand-alone tools such as Microsoft Word documents, Excel spreadsheets, Google Docs, and so on are often used. These tools usually end up as the default with the major drawback and risk of not being shared across the project. Risk is further exacerbated when considering cross-border collaboration.

When utilizing more manual tools, consider augmenting their use with collaboration systems such as SharePoint, Office 365, Google Drive, Team-Work, and other tools—access rights and confidentiality should be assessed in addition to your company's willingness to place documentation in a cloud-based environment. It is not good enough to place these in an online folder structure. A dashboard should be created that provides integration status and easily found links to important documents on one page—in many cases, a simple HTML dashboard can suffice. Of most importance here is that all members are aware of, can easily and appropriately access, and can contribute to information related to the integration project.

A final consideration is to use the project management tools and process currently established in your company. Although very high profile and strategic, an integration effort is still a project. If appropriate access rights are in place, these tools can provide a seamless transition from integration to operational activities.

DAY ONE: STARTING THE INTEGRATE AND ANALYZE PHASES

Congratulations! On Day One you are now managing a new international organization. Two phases are kicked off at this point. It is time to execute what has been preplanned for the integration—the *integrate phase*. Additionally, with access to the full set of people, process, technology, and data of the new organization, further analysis can occur—what we call the *analyze phase*. The analyze phase further develops the integration plans and playbook based on new information available. Integrate and analyze phases occur *concurrently*.

Integrate Phase on Day One

The first immediate task is to kick off the integrate phase; this includes all communication that has been established in the communication plan impacting both internal employees and external audiences such as customers, suppliers, and partners. A full integration team kick-off meeting is completed that includes integration team members now from the entire organization (acquirer and acquired company). Oftentimes integration kick-off meetings are postponed to capture additional information first. Do not fall into this trap as team members will start taking unguided action during this postponement, especially in distributed, international business cultures. Plan to have people attend globally via web meetings, where possible, to set expectations as consistently as possible.

For Day One of the integration phase, address the following:

- Critical "Keep the Lights On" Tasks
  - Treasury, tax, legal, intellectual property, and all international ramifications of asset hand-over, tax and legal filings, funding, banking relationships, credit card processing, payroll processing, and insurance
  - Global employee lists and at-risk personnel
  - Any sales, fulfillment, and customer support changes that need to occur on Day One
  - Technology tasks such as emails, phone numbers, phone tree, help desk
  - Physical and information security

Day One Communication (Planned in Advance)
  - Branding
  - Welcome kits and new printed collateral
  - Vendor, customer, and investor letters
  - Internal team communications
  - Talking points—both internal and external distributed to staff
  - Integration kick-off presentation (described later)
  - Language translation as needed

Integration Kick-Off Presentation
  - Content established in the project charter
  - Global roles, sponsor participation, and commitments
  - Governance model
  - Communication matrix information
  - High-level integration plan and key milestones
  - Risks, dependencies, and open issues

- Immediate next actions for Day One and beyond
- International considerations, privacy considerations
- Review of tools (project portals, admin tools, etc.) that require update by team members
- Other information specific to the integration

Other Actions: Outside of Actions Listed Above, Day One Activities Should Focus on Areas of Highest Priority

- Synergy work streams and initiatives
- Organizational planning
- Projects that support value drivers (sales, operations, retention, etc.)
- Initiatives that help sustain business continuity

Analyze Phase on Day One

In cross-border integrations, there will be a wave of new information, internationally, to consider. You now have access to further information and many additional target staff who will impact your initial discussions. Gain a further understanding of softer skills of the integration, such as attitudes and leadership styles within each international region. Also take on the followings tasks that will have impact on your activities:

- Review all newly available documents and information to determine impact to the integration, including financials and commercials
- Consider feedback from the kick-off meeting
- Review in-flight acquired company projects and programs
- Meet one-on-one with a cross-section of target employees to gain their perspectives. Keep questions open-ended and let them speak their mind. Ideally, capture the following information:
  - Are they happy, worried, or don't have enough information?
  - Do they see the integration plan as being realistic? If not, why not?
  - Do they see specific challenges or risks?
  - Are there any internal political or localization issues that need to be addressed?
  - Are they aware of other items that the integration team should know about?
  - How would they like their role to change (or stay the same) in the new organization?

Expect a substantial level of travel to have teams in place globally for Day One. It is important prior to and during Day One to have face-to-face and one-on-one meetings wherever possible to assess the impact of the integration activity.

There will be updates to plans, priorities, quick wins, risks, issues, negotiations, and many other items during the analyze phase. Aggressive local teams will start making decisions and moving ahead, international cultures will start showing their differences, and communication gaps may materialize—Day One will be a chaotic time. Be expedient with qualified changes to your initial plan, but do not lose sight of the governance you developed during pre-close planning—this is the most critical time to hold it together. If changes to the governance or integration process are needed, make these changes methodically and deliberately with comprehensive communication. The integration management office must appear to be (and be) in full control.

CHAPTER CHECKLIST

Based on this chapter, you should understand

- The purpose and importance of an integration management office (IMO)
- Common cross-border IMO plan and playbook components
- Pre-close and Day One integration phases
- Leading practices for IMO ramp-up
- Key activities for Day One

NOTES

1. Global PMI Partners, Cross-Border M&A Integration Survey, November 2015.
2. Stefan Hofmeyer and ModalMinds, 2013 M&A Integration Survey, published by Stefan Hofmeyer, San Francisco, CA.
3. Project Management Institute, *Project Management Body of Knowledge*, 5th ed. (Newtown Square, PA: Project Management Institute, 2012).
4. Scott Whitaker, *Mergers and Acquisitions Integration Handbook* (Hoboken, NJ: John Wiley & Sons, 2012).
5. Project Management Institute, *Project Management Body of Knowledge*.
6. Whitaker, *Mergers and Acquisitions Integration Handbook*.
7. Global PMI Partners, *Acquisition Integration Framework*™ (AIF), 2015.

CHAPTER 11

Integration Decision Making and Process Strategy in Cross-Border Deals

Stefan Hofmeyer

CHAPTER LEARNING OBJECTIVES—IN THIS CHAPTER, YOU WILL LEARN:

➤ Leadership styles for cross-border decision making
➤ Application of tools to drive decisions
➤ Efficient iteration of process development
➤ Leading practices for process establishment and change
➤ Signs of when to formally stop a process
➤ Timing and integration of technology to support global process

CHAPTER SUMMARY

This chapter begins with a discussion of important factors that drive cross-border M&A success. The chapter then discusses leadership styles and related decision-making approaches, goes through tools for decision making, addresses process development and change, and closes with a review.

PREPARATION AND LOCALIZATION OF DECISION MAKING

Integration-related decisions are made at all levels within an organization during an integration event. Even minor decisions can have a very big impact. Employees are very sensitive to even the smallest decisions affecting their long-term work. If they are not assigned to expected responsibilities, if they do not have the local control they are looking for, or if they sense weak or poor decision-making skills in leaders, they are more apt to take actions that are incongruous with corporate strategy, and when challenged, they may become frustrated and leave.

The *way* decisions are made is important—sometimes more important than the actual decisions themselves. As we look to adjust to new cultures in a cross-border acquisition, it can be awkward at times to refine decision making and process strategy to approaches that are outside our comfort zone. In a recent example of a U.S. manager placed in Germany to manage an integration team, decision making had to be well thought through. Initial perceptions or stereotypes were that a U.S. manager is quick to act, a bit dominant and loud, and not sensitive to local understanding. Decisions established by a process that upheld this stereotype would lead to passive resistance. Adaptation to a local decision-making framework, such as being more inclusive, democratic, and transparent, was essential.

To ease decision-making challenges in a cross-border environment, it is important to assess local decision-making approaches, adjust decision-making style as needed, and telegraph how and why a decision and process change occurs. Understanding the corporate environment in the regional setting is also of critical importance. Table 11.1 provides a decision-making assessment framework to assess the corporate environment.

Establishing a decision-making approach is completed by assessing the following areas.

Acquirer's Decision-Making Process

Having a very sound understanding of the existing decision-making process in the acquirer helps streamline integration efficiencies. Decision making for the integration will most likely follow the acquirer's process and be most

TABLE 11.1   Decision-Making Assessment Framework

Acquirer Decision-Making Process	Target Decision-Making Process	Decision Process Disconnects and Misconceptions	Decision Process Formality	Leadership Style
Characteristics	Characteristics	Actions	Actions	Actions
Typically adopted as the decision-making process	Interfaced with acquirer process	Fill disconnect and misconception gaps	Balance formality versus speed	Consider individual, corporate, and country influencers
Requires reconciliation with target decision-making process	To be understood to avoid local runaway decision making	Ensure transparency Incorporate RACI diagrams	Assess cost/benefit of formality	Consider leader/team mismatches

effective, unless the acquisition is being used as an event to change the status quo of the acquirer or if the target is left as a stand-alone.

How to Assess. Understand the decision-making process within existing programs. Also understand how formal or informal the process is and the impact of specific executives on decision making. Meet individually with select team members to gain their understanding of the decision process—in many cases you will find different understandings. This may be due to different subcultures within the organization, variance of what is espoused versus placed into action, or just plain lack of awareness. Take these situations into account as you establish the decision-making structure for the integration.

Additional Actions to Take. Third parties and new employees typically do not fully understand how decisions are made. As part of an integration team kick-off meeting, the decision-making process should be stated clearly and understood by all. Where necessary, document the decision process flow and utilize tools such as RACI diagrams (see Table 11.4 later in this chapter) to communicate the decision-making process clearly and simply.

Target's Decision-Making Process

Target company decision-making process should also be fully understood to ensure all integration participants are aware of how decisions from the target will be interfaced or integrated with the acquirer. In a stand-alone setting, this is important to help ensure greater transparency into the newly acquired organization. In cases where the target is being fully absorbed, this assessment identifies areas of change management focus.

How to Assess. As with the acquirer, meet individually with select target team members to gain their understanding of decision processes and their expectations for the acquisition—you may find a different understanding between participants that will need to be reconciled. If not a stand-alone integration, take special note of how the decision process will need to change in order to adapt to part or all of the acquirer's processes. Take note of areas that will be difficult to change based on regional and corporate differences.

Additional Actions to Take. Integration team members from the target are critical to engage as they have the greatest adjustment to make and also must set the example for their team members to follow. Ensure that they are fully aware of the acquirer's decision-making process, are engaged and understand the need for feedback and refinement, and where possible, are seen as champions of the process.

Decision Process Disconnects and Misconceptions

A common challenge in an international setting is to have the integration team, and especially the team from the target, not understand how or why decisions are made. This reduces confidence in the new organization that can permeate through the entire company, causing low morale, passive resistance, and employee departures. In these situations team members may fill gaps in knowledge that are inaccurate, negatively influencing decision making at the local level.

> **How to Assess.** To assess disconnects and misconceptions, have team members at both the acquired and acquirer sites come together to assess decision-making processes. These meetings help ensure that a full understanding is established from decision origination to decision execution, with disconnects being identified and addressed.
>
> **Additional Actions to Take.** Transparency and acknowledgment of decision disconnects and misconceptions lay the foundation for integration decision making and decision-making improvements. Special attention should be given to communication and areas where communication can be improved. A tool that can be used for methodical assessment is a RACI diagram, described later in this chapter (see Table 11.4), to make sure integration team members understand who is responsible, accountable, consulted, and informed.

Decision Process Formality

Decision process formality can bring clarity to chaos, but it can also reduce integration speed and efficiency of an acquired organization. Oftentimes, smaller or startup target companies, or companies located in emerging economies, are much less formal in their governance. Mandating tighter governed processes in these organizations may result in inefficiencies and reduced competitive advantage, or may cause governance to be circumvented altogether, causing process breakdowns. The proper balance of formality versus speed should be understood, established, and communicated.

> **How to Assess.** If the acquirer is a serial acquirer, formality of the decision process may already be developed and may either be documented or at least known implicitly. Formality can be assessed by walking through the process with experienced integration participants. For companies new to acquisitions, decision-making process formality from other types of business transformation activity can be assessed as a baseline.

Additional Actions to Take. Decision process formality should be established at the level appropriate for the combined organization. A good rule of thumb is to start with a more formal decision-making process and ease into less formality as work dictates. Informal decision making at integration start, without knowing related consequences, can significantly hurt an organization. Note that online collaboration tools, checklists, and other forms of efficient tools should be used wherever appropriate. Once the formality of the decision-making process is understood, it should be assessed to determine how well it has been accepted in the combined organization. Through interviews and meeting attendance, identify areas of risk and risk mitigation, especially related to passive resistance. If formality does not add value or is seen as bureaucratic or burdensome, make modifications.

Leadership Style

In addition to the role of culture identified in Chapter 7 of this book, it is important to consider common leadership styles in a cross-border integration to establish how to lead the integration and how the new organization will function. The following is a brief summary of leadership styles that can provide guidance for your assessment.

Democratic Leadership. Involves a team guided by a leader where all individuals are involved in the decision-making process to determine what needs to be done and how it should be done. The group's leader has the authority to make the final decision of the group.*

Autocratic Leadership. Controlled by one leader who has total power, and who does not allow anyone else to make decisions.†

Laissez-Faire Leadership. A nonauthoritarian leadership style. Laissez-faire leaders try to give the least possible guidance to subordinates, and try to achieve control through less obvious means. They believe that people excel when they are left alone to respond to their responsibilities and obligations in their own ways.‡

---

* For a definition of *democratic leadership*, see www.businessdictionary.com/definition/democratic-leadership.html.
† For a definition of *autocratic leadership*, see http://dictionary.cambridge.org/dictionary/english/autocratic?a=business-english.
‡ For a definition of *laissez-faire leadership*, see www.businessdictionary.com/definition/laissez-faire-leadership.html.

Transactional Leadership. A style of leadership that is based on the setting of clear objectives and goals for the followers as well as the use of either punishments or rewards in order to encourage compliance with these goals.[*]

Transformational Leadership. A style of leadership in which the leader identifies the needed change, creates a vision to guide the change through inspiration, and executes the change with the commitment of the members of the group.[†]

Paternalistic Leadership. A type of fatherly managerial style typically employed by dominant males where their organizational power is used to control and protect subordinate staff who are expected to be loyal and obedient. A manager with a paternalistic leadership style might be appropriate for a business with a more formal and hierarchical structure where creative thinking is not required of staff.[‡]

Mixed leadership styles exist within and across organizations and countries. Given the fast pace of an acquisition, respect these styles and how these styles impact decision making and decision acceptance. Be vigilant for how these leadership styles impact teams in a new setting. Here are common examples of leadership style implications in a cross-border setting.

Laissez-Faire Leadership Style in a Democratic Setting. Consider a Nordic, laissez-faire leadership style company acquiring a German democratic leadership–style company. The laissez-faire leader will need to provide more guidance or the democratic team will need to become more proactive in their decisions.

New Democratic Leader in an Autocratic Setting. Consider a more traditional Chinese-based organization being acquired by a European organization. The democratic leader will need to make more autocratic decisions while at the same time fostering open communication.

Transactional Leadership Style in a Transformational Setting. Consider an Indian company that incorporates a transactional leadership style after they acquire a creative Israeli startup that has a transformational style. The acquired team may feel burdened by the lack of local decision making and empowerment. Consider leaving decisions

---

[*] For a definition of *transactional leadership*, see www.businessdictionary.com/definition/transactional-leadership.html.

[†] For a definition of *transformational leadership*, see www.businessdictionary.com/definition/transformational-leadership.html.

[‡] For a definition of *paternalistic leadership*, see www.businessdictionary.com/definition/paternalistic-leadership.html.

stand-alone in the acquired organization, with formal interface points to the acquiring organization to maintain structure.

Transactional Leadership Style in a Paternalistic Setting. Consider a U.S. manufacturing company acquiring a Latin American paternalistic driven company. In this case the leaders in the acquired company may need special management as team incentives and decision making will shift to be driven more by transaction metrics instead of by obedient action.

These are just a few examples of conflicting leadership styles in a cross-border setting. Note that a company's mix of leadership styles does not necessarily map to the expected country leadership style trends. Each corporate environment should be assessed and managed based on its unique style to ensure decision making is as effective as possible.

PRIMARY DECISION-MAKING TOOLS, APPROACHES, AND LEADING PRACTICES

The act of capturing information, distilling information, and methodically discussing and making sound decisions helps foster communication across individual, corporate, and country differences.

The following are common examples of decision-making tools and approaches used to maximize decision-making efficiency. These tools are used in combination with governance, such as an integration management office as described in Chapter 10. These tools do not have to be complex. In fact, the simpler they are, the better.

Grid Analysis for Complex Decision Making

Decision making across borders can be very difficult due to varying communication and management styles and the potential for lack of common understanding.

Although it may seem too formal or basic depending on your perspective, a grid analysis spreadsheet as identified in Table 11.2 is one of the best tools that can be used for decision making, and more specifically, for prioritization of initiatives that bring together a diverse team to a common perspective. Benefits of grid analysis includes a clear understanding of:

- Initiatives to complete (and not to complete)
- Initiative prioritization
- Prioritization criteria understanding

TABLE 11.2 Grid Analysis Spreadsheet

Initiative	Increase Revenue	Reduce Cost	Expand Market	Etc.*	Score
Initiative Weight	5	3	5	2	
Initiative 1	4	6	2	4	56
Initiative 2	10	5	7	3	106
Initiative 3	2	9	3	10	72
. . .					

*Additional criteria as needed.

Initiative Development Sessions Initiative development sessions are meetings where team members come together to obtain consensus on work to complete. As an example, let's assume we have internal initiatives we'd like to accomplish to deliver acquisition synergies. In initiative development sessions, comprised of primary integration team members and stakeholders, we start by generating a full set of initiatives. Under most circumstances, resources will be limited and can only accomplish a subset of initiatives during the initial stages of the integration. Prioritization needs to occur.

In our example, progress has already been made by listing all potential initiatives. This is essential for planning, and for helping to ensure that no hidden or side projects are established by team members.

Criteria and Criteria Weighting Sessions The next step is to establish prioritization criteria in a collaborative session. In this example, criteria should be aligned with business drivers and synergies such as "increase revenue," "reduce cost," "expand market share," and so on. To promote quick wins, additional criteria may be "ease of implementation" or "implementation time." Optimally, three to eight prioritization criteria, aligned with company objectives, should be established with criteria being as unique or nonoverlapping as possible. For instance, using *both* "ease of implementation" and "implementation timeline" may skew results as they overlap significantly, and in essence, double their importance and impact during ranking.

In addition to developing criteria, weighting the criteria from 1 to 5 helps determine each criterion's importance in relationship to other criteria, with a rating of 5 being most important. In our example, let's say the business drivers for our acquisition are strongly related to building market share and less to reducing cost. In this case "building market share" may have a 5 and "reducing cost" may have a 3.

In this process, establishing criteria and criteria weight is not an exact science. That is okay. The process of consensus building to determine criteria and criteria importance is of greatest value. This supports clear and consistent understanding across the integration decision makers and the international team. After criteria have been established and weighted, rating of initiatives can occur.

Initiative Rating   Initiative rating is the process of scoring initiatives based on specific criteria, such as: "On a scale of 1 to 5, with 5 being best, how well does this initiative build market share?" This is best completed in real time with a group of senior decision makers. At first, the exercise may seem like overkill as initiatives are each scored by their criteria from 1 to 5 or from 1 to 10 depending on preference. However, through real-time dialogue, each decision maker's priorities and viewpoints are brought into the discussion. This process not only helps in obtaining clarity, it more importantly establishes a deep understanding of each decision maker's thought process.

At the end of the exercise, each initiative will have an overall weighted score, providing clarity of the initiative roadmap ahead. This score can be ranked to determine what needs to be addressed first and what will be postponed to a later date.

Iteration Until Consensus Is Complete   After initiative ranking, more often than not results may surprise decision-making participants. In many cases, initiatives that were thought to be most important do not make the cut. At this point participants should not fall into the trap of doing what the ranking says, or giving up on the grid analysis process. The value here is to go back over the criteria, criteria weight, and criteria score to discuss why ranked items turned out the way they did. Numbers can then be appropriately changed through consensus. This exercise is not just about a tool generating a rank—it is about a team establishing priorities and decisions through a consensus-driven, organized approach.

Pareto Analysis, 80/20 Rule, the Ishikawa Diagram, and the Five Whys

Pareto analysis, the 80/20 rule, the Ishikawa diagram, and the five whys are all good tools to use in combination to assess root cause analysis and risks for decision-making purposes.

Pareto Analysis/Pareto Diagram.   As shown in Figure 11.1, the Pareto diagram identifies root causes or risks related to the decision at hand, with captured frequency of occurrence. Plot these on a bar chart, sorting based on frequency, then graph the cumulative frequency. This provides an understanding of what areas are most important to address.

80/20 Rule.   Coming out of the Pareto analysis, one may find that the 80/20 rule holds true—80% of problems are caused by 20% of root

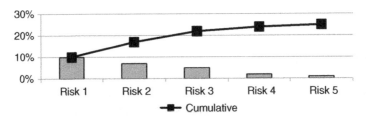

FIGURE 11.1 Pareto Analysis Chart

causes. This rule of thumb helps support decisions by focusing on the areas that have the most impact. Using Pareto analysis, or just the 80/20 rule by itself, provides clarity and focus.

Ishikawa or Fishbone Diagram. As shown in Figure 11.2, the Ishikawa diagram establishes causes of why events occur or develop. Not only does this diagram help in identifying risks to mitigate, it helps in explaining cause and effect relationships in a variety of cases to help in decision making.

Five Whys. If a team member brings up that they'd like to take on an action where a decision is requested, it seems like something your child would say, but ask "why" five times and it will typically lead you to the root cause of reasons that need to be addressed and decided upon.

These tools have their place when decisions can be made based on observation and empirical data. Their results can be compelling to drive decisions. Additionally, just knowing about these tools will enable you to think about decisions and problems in a new organized way, even if these tools are not formally used.

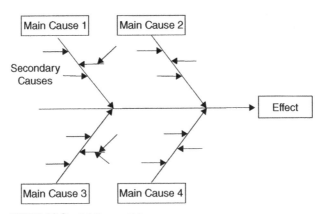

FIGURE 11.2 Ishikawa Diagram

Timing in Decision Making

In the world of cross-border integration, there are very subtle aspects that also enhance decision success. The following are lessons learned from experience.

Timing is important. Decisions made too early typically do not have enough information to be sound, do not have enough backing to be championed, are slow to progress, and when decided upon, are more apt to change later, which hurts the credibility of the decision maker. Changes made too late typically generate rework, lead to frustration by the integration team, and cause "wait then hurry-up" scenarios that affect time, cost, and quality of the integration.

Much like any other activity of the integration, decision *timing* should be planned. As questions or issues materialize, they must be assessed for timing just like any other activity in the project plan. Decisions should be made at the right time when information and champions are ready to take decisions forward.

Political Aspects of Decision Making in a Global Setting

Even the smallest decisions in an international setting have a political angle. What makes things difficult in this environment is the challenge of understanding how each integration participant assesses, approves, and is affected by decisions impacting them:

- Will the participant be personally affected by the decision?
- Will his or her team be affected by the decision?
- Is the person a "yes man" or do they push back on everything?
- Are individuals passive and will they not say much to counter a decision until they need to act upon it, and then do nothing, or rebel?
- Are group decisions being made by the loudest team member? Are passive decision makers not saying anything but meaning "no"?
- Are decision makers saying "yes" but not following through?

Each of these situations must be assessed and dealt with subtly, or they can dramatically undermine the integration.

Closed-Loop Decision Making

Closed-loop decision making is the activity of following up on decisions that were made, and assessing their impact. In the midst of a major international integration, decisions can easily be lost in the shuffle. It is

TABLE 11.3 Decisions List

Decision	Requested by	Decided by	Due Date	Status[1]	Priority[2]	Notes
Decision 1	<name>	<name>	<date>	<O,C,H>	<H,M,L>	<Note>
Decision 2	<name>	<name>	<date>	<O,C,H>	<H,M,L>	<Note>
Decision 3	<name>	<name>	<date>	<O,C,H>	<H,M,L>	<Note>
. . .						

[1] Open, Closed, Hold

[2] High, Medium, Low

important to incorporate closed-loop decision making in a standard process within the governed activities, such as the execution of work stream meetings, integration management office standing meetings, and steering committee meetings.

Steps for Closed-Loop Decision Making

1. **Establish a decision list.** Maintain a list of outstanding decisions to be made, including who requested the decision, who needs to decide, when is the due date, what is the priority, and any specific notes related to the decision (see Table 11.3).
2. **Tie off all items.** In many circumstances, decisions once thought to be strategic and important quickly drop off the radar and fade away. It is important to state these types of situations and formally close the need for the decision. This also helps to ensure that topics do not recur.
3. **Track in-process decisions.** In certain circumstances, important decisions do not get made (1) due to bandwidth issues, (2) due to help needed by others, (3) for reasons of timing. It is important to follow up on these activities in a systematic fashion to maintain project momentum.
4. **Capture rogue decisions.** Especially in an international setting, executives may be aggressive, making decisions locally and begging for forgiveness later. When these local decisions are found out, capture these decisions. This allows for overall transparency and integration control. If decisions go against the overall integration or deal drivers, they should be stopped or escalated.
5. **Capture decision results.** This step, by definition, closes the loop on decisions. Great decisions need to be tracked to ensure they are duplicated across the integration. Mediocre and poor decisions also need to be tracked for remediation and lessons learned. In most cases, mediocre and poor decisions are pushed under the rug. Setting the expectation early that they will be followed up on helps to set a culture of learning

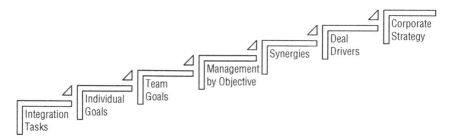

FIGURE 11.3   Line-of-Sight Diagram

from decisions. Capture quantifiable results as much as possible and where possible map these results to synergies and deal drivers.

Synergy Mapping

Establishing a line-of-sight synergy map (Figure 11.3) related to each integration activity provides focus. In the case of deal drivers relying heavily on synergies, mapping synergies to activity establishes importance and identifies areas where synergies do not have related activities assigned. This also aids in decision making by uncovering activities that do not contribute to synergies or business drivers.

As the integration executes to completion, track metrics related to synergies and adjust accordingly. Often the deal team departs and synergy expectations are lost as teams focus on operations and emergencies. Tracking synergies through line-of-sight holds integration tasks to strategic acquisition requirements.

LEADING PRACTICES FOR GLOBAL INTEGRATION PROCESS CHANGE

Process change is a very large topic. In this section, we distill leading practices that have been shown to be effective in cross-border integration settings to support strategic change.

Leverage Existing Leadership Styles

Strategic process change in a global setting must address personnel who are managed by a myriad of leadership styles, from authoritarian to laissez-faire leadership. Unless the acquisition is small, there are a number of leadership styles within integration and operational teams. We must be prepared to address how employee team members are conditioned—for instance, it is difficult to turn a team accustomed to command-and-control into a team that readily picks up kaizen* principles and is self-governing. The lesson here is to not dictate your management style across the entire organization to make process change. Take advantage of how change has been rolled out previously within given regions and companies, and modify your process change methods appropriately for given circumstances. Augment what works in existing local methods over time to best meet the needs of a newly integrated company.

Identify Change That Is Strategic versus Tactical or Busywork

Strategic work involves activities that support long-term corporate goals, whereas tactical or busywork involves activities that address day-to-day needs. During implementation of change, clearly define what is strategic, place emphasis on this, and ensure that time is not fully cannibalized by tactical and busywork. Identify and mitigate conflicts—this may be in the form of communicating why we do activity today, what strategically we will do tomorrow, and how activities will need to change to support the transition.

Identify Active Champions, First Actors, Owners, and Internal Customers

Identifying change participants is at the core of strategic process transformation. To get started, let us define important roles and how they are used to implement strategic process change.

Active Champions. Often executive champions or sponsors are in name only. Successful strategic process change requires champions to be participative and to lead by example. One critical aspect is to have the champion lead a significant portion of kick-off meetings, participate in steering committee meetings, and be active in emails and other communication for the duration. This helps establish clear objectives to the integration and operations teams, and also relays the importance of the integration effort relative to other work. Set these expectations with champions prior to the start of the integration effort.

First Actors. Process change happens when people lead by example. Team members will change when they see their peers changing around them. Necessary process change sometimes comes with a little difficulty

---

* For a definition of *kaizen*, see www.businessdictionary.com/definition/kaizen.html.

at first. Work closely with first actors—individuals who make changes first, to ensure they are involved and ready to set the example for others to follow. This can be actual execution of the process, or it can also be when messaging gets presented in a meeting. First actors can vocally support changes in meetings that will help steer momentum. Don't hesitate to delegate this responsibility to the first actor. Explain to the first actor why he or she needs to act in a certain way and how his or her actions will impact others. For example, tell the first actor, "I need your vocal support in this meeting to let the team know you are on board with our changes" or "If you lead by example, other team members who are more hesitant will follow." Stating the first actor's responsibilities explicitly helps in his or her development.

Process Owners.   A business process can be difficult to view and understand from start to finish, especially when it comes to identifying and tracking synergies. Typically, team members are only responsible for several tasks in an overall operational process. It is beneficial for at least one team member to be assigned to the overall process and be responsible to know how the process executes across all team responsibilities. This helps catch process challenges that occur at hand-off points, adds responsibility for the process owner, and is a good first step for career progression in a newly integrated company.

Internal Customers.   It is important to consider the existence of internal company customers. Every output of a process must have a customer, whether an internal or external customer. If a customer does not need or want the output of a process, then the process is not needed. This seems simple, but if processes are assessed on a daily basis with this test, it is amazing how many reports and meetings, and how much busywork can be avoided, allowing time to focus on real work. By identifying customers and gaining their input, processes become extremely focused, valued, and successful. When establishing a new process or work product, always identify the customers and validate their true needs.

Ensure Communication and Collaboration with the Use of a RACI Diagram

A very simple and effective tool is a RACI diagram—assignment of integration participants who are responsible, accountable, consulted, and informed. Integration teams, especially internationally distributed teams, lose efficiency and effectiveness if these assignments are not agreed to and communicated clearly. Table 11.4 is an example of a common RACI diagram.

TABLE 11.4   RACI Diagram

Tasks	Person 1	Person 2	Person 3	Person 4	Person 5	Person 6
Task 1	R	A	I	I	C	
Task 2		C		A	R	I
Task 3		I	A			R
. . .						

R = Responsible, A = Accountable, C = Consulted, I = Informed

Responsible: Person responsible for getting the hands-on activity done

Accountable: More senior leader accountable for the success of the activity

Consulted: Team members who should provide input to the activity

Informed: Team members who should be aware of the activity

Without a RACI diagram, specific individuals will not be informed or consulted, and others will not be responsible or accountable, causing rework and missed assignments. Setting up a RACI diagram at the beginning of a project is essential for success.

Assess and Align Incentives

We understand how teams are led, we've identified the process participants, and communicated roles to everyone. However, if team participation is not aligned with incentives such as career growth or direct compensation, process change will move at a snail's pace or may not move at all. This is especially critical when dealing with an international integration and dealing with operations team members as part of the integration team where they have other work and related incentives. Further exacerbation occurs when local leadership does not have integration performance incentives—local teams will be aware of this and act accordingly. To counter, it is important to have metrics and benchmarks associated with the integration, synergies, and strategic process that align with incentives.

KAIZEN-BASED LEADING PRACTICES

Kaizen is a Japanese term for a gradual approach to ever higher standards in quality enhancement and waste reduction, through small but continual improvements involving everyone from the chief executive to the lowest-level workers.

Establishing kaizen-based practices and principles is a great way to implement a lasting and positive cycle of strategic process change in an organization. However, the degree of kaizen practices implemented must be governed by the readiness of staff to accept these principles. In this chapter, we do not go over the full kaizen methodology. Instead, we establish a limited set of kaizen principles that have been found to be impactful in specific settings of a cross-border integration.

Core Principles

Kaizen core principles include open-mindedness, job satisfaction, ability to question responsibilities, and shared success.

When to Activate. Kaizen core principles are good if your integration team is used to an environment of collaborative, democratic, or transformational leadership. However, if the existing leadership style is command-and-control or paternalistic, principles such as open-mindedness and ability to question responsibilities will be difficult to execute and may hinder integration efforts. If the target is currently in a command-and-control environment and it is desired to change to a collaborative environment, this may take years to change. Use caution when utilizing kaizen principles when integration speed is of the essence.

Holistic Business View

Supported by process ownership of integration and operations teams, a holistic business view provides a means to optimize output and minimize waste that is generated between process hand-off points. Optimizing a holistic view also establishes a greater tie-in with synergies and provides the standard that each process point should track to.

When to Activate. It's beneficial to spend time to establish a holistic business view and document processes when the processes tie directly into deal drivers and related synergies. Other process areas can benefit from a holistic business view, but given the speed of integration required, will likely not be in the immediate scope.

Continuous Improvement, PDCA, and Metrics

Establishing continued process improvement initiatives can, over the long term, produce significant benefits for an organization. This concept ties in other aspects of kaizen and the iterative concept of plan, do, check, act (PDCA): Plan for process changes, do process changes, check how the changes have benefited the process, and then act on recommendations to continue the cycle.

> **When to Activate.** It is difficult to fully roll out continuous improvement while integrating cross-border acquisitions in a tight time frame. However, implementing metrics (related to the "check" in plan, do, check, act) is a great start as this can tie back to synergies and an executive dashboard to be used to guide further process change. Other aspects of continuous improvement can be planned for, but may not necessarily be implemented during the short integration effort time frame.

Standardization

In a cross-border setting, standardization is valuable. Process and tool standardization are two important aspects. This can be driven down to the basics of what conference call tools to use, how meetings are set, and how meetings are delivered. During integration planning, it is important to set a standard even if it may not be the most optimal—standards should methodically change over time, but there needs to be a starting point. When employees have different first languages and when uncertainties exist, standards, however small, can make a big difference in tying the team together.

CATCHING THE WAVE OF CHANGE

Earlier in this chapter, we discussed decision timing, and in that spirit we also need to address process rollout timing. Process change is not simply about rolling out process when processes have been defined and capabilities are in place. Staff must be ready to receive the process change, champions and first actors must be in place to support the process, and process participants must have a driving need or other incentive to use the process. To use a surfing analogy, this wave needs to build and process rollout needs to occur at the right time—catching the wave. By rolling out the process too soon, the process may be established and no one will use it, causing loss of momentum. By rolling out the process too late, integration team members and operations team members across the globe will have already established their own informal process, making change more difficult. Planning for and identifying when change is needed, and executing change in a timely manner, is the key to success.

When to Use Technology Tools to Support Global Decisions and Process

Enterprise tools can be used to standardize global decision-making approaches and process. However, out-of-the-box tools can bring very inefficient process into organizations, lower morale, and increase cost both in terms of tool expense and time.

When establishing the integration process, first incorporate less automated tools to meet corporate needs, and then investigate, as needed, tools that can be customized prior to your next integration. In a worst-case scenario, a technology tool is rolled out for the first time during the integration and the tool itself needs configuration and understanding, causing a project-in-a-project scenario: Inside the integration project there is an additional project to install, configure, roll out and complete change management for the defined integration technology tool. Wherever possible, avoid this situation.

Tools do play an important role in a cross-border acquisition. Management tools, process automation tools, communication tools, and operations-specific tools play a large role in helping to establish process. The development of cloud-based tools has been a significant evolution to integration work, enabling teams to stand up quickly. However, as mentioned, timing of tool selection and rollout must be considered.

Integration Management Tools   Before an integration is the best time to select and roll out integration management tools (Midaxo, eknow, Deven Software, IBM M&A Accelerator, Microsoft SharePoint, Teamwork, or Excel, Word, and PowerPoint). These tools should be fully functional and well understood prior to integration execution. When selecting tools, choose tools that meet specific requirements of the integration or tools that have been proven to be successful in the past. There are many management tools on the market that have a very complex functionality. Stick to simple tools that are not time intensive and can easily be utilized in a distributed environment. As integration teams typically are a mix of third-party consultants, acquirer team members, and target team members, there will be a major change effort involved. Be aware that the rollout of a tool may cost more in time and money than a manual project effort—always keep this in mind.

Operations Tools   When establishing operational tools, consider their impact on process and determine early on if the tool should drive the process or if the process should drive the tool. For example, in the case of rolling out enterprise resource planning (ERP) systems like SAP, the tool itself may drive the needed process.

At the other extreme, highly configurable cloud-based process management or collaboration tools can be tailored to meet process needs after the process has been developed. In this case, a manual process can be developed first, followed by the rollout of a tool that can be configured. Note that all technology tools are configurable—but at what cost?

When to Formally Stop a Process

If a process is not used, it has a tendency to fade away by itself, even though the integrated organization is set up to support the process. If the integration team and operational owners work around a process, do not use a process, or are not even aware of a process, the process in question should be first looked at to determine its use and see what changes need to occur to make it effective.

This process change can be driven by kaizen methods or other methods related to the leadership style of the organization. If a process is determined not to be of use, it should be formally acknowledged and stopped. A worst-case scenario is when people go through the motions of a process where there is no real customer. In these cases, resolve to end the process and move on. Keep an eye out for processes that have no customer, especially in an international setting where this has a tendency to occur.

CHAPTER CHECKLIST

- **Address decision-making process and leadership style.** Assess the unique decision-making process, culture, and leadership style of the organization and use this understanding to support decision making and process change.
- **Address lack of supporting governance and decision-making process.** Establish a standardized management process during the integration planning phase, including a formal decision-making process. Select, configure, and incorporate supporting technology tools, avoiding situations when technology tools themselves become projects, and establish metrics, including synergy metrics, that drive management decisions. Follow up decisions with a closed-loop decision-making process.
- **Address siloed business view/lack of synergy awareness.** Assign process owners and map synergies to process activities. Roll out the understanding to all process participants as to how they contribute to the integrated company.
- **Address overestimating ability to change.** Understand that it takes first actors to support the rollout of change. Keep technology tools, process,

and change as simple as possible to meet the needs of the integration. Be wary and mitigate passive resistance and stop the process when it has no customer or tangible value.

- **Address lack of a single owner.** Ensure that there is clear ownership and one owner where possible. Utilize RACI diagrams to formally commit team members to positions of responsibility, accountability, consultation, and being informed.

- **Address competing incentives.** Understand that integration team members may have competing incentives, most commonly operational incentives that may not align with integration incentives. Ensure that incentives are in line with the integration and overall corporate strategy.

- **Address lack of follow through/too many changes.** Ensure that decisions and process are rolled out at the appropriate time. Identify internal customers and formalize change approaches. Consider kaizen leading practices. Track changes with a closed-loop approach.

- **Address lack of empowerment.** Consider the changing leadership styles and how that impacts team members who are not accustomed to the style.

- **Address lack of training or communication.** Communicate often using tools that help develop decisions like grid analysis and Pareto analysis. Use tools like RACI diagrams to establish clear responsibilities. Engage champions and first actors to ensure that they are part of communications channels.

CHAPTER 12

Post-Merger Integration Process, Methodologies, and Tools

Thomas Kessler

CHAPTER LEARNING OBJECTIVES—IN THIS CHAPTER, YOU WILL LEARN:

➤ The key questions companies need to ask during strategic selection of M&A targets to ensure a smooth integration post-deal
➤ How to perform an integration due diligence
➤ What to focus on in preparing post-signing communication
➤ How to run the three major events in any successful integration:
   1. Executive alignment
   2. Synergy working session
   3. Integration team launch
➤ How to prepare for Day One
➤ How to manage the first 100 days
➤ How to transition the post-merger integration project to the final owner in the operational organization
➤ Why post-M&A board reviews are important

CHAPTER SUMMARY

This chapter describes how companies can incorporate integration activities from as early as the strategic selection process through to post-M&A board reviews to ensure M&A success. It discusses the integration due diligence steps that provide vital information for the deal decision making. The chapter also elaborates on preparing post-signing communication pre-signing as it sets the tone for the integration activities. It moves on to discuss the importance, steps, and character of the three major events, how to prepare for Day One and what to watch out for during the first 100 days post-closing. The chapter also discusses the steps that ensure an efficient transition from the post-merger integration project to the line organization, and highlights why post-M&A board reviews are important.

THE M&A LIFE CYCLE

The M&A life cycle shown in Chapter 4 is an end-to-end process that spans all five major phases and four major milestones. For a picture of the M&A life cycle, please refer to Figure 4.1. It incorporates every activity from defining the M&A strategy, to selecting the most appropriate target, up to its operational integration. Integration planning and execution has a touch point in each of the five major phases.

Integration Planning and Execution in the M&A Life Cycle

During strategic selection, companies define and link the profile of the acquisition candidate to their strategy. The result of this exercise is a clearly defined and communicable M&A vision.

This vision addresses the reason for the transaction, identifies potential integration challenges, sets the framework for internal and external communication, establishes the baseline for potential changes in the joint organization, and highlights where synergistic values need to be explored.

The vision is the basis for all activities launched during integration due diligence that will help to substantiate how the target could be integrated into the acquirer.

Based on the initial definition of the integration goals, companies should start pre-signing with collating all information gathered during the strategic selection, due diligence, and deal negotiation and devise an integration approach. They should also rethink and address the leadership team question.

In the period between the pre-signing and the closing, the integration management office is activated and the process of an in-depth integration planning starts.

During this phase, companies will sketch out a detailed integration framework that defines the implementation plans for synergies, identifies the most critical tasks at Day One and during the first 100 days, and defines any organizational and business process changes that need to occur. Roles are clarified, the interim organization established, and integration performance targets finalized. Alongside these planning activities a communication plan is established and rolled out that addresses all major stakeholders. If there are parts of the acquisition that will not be retained, a detailed plan needs to be established to carve those activities out into a separate entity to be divested.

Post-signing it is all about integration plan execution, motivation, communication, and progress tracking.

Before companies hand over the integration project into the line organization, an in-depth hand-over needs to be planned and scheduled. This would include an update about all integration objectives and the progress made to date with regard to the set objectives. It would also incorporate any know-how transfer if the receiving unit has not been part of the integration work streams so far. Most important however is to make sure that the overall objectives of the acquisition—the "why" of doing the deal—get communicated and will be integrated into the business units' objectives so that no value is destroyed by the change in hands once the transaction moves from the project organization to the operational unit.

STRATEGIC SELECTION

Why do companies need growth by M&A, and how do they find the best candidate?

Growth is essential. Particularly in today's world, the credo is no longer "the big eat the small"; it is "the fast eat the slow," irrespective of size. Given this changed business reality, new approaches are needed when selecting growth via M&A.

Building Your Strategic M&A Vision Using Lanchester and Other Strategies

The Lanchester strategy has been developed by F. W. Lanchester as a warfare strategy to identify where to invest existing forces best to achieve the largest territorial gains. Sales and marketing strategists have adopted his tactics to define where they can achieve the largest market share gains given an existing market position and budget (see Figure 12.1). M&A strategists also use the strategy when looking to define those regions and markets where an acquisition will enable a shift in market share and change the companies' competitive positioning.

The following M&A strategies can be derived from a review of the marketing and sales strategies. Depending on your relative market share and the resources available to you to acquire companies, you may adopt one of the strategies to gain speed and market effectiveness.

Strategy 1. The larger of two competitors has more resources and thus will typically preserve its resources by just defending its market share. The smaller competitor can try to identify an acquisition target to

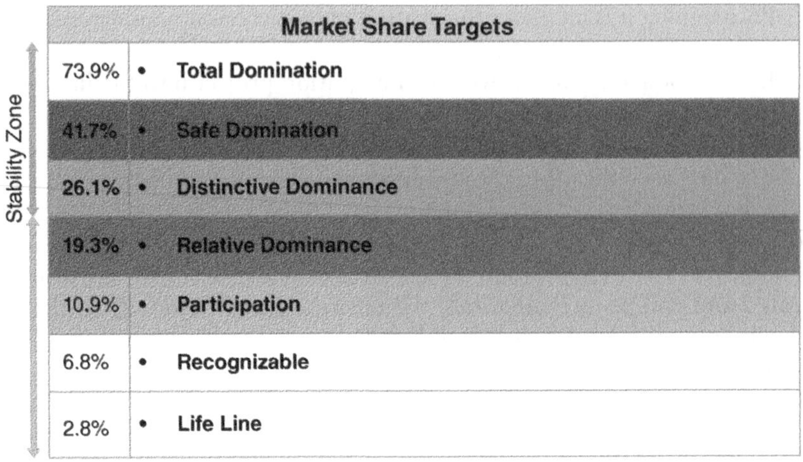

Market Share Targets	
73.9%	• **Total Domination**
41.7%	• **Safe Domination**
26.1%	• **Distinctive Dominance**
19.3%	• **Relative Dominance**
10.9%	• **Participation**
6.8%	• **Recognizable**
2.8%	• **Life Line**

Stability Zone (vertical axis label at left)

FIGURE 12.1   Lanchester Strategy

close the market share gap and get into "shooting range" of the larger, resource-rich competitor. This is called buying market share.

Strategy 2. The larger of two competitors has fewer resources and less market effectiveness. There is a high likelihood that the smaller competitor will gain market share organically, thus an M&A strategy would reflect an inappropriate use of resources.

Strategy 3. The weaker force should always try to compete on a narrower front, fight local battles, and increase combat effectiveness. Thus acquisitions in a specific field that close the distance in that specific area are well-invested resources.

Strategy 4. The stronger force should be mindful of the weaker competitor's tactics and where appropriate adopt them to reduce its advantage and increase resources spent in markets that will stretch the weaker competitor to the breaking point. They cannot fight multiple battles. Thus look toward acquiring in the markets where you cause the biggest stress for the weaker competitor. If the stronger competitor can confuse the weaker one on where to spend its resources, all the better.

Strategy 5. If both competitors are of equal strength, for example, within close "shooting range," look toward opportunities where you can outnumber your opponent at a critical time by placing your well-positioned resources. This could be done effectively through a surprise acquisition.

Beside applying the Lanchester strategy, executives can use the already-described GE–McKinsey nine-box matrix (see Chapter 4) combined with the cash value added approach (CVA) as a valuable way to identify strategic fit and define the areas within the organization that best would grow via M&A.

Identifying Strategic Sources for M&A

A clear strategic intent thus lays the groundwork for a precise M&A transaction charter. Corporate M&A departments and selected operations staff alike may start to look for qualified M&A targets based on the defined M&A transaction charter. Internal sources are typically excellent prequalifiers, as they know the culture (described as the set of behaviors that get decisions done) of their own company best and have already established relationships with competitors, suppliers, or clients, all of which could be good targets.

Good external sources are portfolio investments of venture capital and private equity firms, members of chambers of commerce, trade associations, government trade agencies, and obviously investment banks and the corporate advisory arms of the big audit firms. We even find more and more Internet-based companies such as Axial Markets and Deal Nexus.

Target Screening Process

If companies have a somewhat good idea of who could be of interest to them, it is important to do an initial screening and gain a better understanding if the target is truly a fit or not. Competency and commercial stability, credibility in the marketplace, complementary fit with the company's own business objectives, publicly available financial statements, IT capabilities, innovation track record, sales force effectiveness, and proven timely distribution are key elements to check.

Linking Screening Results to Strategy

Another important step before the first contact is to link the strategic M&A vision and the result of the initial screening to value drivers and synergies. Understanding how the transaction will create value is essential before starting any conversation. At this early stage in any transaction, value drivers and synergies include a large degree of assumptions that need to be validated. Probing the assumptions behind the value creation is one of the most important tasks once you have direct contact with the target.

Establishing Long-Term Relationships with Potential Targets

Existing relationships prove to be extremely valuable in the process of establishing a contact with the target, particularly if the target is a private business, because private companies tend to sell to people they know and like. Therefore companies are well advised to identify the strongest relationship with the decision makers at the target.

Relationships are also important for another reason. Many times targets are not available when you are interested, but become available at a later point in time. Thus building and fostering a strong set of relationships can prove to be a truly important asset for companies that want to grow via M&A.

Selecting the Deal Team

Once contact with the target company is established, one can start thinking about who are good candidates to be involved in the due diligence. The team size should be small to increase the effectiveness of the team. It is important that the team is very knowledgeable in conducting a financial, tax, legal, and operational due diligence. Strong negotiation skills are also essential.

What Are Potential Issues and Barriers?

As part of the initial discussions, companies will want to check into issues and barriers. Creating a list and classifying them into hurdles and true risks is paramount. As with hurdles one needs to define what it will take in financial and human resources (HR) to overcome those; however, with risks the situation is very different. Here the leadership team of the acquirer needs to make a decision whether they want to assume an identified risk or if this risk will jeopardize the deal.

Linking M&A Vision to Screening Results

Ultimately the last step in the strategic selection phase before moving on to due diligence is a sound check of the M&A vision versus the reality found in the initial discussions with the target. This is vitally important as it enables the company to define the goals for the due diligence, and sets the framework for negotiations and key performance indicators (KPIs) to test and probe in the next phase.

INTEGRATION DUE DILIGENCE

Based on the M&A vision and the preliminary discussions with the target, a due diligence approach is developed by the acquirer's deal team. It will at a minimum include due diligence on financial, tax, legal, and HR pension matters. For many companies, due diligence efforts such as environmental, operational, commercial, and information and communication technology are also must-haves. It largely depends on the industry the companies are operating in. A chemicals company typically conducts an environmental due diligence, while a manufacturing business will stress the importance of conducting an operational due diligence, and a consumer goods company will look toward a commercial due diligence.

In recent years, integration due diligence has become a more frequent and regular component of the standard due diligence process. The reason is simply that companies have understood that particularly in cross-border transactions the way an acquisition is integrated is essential to derive the value from the deal that was initially defined.

Essential parts of the integration due diligence are a detailed synergy review, and a cultural assessment of the organization, management, and employees, that is, how culture influences behavior and enables decisions to be taken. Additional focus should be put on the business processes and corporate governance. Identifying differences between the acquirer and target early on is pivotal in establishing the integration plan.

Synergy Analysis

The synergy review should be based on the strategic objectives of the transaction. This should trigger a review of each product and service offered, each regional or global market served, and every existing business process in order of importance. The review should focus on identifying synergies in revenues, operating cost, capital expenditure, financial terms, liquidity, and various taxes paid. Those synergies may come from the existing businesses or may be based on new strategies that the acquisition may enable.

Once companies know what they are looking for, it is essential to identify any hurdles and risks involved in implementing the synergies early on. A rough action and milestone plan with prerequisites and the position on the critical path toward implementation involving departments is also vital.

The end result of this review should be a high-level understanding of the expected financial impact on profitability and cash flow from the various synergies. There is typically a cost associated with achieving most synergies, so do take integration cost, additional employee benefits, and any dis-synergies into account. Integration due diligence teams are well advised to start verifying these initiatives with any data provided in the data room. The more robust these efforts are, the higher the likelihood that companies can tie the effects of synergies to profit and loss and balance sheet line items. This ability will enable financial modelers to evaluate the acquisition with and without synergistic effects, which is an essential step in pre-deal negotiations. After all, every acquirer will need synergies to pay for the cost of doing the deal and any premium they may need to pay based on the negotiations.

Thus understanding the stand-alone value of an acquisition and the value including synergies permits the vital assessment of how much of a premium and cost can be paid.

Cultural Review

Very early on, sometimes even before the due diligence but at the latest during due diligence, companies should start to think about the cultural differences and the way targets get decisions done. Whether an organization is team oriented or individualistic, has a hierarchical or flat management structure, manages information closely or communicates it widely, makes a huge difference in the culture of a company. Understanding where firms are alike and where they differ is essential not only for the integration but in our perspective much earlier when you start negotiating a deal. Figure 4.5 shows a good selection of behavior traits and lets readers adapt the structure to their needs.

Business Model, Process, and Organizational Differences

While synergies and culture build critical elements, it is also wise to use the information available in the data room to assess differences in business processes that may require in-depth understanding as to why the target has organized itself differently and what lessons can be drawn from that, or simply what changes and adjustments need to happen and what that may potentially create in change costs. The more pronounced the differences in key processes such as order to cash, make to deliver, procure to pay, plan to make (sales and operations planning) are, the greater the difficulties to integrate both companies. In addition, due diligence teams typically review the "hire to retire" and "record to report" processes; however, these tend to be easier to adjust and integrate.

Companies also pay close attention to business model differences. Furthermore, reviewing the degree of outsourcing is essential to understanding the integration implications for a proposed transaction. The greater the divergence of internalized versus outsourced value generation, the greater the effort to adjust existing business processes. If the acquired company has outsourced significant elements of its value creation and now the acquirer considers it favorable to insource these business processes, it will require a buildup of internal capacity to insource the business volume. If it is the other way around, the acquirer needs to be prepared to correctly size the acquired organization while adding resources that manage the outsourcing relationship.

In addition to analyzing business processes, companies are typically analyzing the size and the composition of the organization and its functions including the leadership span. It is therefore important to understand the resource allocation as deep as provided and answered in Q&A. Often this is a task that will only be possible to a certain degree.

The Leadership Team

Acquirers are well advised to request as much detail as possible. With regard to the leadership team it is essential to get to know all members and try to identify those who actually would be a good fit to stay with the joint business going forward. Meeting the management one level down from the leadership team is not possible most of the time. Acquirers will typically meet management-level staff only on a very selective basis, such as when visiting the premises for a tour of a plant or research and development center.

Similar to the business processes is corporate governance. Analyzing the set of rules that a company has given itself to govern the way it conducts its business is essential, specifically if they vary widely between acquirer and target. Managing this initiative jointly between those responsible for the integration and the legal due diligence work streams is essential to ensure that all aspects of the governance perspective are captured.

PRE-SIGNING

Having conducted the due diligence assignment, the decision to move forward with the bid is the next important step in the M&A life cycle. Most often this is when companies are granted exclusivity to negotiate with the target and walk the final steps toward signing a sale and purchase agreement (SPA). At this time the attention of the M&A and leadership team is entirely focused on getting the deal done.

This time can be used well by the integration team to prepare key elements of a communication to the organization for release right after the signing has occurred and to define the building blocks of the integration approach in more detail.

Establish the Foundation for Post-Signing Communication

Key elements to draft are the deal rationale—the "why" for the acquirer. For various stakeholder groups this is a key question, so it is essential to have a clear answer—plus it gives much-needed direction from the very beginning.

If the future business model is changing, the integration team should voice how and why it will change and what impact that will have. Communicate as much as can be announced at the time of signing. If more time is needed to orient people on the impact, then it is the perfect time to provide clarity on the time frame before the impact can be discussed with the relevant stakeholders.

Furthermore, an announcement needs to be made if interim management will be put in place to cover for target leadership members who will not transition to the new owner, or because the acquirer does not want to onboard them and would prefer to place their own leadership instead. If the latter is the case then that needs to be announced at signing. Here the following rule holds true: The earlier the acquirer can reach consensus on specific leadership positions and inform the organization and other stakeholders about these decisions, the better for the integration momentum.

Integration KPIs and incentives should be announced post-signing. Most important is to state that the incentive program needs to be self-funding. It should never be a cash investment by the acquirer.

In some cases, the success of the integration is a major factor to support the financial structure chosen to acquire the target. In these circumstances it is sensible to present some elements of the banking case to specific stakeholders to get their full buy-in.

Announcing the integration principles and the integration governance is of utmost importance, as employees will ask who from the leadership team will be responsible and manage the integration.

Establish the Foundation for Post-Signing Integration

The M&A vision, the due diligence findings, and the pre-signing negotiations all should support the deal rationale. These steps should build on each other so that by the time the acquirer has entered exclusive deal negotiations, it can verify the objectives for doing the deal with the synergies as they are initially evaluated, with the first thoughts on integrating the organization and business processes, and with the approach on how to build the integration post-signing. It is also the time to make the right choices about who should support the integration work streams and who can support the integration project team post-signing. These resources should not be nominated just yet but availability and fit should be assessed.

Thus one should collate all of the integration-relevant information gathered up to now:

▪ Business model, product and service information
▪ Organizational and functional information, business processes, geographical footprint
▪ Relevant key people
▪ Synergy evaluations

The next step is to lay it all out and establish the project layout for the initial integration approach. This exercise typically reveals that many data points still need to be filled post-signing once more data become available. Defining the open issues, question marks, critical executive decisions, and most importantly identifying the essential to-do's to get the integration approach advanced to an executable level is important at this stage.

POST-SIGNING

As part of the integration principles communicated at or just after signing, it is important to outline the permissible and especially the nonpermissible information that can be shared while a potential anti-trust investigation is conducted.

Defining Permitted Integration Activities Post-Signing during an Anti-Trust Investigation

Examples of critical activities to avoid during an anti-trust investigation are:

▪ Exchange of competitively sensitive information, and changing or influencing the competitive positioning of the "not yet fully owned" target through changes in pricing, discounts, commercial agreements, sales organization, and so on
▪ Integration or placement of personnel from either side in new positions in the respective other company
▪ Integration activities such as the integration of IT systems, infrastructure, supply chain, corporate identity, marketing initiatives, and so on

Examples of generally permitted activities during an anti-trust investigation are:

- Exchange of aggregated competitive-sensitive data during the due diligence process supporting valuation purposes only
- Agreements at arm's length between the acquirer and the target
- Basic information on integration planning for IT systems, infrastructure, supply chain integration, potential personnel redundancies, compensation schemes, HR policies; this can only be a one-sided information, as no discussions are permitted
- Planning of post-close corporate identity changes
- Any violation may be subject to penalties depending on the jurisdiction you are operating in

If the transaction is not subject to an anti-trust investigation, the time between signing and closing should be used to collate all findings from due diligence and deal negotiations and refine the initial integration plan and hit the road running on the day of signing.

Some targets may not allow joint integration activities until deal closing. In these cases, M&A negotiation teams may want to see if this position is carved in stone, that is, nonnegotiable, or if this rule can be eased by putting a clean team (see Figure 12.2) in place.

A clean team approach is typically an approach used during an anti-trust investigation. Both acquirer and target agree that a group of external advisors receives permission to start analyzing integration activities while the anti-trust investigation is going on. This helps to jump-start the detailed integration planning. The findings are only to be shared with both

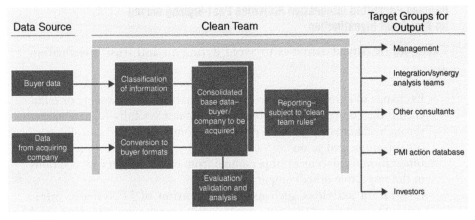

FIGURE 12.2   Clean Team

parties once anti-trust clearance has been provided and official permission is granted.

Holding the Executive Alignment Meeting

The most important event post-signing is to hold an executive alignment meeting. This is a high-powered meeting of the executives and key managers with some members of the executive leadership team (depending on the size and importance of the transaction) to ensure that everyone has a common understanding. Key elements (see Figure 12.3) that will be presented and discussed in a Q&A session are:

- The deal rationale
- The transaction objectives and integration KPIs
- The impact on the business model
- Rules and regulations of the integration process
- Key messages that should be deployed throughout the organization
- Integration governance
- Interim management, management changes, and leadership announcements
- Envisioned Day One corporate design changes
- The implications of the banking case

The next step is to drive communication proactively and to conduct a stakeholder analysis. The purpose of the stakeholder analysis is to listen to

FIGURE 12.3 Executive Alignment Discussion Topics

the concerns of the various groups such as customers, distributors, suppliers, employees, shareholders, local authorities, regulators, press, banking and rating agency analysts, and industry bodies.

Key messages from the executive alignment meeting need to be repurposed to address the various concerns and questions of these stakeholder groups and educate them about the strategic intent and the objectives as much as is suitable.

Setting Up the Integration Management Office

Furthermore, the integration project management office (IMO) needs to be established and a kick-off event needs to be organized to mark the start of the actual project work. The first step here is to set up the post-merger integration project. This initiative entails establishing the various teams, team directory, master calendar, central document repository (e.g., prolonging the data room or setting up a SharePoint portal), and defining the communication etiquette. Additionally the IMO needs to start managing the overall integration process, establish meeting schedules with core teams and steering committee, define work plans, set goals, communicate the KPIs, and manage escalations.

Alongside the initial setup, reporting routines are established and assist in monitoring the progress and the project risks.

Revisiting Synergies and Managing the Synergy Working Session

With regard to synergies, the deal and integration teams need to expand the initial synergy evaluation efforts. Post-signing and post-anti-trust approval, more access to data and exchange among people from both sides—the acquirer and the target—is available.

Experience has shown that a solid synergy template is structured into two parts. It is based on (1) an executive summary presenting a good synopsis of the synergy including timing and financial impact summary, and (2) a detailed financial evaluation.

In detail, the executive summary includes for its descriptive part:

- A description of the synergy
- A brief and clear action catalog of most important implementation activities
- A description of assumptions (market, industry, operational conditions)
- A description of hurdles and risks
- A list of departments responsible for implementation

▪ Prerequisites and positions on a critical path (dependencies on other synergies)

The synergy timing on the executive summary shows:

▪ When work can commence on implementing the synergy
▪ How long the implementation will take
▪ Total months to realization
▪ Number of months to break-even
▪ The probability of implementation over a number of predefined time horizons

The financial summary of the executive summary shows:

▪ The effect on revenue, operating cost, financing cost, and how these effects impact EBIT and EBITDA
▪ The implementation costs as they pertain to operating and financing costs but also to any capital spending that needs to occur
▪ The expected cumulative effect on cash flow and profitability (EBIT).

The synergy calculation template is divided into three parts:

1. A detailed calculation of the specific synergy benefits on revenues, operating and financing cost, as well as capital expenditure savings, effects on liquidity savings, and tax benefits.
2. The implementation cost.
3. Any capital expenditure required to implement the synergy.

The P&L and balance sheet effect section includes:

▪ The link between the synergistic effects and the P&L line items
▪ The balance sheet line items
▪ A remarks section where detailed assumptions can be recorded for later use in the synergy case defense and prioritization

Post-signing it is imperative to revisit the initial synergy thoughts that were hopefully detailed out to a better degree during due diligence. Now, as much more data and access to personnel and experience from both parties is available, a formal revisiting and recalculation of the synergy calculations is needed.

Following the template described above we will be able to prioritize each and every synergy and prepare a summary of the entire collection of synergies to the senior leadership team to review and provide guidance on priorities. This typically happens at the midpoint between signing and closing and is the second most important event during the integration of the acquisition.

The synergy working session is typically organized as an off-site meeting with the purpose of discussing stakeholder analysis findings, prioritizing synergies, and defining the transition teams. At this workshop, key executives and the leadership team meet most likely for the first time, so it is important that the meeting is well organized, and provides room for both sides to align and bond while taking the first steps as a joint management team and organization.

Framing the meeting with the stakeholder analysis sets the scene for the integration challenges that lie ahead of the team. A stakeholder analysis is a review of all the concerns and questions the various stakeholders in the company may have. This typically starts with customers, suppliers, and employees, and continues to include unions, municipalities, regulators, and media. Reviewing and validating the key synergies in detail, their setup, timing, and financial impact, and then prioritizing them connects the corporate strategy with the M&A vision. It also reinforces the expectation that the integration needs to unlock the positive strategic and financial impact expected from the deal while building internal consensus.

Last, following such an in-depth synergy discussion, the leadership team will be in a much better position to choose the right candidates for the transition teams that will implement the synergies.

The event also bears the chance to create a strong alignment of the leadership group and may prove to be pivotal for the team as such. The simple ability to bring the two companies' executives together to socialize and work in a neutral setting is an excellent starting point.

Stakeholder Analysis–Based Communication

"Why is a stakeholder analysis of interest?" companies may ask. The answer is relatively simple—proven results. Listening to what customers have to say is the first thing we learn in business, and listening to stakeholders during acquisition integration apparently is treated differently.

Experience shows that stakeholder analysis faces some steep objections from executives.

Sometimes we see blind arrogance, as executives believe they know everything stakeholders will say. Other times we see fear as executives are scared to hear the responses, and then we experience apathy as executives do not care, or do not want to know in order to not have to respond. Again and again we experience myopic cost-cutting as executives will spend huge sums for a deal but very little to make it work.

Let's draw the attention of those opposed to stakeholder analysis to the grim reality of M&A integration. Initially there are many more questions than answers. "Business as usual" no longer exists and the further one is removed from the decision-making power, the lower is the tolerance for ambiguity. In the absence of frequent credible communication, stakeholders will make up their own version of the reality. Thus executives are well advised to be mindful of what stakeholders think and especially of what they say!

They are also better off if they anticipate rude questions and can answer with predeveloped core messages that reiterate the business case and provide targeted information to eliminate fear and anxiety. Being visible and addressing key concerns with consistent messages and "talking points" in a genuine two-way dialogue with all stakeholder groups is what creates momentum and buy-in and moves an acquirer toward its set integration goals.

Thus the concept of a focus group–based stakeholder analysis is what provides insights and enables understanding of issues, questions, resistance, and barriers, which enables crafting of messages and providing context and answers. If these messages are refined and addressed to the respective stakeholder group using the appropriate channel, venue, and timing, then true dialogue happens and employees from both the acquirer and the target will witness an upward feedback trend with communication that moves and excites people to support the strategic goals of the deal. It moves everyone from a "Why me?" mentality to a "How can I help?" philosophy.

Cultural Alignment

In the section on integration due diligence, we introduced a very basic template to assess behavioral differences in companies. Its simplicity is the reason it is such an easy-to-apply tool to understand where true cultural issues may occur when starting the integration of two organizations.

Using this template in a recent example, we identified very quickly in the first day a major difference in the way both organizations got to decisions. The role of the chapter author was to oversee the management of the project for the client including the cultural alignment work stream. The way the buyer and the seller ran their operations had created two very different realities.

The acquirer ran a V-shaped organizational style (in essence, an upside-down pyramid) that was focused on providing subordinates with the skills and capabilities to manage their responsibilities. This modern behavioral approach met the classical top-down organization where most decisions could only be taken when the business unit manager signed off on them.

By the looks of it, this was a situation that could have lent itself to a major culture clash. Yet using a personal profiling tool that provided insights to the various individuals involved about themselves, their understanding of their role and their function within the system enabled those managers to see clearly what needed to be changed to adopt a more cohesive way of working within the new culture rather than turning against it. It also provided insights to open up and trust the process that accepting and adopting this change was for the better. It ended up deescalating fear and anxiety and made the organization more robust to take on a significant growth not seen in years.

Changing the culture meant conducting group workshops and one-on-one coaching. However, over a period of six months, the organization, aided by a campaign about the acquirer's values, was able to adopt the new behaviors and manage the phenomenal growth opportunity.

Planning Day One and Beyond

During signing and closing there is more to do than time to do it in. Planning for Day One therefore is an essential step. Day One activities are all tasks that need to be done to onboard the newly acquired company and to ensure that the integration and joint business operations will work smoothly.

The identification process involves the work stream leads for the project who are required to:

- Review briefly the due diligence report for relevant task input
- Identify from existing Day One task lists the relevant issues
- Expand the list by important additional tasks
- Participate in a brief workshop to identify any cross dependencies of prior defined tasks and actions

The Day One tasks now need to be prioritized for their business criticality, timing, and monetary impact. The decision grid of planning criteria shown in Figure 12.4 will enable the IMO to assess and qualify the tasks accordingly.

- Priority for integration (business-critical, important, useful)
- Integration phase—when to address (Day One, first 100 days, implementation phase)
- Synergy relevance (resistance to implementation and monetary impact)
- Scheduling of implementation (responsibility, execution, dates)

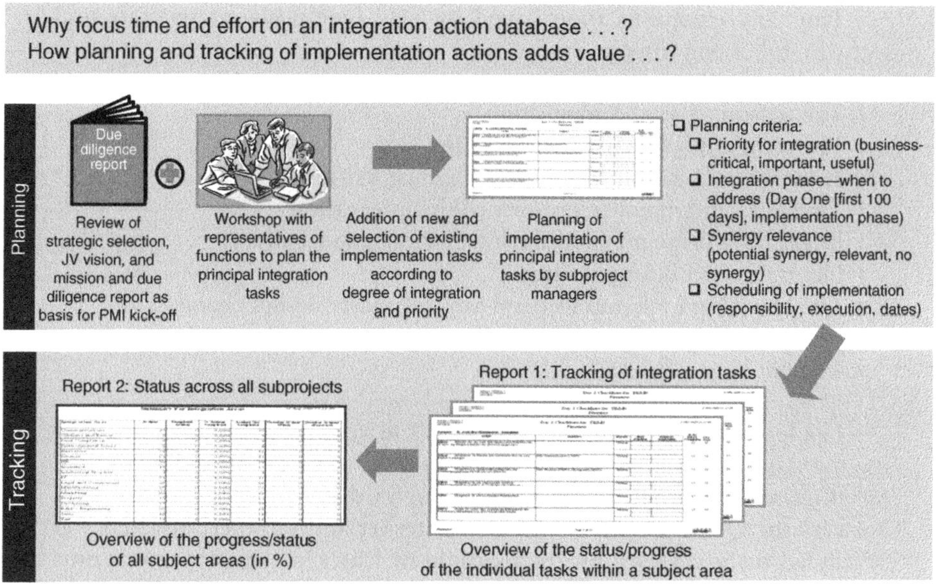

FIGURE 12.4 Day One Task Identification and Management

After this step has been performed, it's all down to execution and frequent weekly tracking and progress reporting. It is literally that simple, and contrary to widespread opinion, exercising this rigor takes out a solid portion of difficulty in integrations.

In addition to the initiatives around Day One tasks, we need to plan the Day One with relevant communications, announcements, town hall meetings, and press coverage. The first day is essential as it lets companies build momentum for the integration ahead and at the same time sets the tone, integration principles, and governance for the weeks and months ahead. It is the event where we onboard all other stakeholders who have not been involved in the planning of the integration and thus it is vital that it be well organized.

We will talk about the integration team launch in the post-signing section and explain this important third event (after the executive alignment and synergy working session).

For now, companies need to focus on organizing Day One. The communication planning typically goes back to the M&A vision and revisits what has been the strategic intent of acquiring, and the link between the M&A vision and the corporate strategy.

Thus any communication issued on Day One needs to reiterate and state the following topics:

- The reason to do the acquisition
- The economic objectives of the deal
- How the acquisition will impact the business model
- Timelines and major milestones of the integration
- Integration principles and the integration governance
- Integration KPIs and incentives
- The Day One look and feel and any corporate design changes
- Presenting any new leadership team members
- The banking case

Leadership teams need to be prepared and oriented about their role during the day, speeches and announcements need to be developed, town hall meetings and video streaming of the same in distant locations organized, answers for Q&A prepared, websites (Internet and intranet) updated and scheduled to be released on the morning of Day One, employee welcome packs prepared, as well as customer, supplier, media communication established, scheduled, and released.

Importance of Establishing an Integration Performance-Driven Incentive Plan

Establishing an incentive plan next to existing plans is always a discussion with the senior leadership team.

Let's take a different point of view. What if the incentive plan would have to be self-funding? In other words, it would only enable participants to benefit when and if they generate the predefined benefits from those synergies. Such a scenario would surely motivate and drive the integration according to the integration goals and the M&A vision of the deal.

Now the next discussion circles around those who are fully dedicated to the integration and those who are requested to split their time between the day-to-day work and integration tasks.

For those who work the day-to-day business and are involved in the integration, the logical argument is to split incentives based on the time spent in the day-to-day operations versus the integration. Is this always fair? No, it is not! Economic benefits are often not correlated 1:1 to the time invested. However, it is a pragmatic way as it would be far too complex to identify the economic benefit of a specific number of hours worked on one versus another topic. For those who dedicate their contribution to either the daily operations or only the integration work performed, their incentives should connect to those activities. This suggestion predicates that there will be an integration-related incentive.

Importance of Closing Activities

Purchase price allocation and closing accounts are typical topics that are started after closing has happened, mostly for legal reasons.

There are companies that take a different point of view. They start a preliminary assessment during due diligence from the point of view to assess any potential pitfalls. This does not mean they perform a purchase price allocation, it means they are looking for value leaks that they will use during negotiations.

Given that "gun jumping" can be very costly, we recommend that, at the most, companies start selecting their professional service providers to perform purchase price allocation and closing accounts during signing and closing but wait on the execution until closing has actually happened. Gun jumping is defined by the Department of Justice as premerger coordination and integration activities such as providing price or terms to be offered to customers or even start negotiations. Joint pre-close planning regarding products, distributors, or employees is also prohibited during an ongoing anti-trust review.

POST-CLOSING

Closing is the most important milestone as it marks the date of successfully completing the acquisition. Now is the time to execute and integrate. A major milestone for this important day was already prepared in the weeks before the planning of Day One. Now it is time to bring all this planning to life.

As the first day unfolds, announcements are made, and employees, customers, suppliers, and the press are informed about the acquisition and the impact it will have on everyone. It is essential to create this upbeat positive momentum in all stakeholders. After all, this transaction is going to add value to the business and therefore motivating everyone to contribute is a major part of it.

The next step in the execution of the Day One activities is the execution of the "integration team launch."

Executing the Integration Team Launch

The "integration team launch" is a structured task–oriented, two-day, off-site planning session of all integration teams. Its purpose is to prepare the integration plans for each synergy, infuse the group with team spirit and momentum, and get the integration off to a fast start.

It is a highly focused session during which the functional integration teams draft milestone plans and activities for capturing the value of each synergy.

The objective of these plans is to establish accountability for results, provide focus on high-priority activities, define the performance metrics of each team, and identify the key communications from teams. The plans focus on:

- The deliverables and decisions
- Additional data needs beyond existing information
- Key responsibilities to implement the synergy
- Reviewing and potentially revisiting the implementation time frames for synergies and integration tasks
- The required analysis to be performed
- Any cross-dependencies and respective communication that need to be managed
- Formulating a recommendation on how to move forward
- Definition of executive team actions and timelines
- Creating a well-documented output as the basis for the IMO to collate and prepare the integration plan

The agenda of the meeting includes an opening and welcome session with a member of the executive team, followed by a briefing of the deal rationale and the ambitions as well as the strategic context of the acquisition before opening the floor for Q&A. Afterward, it is all about setting the expectations of the remaining two days and getting the teams to work and develop the synergy implementation plans.

The result of this initiative will be a solid implementation plan for the synergies that matter. If one does it the conventional way and leaves the building of the synergy implementation plans to the IMO and individual coordination with the work streams, one needs to calculate at a minimum three to four weeks. Think about the momentum that can be generated by doing this planning work differently. It enables the teams to focus much more time on getting to the heart of the synergy issues. See Figure 12.5.

Importance of Successfully Managing the First 100 Days

Managing the progress in the first 100 days, communicating with all stakeholders and aligning the cultures, which means aligning the important behavior traits, decision-making processes, and showing executive presence

Company ABC/Company XYZ
Expedited Planning Charts

Page____ of ____

Transition Team: _____

Value Driver: _____

Deliverable/Action Item	Responsibility	Prerequisite	Cross-Team Dependency	Expected Completion Date

Executive team issues:

FIGURE 12.5   Integration Milestone Planner

are extremely important. We typically experience that employees, suppliers, and customers all sit initially on the sidelines and watch what happens. A well-defined communication strategy that engages stakeholders and gets them to join in is what divides successful from unsuccessful integrations.

Stakeholders need to be pulled in. They need to be motivated by showcasing the success of quick wins, convinced through communicating the new vision to participate and be part of the strategic drive forward. A frequent stakeholder analysis is therefore important for the leadership team to understand what is on the stakeholders' minds, what concerns, fears, and anxieties exist, to react appropriately and drive clarity and eliminate confusion and rumors.

Similarly important is the alignment of the cultures. We define culture as behaviors of an organization that are derived by its vision and values; mainly, however, culture is defined by the ways the leadership team is exemplifying those values in their behavior on a daily basis. Differing behaviors between the acquirer and target need to be aligned. To prompt change, the prevailing behaviors need to be experienced, because physical experience is what creates change. Written and oral communication can support the change process but what moves the needle is experiencing the culture change.

Therefore a series of workshops and one-on-one work to communicate and prepare culture change is needed. Team meetings, town hall meetings, and company events will support this.

Furthermore, managing the progress, supporting conflict resolution, escalating problems and risks to the steering committee, and communicating progress are important actions in demonstrating to everyone involved that the integration process is actively managed and monitored.

Transition from Project Phase to Operational Responsibility

I am always asked when is the best time to transition from a project organization to the day-to-day business in M&A integration. The answer is it depends. It could be 6, 9, or 12 months, depending on the implementation stage of key synergies and integration activities.

In principle, once the large majority of synergies has been implemented, it is time to transition from a project organization into the operations. Not all synergies will be implemented by that time and that is absolutely all right. There just needs to be a time when the operating units take over responsibility to implement the remaining synergies that belong to their business. The same holds true for integration activities that are not linked to synergistic values. Most of the initiatives that had an early priority should be implemented by the time the transition is executed and those that are still in implementation mode need to be transferred.

In order to transition the open synergies and integration initiatives to operations, the project organization needs to prepare:

- A clear documentation of the intended synergy or activity
- A history of the initiatives and actions taken
- The degree of implementation
- The integration cost and economic benefits achieved to date and the desired respectively budgeted objectives
- All project plans, milestones, progress and risk reports, and the desired implementation date
- The people involved and their personal time commitment to finishing the initiatives
- The responsibility at the leadership team

Most important is that the initiatives are transferred over into the budget responsibility of the operating unit and thus it is ensured that the unit has a sufficient budget to finish the started activities and respectively gets additional budget to implement the synergy and integration initiatives.

Furthermore, it is important that the operating unit retain the people who are already involved in executing the initiatives to facilitate the ownership process. In addition, it is most important that the executive sponsor responsible for the initiatives ensures that the transition is as smooth as possible and that transitioning them from the project organization to the operating unit does not change the set targets.

As part of the transition period, the project organization should be asked to pull together a lessons learned presentation, which transparently and openly talks about what was learned during the process, whether positive or negative. Those learnings should be presented to the steering committee, prepared for the leadership of business units, and saved on a secured part of the intranet as a learning repository for future transactions. It may in specific cases also make sense to organize a roadshow to inform a selected group of people within the organization.

Most important, however, is to build a repository of all people who participated on the project including bios and responsibilities, so that the organization can tap into this pool of integration veterans whenever needed.

Post-M&A Integration Board Reviews

The chief financial officer typically will ask for a review of the success of the integration one year and often also two years following the transaction close. This is an important step for the organization as it will demonstrate what successes were achieved during the project phase of the integration and what successes were retained once the project phase ended and the responsibility was transitioned into the line organization. This second review is often not as easy because, with the transition into the line organization, everything becomes a bit blurrier. However, as stated before, it is essential that the line organization retain the synergy targets and integration initiatives and track as much as possible the execution of the same. This will be difficult particularly when the organization is changing rapidly because of serial acquisitions that happen in quick succession and trigger changes to established synergies.

At a minimum, organizations need to track the economic value added on a high level, such as growth in operating profitability and return on equity.

Importance of Corporate Success Celebrations

As a last topic, I would like to stress the importance of corporate success celebrations throughout the entire M&A life cycle. Regardless whether that happens at the signing, the closing, during the first 100 days, or at the close of the project, celebrating successes is an important element in keeping the forward momentum and keeping the people involved in the organization motivated for a time that always is more demanding than anything they typically experience during their regular daily routine. Please keep that in mind.

CHAPTER CHECKLIST

Key questions and issues companies need to consider during the strategic selection of M&A targets to ensure a smooth integration post-deal:

- What do companies need to best perform integration due diligence?
- What items should companies focus on in preparing post-signing communications?
- What elements are needed to run the three major events (executive alignment, synergy working session, and integration team launch) in any successful integration?
- How to prepare for Day One?
- How to manage the first 100 days?
- How to transition the PMI project to the final owner in the operational organization?
- Why are post-M&A board reviews important?

CHAPTER 13

Managing Post-Merger Integration Globally

Eitan Grosbard

CHAPTER LEARNING OBJECTIVES—IN THIS CHAPTER, YOU WILL LEARN:

➤ Present the leading practices that derive from organizing and managing the post-merger integration (PMI) process properly (as opposed to letting the process manage us)

➤ Present approaches for managing a PMI process in a cross-border scenario

➤ Present and discuss the concept of PMI governance and emphasize the project's managerial structure, roles and responsibilities, meetings, management routines, communication and reporting lines, and so on

➤ Assemble the "all-star team"—what is in our power to create the most competent team

➤ Provide an initial checklist for setting up the PMI governance structure

➤ Define key tasks and routines that should be taken care of as the governance is set and the organization starts working accordingly

CHAPTER SUMMARY

This chapter begins with setting the ground for and explaining the nature of the cross-border PMI process. The chapter will continue with an in-depth explanation of the cross-border PMI process and its three components: "routine"—the generic elements that recur in each PMI process; "tailor-made"—specific and unique elements that are relevant for a specific PMI process and not all processes; and the "be prepared for every scenario" element—where the post-merger managing team needs to be ready for every situation that may come along.

The chapter will close with the GPMIP Acquisition Integration Framework, which describes how to transition from the due diligence phase into the post-merger phase. The chapter will present how to set up the integration management office alongside the needed governance to run this type of project, including project structure, routines, fields of work, and so on. In addition to this, the chapter will describe how to kick off this type of project, including the integration approach and how to define it, how to keep track of PMI progress, to navigate it in the right direction, to allocate risks and mitigate them, and so on.

INTRODUCTION

Managing a post-merger integration (PMI) process is challenging enough, but adding the cross-border and cross-cultural elements makes the success of this process seem almost impossible.

In reality, this is not the case. Tailoring two companies from across the globe into one is doable, but it must be coordinated and planned in detail.

However, planning is not enough; there are a variety of additional factors that must be taken into consideration. The process should be managed and a clear governance structure should be put into place in order to maintain the integration moving forward. Also, a significant emphasis should be put on the soft sides of the integration such as people, culture, and communication, alongside other elements such as strategy, business, and organization.

It's actually a mixture of soft skills that should be applied to soften, convince, and move this process forward and a toolbox that will be utilized to properly manage the process.

In order to focus on both worlds in an effective way, in this chapter, we will emphasize the following elements: PMI governance and structure, meeting routines, global PMI management and integration decision making, process strategy, and assembly of a capable multifunctional global team that will execute the plan, tools, activities, and so on.

Managing Cross-Border Post-Merger Integration Projects

One would believe that managing global post-merger integration (PMI) processes is no different than managing local PMI projects. The project manager must follow the same project management methodologies, tools, and routines and the outcomes will be the same.

Right? . . . Not quite so.

Managing a global PMI project is a complex task comprised of many elements. To succeed, one cannot only focus on the straightforward project management components but also be sensitive to different areas such as strategy and business alongside managing people locally and remotely, paying attention to corporate and national culture, understanding business nuances on a global scale, and so on.

Global cross-border PMI projects are multidisciplinary and multidimensional by nature. They are led by one or more project managers managing a team of dedicated experts spread over several sites. As mentioned, the difference in mentality accompanied with time zone differences, language barriers, different points of view related to how a project should be managed, and more, are all part of this complexity, but are only a fragment of the complete picture.

This is why the PMI leader/manager should not only be competent and fit the job description above but at the same time should focus on more than the "trivial" and be able to act in every scenario he confronts.

So, how complex is it to manage a PMI project?

This chapter presents the global cross-border PMI process and debates the elements that distinguish a good process from others.

The Integration Setting Components

Cross-company organizational processes are usually broken down into the typical milestones of a project, including: (1) exploration/study, (2) high-level planning, (3) detailed planning, (4) execution, (5) monitoring results, and (6) corrections/adjustments.

Managing a cross-border PMI process holds more than the generic cross-company process mentioned above, mainly because no PMI process resembles another, especially in the cross-border M&A environment. Comparing these two types of processes reveals that there are many common elements, including: the way the project is managed, the monitoring mechanisms, the structure, and so on, but when going into details, each PMI process is unique and holds different characteristics from others, including integration approach, people, politics, culture, business approach, and so on. These elements, along with others, impact the PMI process and lead toward different scenarios—thus the process and end result are different every time.

A typical post-merger integration process is comprised of three components, as shown in Figure 13.1.

Initiating the PMI process should start with a defined state of mind. One should acknowledge that aside from the fact that not all processes are the same, managing these processes cannot happen on autopilot mode. There are three components that accompany every PMI process and assist the integration architects to allocate the load of work in different conceptual buckets.

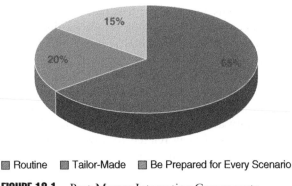

☒ Routine   ☒ Tailor-Made   ☒ Be Prepared for Every Scenario

FIGURE 13.1   Post-Merger Integration Components

The first component, the *routine*, is weighted approximately 65%–70% of the PMI project volume and consists of generic elements that recur in each process no matter which companies are involved, such as setting and managing the integration governance, dealing with the organizational structure, reporting lines, meeting routines, mapping and mitigation of risks, setting of key performance indicators (KPIs), and so on. These elements are usually "packaged" as manuals, checklists, playbooks, or routines and are improved from one process to the next. They are generic by nature, and incorporate tasks and processes that occur in *every* PMI process, regardless of the industry, location of the acquiring and acquired companies, or the type of acquisition. Whether the acquiring and acquired companies are American, French, or Indian, or if it's the Internet, plastic, or pharmaceutical industries (or other industries as well), signatory rights for bank accounts should be transferred, compensation and benefits of employees should be analyzed, key customers should be mapped, and other activities should be taken care of.

In order to meet the "routine" component and execute the PMI process properly, one should acknowledge that: First, this type of process is, in essence, managing a complex and challenging project. The complexity and the challenge both derive from the multidisciplinary, multidimensional, culturally diverse, and geographically spread nature of the process, and business-related complexities as well.

Second, this type of project deals with all (not some, not most, but *all*) of an organization's components. Therefore, many employees at a variety of organizational levels are involved in the process and the main challenges are:

1. Coordinating all parties, getting their buy-in, and moving their areas of responsibility forward. Areas might be of functional essence (e.g., human resources, finance, IT, operations, etc.) as well as mission-based (e.g., strategy, rebranding, cultural alignment, communication teams,

etc.). This is usually handled by the project manager, who is managing remotely and matrix based.

2. Not falling into internal political traps.
3. Emphasizing that these processes are *always* all about people.

The second component, known as the *tailor-made* component, is approximately 20%–25% of the PMI project's volume of activity. It is tailored specifically for each acquisition and its own unique situation. This component should be addressed differently than the routine component as it should start with an initial assessment of the acquiring company, the acquired company, and the differences between the two in a variety of areas, including business elements (strategy, products portfolio, and sales methods), people matters (including culture, communication methods, organizational structure and hierarchy), and the remaining areas (including IT, operations, sales, marketing, finance, and so on).

The sequence of assessing the two companies and defining the gaps between them followed by a detailed work plan to close these gaps usually starts at the due diligence phase (exploration) followed by planning the PMI process in between the pre-signing and pre-closing phase.

The outputs of this assessment will be different in each PMI process we conduct, therefore the implications deriving out of these outputs will influence the PMI execution differently every time.

The outputs will provide an answer to the questions "What should the integration approach be? What integration pace should be applied? What will the integration intensity be (complete integration, partial integration, etc.)? How will we approach the difference of culture?" And so on. This will allow the PMI practitioners to direct their efforts better, thus becoming more focused and efficient.

* * *

The third component, called *be prepared for every scenario*, comprises the rest (between 5% and 15% of the PMI project's volume of activity). This might be the smallest component, but its impact is the highest as it holds the scenarios one is not ready for (e.g., unplanned strike of employees, external political pressure that may impact business decision making such as closing of plants, massive resignation of employees, etc.). Therefore, special attention should be devoted to understanding and planning for these potential scenarios and moreover the importance of managing them correctly and mitigating the risks.

Usually, these "surprises" are in the same recurring areas, such as:

1. **Business-oriented surprises.** It is not unusual to have to face a large or central customer that suddenly decides to leave, and by doing so, impacts the merged company's sales forecast and expected synergies.

2. **People-related surprises.** For example, key people who leave the company earlier than expected where the knowledge they hold is not transferred to someone else.
3. **Regulation-related surprises.** There are cases when the time estimate for regulatory approval is optimistic and the many "road bumps" ahead are underestimated.

One cannot foresee all scenarios but it is definitely possible to estimate them, and classify the potential risks while mitigating them accordingly. This component will be addressed in detail later in this chapter.

The Acquisition Integration Framework™ (AIF)

As discussed, it is difficult to prepare for *all* possible PMI scenarios. The 5%–15% mentioned earlier relates to situations one cannot always anticipate, and one or several of them will emerge at some point in time. These situations happen to be the most impactful and sadly enough also the most negative situations in the PMI phase, but with proper, detailed preparation, the PMI planning process may foresee most of the obstacles and be helpful in being better prepared.

In order to professionally support all the PMI challenges, including *routine*, *tailor-made*, and *be prepared for every scenario* components, a framed program is established to capture all actions needed to be taken in the planning and execution phases of the PMI.

In order to manage the *routine* preparations and tasks, to get ready for the different *tailor-made* specifics, and to try to anticipate most of the *be prepared for every scenario* components, Global PMI Partners has developed the Acquisition Integration Framework™ (see Figure 13.2). This framework provides a 360-degree solution that completely supports these components and activities. The framework and its components will be presented in detail over the next pages.

This framework deals with a variety of areas of practice, including:

- A clear definition of the integration approach
- Clear understanding and definitions of the process and supporting governance, including appointment of leading executives, defining the integrations, reporting structure, and setting PMI meetings and routines
- Concrete plans that build up the overall PMI plan (e.g., high-level plan, key people retention plan, key customers retention plan, communication plan, etc.)

GPMIP's *Acquisition Integration Framework™*, and the underlying tools and templates, provide structure throughout complex global M&A integration programs

GPMIP *Acquisition Integration Framework™ (AIF)*:

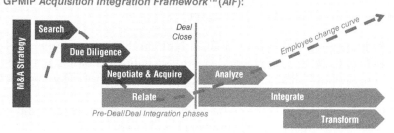

* End-to-end M&A life cycle in 7 intuitive sequential phases—GPMIP expertise focused on the due diligence and integration phases
* Symbolic change curve represents the "people journey," critical throughout M&A and often lowest around close
* Pragmatic, delivering rigor and detail while allowing the flexibility necessary for each specific integration
* Adaptable to clients' internal methodologies, approach, tools, and culture

FIGURE 13.2 GPMIP Acquisition Integration Framework™

■ Other supporting tools and areas of practice that complement the PMI planning activities, including matrices and other tools to measure the process effectivity, risk mapping and mitigation, synergies quantification, quick wins allocation, and so on

All these elements together are utilized to monitor, validate, and promote PMI success.

The overall framework relates to seven sequential phases of the end-to-end M&A life cycle. This chapter describes the phases relevant to PMI activities only.

The integration planning activity usually starts after the due diligence assessment has ended. The due diligence phase (presented in Chapter 9) is used as an exploratory study or starting point and the information collected is the basis for the PMI planning.

The PMI process is captured in the Relate, Analyse, and Integrate phases (described in Figure 13.1). In order to put these phases in the right context, let's go back to the due diligence phase and provide a clear description of this phase.

DUE DILIGENCE

As previously presented, the due diligence is strongly connected with the PMI process. The due diligence, by essence, is the basis for PMI planning and must be fully utilized to start building the integration plan. A list of activities and actions are being executed at this point in time and their outputs will tremendously affect the PMI planning later on.

Activities that are already being taken care of in the due diligence and will impact the PMI include (among others):

- **Risk mapping and mitigation plan** (both on the organizational level as well as work stream by work stream), including definition of a mitigation plan and highlighting red flags that can impact the go/no-go decision making
- Initial *synergies analysis* and definition of revenues synergies and cost synergies as well as quick wins, which will be examined and challenged later on in the PMI phase
- Initial **compatibility assessment** of the two companies, including elements such as strategy, business plans, culture assessment, organizational structure, compensation and benefits, and so on, focusing on business as well as soft human elements
- **Key employees analysis** and short-stay employees, creation of a retention plan for both tiers, and clear definitions of knowledge mapping and transfer
- **Key customers analysis** including actual sales, relationships with customers, key accounts, establishment of key customers map, and an approach plan to secure them

RELATE

After finalizing the due diligence and distilling its findings, the understanding of what type of integration process and approach we're encountering, emerges more clearly.

In the Relate subphase, this understanding is translated into an actual plan. The PMI leadership is given an indication on how to proceed, and this progress occurs on three parallel fronts:

1. Define the suitable integration process that should be conducted—thus defining the *integration approach*.
2. Start laying the foundations of the integration process, in particular the *process governance*, including: project's structure, managerial routines, and reporting lines. Setting up the IMO (integration management office) is essential to kick off the process. The IMO tasks include: defining playbooks and methods, facilitating team kick-offs, and setting the governance and reporting framework.

3. Initial work should be invested in setting up the different PMI plans, mechanisms, and monitoring tools, and putting them in motion. The plan for the first 100 days should include: human capital, finance, technology, corporate services, marketing and sales, operations, integration plans, geographical integration plans, communication plan (internal and external), and culture assimilation plan. In parallel, pre-close additional integration mechanisms should be applied: risks and mitigation actions, synergies and quick wins, D1–100 action plan, mobilization, and communication.

Integration Approach

In order to initiate the PMI activities, there is a need to understand what type of integration the companies are heading to. There is a huge difference between leading a quick business-oriented, cost-cutting, and hostile integration, and leading a balanced, peaceful, people-oriented integration. These two examples lie on opposite sides of the scale.

The *integration approach* (Figure 13.3) consists of a set of elements that provide the acquirer with a framework to define the integration's direction and the most suitable approach in the specific situation.

In a cross-border context, these elements should be weighted differently. The integration approach framework consists of the following elements:

- **Strategy and business compatibility:** Strategic fit, business model compatibility, business continuity

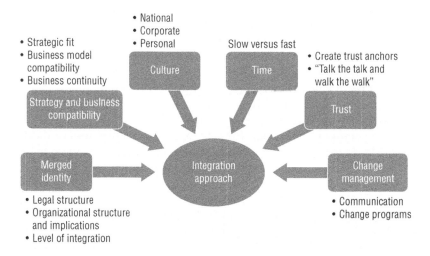

FIGURE 13.3 Integration Approach (Key Factors)

The acquiring company should start the integration process with a clear and defined strategic direction and roadmap. The strategy will be the guiding star for the overall integration process. Any changes to the business model come out of the strategic roadmap and a plan to keep business continuity while leveraging the potential cross-sales and up-sales opportunities, thus enhancing revenue synergies.*

■ **Merged company's identity:** Legal structure, organizational structure and implications, level of integration

Once the strategy is clear, the legal structure should be defined. Which company holds the other? Which legal entity is being liquidated? The legal structure should be carefully communicated as it is not always a clear signal to employees and other stakeholders as to "who's running the show." The legal structure could be more driven from a tax perspective.

In addition, the organization chart should be defined and communicated, who is still working in the merged company, who isn't, who is reporting to whom, which organizational units are to be closed, and so on.

The last point would be the level of integration; on the scale from "keeping as a stand-alone" to "fully integrated" there's a range of alternatives. The acquirer should define the integration's vision.

■ **Culture[1]:** National, corporate, personal

Culture is often an area that gets neglected. Management teams put an emphasis on business-related areas and tend to dismiss culture. After most integrations, the lessons learned argue that culture is a crucial factor that must be handled.

When discussing the concept of culture, the three layers that are usually discussed are: national culture, organizational culture, and personal culture. In cross-border transactions, the organizational culture layer takes a larger portion than the other two layers.

An assessment of the different layers of culture and the gaps deriving out of this assessment in addition to cultural commonalities will provide a better understanding of the culture status and a modus operandi within the integration process.

■ **Time:** Slow process versus rapid process

The common approach in M&A and PMI is "the sooner the better"; thus the integration process should be expedited and completed within 100 days, when most of the integration efforts should be done. In practice, most of the time, "fast is slow and slow is fast." In the context of defining the integration approach, there is a need to decide which changes will happen faster and which can happen at a slower pace.

---

* Also known as "top line synergies."

Appointing a management team, defining the organizational structure, getting to financial alignment, setting new email addresses, and so on, usually happen fast. New location, working processes, compensation and benefit alignment, IT integration, and so on take more time.

■ **Trust:** Create trust anchors, "talk the talk and walk the walk"

In this type of process, the anxiety of employees and management team is constant. Therefore, every rumor or piece of communication gets their interpretation, which usually affects negatively the spirit and morale of the merged company, ending with, for example, key employees leaving, or customers abandoning.

In order to avoid these types of situations, it is important to create trust among all parties involved. Trust anchors arrive in different forms and shapes but communication and consistency tend to be the most efficient anchors. The integration approach framework defines a plan, including: what type of anchors to apply, frequency of applying them, and so on.

■ **Change management:** Communication, change programs

In order to get this complex process in motion and succeed, the change must be managed. Within the integration approach framework, there is a reference to the way that the change should be managed.

A communication plan is a key factor in the change process. Proper, constant communication messages will distinguish between a process that is clear to the internal and external audiences of a merged company, and an unclear one. The communication strategy should be embedded in the integration approach framework.

Foundations of the Integration Process: Governance

Two governance mechanisms are usually applied in the PMI process: (1) integration structure and formation of PMI teams (internal and external) and (2) integration management routines and reporting structure.

Setting Up the Post-Merger Integration Governance Structure The post-merger integration structural organization usually consists of three layers: (1) the integration steering board, (2) the IMO, and (3) the different work streams that assume ownership on different functional areas or mission-based tasks. In order to properly manage this ecosystem, a clear chain of command is needed; thus, reporting lines and procedures should be developed and communicated from Day One (see Figure 13.4).

Proposed Integration Team Organization

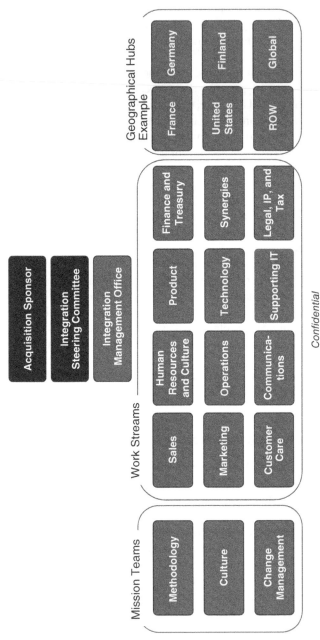

FIGURE 13.4 PMI Structure: Roles

Integration Steering Board* The steering board is usually comprised of three to five senior members (depending on the complexity of the integration process). The balance between acquiring and acquired members varies depending on the type of deal that is being executed. In most deals the majority of board members are representatives from the acquiring company and the acquired company usually gets a "seat" on the board. One member is appointed as the chair and is also the "sponsor" of the integration program.

In the case of a merger, there is a tendency to appoint the same number of board members from both companies. In cross-border deals, the right approach is to appoint people from more than one geographical location. In this situation, the staffing matrix gets more complicated. It can also be that some of the steering board members are exchanged during the project, for example, starting off with sales and human resources (HR) representatives who leave after the initial period, after which production or research and development (R&D) or information technology (IT) representatives are brought in.

Appointing the right people to the steering board is critical for the success of the integration as they need to guide the complete organization and ensure that the PMI process is heading in the right direction. In order to lead the organization toward a safe haven, the steering board should exercise the following responsibilities:

- Establish the vision, objectives, and strategies of the acquisition or merger; provide direction
- Make decisions—support the IMO, PMI leader, and functional team leaders and be the final decision-making level in case of disputes. The escalated issues go up to the steering board, which manages their resolution.
- Communication of leadership position in integration-related aspects—communicate to stakeholders according to the official communication plan in order to ensure their understanding, comfort, and buy-in
- Monitor progress and accelerate the pace whenever needed

The Integration Management Office The IMO is the team responsible for managing the integration's day-to-day activities. One member of the IMO is usually appointed as the PMI leader, a project manager who is responsible for the project's end-to-end responsibilities, including:

- Train and provide tools, insights, support, and direction
- Project leadership—facilitate assignment of leaders, tasks, deadlines, and priorities; capture PMI functional team status reports

---

*Also known as integration steering committee.

- Coordinate interdependencies between work streams
- Integration action planning and execution, including: Day One readiness, 100-days plan, functional streams planning, and horizontal streams planning
- Coordinate project communication with all stakeholders
- Monitor and ensure overall project compliance, risk management
- Synergies capture: planning, tracking, and reporting
- Monitor mechanisms enhancement: Project status reporting to the steering committee, weekly meetings and reports, and so on

Work Streams (Functional, Geographic, Mission-Based). This layer usually comprises a number of teams, each representing one of the following:

- A functional area, for example, human resources, finance, IT, that should take under its responsibility all integration-related tasks within its functional work stream
- A geographical area (dependent on the global complexity) where people are assigned from specific territories or regions. In cross-border processes, there are situations where certain geography gets more attention than others due to different reasons such as volume of business in that territory, headcount, and so on. In that case, alongside the functional stream, there might be a geographical stream as well.
- Specific mission assignment, usually tailored to that specific acquisition. This last type of work stream is usually comprised of cross-company employees and addresses a mission that impacts the company as a whole, for example, order-to-cash process, supply chain flows, innovation approach, or R&D process. In certain cases, the mission-based work streams manage strategic business-related tasks, such as quantifying synergies or valuating new business models.

The work streams have individuals working part-time on the integration and one person who is assigned as the team leader, usually a senior decision-making manager capable of managing the change.

The different work streams are in charge of managing the following tasks:

- Attain process integration
- Execution of activity log steps
- Minimize business disruption
- Communicate up to the IMO and down to team members
- Manage the different functional work streams' activities such as:
  - Objectives, strategies, and tactics

- Task-specific subteams
- Map streams' KPIs, risks, quick wins
- Create and manage a detailed project plan for their PMI functional team responsibilities, including: priorities, timelines, ownership, and due dates
- Report their stream's project status

Setting the Post-Merger Integration Routines The PMI project's reporting lines are usually managed two ways: top-down and bottom-up (see Figure 13.5). The different structural units on the three levels mentioned before must interact with each other constantly. Without a proper set of definitions and rules, this structure and the project's outcomes are doomed to failure.

The top-down approach is utilized to provide guidance downstream to lower-level hierarchies. It will usually start with the integration steering board's defining policy or providing directions to the IMO and work streams. This guidance is usually being defined for the PMI in the form of objectives, priorities, deliverables, timing, and so on. Another use of the top-down approach is to provide temporal updates on the overall M&A status: project status, decisions/priorities shift, major announcements, and so on.

The bottom-up approach is mainly being used for two purposes: first, as a reporting mechanism that represents the current status, including results, achievements, gaps, potential and actual conflicts, and next steps. The second is an escalation mechanism, in case needed, specifically whenever the reality isn't meeting the plan (is not progressing as expected) or in case of disagreements and conflicts that should be settled on a higher level (see Figure 13.6).

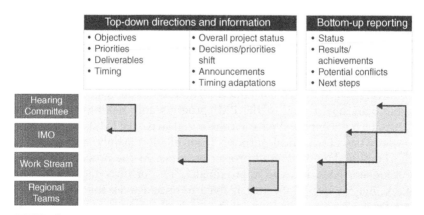

FIGURE 13.5 PMI Structure: Communication and Reporting

Bottom-Up Reporting Frequency

Entity	Frequency	Meeting agenda
Sponsor	Ad hoc	• Status and progress update
Steering committee	Biweekly and ad hoc	• Status report and progress monitoring • Exception reporting • Issue resolution based on work prepared by joint work streams and IMO • Budget/actual report on costs and synergies
IMO	Weekly	• Traffic light report per work streams • Discussion of interdependent topics • Preparation of solutions to issues • Ongoing communication
Individual work stream	Weekly	• Progress of action points to date • Review of action points for the week(s) to come • Resolution of obstacles based on previous guidance of steering committee • Identification of interdependencies with other work streams • Ongoing communication of integration messages and objectives

FIGURE 13.6 PMI Structure: Bottom-Up Reporting Frequency

Steering Board As the project is being kicked off, the integration steering board initially meets once a week and later on every second week or per need. The topics that are usually being reviewed are:

- Status report and progress monitoring
- Exception reporting
- Issue resolution based on work prepared by joint work streams and IMO
- Budget/actual report on costs and synergies

In the case of a cross-border transaction, the leading practice is that the steering board continues meeting as presented with two additions: (1) The time of the meetings changes in order to follow a "global watch." These meetings are virtual via a video call. (2) Some of the meetings are face-to-face, each time at a different site according to the content and events within the integration.

The Integration Management Office. The IMO is the hands-on unit leading the daily monitoring of the PMI progress and making sure all work streams keep the expected pace. At the initial steps, the IMO members meet on a daily basis for tactical purposes (coordination mainly) and weekly for a thorough update on overall project progress. As the process progresses, the frequency goes down to approximately two or three tactical meetings a week, but the overall meeting is fixed to once a week followed by every second week later on. The topics that are usually being reviewed in this type of meetings are:

- Traffic light report per work stream
- Update of blueprint
- Discussion of interdependent topics
- Preparation of solutions to issues
- Ongoing communication

Work Streams. The work streams plan and implement all the integration tasks. These streams might be functional by nature or mission based; in either case, these teams are in charge of translating their post-merger integration plans into actionable activities. Unlike the steering board and IMO, the work streams' work is "around the clock" and embedded in the day-to-day non-PMI activities of the work streams' leaders. Each work stream meets regularly, on a weekly basis, throughout the complete project's life and during these meetings reviews the following:

- Progress of action points to date
- Review of action points for the week(s) to come
- Resolution of obstacles based on previous guidance of steering committee
- Results and decisions based on analysis performed
- Identification of interdependencies with other work streams
- Ongoing communication of integration messages and objectives

Driving these routines does not seem to be too complex—it is actually manageable—but leading these routines globally is a different story. In global PMI processes, the integration goes across continents, regions, or countries. The differences in time zones, culture (national and corporate), and language add challenges to the existing local ones.

At this point, the facilitation of the integration commences and a variety of integration tasks are being taken care of, including: analysis of key staff, negotiation of retention, job offers, leadership announcements, security, communications, brand, facilities, HR, and product preparations for legal close, key customer and key supplier meetings, regulatory filings, and more.

This is why an "all-star team" should be selected to execute all of these PMI assignments and tasks. This team should be comprised of employees and managers who:

- Have knowledge of the business strategy, business plan, and customers
- Have deep understanding of their functional domain and can be helpful in their own team or work stream, but could also consult to other teams
- Have good interrelationship capabilities and work well in a team environment
- Know how to self-manage and have had project management experience

- Are sensitive to other languages and cultures
- Are driven and eager to promote their work stream
- Have senior mandates in their daily line management jobs

Post-Merger Integration Plans, Mechanisms, Monitoring Tools

As previously discussed, at this phase, initial work should have been invested in setting up the different PMI plans, mechanisms, and monitoring tools and putting them in motion.

The Day One and Day 100 PMI plans that include all the functional area activities in addition to all complementary plans such as key employees' retention plan, key customers plan, communication plan, synergies quantification plan, culture plan, and so on, should be ready on a high-level basis.

Work stream owners should have an initial understanding of the two businesses involved alongside the deal rationale and be able to define their initial PMI plan's content.

In parallel, pre-close additional integration mechanisms should be applied: Risks and mitigation actions, synergies, and quick wins.

These elements will be described thoroughly in the "Analyze" section.

ANALYZE

The Analyze subphase is a natural extension of the Relate subphase. Here, the integration team shifts from "low-key" involvement and high-level planning into a large-scale project involving a variety of participants in the organization and a variety of areas that are being taken care of.

This phase is characterized in several ways. As a start, the PMI process shifts from planning only to implementation as well. While the project evolves and participants go into deeper details within the planning process, certain elements go beyond planning. Retention plans are elaborated at this point, so it is clear who the key employees are and what retention plans they will be offered. Global spread of business and offices is clear, key customers are mapped and approached, and other operational tasks are being handled.

The original team that worked on the overall integration approach and started defining the integration governance is now expanding. The team gets staffed, and the expanded team is being debriefed on the deal status and the transaction position.

The process of on-boarding the integration team (mainly work streams) is taking place and several tasks happen in parallel:

- All people involved go through a series of training sessions to get aligned across the following areas: deal status and rationale, integration approach, cross-culture training, and PMI planning essentials.
- Work stream by work stream analysis is conducted, including a deep-dive review of due diligence.
- Integration plan update, including validation of assumptions and clarification of unknowns (to the extent possible), review of in-flight projects and plans, updated integration plans, priorities, product roadmap, issues, negotiations, and so on.
- Day One plan ready, including clear definition of all activities that should be taken care of in the days before and after the closing, such as financial elements (bank accounts, signatory rights), HR elements (salaries, retention plan), sales (key customers), R&D (product development roadmap), and so on.
- 100-days plan ready, covering all integration elements and tasks including, among others:
  - Risk mapping and mitigation plans
  - Definition of KPIs and measuring mechanisms
  - Quick wins allocation and communication planning
  - Synergy analysis: qualitative review and validation, estimates, implementation requirements, allocation and budgeting

In parallel to the on-boarding of the integration team, at this point, the PMI process starts being managed as a "project." Managing a cross-border post-merger integration process requires certain management skills and capabilities alongside project management skills. It takes hard work, discipline, and sensitivity to properly manage this type of project.

In order to excel as a project manager one should stick to the following leading practices:

- Keep it simple: Don't overcomplicate. Focus on the goals and objectives of the project, recruit the needed number of people to participate in the project and not more than that, don't set too many status updates, and don't write too many documents.
- Make decisions: The worst thing that could happen is questioning and decisions "hanging" or waiting for more senior executives to approve. Don't expect to always make the right decisions—you may get it wrong sometimes, but it is better than not deciding.

▪ Following the previous point, assemble a multifunctional, multidimensional team with different skills and strengths. Do not overstaff your team and make sure all are doers—you shouldn't waste time on nonparticipants.

▪ Assemble your plan as soon as possible, develop it as far as possible, and keep your mind open for changes and updates. Make sure your project is managed by deadlines. Keep them tight.

▪ Choose the right tools that the organization will be comfortable working with, whether a simple project management software solution, a designated PMI software, or an Excel spreadsheet. Don't overcomplicate the use of tools as they will be abandoned fast enough.

▪ Be ready to face crises. No project avoids them!

▪ Acknowledge that there are different cultures, personalities, and agendas involved. Try to understand the new ecosystem and motivations as you move along.

INTEGRATE

In the Integrate subphase, sleeves are being completely rolled up and the organization shifts from exploring and planning to full execution engagement.

The integration management office team will be managing the PMI project, taking care of all the PMI efforts, including management of the process, temporal updates to the integration board, management, and assistance and guidance of the functional and mission-based work streams.

In certain cases, this team will also manage high-level tasks such as strategy update, organization chart adjustments, communication plan execution, and so on. The PMI governance, structure, and routines will take another step further and the PMI project will move forward full steam ahead.

Mission-based work streams such as strategy, communication, geography, and so on, will emerge per need, while the functional work streams will emerge simultaneously. Typical functional work streams that start their work include:

Finance. Accounting, processes redesign, treasury, tax, working capital optimization, controlling and reporting, compliance, order to cash, ERP implementation.

Human Capital. Roles and responsibilities, compensation and benefits (C&B), terms and conditions (T&C), leadership, headcount (and reduction), key employee retention and talent, processes and procedures, HR systems, welfare, unions and work councils, culture analysis and implementation plan.

Sales. New territories analysis, account mapping and planning, strategic partnerships, two ways training programs for salespeople, bundling opportunities, customer segmentation, customer profitability, channels, cross-sales and up-sales analysis and planning, sales force management, compensation (quotas), sales support and administration.

Marketing. Products, pricing, branding, PR, collaterals, websites, market segmentation, go-to market strategy.

Information Technology. IT strategy and roadmap, organization, infrastructure, telecom and networks, security, emails, functional and operational systems.

Operations. Products infrastructure analysis and roadmaps, tools and methodologies development, infrastructures, DBA mechanisms, R&D, supply chain, logistics, facilities, quality.

In parallel, there are elements that are being taken care of but are dependent on the context of the integration, such as:

Business Unit Integration. Organizational redesign, governance redesign, transformation reporting and tracking, business unit transition and hand-off.

Geographical Integration. Organizational redesign, governance redesign, transformation reporting and tracking.

Corporate Services. Tax, legal, M&A, real estate, regulatory, government affairs, intellectual property.

CHAPTER CHECKLIST

- ▪ What the PMI process is and how to organize and manage it.
- ▪ What the PMI components are and how to address each one.
- ▪ How to set up the PMI governance, specifically a project's structure, roles and responsibilities, meeting routines, communication, and so on.
- ▪ The key tasks and routines that should be taken care of as the governance is set and the organization starts working accordingly.
- ▪ How to define the right integration approach and follow it.
- ▪ The types of PMI plans, mechanisms, and monitoring tools that exist and how to apply them.

NOTE

1. See also Chapter 7, "The Role of Culture in Cross-Border M&A."

CHAPTER 14

Country-Specific Trends and Tips for Integration Planning

Christophe Van Gampelaere

CHAPTER LEARNING OBJECTIVES—IN THIS CHAPTER, YOU WILL LEARN:

➤ About integration deal planning tips: a suitable approach that factors in cultures and work styles
➤ About cultural tips and hints
➤ About the key integration topics by region in a snapshot

CHAPTER SUMMARY

Dealing with cross-border integrations on a cultural level requires an upfront investment. The acquirer needs to understand its position on a number of cultural scales relative to the target. This chapter recommends creating an awareness of the differences between the target and the acquirer, agreeing on a common approach to address these differences, and keeping the number of cultures within the team to a minimum.

It is up to the acquirer not to misunderstand cultural signals and to adjust leadership to the expectations of various audiences. Decisions and actions correctly framed in a cultural context will carry more weight and ultimately contribute to a successful integration.

OPENING

When preparing for a deal, and before interacting with the management of the M&A target company, take some time to learn about the local culture and the position of your company relative to that culture.

Imagine a person widely considered to be a good boss, an effective communicator, and a highly trusted person within his cultural circle of comfort. The next day, he is transplanted to a foreign place. To his great surprise, he is now perceived to be an ineffectual leader, lousy at communicating, and just plain deceitful. In turn, he thinks of his coworkers as impossible to handle, purposely misunderstanding him, and not following through on their commitments.

In daily corporate life, a normal understanding of individual and personal differences often suffices to be a good manager. This may trick the manager into thinking he knows how to handle international cultural differences. This chapter will provide the reader with some tools to sharpen skills in managing international business relationships.

Being successful in integrating a merger means to be able to master a multidimensional Rubik's Cube and to reconcile individual differences, language barriers, country cultures, regional cultures, organizational cultures, and industry-specific cultures. How to be aware of all these differences? In other words, how can someone move from being "unconsciously unskilled" to being "consciously skilled" and beyond?

Erin Meyer, professor at INSEAD and author of *The Culture Map*, has created an eight-scale model, with each scale representing a specific cultural dimension that integration managers need to be aware of in order to increase their effectiveness.

These are the eight scales:

1. Communication
2. Evaluation
3. Persuasion
4. Leadership
5. Decision
6. Trust
7. Disagreement
8. Time

A crucial point in navigating the cultural labyrinth is to understand the acquirer's own culture relative to the one of the target on each of these dimensions. To someone from Japan, Spanish people may seem to communicate very directly and to-the-point. To an American, Spanish people can appear to be anything but to-the-point.

Figure 14.1 shows how Israel and Russia are very similar when it comes to their communicating, evaluating, trusting, disagreeing, and scheduling habits. But they are diametrically opposed when it comes to leadership style and persuading people.

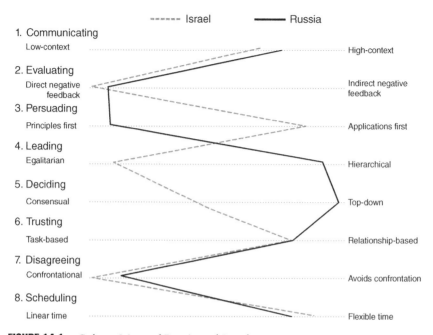

FIGURE 14.1   Culture Maps of Russia and Israel

It is all a question of where the company is on the communication scale relative to the target. And when you are managing a global team, there is a need to understand how each of the team members perceives the other.

A CULTURAL OVERVIEW OF THE MOST ACTIVE M&A REGIONS

A number of countries or regions have been selected based on how they score in various M&A rankings. They are grouped in three categories, in line with their cultural similarity:

- Anglo-Saxon countries (United States, Canada, United Kingdom)
- Asian regions (South Korea, Singapore, Hong Kong, China, India, Japan)
- European countries and regions (Germany, France, The Netherlands, the Nordic countries).

Following is some insight into the cultural scales for each of these categories.

ANGLO-SAXON REGIONS

Communication

Communicating with an Anglo-Saxon is to be literal, explicit, clear, and accurate. The correct transmission of the message is the responsibility of the communicator. A good presenter is somebody who announces what he will say and how he will say it, and he will close by summarizing what he has just said.

When an Anglo-Saxon deals with a more indirect culture, he's faced with a challenge. He will never hear a clear "no." He will have to try to detect it. Is it a hidden "no," disguised as a "yes," or is it a "maybe," or is it a "yes," accompanied by a "no" shaking of the head?

Failing to detect the hidden message will leave the acquirer thinking he had an effective conversation. When he comes back a few weeks later to check on progress, however, he might see that nothing has happened.

When someone is perceived to be a boss or a client, someone from a less direct background will try to convey a negative message between the lines. For them it would never be acceptable to say "no" outright. Look for verbal and nonverbal signals that are more in accordance with a "no" answer.

For an Asian, or someone from any country with a less direct communication style than the United States, being very direct will be very effective when communicating with people from the United States. This means that an American will appreciate a reply to every email. He will appreciate receiving a summary of decisions, notes, and actions. He will consider it to be effective communication when he receives a reply to an email just to say there is nothing to say.

Evaluation

Providing negative feedback: In contrast to his direct communication style, an Anglo-Saxon will provide negative feedback in a subtle and indirect way. He will convey three positive messages to bring one negative message. The negative message will come with *downgraders*, words to make things sound less threatening. He will say something like: "You could have done this *slightly* better." A French person, on the other hand, wanting to convey the exact same feedback would be very direct, and may use *upgraders* in order to reinforce the message, and say: "Your work was *absolutely* worthless" (see Figure 14.2).

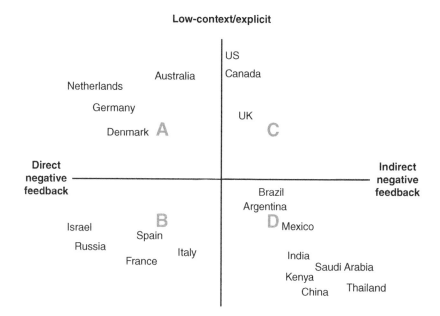

FIGURE 14.2 The Feedback Scale

On the feedback scale, the United States and France are on opposite ends. The way to deal with this is to try to understand where the target's conversation partner is situated in the chart relative to the acquirer's position, and apply a filter that normalizes the message back to the acquirer's frame of reference. An Englishman will need to replace the French upgrader he hears with an English downgrader. "Your work was absolutely worthless" would be filtered back to "You could have done this slightly better." And vice versa.

A note of caution, however: When it comes to providing negative feedback, avoid trying to emulate what works well in the host culture. Chances are subtleties will be missed and someone may feel really offended or patronized.

Persuasion

When the work stream leads need to be activated for an integration exercise, Americans love to come directly to the point. The integration leader may present practical solutions, and propose actions that need to be taken and strategies to be applied. Any question on how those conclusions were reached, what the combined group business model is, or what the pros and cons of alternative approaches are, is received with surprise and is not likely to be treated with priority.

Contrast this to the French way of working: When I receive an email from my French colleague Gilles, author of Chapters 1 and 8, I'm first being put through an extensive exposé, a veritable avalanche of words, and the most important message comes only at the end of the email, by which time I have probably given up trying to digest everything. More on the French art of persuasion further on in this chapter.

Leadership

In the United States, a leader's decision is not set in stone, it's a step in the right direction, but it is subject to change. There is not much distance between a leader and his team. Decisions are quickly taken and acted upon.

Decisions

Despite the low power distance, in the United States or United Kingdom, it *is* the leader who decides, and he would not allow his subordinate to challenge him to the same degree as would happen in Germany or France.

Trust

Trust is built through business-related activities, by working efficiently, and by not spending too much time on what's seen as diversions. An example of this is the sandwich lunch, typical in the United States and the United Kingdom during meetings and negotiations. A South American will wait in vain for a long lunch, where he can get to know his new business partner. Anglo-Saxons tend to trust people who focus on the business at hand and not on social activities. Personal bonds are easily created, and are just as easily dropped. Anglo-Saxons may offer a friendly "Hey, how are you doing?" but they don't really expect an honest answer. They separate their emotional world from the business world.

Cultures where trust is built on relationships are puzzled by this attitude: "Why would you ask the question, if you were not sincere in getting the answer?" For them, trust is all about that connection from the heart, and not from the head: the emotional world and business world are one. People from these cultures leave an American meeting marathon bewildered: there are lots of actions, they've received practical information, but they have not been able to lay a foundation of trust.

Disagreement

Anglo-Saxons are not too keen on showing public disagreement. This may come as some surprise, but in this respect, many countries are more direct than the United States and the United Kingdom. Europeans, for example, who are used to openly discuss topics like politics and religion, will find their American audience disposed to be silent on such issues. The English are masters at conveying disagreement disguised as a qualification ("hmm, interesting"), or as humor, even sarcasm. Humor serves many purposes. In negotiations it can also be used to break tension or introduce a new element. The acquirer will gain the respect of his British target if he can match his humor with some of his own. Even when agreement is likely, do not expect to get it at the end of a meeting. Instead, suggest having "a final decision at the end of next week."

Time

The view on time management is in line with what can be expected given the direct leadership style and quick decision-making characteristics of the culture (see Figure 14.3). Expect U.S. and UK colleagues to be punctual and to handle tasks in a sequential manner. They will expect the same. They tend to focus less on the urgent items that pop up unexpectedly, because they are seen as distractions. Dwight D. Eisenhower said: "What's important is seldom urgent. What's urgent is seldom important." An integration exercise is a high-stress exercise, with milestones that are both important and urgent. In this performance-laced environment, trust is built through being punctual, focused on business, and handling tasks in a timely manner.

In linear-time cultures, tasks have set deadlines, are clearly defined, and neatly ordered. Gantt charts are used to make interdependencies and durations visible. Such an environment is typical and essential in making a cross-border integration a success. There is a big disadvantage, at the same time, when applying a linear-time approach to a flexible-time culture. The approach will be fraught with challenges and difficulties. It will take longer to realize the synergies, implement changes, and have them accepted.

FIGURE 14.3 The Time Management Scale

ASIAN COUNTRIES

Communication

Communication in Asia is contextual, implicit, subtle, and multilayered. The accurate understanding of the message is the shared responsibility of the communicator and listener. Subtle body language like nods and grunts as well as reading between the lines and understanding cultural references are essential.

A non-Asian, who does not have the right contextual reference points, will miss implicit meanings and signals. In China, do not take the messages received up front at face value. Be very attentive to hints. Explicitly check what you think you understood. In order to be sure, check three or four times—a bit embarrassing for both parties perhaps, but still way better than misunderstanding, and acting on a faulty assumption.

Since effective communication is a shared responsibility, it helps to move to a 50% listening mode. Try to pick up signals, even if they are not clear, and check their meaning. Consider practicing some self-deprecating humor. Squarely say that you come from a less-sophisticated communication culture. Request some lenience and patience from the more sophisticated Asian conversation partner. This attitude is likely to create a bond and some goodwill. There is also no shame in asking for help if the communication minefield seems too daunting. Asking for help will in itself be seen as a positive trait.

Consider Erin Meyer's communication scale in Figure 14.4.

Wherever the acquirer is positioned on the slider scale, he will find it to his great benefit to be able to adapt to a higher- or lower-context environment as the need arises.

When working with multicultural integration teams, resort to the lowest common communication denominator: be explicit and low-context. Go

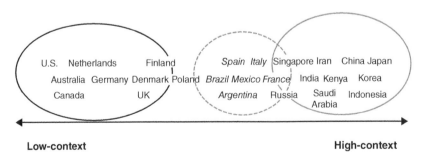

FIGURE 14.4　The Communication Scale

American. Be clear and concise. Recap. Make a list. Set actions. Act. Find and agree on a way within the team to make this low-context approach work.

One effective way during and after meetings is to divide up the task between the team members on a rotation basis:

- One person makes an oral recap of the meeting
- Each team member states verbally what he is supposed to do
- One team member puts everything in writing and sends it around

Clarify, Clarify, Clarify

When initiating a conversation with anyone on the right of the communication scale, ask for clarification. When dealing with someone on the left, try to be clearer. No matter what side of the spectrum the acquirer and the target are on, don't assume the message will come across as intended. When I worked in New York as investment manager for Abacus, a family office, my boss Frank Weil told me: "Christophe, don't *assume*, it makes an '*ass*' out of '*u*' and '*me.*'" I still repeat that message to myself and in every training I give.

Surprisingly, most difficulties in communications actually occur between two parties from differing but equally high-context cultures. Both of them expect each other to be able to read between the lines, and are trained not to be clear and straightforward. With different cultural contexts, however, the messages being conveyed may never reach the recipient the way they were intended to do.

We recommend a simple strategy to position the acquiring company on the scale relative to the target, and adjust behavior and expectations accordingly. To someone from a Chinese or Korean background, Singaporeans will seem to be very direct, even blunt communicators, since they are less contextual. To anyone with a European, Hispanic, or Anglo-Saxon background, Singaporeans will seem to be very subtle indeed.

A Chinese business partner will take the Asian communication approach one step further, by actually *expecting* the other to read between the lines. An acquirer is *expected* to make the necessary investment in time to get to know the specific Chinese context, to decipher messages. This investment and effort will be reciprocated, and together acquirer and target will create a common business context.

In Japan, a first meeting is all about relationship building. Spend time to show eagerness to invest in the relationship. When business cards are exchanged, make the effort to learn the names of the conversation partners by heart, so that by the end of the meeting, you can address them by their name without looking at the card.

In India, another high-context culture, the "Indian head bob" may cause some confusion and wonderment among foreigners. It looks like a cross between a nod and shake, and is often silent. The actual meaning is to indicate anything from "good" to "I understand," to "I'm listening respectfully."

Evaluation

Asians don't like to receive or witness individual negative feedback in a group setting. Ask for and provide such feedback in discreet one-on-one sessions. Give the message ample time to sink in, potentially over several sessions, blurring out what you really want to say, communicating between the lines. Do it in a relaxed setting, laced with food and drink, and do not mention it afterward in the office. In Figure 14.2, Japan and China figure distinctly on the implicit/indirect negative feedback axes.

Persuasion

When wanting to on-board Asians on the M&A project, it helps to make sure the bigger picture is clear and convincing. Asian cultures are holistic—people see the interdependencies and links. Everything needs to come together in one story that makes sense. This is a valuable attitude that comes in handy in a typical M&A project with interdependencies between work streams, entities, and regions.

In Japan, when the acquirer tries an Anglo-Saxon approach and talks to each team member in person to explain the task ahead, the first impression will probably be that the message is clearly received. He will most likely not catch that he's approaching things the wrong way. Later on, he will notice that the local target team is not making much progress. What was lacking in the communication was the holistic approach: Every team member needs to see how his task fits in the bigger integration picture. They would not expect the acquirer to define each and every integration task. In Japan it is more effective to set a team task, without distilling it down any further. The team will then work and decide internally what needs to be done to achieve the goal.

To get something done in India, again, clarification is key. Indian team members will not ask for it, it is up to the acquirer to double-check that the message is well understood. Ask the team to confirm in writing how they understand what needs to be done. Follow up closely on the actual delivery of actions.

Leadership

Asian countries, together with Russia, typically have a strong hierarchical leadership structure. The ideal distance between a boss and a subordinate

Denmark	Israel	Canada	U.S.			France	Poland	Saudi Arabia	Japan
Netherlands		Finland		UK	Germany	Italy		Russia India	Korea
Sweden	Australia				Brazil	Spain	Mexico	Peru China	Nigeria

Egalitarian   **Hierarchical**

FIGURE 14.5   The Leadership Scale

is high. Those who are higher up are expected to mentor and protect those below. In return, the lower levels owe loyalty, respect, and obedience to the ones higher up.

Here are some tips on effective acquirer leadership in a hierarchical society (see Figure 14.5):

- Only interact with the person at the same hierarchical level. A CEO who negotiates a deal, and meets team members of the target company, needs to know beforehand who his same-level counterpart is, and should address him first.
- Display the symbols that go with the leadership territory, and act accordingly. Don't call a boss by his first name: "Jim" is not acceptable, "Mr. Jones" is—and at the least, it's "Mr. Jim."

Decisions

Decision making in Asia is not consensual. The boss decides. That does not mean the boss does not solicit input from his team. He will do that via informal discussions. Meetings are called to confirm a decision already made. Contrast this with how other regions measure the success of a meeting (Table 14.1).

Even though, in general, the adage in Asia is that "the boss decides," in Japan there is a model similar to the one in Germany, with strong hierarchical structures, but a consensual decision-making model, called the *ringi* system. Lower-level managers discuss a new idea among themselves (see Table 14.2). They come to a consensus and take it one level up. The

TABLE 14.1   Successful Meetings

A meeting is a success when:	Asian	Anglo-Saxon	Germany/France
A decision is made		X	
Various viewpoints are debated			X
A decision is confirmed	X		

TABLE 14.2   Cross-Cultural Decision-Making Strategies

Top-Down Decision Making	Consensual Decision Making
A decision is quickly made, has more feeble roots	Takes longer, has deeper roots
A decision is prone to changes	A decision is final, difficult to uproot
Soliciting feedback from team members on decisions may be perceived as weak	Take time to connect with your team members
Decide and implement	Facilitate and decide
Follow the decision taken	Provide input into the decision-making process

higher-level management discusses the new idea and comes to its own consensus. This process continues until the idea comes to the highest management level and the idea is (or is not) implemented. The implications in a merger integration setting are significant. Less consensus-prone managers may think ringi is time-consuming and futile. Yet, as many seasoned professionals will confirm, without local buy-in, Japanese integration efforts will not go as planned, resulting in delays, lost synergies, and lost trust.

Trust

Building trust in Asia is based on building relationships, on taking time for social talk, a long lunch or dinner. Building on mutual interests lays the foundation of further cooperation. An acquirer who is not used to this needs to invest in opening up, in showing his true self. Have long drinking sessions; pick up the phone instead of sending an email; build emotional, affective connections for a trusting relationship to develop.

Becoming familiar with one another is a bond not easily entered into, and once that bond is created, it is not easily dropped. Such a bond is a critical element to lay the foundation for further cooperation; it is the equivalent of a contract in the West. With East-West investment activities becoming more important, managers who understand and trust each other on an emotional level as well as a cognitive one have a critical advantage on those who don't.

In China, trust and loyalty are to the individual, more than to the company. Acquiring a company without acquiring the trust of the employees and management may soon result in the target becoming an empty shell after key sales managers have left, taking their customers and subordinates with them.

Disagreement

Asian cultures do not like direct confrontational disagreement, and they feel much stronger about it than English speakers or Europeans. It disrupts group balance, and makes people lose face. It is a difficult concept to grasp for someone from a society where group discussions are the way to come to consensus, and where people sometimes like to shock each other into opening up their minds to different points of view, even with a soft tool like humor. The biggest contrast on the disagreement scale is between Asian societies and cultures like France, Israel, Germany, and The Netherlands, as shown in Figure 14.6. Anglo-Saxon countries figure neatly in the middle of the scale.

The scale includes a second axis, lining out how emotionally expressive people from various countries are in general. This helps to read reactions and behavior in a meeting or negotiation. Someone from Japan is typically not too emotionally expressive and tends to avoid confrontation. That person may need to put in quite an effort to surmount inner objections against the signals he receives from someone from Israel, who is direct and confrontational. Add to that that both countries are on opposite sides of the hierarchical and feedback scales, and have entirely different contextual references. You may not be surprised that it is difficult to integrate companies from each country, or even come to an agreement to enter into a deal or partnership.

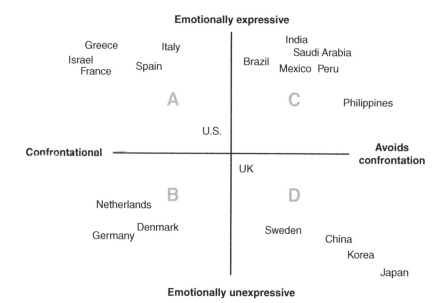

FIGURE 14.6 The Disagreement Scale

Just remember that both sides have similar goals and aspirations, just different perspectives, and they are used to taking different roads. Disagreements are therefore often not to be taken personally; they find their origins in culture.

Time

Asian cultures appear across the time management scale (see Figure 14.3). Japan is there with Germany, the United States, and the United Kingdom. China and India are on the opposite side: interruptions are accepted; tasks are more easily changed and rearranged. People tend to work on several things at a time, instead of sequentially. The same goes for meetings. They start on time, but a linear agenda is not necessarily followed to the letter, and new topics may pop up on the agenda. Meeting participants who check their emails, leave the meeting for calls, or hijack the agenda are not considered to be rude, they are just being flexible.

EUROPEAN COUNTRIES AND REGIONS

Europe is composed of close to 50 countries and 500 million people who are joined by a political and economic community. There *is* such a thing as a European culture, but within it, the continent has many different traditions and languages that lead to major cross-cultural differences.

Communication

Styles vary across the continent. The Netherlands, Germany, and the Nordic states are comparable with the direct, low-context style we described for the Anglo-Saxon cultures. Southern European countries like Spain and Italy are more high-context, with meaning being communicated on more than one level. France is one of the most contextual countries in Europe. When it comes to communication, the French are closer to the Asian cultures than any Anglo-Saxon or European country. Speaking from a less contextual point of view may mean to the French that you are stating the obvious, or treating them in a condescending way.

Evaluation

France is the direct opposite of the United States: subtle and contextual in its communication, but very direct in its feedback. In general, Europeans need to seriously downgrade their feedback style with Anglo-Saxons and Asians.

Persuasion

In Germany, before persuading an audience, make sure to first present a solid case as to how the conclusion came about. Clarify the groundwork, the methodology used, and how conclusions were stress-tested. Prepare to build arguments, and start with the theory to then move to the practical implications.

The French too want to hear the principles first, and only later the practical application. They cannot be persuaded without having laid out a foundation. If an acquirer wants the French team to act on the merger and to work on their integration tasks, he will have to explain everything from the ground up. Start by explaining the original company vision, business model, and implementation strategy. Tell them where there was a gap in the business model, and how the acquisition makes sense in filling that gap. Give them the impact on the combined organization, on the acquirer, and on them as the target. Initiate a dialogue over the pros and cons, solicit feedback, and get buy-in. Only then is it time to start working on the integration action plan.

Italians and Russians like to be approached in the same manner, as shown in Figure 14.7.

Leadership

Even though leadership is relatively hierarchic in Germany, with formal titles and positions, German managers do expect to be challenged by their peers and subordinates alike. The culture of persuasion continues in the leadership style, and decision making in Germany is more consensual than in Anglo-Saxon countries.

The Dutch do not care who's the boss in the room. They score very low on Geert Hofstede's power distance chart. Holland is one of the most egalitarian countries on the globe. Status is less important than being a good team facilitator. A leader who rides his bike to work shows he is "one of the team." Try this in China, and you will humiliate your team in the eyes of others.

| Italy | Russia | Germany | Argentina | Sweden | Netherlands | Australia |
| France | Spain | | Brazil | Mexico | Denmark | UK | Canada U.S. |

Principles first   Applications first

FIGURE 14.7 The Persuasion Scale

A Swedish health care company acquired a Polish company in 2013. The personnel in Poland were used to a hierarchical leadership style, receiving only negative feedback. Some people were emotionally touched when their new leaders gave positive feedback. Getting them to accept the concept of 360-degree feedback was more difficult, revolutionary even. It took over a year to implement, as the target personnel was afraid to get fired for giving feedback on their leaders.

Table 14.3 shows a comparison of egalitarian versus hierarchical leadership.

Trust

Establishing a trustful relationship in Europe differs in each country, and even in every region within the country (see Figure 14.8). European countries

TABLE 14.3 Egalitarian versus Hierarchical Leadership

Egalitarian	Hierarchical
Minimize use of titles	Maximize use of titles
It's okay to disagree with the boss in front of others	Defer to the boss's opinion, especially in public
People will move to action without the boss's go-ahead	The boss's approval is needed before undertaking action
People take initiative to solve issues beyond their immediate realm of responsibility	People stick to their roles, and defer to their superior
Meetings between parties can be many to one, or one to many, with hierarchical levels being mixed	Meetings between parties need to match both on a hierarchical and quantitative level
It may be okay to jump hierarchical levels in communication	Communication follows a hierarchical chain
No seating arrangements or specific speaking order	You are seated and spoken to in order of position
New ideas are generated during a meeting	Give clear meeting instructions beforehand, so your team can prepare and align
Challenge the boss	The boss is right
In emails, copying the boss may indicate lack of trust	In emails, copy the boss
Use first names	Use last names and titles
Decisions take time	Quick decisions

									Saudi
U.S.	Denmark	Germany	UK	Poland	France	Italy	Mexico	Brazil	Arabia
Netherlands		Finland				Spain	Russia	Thailand	India
	Australia			Austria			Japan	Turkey	China Nigeria

◄───►

Task-based   **Relationship-based**

FIGURE 14.8   The Trust Scale

span the spectrum on the trust scale, with trust in The Netherlands being very much task-based like the United States. France, Italy, and Spain lean much more toward the Asian relationship-based side of the spectrum.

Disagreement

The Dutch, Germans, and French will disagree in public. For them, the honest thing to do is to state their beliefs, to engage in a dialogue, and to come to a common understanding. This can only be done by discussing thesis and antithesis, by stating bold arguments, by playing the devil's advocate. All this comes across as very confrontational in other societies, specifically Asian cultures where one strives for harmony.

Time

European countries, too, figure a bit across the time management scale. Italy, Spain, and France are most flexible. The French may arrive late to meetings, talk at length during them, or delay them, and not get through the agenda. The French may switch from one agenda topic to another. Time is there to be used, enjoyed, or wasted—sometimes all at the same time, like during a strike. The Germans and Dutch are ultra-punctual. Not showing up at meetings may cause them to stop the business relationship. Wasting time is a sin, hence the rarity of strikes.

SUMMARY

Be aware of cultural differences and approach them with respect. Effectively managing them will enhance understanding and deal success. Armed with cultural knowledge, we recommend the reader frame his behavior and explain that the way he acts is different from his counterpart's.

In a multicultural, cross-border integration team, it is key that the integration leaders understand their position on all of the cultural dimensions.

It's always good to have someone on the team who has some experience in facilitating this kind of cooperation.

Consider having culture workshops with your teams. They may be more rewarding than a traditional team-building event.

Give the process of mutual cultural adjustment some time—everyone will have to move a little bit out of his or her comfort zone, but the effort is worth it on a business as well as a personal level.

CHAPTER CHECKLIST

■ Integration managers need to be aware of culture differences in eight domains: communication, giving evaluations, persuading your team, leadership, making decisions, gaining trust, disagreeing, and time management.
■ Cultural issues can be grouped by three major M&A regions: Anglo-Saxon, Asian, and European.

BIBLIOGRAPHY

Ehrenfreund, P., N. Peter, K. U. Schrogl, and J. M. Logsdon. "Cross-Cultural Management Supporting Global Space Exploration," *Acta Astronautica*, 2010.

Hofstede, Geert. *Culture's Consequences: Comparing Values, Behaviors, Institutions, and Organizations Across Nations*, 2nd ed. Thousand Oaks, CA: Sage, 2001.

Lewis, Richard D. *When Cultures Collide*, 3rd ed. Boston: Nicholas Brealy International, 2006.

Meyer, Erin. *The Culture Map: Breaking through the Invisible Boundaries of Global Business*. New York: PublicAffairs, 2014.

CHAPTER 15

M&A and Post-Merger Integration Considerations for China and Japan

Robert Ping Yu, Masaki Yamamoto, and Makoto Ideno

PART 1: CHINA

PART 1 LEARNING OBJECTIVES—IN THIS PART, YOU WILL LEARN:

➤ Current trends of cross-border M&A in China
➤ Common pitfalls when entering the Chinese market
➤ Critical issues and approaches that could make or break an M&A deal
➤ China outbound M&A trends and issues

PART 1 SUMMARY

Part 1 elaborates on trends and issues involving both inbound investment into China by foreign companies and China outbound investment. It describes the motivations behind the inbound and outbound investments, and points out the critical issues that have a significant impact on the success or failure of an M&A project. It also provides some approaches to deal with the issues.

OVERVIEW OF M&A TRENDS IN CHINA

Since the market reform was initiated to shift from a centrally planned to a market-based economy in 1978, China has experienced rapid economic and social development. Joining the World Trade Organization in December

2001, China has shown accelerated growth and progress. With a 1.3 billion population, China had become the world's second largest economy, a title Japan had held for more than 40 years. It has become a major player in global trade and a key factor in the world economy. Over 90 percent of Fortune 500 companies have entered the Chinese market, although the successes of such investments seem to be mixed.

Globalization, industry consolidation, and maturing domestic markets drive companies to become global in scope and scale to effectively compete and thrive. Factors such as low-cost manufacturing, research and development (R&D) resources, and a large consumer market have attracted ever-increasing amounts of foreign direct investment in China. Cross-border mergers & acquisitions (M&A) have become a global expansion strategy for multinational companies (MNCs) and one of the most prevalent forms of foreign direct investment (FDI) in China. As labor costs continue to rise in China, many manufacturing-based FDI have shifted to southeast Asian countries, and this has somewhat slowed the growth of China's inbound FDI investment. However, as China's economic reform deepens, name-brand consumer products will be in high demand, and new investment will likely to continue to flow into China to capitalize on this growing trend.

In the meantime, an increasing number of Chinese companies are not only very active participants in domestic M&A deals but also have gone overseas to seek investment opportunities. This trend is evidenced by data from the published reports of the Chinese Ministry of Commerce and the National Bureau of Statistics as shown in Figure 15.1 and Figure 15.2. Figure 15.1 shows FDI inflows from 2000 to 2014, while Figure 15.2 illustrates outbound investment volume by Chinese companies from 2005 to 2014. According to this Chinese government report, outbound M&A values typically exceed half of all outbound investment overseas.

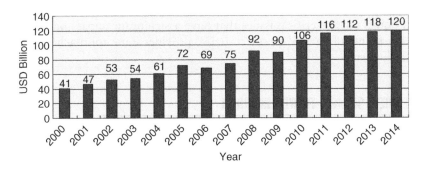

FIGURE 15.1 Foreign Direct Investment in China (2000–2014)

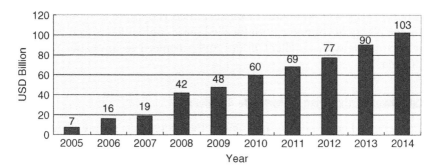

FIGURE 15.2 Outbound Investment (Nonfinancial) from China (2005–2014)

The data in Figure 15.1 show that inbound foreign direct investment to China continues to rise and reached an all-time high of $119b in 2014, although the rate of growth has been nearly flat since 2011.

From Figure 15.2, we can see that outbound investments made by Chinese companies have grown sharply since 2008.

To better understand this M&A trend, we need to look at the driving factors in China's economy.

Structural Shifting in China's Economy

Even with the double-digit growth seen in the first 30 years after the market reforms, China remains a developing country (measured by per capita income). Growth is still important for China; however, healthy and sustained growth has become the top priority. Heavy foreign direct investment and rapid economic ascendance have resulted in many challenges such as overly export-dependent industries, labor-intensive and less energy efficient manufacturers, significant rise in the cost of labor, imbalanced urbanization, and environmental pollution. China also faces demographic pressures related to an aging population and a shortage of skilled labor.

As such, the Chinese government has initiated a major shift in economic structure in its 12th Five-Year Plan (2011–2015). The plan encourages state-owned enterprises (SOEs) to deepen reforms and shift to more innovative, greener, and energy-efficient businesses. It encourages the development of services, energy-efficient, and high-tech industries and takes measures to address environmental and social imbalances and to reduce pollution with a reduced annual growth target of 7%. With various policy measures, the Chinese government is in the process of steering its economy from a world factory ("Made in China") and export-dependent economy to a more innovative ("Created in China"), more domestic consumption and service-oriented economy. This will stimulate more sustained economic development and provide plenty of room for both local Chinese companies as well as foreign multinationals with excellent brand and advanced technologies to thrive in China.

State-Owned Enterprise Reforms to Accelerate

With renewed emphasis on improving efficiency China's State Council has issued guidelines and plans for state-owned enterprise reform. It will allow SOEs to have mixed ownership such as employees and it also encourages SOEs to become publicly traded companies. As a pilot program, the plan identified six large SOEs to open up for private investment and to improve corporate governance. Another pilot aimed at improving management efficiency will allow the SOE boards of directors to appoint senior management teams and set performance measures. With more reforms coming, more market-based competitors can be expected and the environment will be more attractive to foreign investors.

Over-Capacity in Many Industries and Others Going through Consolidation

Due to the global economic slowdown, and the lack of demand after the 2008 global financial crisis, many industries received investments from the government's economy stimulus measures that resulted in high inventories and over-capacity. In addition, declining exports, the rise in domestic competition, and industry consolidation are becoming the new norm. This leads to more companies starting to "go overseas" in order to expand distribution networks and access the global market. Going overseas also helps bring back better technologies and management skills to enhance competency at home. This kind of activity along with industry consolidation has been driving a sharp increase in domestic M&A as well as outbound M&A deals. This trend is expected to continue for at least another decade, especially in outbound investment by Chinese companies, both SOEs and private companies. How to execute their global strategies and maximize the return on such investments and lower risk is a top concern for many Chinese companies looking to expand overseas.

SOE restructuring, industry consolidation, and the government policy to increase domestic consumption will drive more M&A activities and deal flows both inbound to and outbound from China.

In this chapter, we identify some of the critical M&A issues in China related to inbound and outbound activities. We will also share our perspectives and practical approaches to tackle these issues based on our extensive cross-border M&A and post-merger integration (PMI) project experience.

ISSUES AND APPROACHES FOR INBOUND M&A IN CHINA

In this section, we will discuss some of issues encountered by foreign companies when investing in China.

Although there could be many strategic or operational reasons for inbound M&A into China, typical objectives of a foreign company coming to China and acquiring or entering into a joint venture with a Chinese company can be categorized as follows:

- **Outsourcing or cost reduction:** This could be in the form of establishing a joint venture or a directly owned manufacturing base or an R&D center. It is largely driven by supply chain cost reduction or accessing a larger human resource pool in China.
- **Market access or market expansion:** The main objective is to seek growth internationally by entering the Chinese market, the largest or one of the largest markets in the world, depending on the specific industry. This is typically accomplished via an acquisition or a joint venture with existing distribution networks in China.
- **Acquiring strategic assets and setting up joint ventures with local strategic partners:** Many deals are motivated by the need to comply with foreign ownership control policies and the desire to get more favorable treatment as a "local player" due to China's increased regulations on antimonopoly and national security.

No matter what the strategic rationale is, cross-border M&A remains more complex than domestic transactions and the success rate is considerably lower. For example, a research report found that only 17% of cross-border acquisitions created shareholder value, while 53% destroyed it. There are common issues that are critical to determine the fate of an M&A deal in China.

Key issues and challenges:

- The common problems of M&A such as uncertainties in valuation and control of target companies are complicated by a lack of local knowledge, relationships, and the changing regulations in China.
- Significant differences in culture, management styles, market environment, competitive landscape, legal systems, accounting, and tax policies.
- Strategy disconnect, intentions "lost in translation," or policies not localized.

Although there have been successful and profitable entries into the Chinese market for companies such as Starbucks, Yum!, Coca-Cola, Carrefour, Apple, and others, there are many high-profile failures by some well-respected Fortune 500 companies. For example, Mattel, Best Buy, and Home

Depot all closed their China stores in 2011. eBay was basically pushed out by local competitors. Google, although political factors may have played a role, never had a comparable market share as they had elsewhere before they exited China.

In hindsight, we have seen many analyses and commentaries as to what went wrong with those market entry ventures. Some suggest wrong strategies, some found culture misfits, and others point to the market timing as a factor. However, very few analyses discussed how those companies executed their strategy after entering the Chinese market. From many published news reports and interviews, we have seen that commonly known problems of government protectionism, corruption, or Chinese customer characteristics were not the key reasons for failure. In reality, a lack of localized strategies, inappropriate headquarters control, and misunderstanding of local competitions are some of the crucial causes of failures.

Understanding the issues and proactively mitigating the risks will greatly increase the chance of success of companies investing in China. Some of the key approaches include effectively handling the management style and cultural differences, installing the right local management team, balancing the priorities of growth versus process, and maintaining flexibility and making timely adjustments when necessary. We will address the key issues in the following sections.

Issue No. 1: Understand the Difference in Behavior, Culture, and Environment

As we learned in Chapter 7 of this book, culture is the number one issue for cross-border M&A. Since there are distinct differences between the culture in China and most of the countries in the Western world, this issue becomes more pronounced and is the most crucial of all. There are many aspects and layers of culture such as national, regional, generational, social, and corporate. We will primarily discuss business and corporate culture.

Cultural differences are also the root of conflicts and disagreements between overseas and local Chinese companies. This is reflected in both business negotiations before the deal and integration execution after the deal.

Guanxi The way the Chinese conduct their business tends to differ from foreigners. Chinese are very particular about having a good relationship or "Guanxi" with each other, especially in business. There is an old saying in China: "Guanxi first and business later." They invest significant effort in socializing and in building relationships with others, as they believe that Guanxi is the foundation of a successful business. The relationship building over time allows them to develop trust with each other and minimize commercial and legal risks while doing business. This factor affects the working relationships with Chinese teams in all phases of the M&A process.

Originally, Guanxi signified the personal connection between two people in which one is able to receive a favor or service from the other as reciprocity for favors or services given before. It describes the basic dynamic in personalized networks of influence in Chinese society and has been expanded to describe a network of contacts that an individual can call upon when something needs to be done, and through which he or she can exert influence on behalf of another. Reciprocal favors are the key factor to maintaining one's Guanxi web. Giving a favor could simply start with saying something that makes the other person feel good or it could be a free service that saves the other person trouble or makes that person looks good ("save face": boost or maintain someone's prestige and/or social status). There are many forms of Guanxi building, but one needs to be careful of falling into the trap of corruption, on which many countries have specific rules and laws, which will not be discussed here.

In regard to Guanxi, there are also many stakeholders that need to be managed appropriately in addition to the shareholders of the M&A target company itself. Some are apparent, such as industry players, industry regulators, the State Development and Reform Commission, the Foreign Exchange Commission, the Ministry of Commerce, and the State-Owned Assets Supervision and Administration Commission of the State Council. Some are less visible, such as local governments at the city or provincial level. Building a good Guanxi, for example, could mean that your M&A project brings benefits to the society in the city of your project's location.

In order to make M&A projects more successful, acquiring companies need to leverage the personal relationships developed by the local executives over time and avoid demanding immediate favors or reciprocity.

In addition, Chinese companies tend to be more hierarchical. They pay more attention to social status and involvement of senior executives from the acquiring companies. It is highly advisable that they handle negotiations at the appropriate time. Subsequent change management initiatives are considered to be a form of Guanxi building and therefore need to be handled with the utmost care.

Management Style When it comes to M&A success, one of top concerns for the acquiring foreign companies is how to manage the people to implement the business strategy and make changes when necessary. Understanding style differences and recognizing the mentality and the motivation of Chinese management enables more effective partnerships and execution.

In Western companies, typical top management sets the vision and strategy for the business and empowers the teams to execute. They encourage two-way communication with employees and encourage bottom-up input in decision making. In China, management tends to be autocratic and top-down. They manage teams at a micro level. This can be very efficient for critical missions. With the direction set at the top, employees simply follow the orders and execute. However, this discourages ownership at the lower level and makes accountability ineffective.

Not only are there apparent differences in management styles between China and the West, but there are internal differences between Chinese companies. From this perspective, business organizations in China can be categorized in two groups:

1. SOEs or formal SOEs
2. Nonstate or privately owned businesses (could be publicly traded companies as well)

Although it might be difficult to accurately portray and generalize the management styles and culture differences between the two groups, a few distinctions can be made from the perspective of M&A projects.

A typical SOE management team consists of both a general manager and a party secretary general. The general manager is typically in charge of business operations, while the party leader controls the overall strategy and human resources. Although many decisions are subjective and made ad hoc, some are decided by committees. The SOEs are typically vertically organized and managed through autocratic authority and seniority. Accomplishments and rewards are managed as a group versus individuals; accountability can be very unclear and is often difficult to track. Since competitions for SOEs are relatively few and far between, their operating efficiency becomes an area for improvement. One of the main concerns for their management teams is to meet the requirements set out by the government (the most important stakeholder) while making no mistakes. The management teams at both the top and middle level are therefore very sensitive to risks and are more resistant to change initiatives—even when market conditions would require them to do so. Therefore, when negotiating deals or initiating post-deal strategy and operational changes, identifying common ground and aligning interest is key. Carefully articulated and less risky benefits that can satisfy the management team as well as the key stakeholders tend to be more acceptable and are implemented with less resistance.

A typical private business, on the other hand, is dominated by a single entrepreneurial but equally autocratic leader. These leaders will be very aggressive in pursuing changes for market gain since they often operate in a very competitive market environment. Final decisions are usually made by the dominating leader, despite the presence of board members and various company committees. Middle managers at key positions tend not to have sophisticated management skills, but are proactive and open-minded about changes and improvements. They are very open to new market opportunities and actively seek advanced technologies to boost the competitiveness of their core products or services. Emphasizing upside potential and benefits in negotiations would be desirable and welcomed.

In addition to what we described previously, there are also generational differences. Even Chinese managers sometimes struggle to cope with the so called "post-90" younger generation as they adopt Western influences and values. Recognizing those issues and learning to deal with them requires patience and experimenting.

Other Factors   Most Western acquirers come from an environment where business operations are highly transparent, with standard and mature processes supported by reliable financial data and a well-developed legal system. In China, however, things are much less transparent, business practice is changing, and the legal system is evolving. There are multiple parallel and inconsistent financial data and companies can be heavily affected by government bureaucracy. As a result, there are many uncertainties and ambiguities during an M&A project. Managers need to be ready and mentally prepared.

To add to the complexity, communication barriers present challenges for everyone. Lack of clear communication and the different language interpretation issues will cause employee anxiety, mistrust, and uncertainty about their future, and some managers or talents may leave. In the absence of official "news," rumors often travel faster than email announcements.

It is a good practice to publish weekly or monthly newsletters in local languages, with news from the Chinese human resources (HR) department as well as from the acquiring company's management team, and to clarify the integration roadmap and initiatives. Identifying key talent and developing retention plans and early incentive announcements (before deal close) would be another way to manage the risk.

Understanding those differences and risks and being prepared to handle them with the right team would greatly enhance the effectiveness and chance of success of M&A projects in China.

Issue No. 2: What Is the Right Profile for the Integration Management Team?

The high-profile failures of some well-respected Fortune 500 companies when entering China have sparked many discussions. There seems to be a consensus that a foreign company needs to find local talent to help it adapt to the local environment and to better manage the deep cultural gap, the language barrier, and differing management styles.

Language Is Not the Issue Language barrier issues seem to be apparent since most of the locals in China are unable to communicate well in English, especially in the second- or third-tier cities, and many foreigners only know a few words of Chinese. One might argue that with the help of interpreters the issue can be resolved easily. However, being able to speak the language does not mean that the parties will be able to converse effectively. Some expatriate managers have hired bilingual executive assistants to help with the communications, and other companies hired local managers to deal with the language issue.

However, as those companies found out, an effective manager would not only be able to understand the language but must also be familiar with both the Chinese culture and that of the foreign company. Therefore, some companies, especially the larger multinationals, were lucky enough to find a native Chinese-speaking manager from the home office (where the company headquarters are located) and send them to the battlefield (China) hoping that this would be that silver bullet. Those managers have typically come out of China and worked in the foreign companies for a few years and have shown promising ability in a functional area such as marketing/sales or product development or have done well in project management and earned a level of trust from business unit leaders. A few of them were able to hit the ground running but many cannot deliver the expected results in the first few critical months or even years after the close of an M&A deal. There could be many reasons, but the main challenge is that the "rising stars" had very little work experience, if any, in China before they left China to study abroad and later on joined a foreign company. Some of them become successful in certain functional areas in the Western business environment but they rarely have the necessary experience to deal with the social, market, and legal complexities in such an emerging market as in China. It would be challenging enough for them to lead a single functional area of an acquired Chinese company, not to mention the cross-functional and cross-border teams. A better option would be to look for those who have been working for multinational companies in China for many years with multiple roles after returning from abroad, those who have a better understanding of both the Western corporate culture and what it takes to navigate the waters in a local Chinese company.

With a larger budget and bigger resources, some of the serial acquirers have been able to find and train this type of manager and were able to develop strong in-house capabilities over a period of 10 to 20 years. Many other companies, however, don't have the luxury to maintain a dedicated team of PMI specialists and have to "borrow" part-time resources who typically have line-management roles in sales, marketing, finance, HR, or even legal in an acquiring company's business unit. There are even companies that put a generic project manager in charge of the entire M&A and PMI program.

A Project Manager Is Not Enough As we all have seen, during a full M&A project cycle, there could be many obstacles that require an experienced PMI leader or a PMI team to proactively manage the many conflicts between the acquirer and the target in China. Not only should the PMI leader have the skills as a super project manager to identify and coordinate the many interdependencies across the various integration work streams, he or she also needs to possess the leadership ability and the political sensitivity to deal with a broad range of cross-functional teams, from the steering committee and CEO at the top to work stream project members at the bottom, over whom the PMI leader very often doesn't have direct authority but still needs to lead and exert influence.

Having realized the significant challenges and importance of the local management role during the transformation period after the deal is closed, some companies have done well by bringing in senior executives who previously have successfully managed integration projects in China. Others find hiring highly experienced and specialized consultants as interim general managers very effective during the critical transition period. They typically are bilingual and have a deep understanding of Chinese culture and the ways business is conducted in China. They have also managed many operational teams both in China and abroad, and can handle the uncertainty and the changing environments very well. Not only are such external resources sensitive to critical issues, they can also effectively move the integration team forward with the ability to resolve the challenging matters at the appropriate management level. Sometimes, they are set up as the interim CEO of the acquired company before a permanent candidate can be identified and brought onboard.

To ensure a successful return on acquisitions in China, companies need to be mindful of this crucial issue at an early stage and be prepared to bring in the right team to handle the complexities often not seen in their home countries. The fast-paced emerging market in China is quite different from that of a well-developed and mature economy.

Issue No. 3: What Is the Appropriate Governance and the Level of Control?

A crucial aspect in M&A projects is to identify and establish the required level of management structure and control. In a cross-border situation, key decision makers often lack the information on the ground and the necessary experience to properly assess a program prior to making key decisions. This could lead to inadequate planning, poor execution, or insufficient monitoring and control. The following section addresses some of the common issues and provides recommendations based on the experience we have accumulated over the years.

Reporting Line and Decision Making   To ensure control and compliance, many companies have sent expatriates to China only to learn that they need to adapt to the local environment. Thereafter they hired local resources on the Chinese management team, or found seasoned executives with international experience in running businesses. However, reporting lines are such that a China country manager or integration director often needs to go through layers of management before reaching the top management at headquarters. Examples of such layers are the manager of the APAC division, or a senior executive from the international business division. More often than not, those managers outside China typically don't have a daily view of situations on the ground. Even though they may have visited China a few times, they don't have the comprehensive knowledge of the local cultures (which sometimes can be quite different in different cities in China. For example, people born in the north part of China are typically more straightforward than those from the south), but have the responsibilities to make key decisions that impact the local situation and integration result.

Due to the information imbalance and lack of understanding of the dynamic and fluid business environment in China, they tend to take longer to move forward with making decisions. To complicate things, headquarters processes may dictate lengthy discussions and consensus building, greatly affecting the speed of executions at a time when swift adjustments to integration plans or ad hoc decisions are required. This may partially explain why smaller foreign companies often do better in adapting to the environment in China than some of the larger Fortune 500 companies.

Integration Management Office   We have seen more successful approaches where companies gave their local integration management office (IMO) team more authority and flexibility in making the necessary decisions, allowing them to be more independent and report directly to both the headquarters and the local company CEO or country manager. This helped the PMI to maintain a balance between process compliance and progress effectiveness, between strategic control and operational flexibility. However, the steering committee would also need to set reasonable boundaries on "go/no-go" decisions, so that key decisions with great risks can be managed. Other alternatives include setting shorter deadlines for decision feedback from the headquarters or the steering committee, having more frequent steering committee meetings even if not every member can be present at those meetings so that key decisions get made quicker.

Set the Right Priority As companies enter into emerging markets such as China, growth and market share often override the significance of synergy and profitability. Management is more focused on controlling key functions such as financial reporting, HR, and audit and aligning key persons than on an acquisition strategy to drive change and move forward. Senior executives need to be visible, especially the local CEO, and be up front in breaking down the resistance to change by applauding small and early achievements. Such actions motivate alignment to changes. The IMO needs to leverage the existing management team, but establish key control points within the acquired company.

Issue No. 4: M&A Strategy Execution and Localization

Generally, there are two types of pitfalls in executing the M&A strategy. The most common one is the strategy disconnect between the deal team and the PMI team. As the deal closes, the deal team typically moves on to other projects and rarely has the opportunity or interest to constantly reengage the PMI team on strategic and due diligence issues. Additionally, during the course of PMI, work stream leaders may go through changes or replacements, and the strategy message is often lost in transition. In other cases, due to communication issues, the real contents of M&A strategy are not translated correctly to the team on the ground.

Strategy Clarity It is the responsibility of the project steering committee to set and enforce the expectation of strategy clarity and consistency throughout the entire M&A project life cycle. It is the responsibility of the integration management office to ensure the strategy messages get interpreted and transferred, and the actual sources of value can be understood by the entire team and every member of the PMI team as well as the employees of the target company. Ideally, IMO managers would join deal teams early on, in order to identify key issues and risks in the due diligence process, assist the culture assessment and fitness evaluation, and validate synergy estimates with business unit leaders.

Localization The second pitfall, which is often more fatal than the first, is that the M&A strategy was not adjusted or localized to fit into the fast-changing business and social environment as well as the competitive landscape in China. Traditionally, some people may say, "We only change tactics but not the strategy."

Well, this may work in a well-developed market and system in the West. However, in an emerging market such as China, many uncertainties exist. The legal system is less than perfect, new government regulations come out every year, and competition is often fierce and cutthroat. Top management needs to adjust their perspective and to adopt an emerging market mind-set. They also need to be flexible and be prepared for the shortened cycle of many business operations to meet the changing market needs in China. A leading practice is for top management to set boundaries, but to not dwell on stringent processes and rules. If progress falls short of expectations during the first-100-day review, there should be a serious review of the initial strategy by functional area, to assess the impact of the actual local conditions on the ground. One cannot stick his or her head in the sand to tough it out. Additionally, a well-constructed governance structure and localized management team would also be important to ensure timely monitoring and practical decision making. Failure to adopt a localized strategy has been one of the crucial mistakes for some of the well-known brands that entered China but failed, and this lesson learned is invaluable to other future corporate investors.

CASE STUDY

How Starbucks maintains its global brand image, but still manages to localize its operations and product offerings.

Unlike many other foreign brands that sometimes use price cuts to fight for market share with the local competitors, Starbucks maintained its brand integrity by maintaining its global standard services to create the same exceptional experience as elsewhere in the world. One of its successful practices is to bring their best baristas from established markets to China to train new employees. Not only do they teach superior skills of coffee making, but more important they bring Starbucks culture and global standard of service to each local store in China.

In contrast to Home Depot or Mattel, Starbucks did not fall into the trap of "global products," or "global platform"; they offered a highly localized menu of beverages that is particularly tailored to Chinese consumers' tastes from their extensive research and analysis. It even gives each store the flexibility to choose from a wide variety of its beverage portfolio that fits the particular local customers, as taste may differ across different regions in China. It is critical for global brands to adapt their businesses to local markets in order to succeed in China, and Starbucks did just that.

ISSUES AND APPROACHES FOR OUTBOUND M&A FROM CHINA

As mentioned earlier in this chapter, China's outbound foreign direct investment (OFDI) expanded significantly from 2005 to 2014. A lot of investments initially targeted the developing world but the focus has been shifting to North America and Europe. Since 2009, Chinese direct investment in America and Europe has increased significantly. For example, Chinese investment in the United States grew from less than $1b annually before 2008 to $2b in 2009 and $5b in 2010. The deal flows are poised to grow more beyond 2014 through the next decade, according to many economic estimates.

Overall, as shown in Figure 15.3, outbound M&A has grown sharply since 2008 and has reached $56.9b in 2014. In comparison, just two months into 2016, Chinese companies have already made roughly $55b in outbound M&As according to data reported by *China Daily*.

With such increased activity in outbound M&A, some companies have achieved their initial goal of "going global." However, they encountered many social, legal, and operational issues that needed to be resolved. To understand the challenges, we need to look at the types of investments and the motivation behind them. Outbound investments for Chinese companies can be grouped into the following three categories:

- Acquiring natural resources
- Acquiring distribution channels
- Acquiring advanced technology and well-known brands

In the past, since the double-digit growth rate in China outweighed the potential offered by overseas opportunities, OFDI from China in the early years was focused on developing countries, investment in developed economies, such as Australia and Canada, was limited to securing natural resources and building

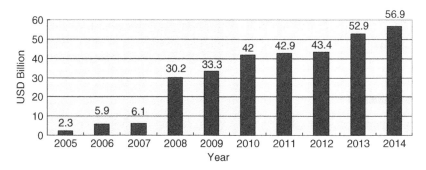

FIGURE 15.3   Outbound M&A from China (2005–2014)

the infrastructure necessary for cross-border trade. Maintaining control at board level to implement strategy is achievable and relatively less complex.

This began to change in 2008 when investment flows to Europe and North America grew sharply. The emerging trend behind Chinese investments in developed economies was driven by business and government policy that pushes Chinese companies to look abroad. As export trade slowed down after the global financial crisis in 2008, access to improved distribution networks became more important to Chinese companies. They sought to build and improve control of their export distribution channels.

In addition, as capacity over-builds and domestic competition heated up, more Chinese companies started to look overseas for ways to resolve overcapacity or low value added price competition issues. Publicly traded companies tried to leverage the size of the global market as additional growth potential when their domestic market space became more saturated and the overall Chinese market slowed down during 2010–2015, mainly due to a reduction in industrial output, sluggish property investment, and a contraction in exports. However, a key motivator for many Chinese companies doing overseas M&A deals is the need to acquire advanced technology or well-known global consumer brands to upgrade their product offerings, to move up in the value chain in areas previously conceded to companies from the developed countries, and to augment managerial skills and staffing to remain globally competitive.

The North American market is important to Chinese firms for its market size in terms of export trade from China, availability of abundant innovations and global brands, advanced technology, and management practices. The European market also became attractive due to the fact that the European Union is an integrated market, has a single currency, a good regulatory environment, and availability of acquisition targets at more attractive prices in recent years after the financial crisis.

Several large-scale acquisitions have been made, such as Sinopec Shanghai Petrochemical Co.'s (Sinopec) $2.5b investment in five shale oil and gas fields owned by Oklahoma-based Devon Energy Corp.; the $2.6b acquisition of the movie theater operator AMC Entertainment Holdings by China's Dalian Wanda Group Co.; the $1.8b successful bid of Zhejiang Geely Holding Group to carve out Volvo from Ford; and the record-breaking $43b cash buyout of Swiss pesticide and seeds giant Syngenta by the Chinese state-owned chemical company ChemChina announced on February 3, 2016.

The Challenges

Key impediments for Chinese firms when setting up shop overseas are their inexperience and lack of capabilities rather than political or social issues. This puts the Chinese firms at a disadvantage on pre-deal target sourcing, due diligence, and negotiations. On top of that, as the Chinese companies rush out to secure deals (many of the deals were such that Chinese firms became the largest shareholder but not necessarily have the majority of shares of the foreign companies they had invested in), they may not consider PMI as important as the M&A deal itself, or they simply don't have the power to initiate an integration agenda due to the lack of majority shares or negotiation compromise when signing a deal to leave the current management team and many of its practices unchanged. This would make the outbound investment even more challenging and risky.

Some of the key challenges for Chinese companies going overseas are:

- Lack of management capability and control in foreign countries, especially in the West
- Huge differences in culture and management styles
- Lack of understanding of local legal, financial, labor, environmental compliance systems, and foreign market risks
- Poor brand recognition and general concerns over product quality toward Chinese brands by foreign consumers
- Lack of unique technical or product competitive advantages other than price

In addition to the typical issues in cross-border projects that we discussed earlier, some unique challenges that may derail the efforts of the global strategy for many Chinese companies remain.

People Management

People management can be very tricky for Chinese managers because of differing management styles. A top-down micromanaging style can put a lot of stress on Western employees who are not used to it and may feel they are not being fully trusted to manage their own work. This can lead to employees being less motivated, depressed, or simply leaving the company, especially in Western countries. What motivates Chinese employees is not always the same as what motivates foreign employees. This is one of the key culture issues that makes it very challenging for Chinese managers on the ground to control local employees and execute planned strategies.

Management Issues

Due to different governance structures in foreign companies, especially the larger ones, simply becoming a major shareholder and controlling the board doesn't guarantee complete control of the company's daily operations. Sooner or later, companies will need a strategy and a solid plan to transform and integrate the acquired business based on the acquiring company's business strategy and deal rationale in order to realize its expected deal value. After all, many of the large M&A deals made by the Chinese companies were secured through bidding and a relatively high premium was paid for the targets. Even though plenty of due diligence has been performed to identify risks and issues, there is no substitute for a well-planned and well-executed post-merger or post-investment integration. Just as foreign companies need excellent PMI teams when entering into the Chinese market, Chinese companies also need a sophisticated PMI team to implement the M&A strategy and capture the value when investing overseas. There are no shortcuts.

Local Experts Needed

When dealing with M&A projects in foreign countries, a comprehensive and pragmatic approach needs to be taken to study and understand the local cultural, social, legal, and regulatory environment. Engaging local experts to assist with these tasks would be very helpful. Most important, the issues of corporate control and governance need to be understood and well prepared for with realistic post-deal measures. Optimistic assumptions can come back and bite the returns out of the investment. Thus we strongly recommend that Chinese firms going abroad equip themselves with highly experienced deal and integration teams, ideally including hired local experts as well as seasoned executives with international experience. This would greatly increase their chance of success in their overseas ventures.

CHAPTER CHECKLIST FOR PART 1: CHINA

- Inbound case to China
  - Understand culture differences down to the regional level
  - Manage Guanxi (relationship) proactively and build trust first
  - Recognize the motivation of the Chinese management team
  - Understand the motivation of Chinese employees and generational differences
  - Keep clear and frequent communications with the employees of the target company
  - Secure talent with international experience
  - A project manager is not enough; a seasoned PMI team is needed
  - Set up an appropriate reporting structure between headquarters and the local PMI team
  - Set the right priority between growth and profit
  - Maintain a clear and consistent integration strategy
  - Adjust the M&A and PMI strategies based on the local situation

- Outbound case from China
  - Understand the management styles in Western cultures
  - Leverage local resources to minimize uncertainty in foreign legal, financial, and labor issues
  - Create a dedicated and well-qualified local PMI team
  - Establish a structured governance system
  - Go beyond controlling the board and motivate the middle managers

PART 2: JAPAN

PART 2 LEARNING OBJECTIVES—IN THIS PART, YOU WILL LEARN:

➤ Current trends of cross-border M&A and PMI in Japan
➤ Critical issues and approaches in outbound and inbound M&A
➤ Practical approaches for problems we will face

PART 2 SUMMARY:

Part 2 describes key issues and practical approaches to solve the problems Japanese companies face when they purchase foreign companies and when a non-Japanese company purchases Japanese companies. The issues are categorized for outbound from Japan and inbound to Japan. We have to carefully treat organizational issues peculiar to Japanese companies. On the other hand, simultaneously, we have to quickly install and utilize standardized PMI methodologies in integrations. Moreover, we need to have some knowledge to avoid pitfalls that occur when working with Japanese companies. Otherwise we will lose the expected outcomes from the integrations.

OVERVIEW OF M&A AND POST-MERGER INTEGRATION IN JAPAN

Japanese companies think of M&A as one of the major corporate strategies in addition to traditional organic growth. The number of mergers and acquisitions conducted by Japanese companies has grown since 2011 in both "In-In" and outbound deals. In-In denotes Japanese companies buying other Japanese companies.

Additionally, acquirers have started to pursue bigger deals than before. There are lots of cases. Tokyo Marine Holdings, a leading Japanese insurance company, purchased HCC Holdings for $7.5b. Meiji Yasuda Life insurance bought StanCorp Financial Group for $4.9b. And Nihon Keizai Shimbun, a major economic press, bought the Financial Times group for 844 million pounds. In order to understand these mega-deals, we need to learn a bit of background about the Japanese economy.

Matured Economy

The Japanese domestic market is saturated in most industries. Some economic data show that Japan's gross domestic product has been saturated since around 2000. This is due to the declining population and workforce. Therefore the market is required to be reconstructed and domestic companies are forced to be merged for more economic efficiency. To name a few, retail banking service, retail store chains, and petroleum industries are good examples of domestic M&A in Japan. This trend will continue for a while as it is difficult to write scenarios for growth in the domestic market.

Growth Strategy

As we cannot expect more growth in most of the Japanese market, many companies try to expand their business into the global market. Some companies are getting better with the help of the government-led economic stimulus package. They are pursuing the next growth strategy and they have two options. One is to start a new business, and the other is to expand their current business from local to global. As a result, many Japanese companies conduct M&A against foreign companies to expand their activities.

In this Part 2 of this chapter, we can identify post-merger integration (PMI) issues following both inbound M&A and outbound M&A conducted by Japanese companies. And we can try to propose practical approaches to solve the PMI issues.

ISSUES AND APPROACHES FOR OUTBOUND M&A AND POST-MERGER INTEGRATION FROM JAPAN

Many Japanese companies invest a lot of money and assets for M&A deals. But most of them do not regard the post-merger process as important. In many cases, the operations in the acquired foreign companies are kept as completely the same as before. Although they buy a new technology or add a new business, they seem to believe it is better to keep the operation the same as before. They literally put in practice "When in Rome, do as the Romans do." However, this laissez-faire policy sometimes brings little or no governance to control the acquired company and cannot take appropriate actions once the new organization worsens financially. Parent Japanese companies, in some cases, even fail to notice the fact that the acquired company is in a crisis situation.

There are several reasons for their reluctance to control acquired companies. We have to clarify the critical factors coming from Japanese culture and its characteristics.

Issue No. 1: English Conversation Capability

A majority of Japanese business persons, in general, are not good at English conversation compared to other major developed countries. The score of the Test of English for International Communication (TOEIC) shows that Japan was ranked fortieth out of 48 countries in 2013. English itself is a communication infrastructure in global business. Therefore poor English capability causes misunderstanding and troubles in global business scenes. And it often occurs when Japanese companies purchase foreign companies.

Issue No. 2: High-Context Culture

Even if your Japanese counterpart can speak English proficiently, his or her communication may depend on an "A-Un" style, a form of traditional nonverbal communication, which is not saying any words or expressing any thoughts among insider members. Japan is an island country and historically developed in isolation from other countries. Therefore the Japanese have developed a monocultural identity and don't need special efforts to understand each other. It might be a generalized idea, but it is still true.

Issue No. 3: Slow Decision Making

Japanese decision making is often based on mutual consensus without discussions. The reason is that the Japanese community originated from a village community. The role and responsibility of each member is very vague and naturally occurring. In the village community, even important issues are not discussed and critical decisions are suspended. Slow decision making is still very comfortable for many Japanese businesspeople.

Issue No. 4: Bottom-Up Problem Solving

In general, each employee is very capable and highly committed to his or her job. So they are very good at kaizen, or continuous improvement, based on bottom-up problem solving. However, depending on kaizen too much is a double-edged sword. They can improve the situation gradually but are not accustomed to the revolutionary change that is required, especially after mergers and acquisitions.

Issue No. 5: Inclination to Avoid Changes

Traditional Japanese businesspeople prefer stable organizational systems. Japanese companies were operated under a lifetime employment system for a long time. So the workers have little or no resilience to downsizing or layoffs. The current government-led employment safety-net system is not sufficient to cover the drastic changes that Japanese companies have not experienced before. They try to avoid restructuring themselves even after integrations.

Due to the previous five factors, when Japanese companies try to merge with foreign ones, their integration is implemented very slowly and they hold insufficient traditional structures and processes. Therefore there is lots of room to improve. We can maximize the outcome of integration by focusing on post-merger phases as follows.

Crystallize Goals and Strategies

As the first step, the strategy of the new organization should be clearly defined and shared with all members, including purchased companies. The corporate strategy in some Japanese companies is sometimes vague and not shared with employees. Their employees have to work without fully understanding vision and strategy. What is required at Japanese companies is that they get away from their traditional comfort area where mutual nonverbal understanding exists. And then crystallize and declare their goals and strategies to new foreign participants who have different cultural backgrounds and perspectives.

Document Operational Process

Japanese operational knowledge should be defined and shared with related members. The operational process is often generated empirically from task-dedicated blue-collar workers. They have often developed the accumulated knowledge, but they rarely share this with others in their workplace. In order to introduce efficient operation in a new organization, it is necessary to put the accumulated knowledge down in writing.

Define Key Performance Indicators

Key performance indicators, or KPI, should be also defined and assigned to each role in new organizations. It is still not easy to share the same directions even though the management members try their best to deliver their strategy to the new organization, due to the difference between Japanese and other cultures. We need not only strategy sharing but also more practical guidelines to move forward after cross-border integrations. Our experience shows that well-defined appropriate KPI setting is critical to manage new organizations with multicultured members.

Use Standardized Process for Post-Merger Integration

The PMI process, which is standardized and accepted for globally successful companies, should be used as an inevitable element for integrations. Japanese companies sometimes make light of the PMI process and omit it. And they try to keep the same operation in acquired companies as before. However, it generates various types of problems after integrations. The standardized PMI process is an efficient and productive way to share mutual understanding among culturally different companies at the early stage of integrations.

Communicate More

More communication should be actively conducted. Culture and language barriers generate bad communication and, as a result, many concerns remain unsolved in the integration processes and may cause serious problems as the integration proceeds. The concerns should be identified at an early stage and shared to find solutions for them. If your company was purchased by a Japanese company and the company has not announced their managerial concerns, then you should point out your concerns proactively from the purchased side's perspective. Otherwise chaotic situations may be generated later. Proactive communication from both sides is also a key to success.

ISSUES AND APPROACHES FOR INBOUND M&A AND POST-MERGER INTEGRATION IN JAPAN

Now we move to inbound M&A and PMI instead of outbound. Our experiences show that major purposes for purchasing a Japanese company can be categorized as follows:

- To enter the Japanese domestic market
- To acquire Japanese technological advantages
- To incorporate Japanese-trusted brand names

Some pharmaceutical and retail multinational blue chips had purchased Japanese companies for the purpose of entering the Japanese market during the last two or three decades. As Japanese GDP is used to being ranked second in the world and Japan still has over 126 million people, some market segments are still attractive for some industries.

On the other hand, the trend has shifted to the pursuance of technological advantage and brand names for market entry purpose. Some industries, like medical devices and electrical appliances, are interested in incorporating Japanese technological advantages into their research and development (R&D) and manufacturing departments. And Japanese brand names are also valuable for emerging new powers, including well-funded Chinese apparel and food companies.

Although their purposes are different among purchasing parent companies, our experience shows that there are common and critical issues for success when integrating Japanese companies. The key idea is the well-balanced approach between global standardization for outcomes and cultural adaptation for processes.

Issue No. 1: Necessity to Install Reporting Systems Quickly

Most companies that purchased Japanese companies and are performing well, have well-established reporting systems that include budget-planning and performance-tracking systems, by which top management can grasp and control real business by each department separately. Generally speaking, we have to consider cultural differences. However, as to reporting systems, in most cases there is little need to re-tune your original systems. You might not have to translate the original language in the original system.

Japanese employees may initially complain about it, but they can make full use of it soon if you provide appropriate supports. You can install reporting systems immediately after integration.

However, in many cases, it is the first experience for Japanese employees to work for a company that is purchased by a foreign company. Therefore, explanations are needed for why new reporting systems are important to the new parent company and how to fill the reporting formats with appropriate guidelines and templates. In other words, Japanese employees may be averse to change if they do not understand the reasons and procedures, but once they understand them, they become very dedicated and cooperative.

Issue No. 2: Lack of Clear Definition of Expected Result

Even if a purchased Japanese company is a well-known major player in the industry, it is not common to have well-organized job descriptions or roles and responsibilities defined clearly for each position. We can adapt the same approach as the reporting systems to this issue. We can translate and adopt the parent company's job descriptions directly as in the first step.

The point is that we have to consider definitions of expected results and expected processes "separately." The definition of expected results is required for each position because most Japanese companies lack it. But some cases might not have to be changed, because the current processes are often optimized for their local business environment.

Japanese nonmanagerial staff and workers are generally more capable and committed to their tasks than those of non-Japanese parent companies, especially in the operation and manufacturing departments. Coerced introduction of the parent company's standardized process might bring unproductive confusion. We need to clarify expected results for each position, make employees commit to the result, and then delegate how to achieve it.

Issue No. 3: Loss of Respect for Employees' Dignity

Japanese employees are sometimes very far from "homo economicus." They do not necessarily prioritize monetary benefit when confronting personal decisions. We wouldn't say that an attractive retirement package does not work for targeted low-performing employees at the downsizing stage after integrations. But in cases where Japanese employees feel their past contribution was denied or they were strongly insulted by a new foreign employer, they will pretend to obey but secretly betray new bosses, and sometimes attack them with their labor union.

A certain global pharmaceutical giant integrated some midsized competitors and tried to optimize the size of its sales force in Japan. Following their standard downsizing process, they designed early retirement packages, which were very attractive, identified the targeted employees to be fired, and then announced them in the very short term. It was common and reasonable for the parent company's culture.

But many Japanese employees felt insulted by this downsizing action, even if the retirement package was appealing from a monetary perspective. They were supported by the labor union and leaked internal information to a major economic press. In the end, the parent company had to retract the original downsizing plan and make a promise to sustain full employment.

From another standpoint, we can take advantage of employees' mentality. If employees wish to be treated with full respect for their dignity, the retained employees will show their strong commitment to new bosses and new organizations, and nonretained people will accept mediocre packages if asked to leave the company. We have to utilize effectively the peculiar sensitivity of Japanese employees.

Issues No. 4: Too Much Dependency on Fluent English-Speaking Members

The management members coming to Japan are apt to trust and depend too much on fluent English-speaking Japanese. However, unfortunately, English-speaking capability does not accord with functional or managerial capability in most Japanese companies, partly due to the excessive emphasis on reading and grammar capability in the past education system for English in Japan.

It is understandable that expats from parent companies depend on them, but this tendency can devastate their integration effort. We observed lots of cases where expat members made wrong decisions by depending on biased and incorrect information from Japanese with very limited English-speaking capability.

Moreover, these employees will be easily promoted to managerial positions only due to their English capability with recommendations from expat members even if their functional performance is mediocre. A certain Japanese automobile manufacturer was bought by a German automobile giant. In this case, many skillful procurement staff members were fired or left voluntarily. The remaining and newly hired staff were surely able to communicate well in English, but most were amateurs and mediocre performers in function.

Our recommendation is that foreign expats must not hesitate to use more than one translator in order to communicate with and get information from functionally capable employees who cannot speak English well. It is true that there are some risks in using translators because a translator might manipulate and control sensitive nuances of the conversation for his or her own benefit. Sometimes a translator might behave like "fox that borrows the authority of a tiger," which means a person who swaggers about under borrowed authority. Despite the possibility of the risks, it is better to use two or three translators.

Issue No. 5: Malfunction of Integration Management Office

We have also observed that some experienced parent companies struggle against unexpected obstacles in the integration process of Japanese companies. A certain European electronics company purchased a medical device division from an American company. Its highly vaunted integration management office teams were sent to each office in order to facilitate local integrations. Like their past records, the integration team succeeded in every country except Japan. The two sales teams that originated from each company still have deep antagonism for each other even five years after the initial integration.

These frictions are often caused by ignoring the previous five issues that are not necessarily the same as those in Asian developing countries or in developed Western counties. We have to care about these issues described earlier.

It may be necessary to put additional local Japanese-native IMO support members in order to bridge the dispatched headquarters IMO team and the local employees. The IMO support members should be familiar with the cultural and organizational issues and should be able to handle the obstacles they face.

The IMO support members can be internal or external. If the parent company has a plan to purchase more Japanese companies in the near future, it is reasonable for it to have its own IMO team especially for Japan, otherwise it could be useful to hire external inbound IMO specialists.

Don't underestimate the obstacles you will face when purchasing Japanese companies. And remember that you will face many more difficulties to incorporate their capability than you expect. You have to prepare and adopt appropriate approaches to tackle these obstacles.

CHAPTER CHECKLIST FOR PART 2: JAPAN

- Outbound case from Japan
  - Crystallize goals and strategies
  - Document operational process
  - Define key performance indicators
  - Use standardized process for PMI
  - Communicate more
- Inbound case to Japan
  - Install reporting system quickly
  - Define expected result clearly
  - Respect employee dignity
  - Don't depend too much on members who are fluent in English
  - Utilize an IMO

CHAPTER 16

Cross-Border Synergy Program Management

Michael Holm

CHAPTER LEARNING OBJECTIVES—IN THIS CHAPTER, YOU WILL LEARN:

➤ How to define synergies and validate them pre-signing
➤ How to structure your synergy program
➤ How to take critical actions to capture synergies
➤ How to implement post-closing due diligence, leading practice sharing, and peer review
➤ How to track synergies

CHAPTER SUMMARY

This chapter begins with an introduction and what benefits to look for in cross-border deals. Next, synergies are defined and how to validate them pre-deal. The chapter then explains how to structure a synergy program and how to track synergies until realized.

INTRODUCTION

The value of an acquisition can be divided into two categories:

1. The stand-alone value
2. Synergies with buyer's business

The *stand-alone value* is how the target is expected to perform in terms of growth, cash flow, revenues, costs, and profits over the next years, normally over a five-year period. A discounted cash flow (DCF) model is used to calculate that future value back to today and, in part, used to price the target (the other being the synergies). Two versions of the stand-alone value are usually built by the buyer into the DCF:

1. **Base case** for the business: Determined from historical trends and performance looking at the target and its industry peers, and the buyer's view of the possible future performance of the business. Normally there are versions on the conservative side (not to overvalue the target) and on the best-case side (to understand the dream scenario). The true value falls somewhere in between and the understanding gained by exploring is valuable.
2. **Management case** for the business: How the seller's management believes that the business will perform going forward. This is normally optimistic since it increases the price of the target. Overly optimistic management cases could be mitigated and reality checked with earn-outs or bonus discussions.

The two cases and scenarios within the cases are used to model the sensitivity of future expectations for the business (see Figure 16.1).

The synergy case, or *synergies*, is how the buyer and target business can be combined to create value above the stand-alone value. This is where 1 + 1 > 2. Both buyer and seller normally build a synergy DCF. The seller builds it to understand the value of the business to the buyer and adds part of it to the management case to increase the initial asking price of the target. The buyer builds it to understand the value and sensitivity in how the two companies can be combined. The possible financial synergies are usually between 20% and 40% and operating synergies are between 60% and 80% of the total synergy value for a private equity acquirer. For corporate acquirers, these percentages are harder to generalize and depend on the situation at both the acquirer and target.

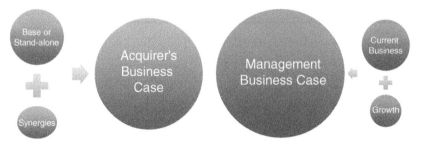

FIGURE 16.1   Picture of Base Case, Management Case, and Synergy Case

Both buyer and seller put the synergies into their valuation of the target and the buyer in the end has to include (or pass on) on average between 15% and 50% of those in the bid price. In some deals the buyer openly states which synergies are included and excluded in their DCF and valuation. In other deals it is cloak-and-dagger to try to expose how the other party has calculated. The saying goes "there are no rules in love, war, or M&A." Depending on the buyer's level of confidence the synergies could be included to a minimum or almost fully in the DCF. So, the next question is how long in time the synergies will last and how to reflect that in the DCF. There has to be an end in time for revenue synergies when the market, competitors, or other factors have resulted in that it is no longer an advantage but the norm.

When comparing in-country versus cross-border deals, the biggest factors that affect how to manage synergies are:

- The need to understand the target's business and operating models on a deeper level bottom-up in order to validate synergies—there could be different logic and key performance indicators (KPIs) for target compared to acquirer.
- The realization of synergies could be different within the target than the norm for the acquirer.
- Communication is needed to form an understanding and alignment between target and acquirer. That requires leadership to allocate time pre-deal and normally delays post-closing analysis and execution.
- To what degree unions and work councils are a factor in the process. For example, in a redundancy or factory closing situation.
- How local laws, regulations, tax, or accounting practices might impact the synergies (see Chapter 3 for a more detailed discussion).

Corporations have an advantage over private equity companies regarding synergies when bidding for the same target. Private equity can only add value to the stand-alone target or in the next step get synergies when merging with another target. Corporate bidders have a potentially synergistic business that should enable them to bid higher for a target. However, private equity can, to a certain extent, leverage more on the debt side depending on track record and how their fund is set up. A typical acquisition business case is described in Figure 16.2.

The diagram shows that there could be value lost in the integration. An example of this is, if the transaction is over the threshold for competition clearance procedure, there might be remedies demanded by the competition authority. The remedies would then reduce the value as units are spun

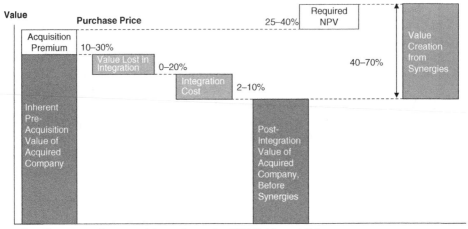

Note: Percentages shown are of the purchase price. NPV, Net Present Value

FIGURE 16.2 Acquisition, Synergy, and Integration Value Analysis

off or markets exited. Another source of lost value could be customers who adjust their buying volumes when two of their suppliers merge. The adjustment could be done to ensure that they also feed their number two and three suppliers. The percentages are typical of midsized to large transactions.

Last but not least, it is possible to slip in other improvements in the organic legacy business of the acquirer during an acquisition. The threshold for accepting changes internally and in the market is lowered both at acquirer and target just after an acquisition. These changes could be:

- Closing loss-making business units
- Office moves
- Redundancies and organizational adjustments
- Portfolio adjustments in products and services
- Renegotiation of contracts with customers or suppliers
- Exit from markets or customers
- Supply chain adjustments
- Price increases

However, these need to be carefully managed and perhaps included in the synergy program. Communication, rhetoric, and logic have to be clear to the organization, as should be the timing connected to the acquisition. For example, that the acquirer has just acquired the target, which leads to some necessary adjustments to the business.

DEFINING AND VALIDATING SYNERGIES

Synergies can be divided into these categories:

- Cost
- Revenue
- Tax
- Balance sheet items such as debt (or lack thereof) and other items that can be leveraged (e.g., facilities that can be sold and space rented instead to release working capital)

Revenue synergies, such as cross-selling new products, or selling them to new markets, are the most difficult to quantify and capture as success depends on the market and customers buying the added value at the business case price point. Some acquirers simply exclude revenue synergies from their valuations and what the purchase price is based on. It is kept as the upside in the transaction, but there is so much risk or uncertainty that it cannot be part of their business case. For other acquirers, revenue synergies form an essential part of the acquisition rationale. They take the cost synergies out of the valuation model and see those as an upside but not material in the deal.

Cost and balance sheet synergies, such as employee redundancies and resource rationalization, are more easily calculated and captured although the time it takes to realize them in the post-closing landscape is sometimes underestimated. It will take time after Day One until synergies are running at 100%; for example, supply chain synergies, redundancies, supplier contract renegotiation due to increased spend, and bargaining power. Employees are very sensitive when it comes to cost synergies and the IMO (integration management office) and the synergy work stream needs to keep communication focused on revenue synergies to mitigate employee morale risks, while quietly working on realizing the cost synergies.

Tax synergies include the target's operating losses in previous years that can be carried forward or used to reduce tax liabilities on future capital gains for the acquirer. The tax losses could reside in the target or subsidiaries to the target.

A synergy is an action or activity over time that results in a positive dollar value. It is often an estimate or calculation by the deal team that is plugged into the DCF. The estimate can be fully or partially supported by facts and some acquirers leave it at that until after the acquisition has been signed. Input to the synergy calculation could come from internal line management, the due diligence, and deal team research. However, to validate the feasibility and the value of a synergy, there is some work to be done. This is especially true in cross-border deals as the market and business operations differ between the countries. The method is a top-down and bottom-up exercise. A simple one-page template can be used to validate each synergy, and the key things to capture are:

- Which manager will be responsible for realizing the synergy (the owner)
- Sign-off of the synergy target by the owner
- Description of the synergy
- Target value of the synergy
- How the synergy will be captured
- Facts and analysis that support the synergy value
- The timeline and investment cost it will take to realize the synergy
- Interdependencies and any prerequisites

An example: The target's product is to be sold through the buyer's sales organization in region X consisting of five countries, which is treated as a new product launch in the region. The regional sales director is responsible for revenue synergies valued at $9m over three years ($1m year one, $3m year two, $5m year three) that are dependent on other functions for:

- Sales staff to be trained on the new product
- Sales incentives are available for the new product; for example, bonus or commission
- Marketing collateral being translated and rebranded
- Market communication supporting the sales launch
- Delivery and support organization being ready
- Pre-sales engineer allocated to the region
- The product being added to financial, customer relationship management (CRM), and other systems

The regional sales director signs off and assumes responsibility for the synergy in the template. The regional sales director and the deal team can then make a simple time plan for what needs to happen after closing the deal and when revenues for the first sales can be recognized in the DCF. The organizational experience and readiness in launching new products in new markets is a factor. If this has been done a sufficient number of times, then the synergy can be validated more accurately.

In the example, the revenue synergy has been broken down to regional sales director level but it could also have stayed on the vice president sales level. Execution and the probability of capturing the synergy is increased the lower it has been broken down, responsibility assigned for synergy and interdependencies during validation. There is a balance between how low in the organization you involve staff in synergy validation and the need to keep the pending deal confidential.

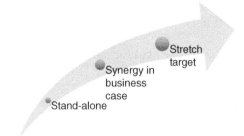

FIGURE 16.3   Stretch Targets

It is also recommended that the revenue synergy targets are stretched if possible (see Figure 16.3). How much stretch depends on how familiar the organization is with working with stretch targets and any target should preferably align with how revenue targets are set in the normal course of business. Some companies that acquire often are able to be very aggressive in setting and achieving stretched synergy targets.

On cost synergies there are a number of considerations needed before execution starts. If it involves redundancies, the criteria used in selecting employees to be made redundant need to be explained easily to those employees. It could be closing down an overlapping product line where the impact on the brand and customers needs analysis. If it involves closing one factory out of many, the selection criteria should be clear within management, the possible ramifications known, and a risk mitigation plan prepared. The time it takes to close down a factory and when the cost synergy starts to positively increase the bottom line is normally underestimated.

For cost synergies (see Figure 16.4), for example, moving production, ramping down, and closing a factory, the same template and method of validation by line management applies:

FIGURE 16.4   Cost Synergies

▓ Analysis of scope and cost of moving production and closing factory
▓ Training of factory staff in receiving factory

- Dismissal or transfer of staff in closing factory
- Incentives to staff in closing factory to work hard until their factory is closed
- Resources needed and time plan for moving production line
- Supplier changes due to move
- Real estate solution for closed factory
- Changes to production, financial, human resource, and supply chain systems
- Logistics changes
- In case of cross-border, regulatory, tariff, and tax implications
- The time plan when the costs for closing down will occur and when the cost synergies will impact the bottom line

Another way to validate synergies is to calculate how long it would take to achieve and the cost to do so through internal benchmarking. For example, the company may have closed three factories in the past five years and can calculate what is realistic for the acquired company. It should not be left to the M&A deal team only to validate synergies—involve the management that closed those factories in evaluating cost synergies. That was an obvious example perhaps. The same obvious internal benchmark is for redundancies in a country.

If there is no internal benchmark, it is possible to use an external research agency that can, without mentioning who is contracting them, approach those in your industry sector or a similar niche that have realized such synergies in the same country as the target. Alternatively, a local consultancy specializing in supply chain can be brought in for an analysis if it is, for example, a factory closure. That is of course using external resources in pre-deal evaluation due diligence, which might be a stranded investment if the deal never happens.

If the synergy is cross-selling, then the benchmark could be how long new product introduction takes in a new market at the acquiring company or the relevant parts of the process.

You can also do a minimum to maximum scenario analysis of possible synergy outcomes to understand the sensitivity (see Figure 16.5).

For cross-border deals it is more important to validate synergies through both deal teams' research and analysis, as well as line management locally or in the region.

Negative Synergies

Negative synergies, or the risk of them, also need to be validated. Negative synergies could be:

Work Stream	Minimum Scenario « Incremental Evolution » (€M)		Maximum Scenario « Quantum Leap » (€M)	
	Cumulative over 3-year period	Recurring gains as of third year	Cumulative over 3-year period	Recurring gains as of third year
Purchasing	5.6	3.4	8.4	5.1
Production	Nd	Nd	Nd	Nd
ICT	−1.7	−0.1	−4.7	−0.8
Finance & Accounting	−0.1	0.7	−0.1	1.5
Legal	0.1	0.1	0.1	0.2
HR	0.1	0.3	0.2	0.5
Logistics	0.8	4.0	-0.5	8.1
Sales	0.4	1.3	−0.5	3.0
Marketing	1.0	0.7	2.0	1.3
Supply chain	0.7	0.4	1.4	0.7
Total	**7.0**	**10.8**	**6.2**	**19.6**

FIGURE 16.5   Minimum to Maximum Scenario

▪ Remedies needed to satisfy competition authorities
▪ Revenues of the acquirer's legacy business in a market can be negatively impacted when introducing the target's products to customers who will be unable or unwilling to do business with a combined entity
▪ Implications of culture clashes (e.g., attrition and lost productivity in a professional services acquisition where there is an exodus of managers and disengaged employees)
▪ Taxes or regulatory costs can increase (or decrease) when thresholds are exceeded
▪ Underfunded pension obligation
▪ Back office systems such as IT, financial, or HR might need to be scaled up due to an acquisition

Some of these could be considered integration costs instead of negative synergies, but many companies separate them out.

Complementary versus Overlapping Synergies

Another way of viewing synergies is if they are complementary to, or overlapping with, the acquirer's business. Complementary synergies are then more easily managed and less controversial in execution. This could be, for example, presence in a new geographical market. To execute on overlapping

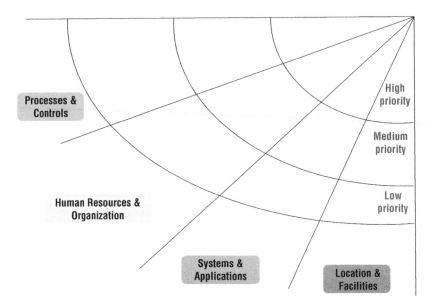

FIGURE 16.6   Synergy Spiderweb

synergies, there needs to be more alignment in between the organizations; for example, merging in a geographical market where both have operations.

Synergies can be very close to each other and overlap or disturb so that the sum is less when you combine the two synergies. An example is if a revenue synergy A is $5m and synergy B is $10m, you would expect $15m if you execute both but the end result might be $13m because they overlap. A synergy from the target can also cannibalize an acquirer's revenue.

A synergy spiderweb can be used to prioritize synergies (see Figure 16.6).

In summary, synergies are educated guesses until a line manager has assumed responsibility, resource needs and interdependencies are signed off, and they are included in budgets and financial plans. The objective post-deal is to update the budgets, allocate resources, and put the necessary incentives in place as quickly as possible.

STRUCTURING SYNERGY PROGRAMS

Once the deal is signed, it is time to structure the synergy program. How this is done depends on the scope, value, and complexity of the synergies. Figure 16.7 illustrates three options. Synergies can be grouped together into revenue and cost synergies or, depending on how the combined company will

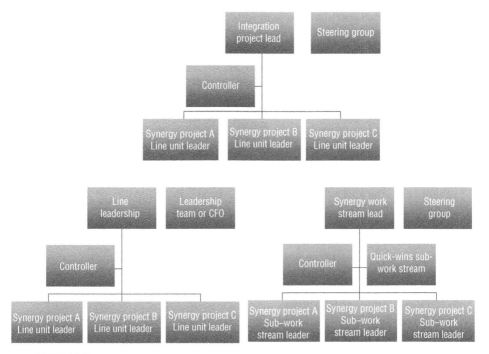

FIGURE 16.7   Different Synergy Structures

be organized, according to functions (sales, operations, IT, etc.), geography, business units, or by products. It also depends on the rationale of the deal and what is mission-critical.

Regardless of structure, there are five decisions and areas to address. First to consider is *governance* and who besides the deal champion needs to have oversight over the synergy program. Candidates are the CFO or a delegate from the finance organization, representative of the acquired company, human resource representative, head of sales, or head of operations. The selection criteria are that there are synergies within the executive's area of responsibility or resources needed from the executive's organization to support synergy capture.

Second is to decide whether or not a *synergy work stream lead* is needed or who reports the progress to the governance team and manages the synergy program. A synergy work stream lead does not have to be full-time. What influences the decision besides scope, value, and complexity is how experienced the organization is in cross-functional projects and cooperation. Does there need to be a co-lead so that both sides of the integration are represented? Another aspect is how much the synergies need to be managed and facilitated. Is it the integration project lead, the synergy work stream lead, the finance work stream lead, or someone else driving and managing the synergy program?

Third is how widely the synergy targets, scope, and results are *to be communicated*. Companies have put up the synergy targets, the name of the manager responsible for the target, and results posted on large charts in the main lobby of main locations and on the intranet. It depends if the whole organization can contribute to the achievement of the targets or if it is focused in a few units. In cross-border deals there needs to be a sensitivity to what local management recommends in terms of visibility of targets and owners. There may also be constraints on releasing information considered to be prejudiced, if certain processes have not concluded (e.g., employee or union consultations related to synergy targets). But for 80% of all deals it is recommended that a high level of visibility is created to control speculation and rumors. This visibility can then be regarded as public information and needs to match what has been said to the media and communicated in announcements. The mind-set throughout this communication to the stakeholders is key for the acquirer to get return on investment (ROI). A positive, open, and sharing spirit will enable synergy teams' work.

Fourth, *who are the owners* for each synergy target in the organization? This has to be at the right level in the organization. A revenue synergy target on a company level of $100m needs to be broken down per region, country, sales representative, account, and business or product line, and assigned to one individual, the owner, similar to how a sales budget allocation process is done. It is also recommended that each owner analyze (alone or in a team) and document the target and details in a plan with resources and toll gates or milestones on how to realize it. The synergy analysis and documentation done pre-deal is input to this exercise.

Fifth, divide the synergies into *low-hanging fruit* or quick wins that are easy to capture and more long-term synergies. This enables more focus on the decision process needed to move into executing the realization of the quick wins.

All synergy target owners, or grouping of target owners, can be together for a kick-off doing reviews of plans and putting requirements on central functions such as finance, human resources, product owners, and so on.

CRITICAL ACTIONS TO CAPTURE SYNERGIES

There are a number of critical actions that cut across most synergy scenarios. They have to do with leadership, people, accountability, business dynamics, business and operational knowledge, interdependencies, involvement of the target's management, stringent systematic approach, analysis methods, and tools. Every day lost in capturing a synergy results in lost revenue that cannot be regained. That revenue is lost forever and this needs to be balanced with how fast it is possible to proceed, considering the resources that need to be allocated to a synergy.

It is necessary in most cases in the post-closing landscape to analyze actions that need to be taken to capture a synergy and their impacts in a cost-benefit analysis. The time spent on analysis by the synergy team depends on how well the synergy was validated pre-closing. The parameters of such an analysis could include impact on:

- Customers
- Market
- Suppliers
- Employees
- Time plan
- Costs to capture synergy summarized
- Revenues or cost reductions = synergy value
- Resources needed versus existing resources

It starts with putting the right governance in place from the board down to the accountability and mandate of the target owner. *All levels of leadership need to add value and to support the owner* until the synergy has been realized. The board might track it on a quarterly basis in a balanced scorecard or traffic light report. Executive management should review on a monthly basis and middle management should be hands-on as required. If the leadership does not get involved and follow up, then the organization will assume that the synergies are not that important.

Target owners must be *experienced line managers* from the A-team and be given clear mandates. The target owner selection process should be a rather open process between acquirer and target's management as the talent and individual capabilities are not known across the combined company. Speed is needed to capture the synergies, but also a period of reflection and discussion before announcing the owners. Human resources and integration management office should be involved in the process. The momentum will be lost and the time to take action will increase 10 times if the wrong manager is picked or if the mandate is unclear. Within cross-border deals it is even more important to increase sensitivity to nuances in communication and to use the period of reflection to ensure that the best person is selected regardless of origin.

Accountability and target owner mandate need to be stated and communicated. Target owners will run into all kinds of issues and it is important that there is an *issue escalation procedure* in place to make sure that the leadership gets involved in resolving the issue. Any business is dynamic and certainly so over the two- to three-year period it normally takes to capture all synergies in a merger. So the leadership needs to be involved to understand how the market or business has changed, and be prepared to adjust accordingly.

Business and operational logic may differ between acquirer and target. It is essential that everyone involved in the merger recognizes that they need to learn and explore that difference in order to be successful. There might be two best ways of getting things done within the company or value to be found by changing or merging into one way of operating. Leadership and employees need to be in a *learning mode* and a quest to understand the logic.

Dependencies and Interdependencies in the Realization of Synergies

There will be dependencies on other units in the combined company to capture synergies. These *dependencies or interdependencies* need to be understood and deliverables and time plan agreed. The leadership and IMO need to be very active in flushing them out. Interim ways of working might be adopted until the dependencies have been delivered. It is clearly not the preferred way, but most functions and synergy teams can live with, for example, a Microsoft Excel solution for a while.

The acquirer's deal team and some line managers will have been involved in the transaction pre-deal. It is leading practice to create open communication around the deal rationale and the synergies within the leadership. More involvement of the acquirer's management and key staff is possible after the deal has been made public, and post-closing the target's key staff and management can also be included. In cross-border deals this should be done with care so that the target's way of working is followed. To gather all of the target's management in alignment workshops will not be effective if it is a "command-and-control" culture.

There have been occasions where leaders (at the acquirer or target) have openly agreed to take action, but have done little in reality. An executive might just wait for a retention bonus or already be on the way out of the company. The damage to momentum in synergy capture and integration can be considerable. Such lip service could normally be detected after alignment workshops or if the first actions to capture synergies are not executed. This is more important in cross-border deals where language, corporate culture, or other reasons might also slow down synergy execution. IMO and synergy work stream need to pay close attention and find the real reason for not executing actions.

Is a Stringent Synergy Structure Needed?

Last but not least, a synergy does not exist until the acquirer has been able to collect and account for it in the company's books. Before then it exists in theory only.

The stringent structure that is being discussed in this chapter might feel heavy, overworked, only applicable to M&A transactions with a large synergy scope, and requiring a lot of time from the organization. It might also be that internal costs to capture synergies were not part of the acquisition business case or DCF. However, the structure works and can mitigate part of the result seen in a PricewaterhouseCoopers (PwC) study (see Figure 16.8). Where the planned versus actual synergy effects differed was between 7 and 12 months, indicating that deal-makers were too optimistic regarding the time it would take until synergies would be captured.

The alternative approach to a synergy structure and tracking, as described in this chapter, is to put line management in charge of breaking down the synergies within their responsibility and realize them without a separate synergy execution and tracking project. This could be appropriate if the synergies are few and of low value compared with the overall target revenues. Line management experience in managing cross-functional teams

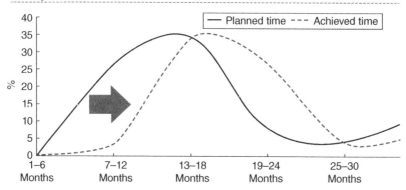

What was your planned timeline to realize the full synergy effect and how long did it actually take?

FIGURE 16.8 Picture with Relationship between Planned versus Actual Synergy Effects over Time in a Study
Source: Thomas Fossum, PwC Sweden, Presentation on Post-Deal Integration, November 11, 2015.

needs to be considered or if the synergies are more or less within organizational silos. It is recommended (see Figure 16.9) that:

- Synergies are included in budget
- Synergies are included in bonus or other incentive schemes
- Synergies are fully included in long-term (2–4 years) business plans
- Synergy tracking responsibility is given to someone outside line management (e.g., within the finance organization)
- Governance is set to follow up on actions taken, results, plans, and decisions on corrective actions

Earn-outs can be used to bridge the difference between seller's and buyer's valuations of a business. The driving factor for including an earn-out is often how the parties view the future revenue potential and the potential in the market. So, an earn-out construction is made tying a percentage of the price of the business to hitting a revenue or profit level in the future. For example, 20% of the price of the business will be paid out if the revenues have increased from $80m to $100m after two years (hence 80% will be paid at closing). The consequences for the post-merger integration project could be that the target needs to be kept at arm's length for two years while the earn-out receiver(s) are focusing on hitting their earn-out. Integration and synergy capture is done if supporting the earn-out and any interferences with the target's business can be vetoed by sellers if the share purchase agreement is structured in favor of earn-out receiver(s). Accounting and finances will be kept as is in the target to ensure that the revenues are calculated correctly.

An earn-out scenario could contradict some of the deal synergies. The suggested remedy to create a win-win is to decouple the costs from the

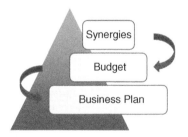

FIGURE 16.9   Relationship between Business Plan, Budget, and Synergies

revenues and define the delta between the seller's and buyer's revenue expectations per product line or market or customer. The resources, cost, and initiatives that will be needed to drive those revenues could be defined. How to measure earn-out fulfillment, the costs that can be spent, and alignment on strategic intent are also key items that could be included in an agreement with sellers. This will remove a barrier and enable a more complete integration between the two businesses during the earn-out period.

The task of realizing the synergies in the transaction depends on the scope of the integration and how much the target will be integrated. A Haspeslagh matrix (see Figure 16.10) can be used to determine how different targets should be integrated if you are contemplating a few acquisitions and could be used as input to the decision on which one to acquire first. The Haspeslagh matrix can also be used to map out how the organization's units should be integrated to understand the impact on synergy realization that will depend on those units. For example, it might be easier to capture certain types of cost synergies in absorption than in symbiosis.

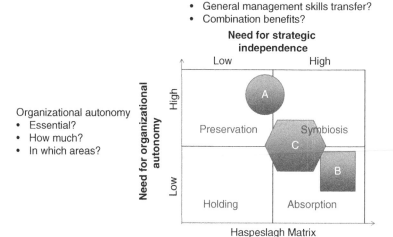

FIGURE 16.10   Haspeslagh Matrix
Source: David B. Jemison and Philippe C. Haspeslagh, *Managing Acquisitions: Creating Value through Corporate Renewal* (New York: Free Press, 1991).

POST-CLOSING DUE DILIGENCE

A leading practice is to review or revisit the important due diligence findings, synergy assumptions, strategy, integration approach, business case, and other key decisions in a *post-closing due diligence workshop*. The recommendation is to do this between two to four months after close. Both acquirer's and target's leadership should participate. The objectives of the workshop are:

- Validation of strategic facts and views on the future
- Alignment on the way forward
- Discovery of further synergies
- Ideas for business and operational development
- Corrective actions based on feedback from synergy teams

The reasoning for post-close due diligence is that the acquirer and target have been looking at the other company's business from an outside-in perspective pre-deal and should have increased understanding two to four months after closing. Assumptions need to be validated with real numbers and current business environment conditions included in the analysis by the experienced leadership of both companies. It is important to look at how business and operations differ compared with the due diligence conclusions and how the leadership decides to act on those differences. One could use the analogy that before closing the acquirer looked at the car from the outside and now two to four months after closing they have been driving it for a while and have gained insights into the business, operations, and people. Both the acquirer's and target's deal teams, leadership, and integration teams could participate. The scope of the post-closing due diligence workshop could be to review (see Figure 16.11):

- Original M&A strategy, analysis, and assumptions to define if there is a delta compared with today's understanding
- Review due diligence reports and recommendations
- Suggest improvements and lessons learned in due diligence
- Review the business case that the acquisition was based on and the results received so far in the business
- Review the closing/Day One actions and lessons learned
- Review remaining actions in the sale and purchase agreement
- Review synergies and execution so far, review discarded synergies pre-deal, and explore new synergies or opportunities for improvement
- Update risk analysis and determine future risk scenario

FIGURE 16.11 Workshop and Analysis Topics for Post-Closing Due Diligence

- Go through the integration work stream charters and results
- Review the integration escalation process and escalations so far
- Determine corrective actions and mitigation

It is a leading practice to look for more synergies at least once more in the period 6 to 12 months after close. The original synergies are by then either captured in quick wins or synergy teams are well on their way through execution, so what else could be of value that could be uncovered by a cross-functional group? A *post-closing synergy exploration* could be done in that period. The participants in this exercise can be the innovators, R&D, sales, and intrapreneurs in the combined company. Looking outward, new opportunities always exist in today's dynamic business environment and new value can be uncovered if the workshop is timed right.

Another area of focus at this time is to look inward at ways of working and leading practices by comparing practices between the merging units. This is normally a different set of participants, such as business process owners, controllers, and other operational staff. The interest is to look at different sets of KPIs to determine if there are efficiency gains in changing or merging ways of working.

An example is a cross-border merger where two companies with +80% market share in the home country and a 100-year-old business model merged with an economies of scale rationale. The biggest surprise was that there were still gains and tweaks to their way of operating and handling the resources. These were not visible by looking at the due diligence material and the financial KPIs. Leading practice teams had to peel away a lot of differences in definitions and perceptions to get down to what actually took place on the floor when delivering to customers and then compare the impact on costs and revenues. The perceptions that had to be dealt with were different tastes and customer patterns, buying power of customers, currency differences between the countries, and so on. In the end, the teams found leading practices from the other that could be quite easily be implemented and showed up on the bottom line shortly after.

Peer reviews can be helpful if another division or business unit has recently acquired and can advise on what to do and what not to do when reviewing the synergy plans with the synergy team. So, it will be the synergy team from a completed transaction done by another division that conducts the review. Peer reviews are used to fast-track and capture learnings that have not yet been entered into the acquirer's processes and methods. The peer review team will use the decision material, analysis, and plans made by the synergy teams and challenge their conclusions. A peer review can be done after synergy teams have made their plans.

Tracking Synergies

A *synergy tracking process* needs to be put in place and a synergy tracking responsible owner needs to be assigned. A finance controller who can set up how to separate out synergy revenues or cost reductions from financial reporting would be ideal (see Figure 16.12). The frequency of reports depends on when the data are available from financial systems, but it is suggested that target owners report progress in parallel or near real time through a simple mechanism. This feedback loop outside the financial system is needed to troubleshoot, correct, and adjust when target deadlines are missed, as well as to communicate early wins and positive news to inspire the staff involved. Progress needs to be reported back to synergy owners and teams on a regular basis.

The objectives for tracking synergies are:

For leadership

- To monitor the actual impact of the integration project on the business
- To report back to shareholders, customers, and employees

Performance Report	
Team: Soft Dial Tone Team Lead: Date:	% Completion: 30% Target Benefits to Date: Actual Benefits to Date:
Recent Activities	
Achievements	
Implementation Progress	
Benefits Progress Identified Approved WIP Implemented Realized $	
Deliverable Completed	
Outstanding Issues: Decision to Be Made	

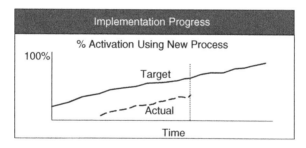

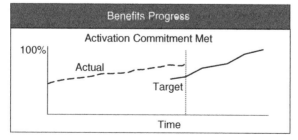

FIGURE 16.12 Synergy Tracking

- To provide the necessary input to steer the integration process; facts-based decision making
- To provide proof that the integration process is delivering value

For joint team management

- To provide an unambiguous feedback mechanism for each work stream
- To monitor mutual work stream interdependencies and their impact
- To enable decision making and clear roadblocks
- To identify and broadcast any wins realized

Synergy tracking using financial data can be quite difficult when a target is integrated in many pieces into an acquirer and using the acquirer's financial systems. A number of options exist for how to reconstruct the business to be able to compare the target's business and synergy results with the acquisition business case (stand-alone and synergies).

An example of the challenges with synergy tracking follows. The target's main product has been integrated into a business unit at the acquirer and there is no possibility to book sales and revenues into two different product codes due to what is available in the current financial system set up under that business unit. The result is that sales have to be manually separated out or by the use of business intelligence tools, which does not give the full picture of the costs associated with those revenues pre-deal. Delivery and supply chain costs might also be mixed. The result is that those costs need to be estimated manually or with a percentage that mirrors how they looked pre-acquisition to build up the stand-alone profitability of the product and its contribution to the bottom line.

CHAPTER CHECKLIST

- What synergies are and how to validate them
- Different ways of structuring a synergy program
- What actions could be needed to capture synergies
- How to mine for more synergies or deal benefits
- How to follow up and track synergies

Unique Cross-Border M&A Transaction Scenarios

Managing Carve-Outs and Transition Service Agreements

Andrew Scola

CHAPTER LEARNING OBJECTIVES—IN THIS CHAPTER, YOU WILL LEARN:

➤ How carve-outs differ from integrations
➤ How deal rationale impacts the integration of carve-outs
➤ Why transition services are necessary
➤ How transition service agreements are structured
➤ Carve-out leading practices around people, process, and technology
➤ Managing and exiting transition service agreements
➤ Why transformation activity often follows on from carve-outs

CHAPTER SUMMARY

This chapter describes what divestitures are, how they differ from integrations, and what the end state of a carve-out can look like. It goes on to describe the key contract associated with carve-outs, the transition service agreement, how it is structured, managed, and exited successfully. Carve-out activity is described from the perspective of people, processes, and tools, and the chapter concludes with a description of what often happens after carve-outs are completed, that is, a transformation.

INTRODUCTION TO DIVESTITURES AND CARVE-OUTS

A *carve-out*, also known as a *separation*, is normally used to refer to the result of the sale (divestment) of a part of a business; however, it may also be used when referring to the permanent division of an organization into

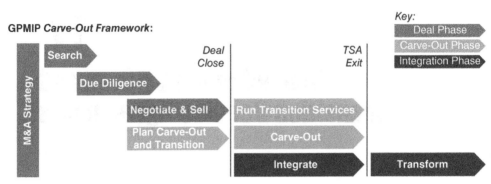

FIGURE 17.1   GPMIP Acquisition Carve-Out Framework™ (ACF)

two or more smaller parts without any sale, or in preparation for a future sale or initial public offering (IPO). It is an end-to-end process as depicted in Figure 17.1. It incorporates every activity from defining the divestiture strategy, selecting and preparing the asset for sale, and going through the motions of setting it up and dealing with the post-close cleanup after the asset has been sold.

A carve-out on the part of a seller is simultaneously accompanied by either the standing-up of a new business, for example, from a private equity buyer, or more commonly the integration of the sold entity (the target) into the acquirer. As with any M&A program, carve-out processes need to be tailored to the specific context, but the majority of the activities described in this chapter will be relevant to all of these types of carve-outs.

The sale transaction between the parties of a divestiture follows a similar path to other M&A deals, but the implications to both the seller and buyer are significantly different from a classic integration, if the target is part of a larger business.

THE CONTEXT OF DIVESTITURE IMPACTS CARVE-OUT PROCESSES

The complexity and timeline of the carve-out program depend largely on the level of integration of the target into the seller organization. For example, the carve-out of an established global product line from a larger portfolio managed together with centralized support functions and systems is likely to be far more difficult to carve out than a recently acquired one-country bolt-on business that is integrated only for the purpose of financial and management reporting.

In addition to level of integration, there are several other important contextual variables that are likely to impact the separation. These include:

- Deal rationale for the sale: financial resources required for another purpose, nonprofitable business area, noncore product or service, management focus, opportunistic approach, regulatory mandate, toxic brand, geographic retraction
- Deal rationale for the acquisition: strategic growth, cost synergies, defensive position, geographic expansion, bolt-on business, future M&A strategy
- Business type of the acquirer: corporate competitor, diversified conglomerate, financial investor (private equity, pension fund, or sovereign wealth fund), management buyout, IPO
- Market announcements and expectations of the deal
- Share or asset deal
- Scope of the business impacted
- Cross-border or multilanguage businesses
- Cultural differences
- If any carve-out activity was started prior to the deal
- In-house M&A program capabilities of the buyer, seller, and target

Each of these impacts and shapes the carve-out scope, structure, and approach. Throughout this chapter, references are made to specific deal variable impacts from the list above.

The first question to answer when integrating a carved-out business is always "What does the buyer want to do with the target?" or to put it another way, "What does the end-state look like for the target?"

- Stand-alone business: no integration
- Autonomous business division or unit: minimal integration
- Integrated into acquirer: full integration

A classic cross-border carve-out is a business unit divestiture to generate cash for another business purpose, where the carve-out is announced and begins after a sale is agreed, and the target is integrated fully into an industry competitor. The underlying rationale is based on which owner can best grow the business. This can be assumed to be the typical carve-out scenario.

DIVESTITURE PROGRAM OVERVIEW

The early deal phases for carve-outs mirror those of M&A integration, described in Chapter 2 on strategy and Chapter 9 on due diligence. However, there are some specifics to carve-outs and some consideration specifically for the divesting company, as illustrated in Figure 17.1.

Who to sell to is a key question and when considering who to approach, the seller is advised to think carefully. Whether the seller approaches several strategic and financial buyers, and considers an IPO at the same time, is largely dependent on the quality of the assets sold. While strategic and financial buyers may be interested in buying a number of assets, an IPO requires the sale of an entire entity that can operate independently.

The information that needs to be prepared is very different for each of these trajectories. Strategic buyers focus on understanding commercial and operational data, including property, product development, price policy, and customer relationships. Financial buyers are likely to also focus on the restructuring and reorganization potential or the stand-alone capability of the organization and, depending on their funding structure, to exit the ownership within five to eight years.

In the case of an IPO, the company needs to satisfy all requirements by the country's regulator to be placed in the capital markets. It is possible to prepare a divestment simultaneously for a sale or an IPO.

The seller needs to decide whether to engage in vendor due diligence (VDD) or not. The benefits are that a VDD simplifies and accelerates the transaction process. It supports a structured divestiture process, and eliminates possible drawbacks and risks leading to potential price reductions or late failure of the transaction. It also provides a decision point for the seller to define the perimeter for the carve-out, what to sell and what to keep. The VDD builds up a profit and loss for the asset to be sold and states how the seller intends to manage important aspects of the carve-out across the functional areas such as IT, HR, staff selection, key systems, and data security. The VDD identifies confidential information early on that is not supposed to be disclosed to potential investors such as competitors prior to signing, or in some cases, close. The VDD provides important negotiation data, and typically leads to strengthened price discussions. It is a convenient and efficient way to answer questions arising through an auction process and thus reduces the extent and time of the potential buyer's due diligence. More important, it provides a strong impression on experienced investors who are specifically seeking properly functioning and well-kept assets.

After signing, and prior to the deal close, a very important planning phase runs in parallel with negotiations focusing not only on setting up the carve-out program, but also establishing how the seller will continue to run the target during the transition phase.

After close, the carve-out, transition services, and the buyer's integration phases are interrelated and run together. A transformation program usually follows straight after integration within the acquirer's business. The following sections detail these carve-out phases.

PLANNING A CARVE-OUT AND TRANSITION

Depending on what is sold, the seller will evaluate various divestment options, and the approach will largely depend on whether a discrete business unit is being divested, or a collection of assets such as brands, plants, and real estate.

Some strategic divestitures are planned a long time in advance and the management team starts to prepare the business by carving it out operationally and functionally. This may follow a market announcement about strategic directions or may be just internal preparation. Carving out the target prior to the sale simplifies the sale and separation overall because the seller can hand over operational control of the business at the agreed close date without having ongoing obligations to service the business. However, since the end-state operating model of the carve-out cannot be known, the carve-out will have to be set up as a stand-alone business, which itself may be less efficient than carving-out for an integration because the processes and systems may reflect the larger seller organization's own, and be too heavy for the target. As a stand-alone business, there are likely to be zero or negative operating synergies.

For the majority of deals, the carve-out is announced internally at the same time as the deal is signed and announced publicly, so carve-out planning starts at this time without preparation. In this phase, the carve-out plans are created at a high level, and the transition services are defined and agreed upon between the buyer and the seller.

Transition Services

A transition service agreement (TSA) is a contract between the seller and the buyer that covers post-deal support for the target to continue operating until such time as it can be set up independently or integrated into the acquirer. They are common practice during divestitures and negotiated and signed prior to the sale and purchase agreement (SPA), or occasionally prior to the deal close if the TSA is complex. The SPA will contain a TSA master schedule, which will contain high-level details of the transition services, and refer to one or more separate TSA documents. The details cannot be known until analyzed by the buyer's and seller's staff as the operation details of any company are complex and internal information. It is very hard for a buyer's

TABLE 17.1 Benefits of Good Transition Service Agreements

Seller	Buyer
Removing deal uncertainty	Assuring business continuity
Higher deal price	Allowing time to plan and implement integration
Quicker deal because buyer can conduct deep-dive due diligence after deal close	
	Allowing time to stand up any new business areas, processes, and systems
Ensuring services are more than outsourced services	
Cover cost of delivering services and set punitive costs for delays	Define service levels
	Clear end date for carve-out to be independent of seller
Clarity on TSA exit	
Establishing good reputation for successfully delivering carve-outs	Better grip on the target

deal team to decide on TSA details without involving a lot of resources in their and the seller's organization, which in most transactions is not possible until the deal has been made public.

Although the terms are often drafted by the seller, who may lay down maximum TSA timelines or charges early in the TSA negotiations, they must be agreed by both parties to the deal. The costs for the TSA could be staggered in such a way that they encourage the buyer to quickly exit the TSA. For example, a first period is free of charge, a second period is according to seller's cost with a small markup, and a third period where remaining services are provided at market price or punitively high cost set by the seller. Without a TSA, the seller would have no obligation to continue supporting the target after the deal closed and the operations of the business could be at risk in many areas. A clear and comprehensive TSA benefits both the seller and the buyer (see Table 17.1).

Transition service agreements should be broken down logically to align with the needs of the target. For large carve-outs this may require separate TSAs by geography or business unit, but most agreements are broken down at a relatively high level into services that define either process areas (e.g., order-to-cash) or functional areas (e.g., HR systems and services).

Between the TSA document itself and the TSA schedules, the specific elements include:

- Reference to the master schedule by a unique identifier
- Termination date
- TSA type

- Seller (provider) business unit, function, process owner, and contact information
- Buyer or target (recipient) business unit, function, process owner, and contact information
- Process name or functional area
- Process or functional area description
- Detailed breakdown of scope
- Explicit exemptions
- Any third-party or major internal interdependencies
- IT systems and infrastructure dependencies, including licenses
- Data management and any conflicts of interest
- Service level key performance metric
- Explanation of service delivery costs, including resource estimates and historical costs
- Monthly fee schedule
- Criteria and costs of extending TSAs past termination date

Although by this stage the buyer has performed due diligence on the target business, it is likely to still be dependent upon the seller to provide detailed accurate information surrounding the TSA scope and breakdown. Where gaps and omissions are identified later, it is in the interest of both parties to find agreeable solutions by providing additional services if necessary.

Reverse TSA and Long-Term Transition Service Agreement

TSAs are normally no longer than 18 months in duration, and cover the provision of services from the seller to the target. There are also two less common types of TSA.

Reverse Transition Service Agreement. In some cases, at the time of deal close, the carved-out business is providing services to other parts of the seller organization. For example, if a carve-out is an international business, then in some countries it may be providing shared services functions across the entire seller organization. If it makes sense to transfer these functions with the deal, the seller would require these services to continue being delivered until it could reestablish its own independent functions. In this case, a reverse transition service agreement is signed in parallel.

Long-Term Transition Service Agreement. Where there are very long business cycles, the provision of transition services may be required for a far longer period of time. This may be necessary in areas such as in heavy manufacturing, construction, or where there are long-term government contracts in place. In these cases long-term TSAs may be signed to ensure continuous services or supply. These contracts may also be accompanied by other agreements such as new sales contracts.

PROGRAM STRUCTURE

As with an integration, a governance structure needs to be established early in the carve-out process to ensure that all plans and activities are coordinated. For cross-border separations, the need to have a clearly defined governance model, with defined roles and responsibilities, becomes even more important.

A key difference with carve-outs, compared to integration, is the structure of the program teams across the seller, target, and buyer. Figure 17.2 shows an example of a carve-out program. Depending on the contextual variables of the deal, there can be three distinct functional teams.

1. The seller teams represent the interests of the seller to ensure that the organization is not impacted by the carve-out, continues to operate and grow, that the carve-out is achieved as quickly as possible, and that the integrity of the seller's data and systems is not compromised in any way.
2. The target teams, initially still reporting through the seller business, represent the interests of the target itself. Throughout the carve-out planning and TSA negotiations, the functional leads of the target ensure that the target business is able to operate effectively and that the TSAs are comprehensive. It is in the interest of the seller to set up a semiautonomous team to represent the target itself to demonstrate to the buyer that this independent functional team concurs with the TSAs and carve-out plans, and to provide continuity for the program throughout the carve-out and integration processes.
3. The buyer teams represent the acquiring organization, and focus on the integration planning.

Functional counterparts work closely together across the businesses, as appropriate, to coordinate plans. Escalation paths and program reporting follow these business lines, to business relationship group/TSA management forum, up to a steering committee with representation across all business teams. At the highest level of escalation, with decision-making authority over the deal itself, it is likely that there is a direct relationship between the seller and buyer executives.

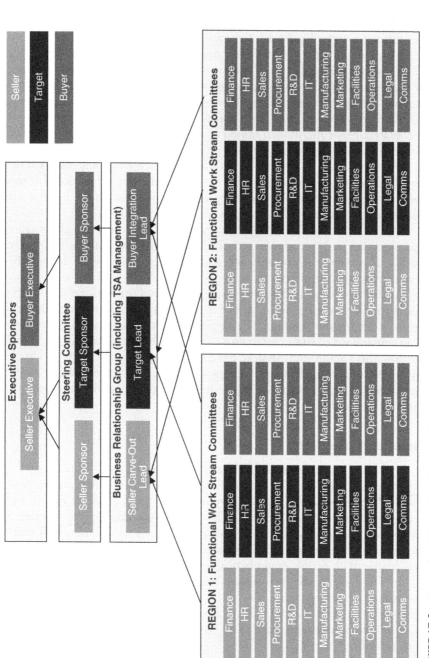

FIGURE 17.2 Example of Carve-Cut Program Structure

This default program structure may need to be tailored in numerous different ways. Figure 17.2 shows a cross-border deal in two regions (e.g., EMEA [Europe, Middle East, Asia] and North America), where the program structure reflects the business model of the seller and the target, in which functional ownership is regional. There may need to be several regional groups reporting through one global business relationship group, and there may need to be country teams below the regional teams, possibly in a matrix reporting model, taking responsibility for local carve-out and integration activities (not shown).

If the end-state is a stand-alone business, then there will be no functional teams representing the buyer at all, and the target functional teams should be given more authority to represent the interests of the buyer early on, and escalate risks and issues early and openly.

Once set up appropriately, the management of the program governance and reporting and its cadence and escalation should be managed carefully. Details of running the program office are described in Chapter 10 on integration management offices.

More important, at close, the target integration team, along with everyone in the target organization, will of course start to report through the new business owner, the acquirer. The target integration team is likely to have been constrained to some extent up to that point by the seller. The target and buyer teams should immediately have full and open workshops to ensure alignment on all carve-out and integration plans. If there are risks or issues, omissions, or organization or leadership gaps, these should be communicated immediately.

Carve-Out Phase—People

For most businesses, the most important resource is talent—the experience, expertise, and creativity of the people who run it. All M&A deals are challenging because at the same time as requiring the most professionalism and dedication from its staff, the company is often putting people through a tough time, personally and professionally. There is no escaping this completely, but recognizing that this is the case, taking people matters seriously, and dealing with people empathetically will really mitigate risks.

In a carve-out, the deal-makers need to agree at a high level on the intention for staff transition. There will neither be a right solution, nor easy boundaries to draw, but all staff related in any way to the target business must either transfer with the deal to the target or acquirer business or stay with the seller.

The mechanism by which staff can be identified, consulted with, and transferred is subject to local employment law regulations, which vary greatly between different countries. Broadly speaking, North American and Asia Pacific regulations are more protective of the employer's rights than European regulations, which champion employee rights. The cost and complexity of carving out employees in Europe is far greater, and the achievable timeline many times slower. It is common for large cross-border carve-outs to proceed at quite a different pace across regions, with the mainland European countries often the last to complete the deal and successfully carve out the employees.

Because of these implications of transitioning staff, usually only staff who support the target business 100% are transferred with the carve-out, and all others remain with the seller. Shared service functions within the seller organization typically will not transfer any people, and the TSA period is used to recruit and build a new team, or switch over to the acquirer's corporate services.

The seller and buyer need to agree on a joint communication plan, where an important part is how to inform and motivate employees during the TSA period and beyond. The new owners need to be visible to the employees and rumors managed in communication as people might suspect a hidden agenda. Transparency, honesty, and clarity are key to show a clear plan of when decisions will be made affecting employees. It is, of course, an easier message if the buyer can announce that it will invest in the business.

There may be examples where key individuals find themselves on the wrong side of the line from their personal perspective. For example, a talented manager within the seller may be rotated around to a management position in the target at the time of the deal, but prefer to cycle quickly back into the acquirer prior to close in order to remain with the seller. While the preferences of key individuals ought to be sensitively understood and taken into consideration, the buyer needs to be aware of any key changes to avoid losing any stars. Identification of key resources and retention planning for those individuals is common practice.

As with an acquisition, leadership and organization announcements are important immediately after close to ensure that governance is clear. The easiest transitions are those where the existing leadership team of the target remains in place, and the reporting line into the acquirer is announced. Providing the management team is supported by the acquirer, it reduces risks to continue with existing management teams in place. If the acquirer wants to make new leadership announcements, then these should be planned in advance, coordinated with a settlement or swapping out of existing management, and announced as early as it is appropriate to do so. Where the acquirer has been able to assess the target staff down two or three levels, quick announcements on a top-down basis are advisable.

Carve-Out Phase—Processes

Careful and complete process definition is important during carve-outs, especially for the buyer. Across all areas of the business that are impacted by the carve-out, it is advisable to perform an analysis of the changes, and the tool used to structure this is called a *process blueprint*. The process for using the blueprint can be used on either the carve-out or integration side of a divestiture.

The blueprint is ultimately owned by a functional work stream lead, but there may also be business process owners for some or all functional areas, on both sides of the deal, who have more direct expertise in the processes within the blueprint. The blueprint includes all business processes within a particular functional area. It is broken down further into processes at different levels of detail, and can run to hundreds of rows. The appropriate level to go down to will depend on the complexity of the business, resources available to complete the exercise, and the available information. The more comprehensive the blueprint, the more one mitigates the risks of aspects of the business not being prepared.

As shown in Figure 17.3, the blueprint shows, against each process or functional area, both the process detail and any systems used by the carve-out, the business, and the buyer currently.

Blueprints work as well for cross-border M&A as any other deal, and the value that they are likely to bring is higher because of the likely complexity of the process changes. In addition to functional breakdown, it may be useful to use region, country, or offices to further break down the blueprint, and this should be done where there are differences between locations. In a highly centralized organization with global processes, this will not be necessary, but if there are distinct processes impacting the carved-out entity then this will be helpful.

Once as-is processes are understood and documented, then the next step is for end-state processes to be agreed upon. For the seller producing a blueprint, the end-state will mean the retained business operating without the carve-out. For the buyer, this means the acquired business, either stand-alone or integrated into its own business. There are various choices from which to select the end-state process. The carve-out may have the same process as the seller at end-state, may continue to use a distinct process already in place within the carve-out, may be integrated into the buyer's process already, or it could have a completely new process or some form of hybrid. The latter, where elements are taken from different businesses, is often referred to as "best of both," and having examples of these helps to demonstrate that an acquirer isn't simply throwing out everything of the acquired business (carve-out or otherwise) and looking to retain the best processes.

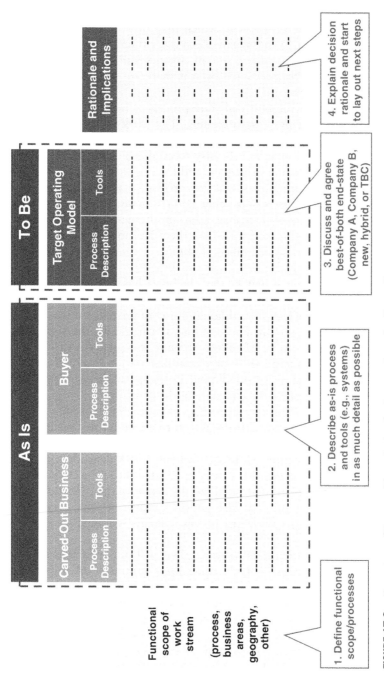

FIGURE 17.3 Overview of Process Blueprinting for Integration of a Carve-Out

New processes at end-state might be the best permanent solution, but could also be an interim process, which may be required for example to achieve TSA exit in a given timeline when there is no time for the right end-state process to be adopted, or system changes will not be ready in time. These may need to be considered even if these are temporary "backward steps" for the business.

The selection of the best end-state process is iterative, and of course, will depend on each process, in context. The work stream lead, or leads, across the businesses will start by analyzing the most appropriate end-state. In most cases, it will be relatively easy to establish the required end-state, working from the guiding principles, and looking at the system dependencies, scalability, operating costs, and the perceived maturity of the processes. Naturally, if the process is dependent upon systems or teams that will no longer be available after TSA exit, then an alternative end-state must be defined. Once defined, processes where there are no easy or obvious end-states can be more easily identified, and more a detailed investigation will often follow.

In an industry sale, it may be that the buyer has established centralized processes that the carve-out needs to adopt. This does not have to be done in one jump prior to TSA exit, although for core processes it may be easier to do this, and is common. For stand-alone carve-outs, the suitability of seller processes needs to be taken into account. It is often the case that even efficient processes in large seller organizations are too heavy or no longer efficient when applied to the stand-alone business and therefore new lighter processes are required for the end-state of the carve-out.

The blueprint will usually stop short of getting into specifics about the timeline or activities required to transition to the end-state, but it can contain contextual information, for example, decision rationale, synergy and operating cost implications of process changes, TSA dependencies, and so on. When approved, blueprints can be translated into project charters and detailed integration plans that build out the details of the transition of these processes during and after the TSA phases. Cutover of some processes can continue early, but typically many process changes will be done just before or at TSA exit.

Processes in multinational organizations will of course depend on the structure of the business—highly centralized multinational organizations provide greater challenges in this area, and big bang approaches become increasingly risky. Consider de-risking process changes by prioritizing the big ones. The major ERP-dependent processes such as procure to pay, order to cash, and record to report are often cut over first in a big bang approach, leaving other processes to follow after the stability of the enterprise resource planning system is established.

Carve-Out Phase—Technology

Technology infrastructure and systems are usually on the critical path when it comes to the carve-out timeline. They must be taken into account and planned around, but they follow the above sections on people and processes because technology should not overwhelmingly determine end-state processes. It is a frequent lesson learned from carve-outs that existing systems from the seller are completely inappropriate for a new smaller carve-out entity, which often does not need the same level of process and can struggle to maintain and pay for the inherited systems.

A carve-out is an opportunity to move away from old or inappropriate systems. However, the carve-out must not be used as an excuse to start developing several new systems. Not only will the seller not wish to allow this under the TSA because it will extend the timeline, but the carved-out business may become overwhelmed by "unnecessary" changes at an already busy time. Any new systems must be carefully prioritized.

Where the carve-out becomes a stand-alone business, a "clone-and-go" approach is often the default. A clone-and-go involves replicating the seller's system, including the data and necessary underlying infrastructure, then meticulously removing all data that are not transferring with the deal. This is usually specified in the TSA and managed by the seller, so that their data are secure throughout. The scope, scale, and history of these data need to be clearly defined and agreed to by both parties.

Alternatives to clone-and-go are to move straight to the acquirer's system by migrating data, to acquire a new fit-for-purpose system for the carve-out business, or to stop using a system if a process is simple enough. Caution should obviously be taken before committing to a migration to a new system, and data migrations between systems managed by different companies within a short time period can be the cause of significant system and operational issues.

To support understanding and defining system changes around carve-outs, the process blueprint shown in Figure 17.4 can certainly include system dependencies next to process steps. Keeping end-state design process-centric ensures that the integration team focuses on the process changes while keeping the system dependencies clearly in mind. To support this, a systems landscape document can also be created to focus on the as-is and end-state systems, including details such as the geographic scope of each system, who manages and supports each system, and any outsourced or cloud-based services.

While it would be usual to make decisions about whole systems, which are likely to impact multiple end-state processes in the blueprint, it is possible to decrease or increase the functional scope of a system. It may be

Business Area	Process	Pre-Close			End-State		
		Seller	Carved-Out Business	Buyer	Seller	Carved-Out Business	Buyer
Finance	Process 1	System A	System A	System L	System A	System L	System L
	Process 2	System B	System B	System M	System B	System M	System M
	Process 3			System N		System N	System N
HR	Process 1	System C	System E	System O	System C	System O	System O
	Process 2	System D	System D	System P	System D	System P	System P
	Process 3						
Sales	Process 1	System F	System F	System Q	System F	System Q	System Q
	Process 2	System G	System G	System R	System G	System R	System R
	Process 3	System H	System H		System H		
Procurement	Process 1	System I	System I	System S	System I	System S	System S
	Process 2	System J	System J	System T	System J	System T	System T
	Process 3	System K	System K	System U	System K	System Z	System U
and so on	and so on	and so on	and so on	and so on	and so on	and so on	and so on

FIGURE 17.4 System Landscape

required, for example, to clone a certain seller system purely for the functionality that it provides in one country that is otherwise not supported by the buyer's system.

System cutovers are critical to success, and while inherently more risky than typical system go-lives, carefully implemented integration and cutover plans should mitigate the risks. Delays around system go-lives are particularly problematic around carve-outs because of the dependencies of processes and the TSA exits (see "Exiting the Transition Service Agreement" further on), so special focus should remain on any development and testing activity required within the carve-out or subsequent integration programs to ensure that they do not slip.

IT infrastructure changes will be required in addition to the system changes. These range from server and data center moves to network equipment, mail, and calendar provision, personal computing and telephony provision and support, and so on. Wherever possible, details of major infrastructure changes should be spelled out in the TSA as well.

MANAGING THE TRANSITION SERVICE AGREEMENT

The TSA starts the day the deal closes, but in reality the behaviors start as soon as the deal is agreed, and affects everyone involved in the seller, the carve-out, and the acquirer after the announcement is made. It is natural that people start to think about the implications on themselves, their teams and co-workers, and their jobs. It is important that the announcement be as clear as possible about the intentions for people. In the seller, teams that are supporting the carve-out for the duration of the TSA, but not transferring, will inevitably start reprioritizing their own commitments, regardless of the TSA detail. A brand marketing manager in the seller, for example, who is responsible for a portfolio of products, is less likely to give the same amount of time and energy to campaigns for divested products while waiting to hand them over to someone else.

For this reason, it is important to actively manage the TSA early to ensure that the commitments within it are delivered. The TSA and any accompanying documents will be as detailed as the deal teams were able to make them given the available information, but there will always be a requirement to make interpretations of the TSA. To manage this, and to monitor the services provided and prepare for the exit of the various elements of the TSA, a TSA manager is appointed on both sides. The TSA managers do not need to be executives, but must have immediate access to the executive sponsors to escalate issues. TSA managers should have weekly calls or meetings to discuss progress, service levels, and progress on both sides.

Adding, changing, or exiting TSA services need to follow a strict process as the impact could be that the seller reassigns its staff to other tasks and it will be hard to resume the service in case of mistakes. Sometimes a part of a TSA service is carried out for the seller by a third party where the seller needs to follow the outsourcing contract and give notice to discontinue a service, or for the outsourcing partner to participate in cutover activities.

Although the roles of TSA managers can be adversarial because in many areas the objectives, costs, and concerns will be opposing, the M&A reputation of both businesses is at stake. A firm but reasonable attitude is required on both sides to ensure a successful carve-out, which neither party wants to see at risk. Transparency about progress and risks on both sides is essential. If projects to prepare for system cutover are not progressing on track, for example, both sides need to recognize and plan accordingly, even if there are cost implications. It is better to make tough decisions about transition services, and accept additional costs if necessary, than to see failed TSA exits or impact business continuity.

Good faith is required in particular around service levels. A service level agreement (SLA) may be signed along with the TSA that defines the precise metrics that the transition services are expected to be delivered to. However, there are many reasons why this may not be done, including former service levels not being quantifiable, and therefore it is common for the seller to agree to continue delivering "the same level of services" to the buyer under the TSA. The TSA manager within the seller should endeavor to make sure that the business is indeed delivering the services at the same level as before. The executive sponsors may need to ensure appropriate resourcing to protect this obligation, and be prepared to ring-fence or if necessary fight internally to do so.

Exiting the Transition Service Agreement

The approximate timing and the approach for TSA exit should all be planned at the time the TSAs are drawn up. It is quite normal for TSA timelines to determine the integration approach and even end-state design as TSA exit is a priority. The carve-out and integration program progress should be shared regularly between the TSA managers so there are no surprises, and TSA exit should be counted down.

It is usual for TSAs to be exited in phases or clusters, grouped according to the way the transition services have been defined within the TSA, which will normally be by geography, by processes, or by major systems.

Allow one month of contingency after major go-lives before TSA exit, particularly for the final TSA exit, which is often aligned with the ERP system cutover. Cutting back becomes nearly impossible when the services are not provided by your own organization—the seller will have planned the reallocation of those resources immediately and will not be obligated to support failed TSA exits.

Many TSAs allow the buyer to set specific TSA exit dates, but have an aggressive final deadline for TSA exit, by which the carve-out must be independent of the seller's processes, systems, and organization. Failure to carve out within this time will result in the need to negotiate an extension, for which the service costs are often punitive. It is not in the seller's interests for any carved-out businesses to fail so unless impossible or unreasonable, the seller should agree to limited necessary extensions.

Transformation

"Mission accomplished" is usually announced at the final TSA exit, sometimes before, but there is often very much more work to do before the carve-out is really running in business-as-usual mode. The TSA period normally only allows for absolutely necessary process and system changes, may have left several cloned systems that were intended as interim stages only, and processes that are heavy because they were suited to a much larger organization or a different operating model. A second phase of change activity is therefore scheduled after the TSA exit, which could be called "transformation"—the purpose of this is to optimize the now independent business, or where appropriate to integrate it into the buyer.

Often these are larger, longer projects that are able to move from interim processes to desired end-state processes. These do not normally fall within the integration budget or program.

CHAPTER CHECKLIST

- There are many similarities between integration and carve-out programs. Often a carve-out and an integration of that carve-out are run in parallel by the seller and buyer, respectively.
- Carve-out specifics depend greatly on the context of the divestiture, and whether a buyer has already been identified.
- Transition periods are necessary for business continuity during the separation, and transition service agreements are signed alongside almost every divestiture deal agreement.
- Managing the people issues is central to successful carve-outs.
- As-is and end-state processes should be comprehensively mapped out using process blueprints.

- Clone-and-go approach is the default for processes and systems, but may not always be appropriate.
- Careful and transparent management of TSAs is essential to the successful running and exit of TSAs.
- Transformation may be required post–TSA exit to optimize the new business.

CHAPTER 18

Joint Ventures

Thomas Kessler

CHAPTER LEARNING OBJECTIVES—IN THIS CHAPTER, YOU WILL LEARN:

- ➤ What the process steps are to set up a successful joint venture
- ➤ How joint venture characteristics link to joint venture strategies
- ➤ The most commonly used deal structure for joint ventures
- ➤ How to structure a successful joint venture agreement
  - ➤ Definition of the business
  - ➤ Completion actions
  - ➤ Directors and management
  - ➤ Funding and financing the joint venture
  - ➤ Restrictions and rights of shareholders
  - ➤ Business planning and accounting
  - ➤ Termination
  - ➤ Confidentiality
  - ➤ Other key joint venture clauses

CHAPTER SUMMARY

This chapter describes how to set up a successful joint venture. It leads the discussion through the design steps, strategic characteristics, and most commonly used deal structure. It continues to discuss how to set up a proper joint venture agreement and describes the most important elements of any joint venture contract.

THE JOINT VENTURE LIFE CYCLE

Joint venture (JV) life cycles are very much dependent on the objective of the JV. Companies that are interested in contractual JVs will "borrow" the necessary resources required to achieve their business objectives. Borrowing resources as described in the resource pathways framework by Laurence Capron and discussed in Chapter 4 of this book will entail setting up contractual structures that describe and guide the JV partners on how to work closely together and provide the products and services bought by their customers.

If the objective is to establish a JV company, then the JV life cycle incorporates all steps of a typical carve-out and those of an acquisition. For the assets to be contributed to the JV company, the carve-out steps are relevant. In order to combine both partner operations into a JV company, the steps performed for an acquisition are also relevant.

Process Steps

The first step, as in every transaction, needs to be the *alignment of strategic corporate goals with the M&A vision*. Essentially companies will perform all steps necessary that we described in the strategic selection process previously. This alignment may result in a JV company to be the desired approach to implement the corporate strategy.

The next step is to contact the future partner and to establish a solid *basis for a joint business*. The discussions will include:

- The strategic and competitive positioning, including business, financial, cash flow, and marketing plans
- The contributions of each side and who gets what out of the JV
- The legal and tax structure of the joint company and who controls what as part of the JV
- The timing of the transaction and when to start approaching the market
- Any approvals needed by third parties

After that, each party needs to think through how they will *carve-out any potential assets contributed* to the joint venture. This entails all steps described above, including tax structures, operational carve-out, and transfer of staff.

Most important beyond the operational aspects of the carve-out will be the *valuation of the contribution*. Based on the valuation, both parties identify the value they contribute and thus define the share each partner will initially own in the JV.

An important next step is to carry out the *due diligence* on each other's business or asset contributions and to validate the value of the assets, contracts, and client relationships that are transferred into the organization.

As part of the due diligence, both partners need to engage in designing a *high-level post-merger integration approach*. Given that no signing has occurred and anti-trust approval may still be necessary, it is essential that any joint integration planning wait until anti-trust approval has been received.

Contract negotiations are the next step leading to a central milestone: the signing of the sale and purchase agreement (SPA) between the JV partners.

Alongside preparing the final contractual agreement, both companies need to establish a *joint communication strategy* on the "why" for the deal, who is going to be on the leadership team, and what the strategic direction is going to be for the joint business development.

With signing in close reach, both partners need to start the *carve-out preparation phase*. Resources need to be identified, and actions defined and prioritized so that the start of the actual decoupling of the assets can kick off once signing and anti-trust clearance have taken place.

During signing and closing post-anti-trust approval, the *final integration planning* needs to occur, which includes integration actions, detailed synergy development, cultural alignment, and planning for Day One. In addition, finance needs to start thinking about closing accounts and the purchase price allocation.

Post-closing transition teams need to launch the integration of both sides, and the business plan is implemented.

Ultimately it is then all about executing the business, marketing, and integration plans.

Designing the Joint Venture Strategy

A cornerstone of the JV strategy is to define the joint venture type, meaning the type of activities that are brought together and that will be the driving force between both firms, and last, the deal structure. The next sections will explain in more detail these foundational principles. The strategy section will close with walking through our approach of establishing a JV agreement that highlights the key elements and serves as a solid checklist for companies establishing a JV company.

Joint Venture Types

There are essentially three ways to establish JVs. One way is to establish a JV company, another is to establish a contractual JV, and a third way is to co-own assets.

All three JV types are different from a legal point of view. JV companies are typically established as limited liability companies. Contractual JVs are not a legal entity. The ventures hold title to the relevant assets and the parties agree by contract to provide one or more services and relevant operating assets usually on a long-term basis. As for co-ownership, here the parties co-own assets. Contractual JVs and co-ownership structures can be found frequently in Asia, while JV companies are preferred in North America and Europe. Nevertheless, JV companies do get established in Asia on a frequent basis. They are just not automatically the default choice.

Joint Venture Characteristics

What is the nature of a JV? In talking about successful JV characteristics, one thing comes to mind immediately. JVs are swaps of complementary capabilities, nothing more and nothing less. The concept of swaps fits well with the resource pathway because a resource, know-how, or complementary skill exchange is the underlying basis for a swap. Thus, many JVs are established around a swap of:

- Product for market
- Research and development (R&D) for manufacturing
- Procurement for market
- Value chain swaps
- Step approach to divestiture

For example, in a *product for market* JV, one partner provides a technology or product to a foreign market asking the partnering firm in the joint venture to provide access to solid and existing commercial relationships in those markets.

R&D for manufacturing JVs capitalize on low-cost manufacturing in one country while leveraging the R&D capabilities in another country.

Procurement for market swaps leverage the strength of a supplier to provide low-cost raw materials while capitalizing on the buyer's ability to market the final product in their marketplace. We have witnessed this strategy as a particularly helpful one in the chemicals industry where an environment of volatile raw material prices on the one hand and high investment cost to replicate a raw material production on the other hand enabled two competitors with unequal strength to form a joint venture and benefit from aligning their respective strengths in raw material production and market penetration.

Value chain swaps are an exchange of one part of the value chain for access to another part of the value chain. The oil and gas industry is a good example where upstream and downstream activities are swapped.

Step approach to divestiture is used by large conglomerates that establish joint ventures with competitors in order to gain scale and efficiency. We have seen this approach used by Siemens and Philips. In case the JV is not able to achieve the desired efficiencies, one of the partners will opt out and sell to the other partner. Typically, the buying partner is the partner that is closer to the core of the business the JV is focusing on. Siemens had other businesses outside of fixed and mobile networks and when they recognized that the joint venture with Nokia would not yield the desired results they decided to sell to Nokia. A similar approach was used and implemented by Philips with LG in LCD flat-panel production.

Deal Structure

The typical deal structure for a JV company is that both partners set up a new entity and contribute either assets and liabilities or the shares of an existing subsidiary into a newly formed JV company.

In the case when assets and liabilities are contributed, we are talking about an asset deal. The ability to cherry-pick assets and liabilities that will be contributed to the joint venture is a significant advantage of this approach. This will also trigger an asset step-up for accounting and tax purposes with respect to the assets received. Contracts with suppliers need to be renegotiated and employee contracts need to be novated for everyone transferring into the JV company. For a schematic picture of a JV structured as an asset deal, see Figure 18.1.

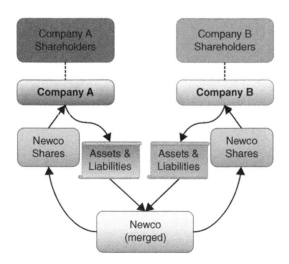

FIGURE 18.1 Schematic Picture of an Asset Deal Paid for by Cash or Paid for by Stock

In the case when an entire entity is contributed into the JV company, we use a share deal approach. This approach could result in a largely tax-free structure. For this, the contribution needs to be paid for with voting stock of the JV as consideration.

Ultimately deal structures are as manifold and complex as legal entity, tax structures, and local laws permit. We therefore stress the importance of involving legal and tax experts to address the specific issues that companies may find in their organizations. In this respect, it goes without saying that companies not only review the impact a specific structure will have on the joint venture but even more important what the consequences will be on the contributing parent company.

Introduction to Structuring Joint Venture Agreements

Structuring successful joint ventures is largely based on designing an agreement that incorporates all operational success factors shown in Figure 18.2 as we know them today. These success factors are:

- Focus on complementary skill development and an even balance of skills
- Handling fear and suspicion through appropriate legal and operational structures
- Ensure an equal balance of strength so that no partner solely relies on the other

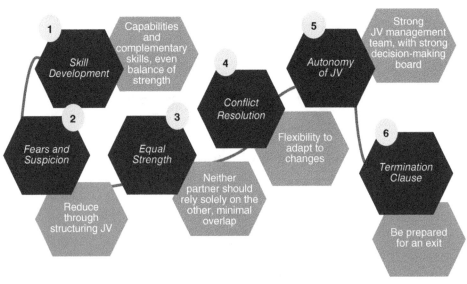

FIGURE 18.2 Operating Characteristics of Successful Strategic Alliances

- Establish mechanisms that enable amicable conflict resolution
- Most critical of all factors is the full autonomy of a strong JV management team and a board that is willing to actively drive decisions
- Last, it is important to establish procedures and a framework for terminating the JV

Following this introduction, the next step is to dive into designing a solid JV agreement. It goes without saying that crafting the joint venture agreement requires business and strategic thinking as well as a strong legal focus to make it a good solid contract. See Figure 18.3.

The introduction of the agreement should name all parties involved, including the definition of their ownership. It also should focus on defining the terms and the common behaviors applicable in the JV going forward.

Definition of the Business

In the definition of the business section, the company describes what the JV will do as a business, and what products and services it will provide and sell. It also will define its location and the regions it will carry out its business. Highlight what is defined as performance in the agreement to ensure this is clearly understood among the parties. Last for this section it is important to include a "good faith" clause. This states that all JV parties will commit to implement the strategic vision designed to move the JV forward.

Completion Actions

This section of the JV agreement describes what actions the partners have to perform before the JV can be completed. Post-signing both parties should

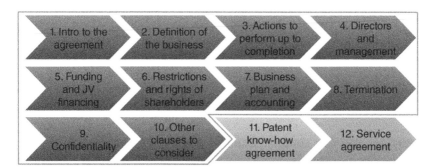

FIGURE 18.3 Core Elements of a Joint Venture Agreement Augmented by Additional Agreements for Patents and Services

set the location and, as soon as possible pending the approval process, the closing date. It is wise to appoint the management team as soon as the approval process is successfully completed, so that the integration of all contributions can start.

Among the actions should also be triggering the closing accounts so that right after the closing both partners have a solid basis to clear any value adjustments. The same holds true for the purchase price allocation. This also can be started between signing and closing and should be finalized as soon as possible post-closing to establish the appropriate opening balance sheet for the JV company. Other typical actions are any regulatory approval processes, and defining the process of transferring financial funds so that this can be executed right after closing.

Actions to abstain from during signing and closing are any changes to the technology, assets contributed, or actions that would change the business in such a material form that it would significantly impact the valuation and strategic orientation of the JV as negotiated.

Directors and Management

The JV parties need to be clear who and how many they will appoint for a leadership position in the JV. Based on this cornerstone the discussion about who will fulfill what role is necessary. This will start from chairman, CEO, and CFO, to any other C-level role that is required to run the business.

Any nonexecutive board members or supervisory board members also need to be named. In this section, companies further need to define the frequency, location, calling process, and quorum of board meetings.

This also includes defining a process to establish the board meeting agenda, associated documentation and distribution of such documents, as well as to negotiate how to deal with items not on the agenda that are brought forward at or shortly before a board meeting.

Essential to the independence of the management are the rules that define which business transactions need approval and what the required voting power will be and which business transactions can be performed by the management team without ownership or board approval.

Last, this section is well placed to define the location, calling process, and quorum of the annual general meeting of the JV company.

Funding and Financing the Joint Venture

Funding and financing the JV is an essential section in the agreement. Companies should think through the financial requirements and terms and conditions that are needed to fund the JV company properly.

This starts with the initial funding and establishing clear rules about who will be funding the operations and what the funding party will receive in return for such funds.

It further sets the baseline for subsequent funding, for example, it defines the threshold at which subsequent funding needs to be approved and who will provide what form of security if a financing institution is incorporated in a subsequent or even the initial funding round.

Companies also need to set the rules for potential third-party ownership if outside parties, for example, parties that do not belong to the JV partner group companies, are involved in providing financing.

Restrictions and Rights of Shareholders

The rights and restrictions section of the JV agreement defines what the partners are permitted to do, what their rights are, and what they are precluded from doing.

A solid noncompete with regard to business, geographies, clients, employees, and associated subsidiaries or companies will define that the partners are under no circumstances to compete with each other or poach the other partner's customers and employees.

If in the previous agreement sections the partners defined that upon providing the initial financing and contributing assets the parent would receive, for example, shares in the JV company, then they need to define in this section the transfer and issuance of shares as the corresponding right of the contributing party.

Typically alongside these rights both parties will reach an agreement on the lock-up period. A lock-up period defines the holding period for shares during which no sale may occur.

The parties need to also agree on the rules to issue preemption rights to acquire shares for sale by any other joint venture party, including the order of these preemption rights. For some companies it might seem slightly delicate but it is nevertheless important to establish a framework about the terms under which any one party may acquire the shares of an insolvent shareholder in the joint venture.

Looking from a selling shareholder's point of view, the partners need to set rules to transfer shares to nonshareholders. If this was to occur, appropriate tag along or drag along rights need to be predefined in the contractual agreements. A tag along right represents the right to sell with another party without mutual consent to ensure a shareholder does not end up in a potential minority position, which largely impacts their rights. A drag along right represents the right to demand of another shareholder to sell their shares with the selling party to ensure a majority of shares will change hands.

Finally, JV partners may discuss exit strategies that may be structured using call or put options. These would provide a minority partner the right to exit the joint venture and another party the right to acquire their position in the joint venture. This often happens when we have three or more part joint ventures. In case options are used to structure an exit the contract needs to define the option expiry date, notice, the exercise date, and how the price for the underlying shares is established at the exercise date.

Last, this section of the JV agreement needs to set the parameters for the necessary voting power to agree on any future issuance of new shares.

Business Planning and Accounting

In this section business planning, accounting, and taxation will be established. Key questions to negotiate are which accounting laws to apply and which tax laws the JV will have to follow. Where documents will be stored might be an important question to define when the joint venture covers countries that have very different laws. If documents or copies thereof are stored in a country where easy access to books and records is given, then it will eliminate the fear and suspicion factor to some degree.

Regular reporting about the business development, such as monthly management accounts, audited accounts of the JV company, and any data required to support compliance requests and file tax returns in the country of the parent's origin, may be a mandatory requirement. Further with regard to reporting, the parties need to decide what planning and reporting documents the JV company will provide to the board to ensure proper decision making. This typically includes an annualized updated business plan, cash flow planning including working capital and capital expenditure requirements, monthly profit and loss and balance sheet, operating budgets for subsequent years, and the deadline of submission of such documents and budgets. Most important on budgets is to establish a default clause detailing how to deal with an impasse if the board cannot agree on the business plan and operating budgets.

Furthermore, a point of discussion will typically be the ownership of tax reliefs and trading losses if they occur. This should be clearly defined in the agreement.

Termination

We discussed in the introduction the need to define the conditions under which the JV company would be terminated. Termination may be necessary beyond the situation that one partner wants to leave the JV. Other causes for a termination might be an initial public offering, a court order, or that the JV is in violation of applicable laws. Sometimes unanimous resolution by shareholders and creditors or simply reaching a predefined date and the appropriately provided notice by one shareholder will cause a termination of the JV.

If that occurs, both parties need to follow a preset plan that was determined before the signing of the deal. This should include rights to trade names, licenses, and other contributed IP and return thereof as well as returning any other rights or liabilities or guarantees provided to those that own it. When dissolving the JV, its assets and liabilities may need to be distributed among the shareholders. If shared ownership exists they need to be split according to predefined rules (ownership or other means).

Termination clauses define regularly the applicable valuation methodologies to sell the shares in the JV to another party. We have witnessed several approaches with regard to valuation and termination. One way is to appoint an independent third party to carry out the valuation to eliminate bias and facilitate the termination among the parties. A completely different approach to the commonly thought approach of facilitating the termination is to make it more difficult by establishing significant discounts that would apply in case one party wants out prematurely. This later approach has the objective to retain the strength of the JV from the beginning, and was used for example by Reuters and Dow Jones when setting up their JV called Factiva.

Confidentiality

Any JV agreement needs to define the extent, nature, and treatment of confidential information, as well as what it covers, including information acquired about customers, suppliers, business assets, or affairs while being involved with the JV or during the negotiations toward forming the JV.

The agreement also should identify circumstances where confidentiality does not apply (i.e., court order) and clarify that each party involved has to ensure confidentiality can be adhered to (i.e., technically, clear order, etc.)

Last, the timing of the confidentiality agreement including "lockout provisions" preventing one partner from conducting parallel negotiations should be established to ensure you are on a solid path toward signing a successful deal.

Other Key Joint Venture Clauses

Beyond what was discussed earlier, there are a number of other clauses that need to be discussed and set straight.

Warranties. Define the warranties that will apply for all parties directly or indirectly involved in the strategic alliance. This should include the minimum service levels and product qualities that need to be met.

Variations and Waivers. Define the necessary exceptions and flexibility to clauses needed in this agreement.

Cost. Define how the parties will split the cost associated with the transaction.

Good Faith. The JV parties establish a mutual understanding that each party is acting in good faith. The agreement should specify what this means to all involved.

Third-Party Rights. Define the limitations any third party may apply.

Notice. Define what the term "notice" under this agreement constitutes.

Interest. Define the interest on late payments.

Language. Define the language of the JV.

Legal. Define the governing law, jurisdiction, and the process and location of any potential arbitration, as well as the term force majeure, what a notice constitutes.

As the parties discuss within this JV agreement or in a separate agreement the use of intellectual property (IP) rights and know-how, they need to address a clear definition of the obligations and rights of the licensor and those of the licensee. Typically the licensor will be required to provide mandatory updates and upgrades of any know-how or technical assistance provided as well as regular quality controls and checkups. With such rules comes the need to specify the duration of the license, and the rules that will govern the protection of any patents provided.

Thus a related question that always needs to be resolved in IP transfer or license agreements is the ownership rights of any development triggered or performed by the JV during its existence. This is a sensitive area, particularly with a view toward a potential termination of the JV in the future, because at that time the partner companies no longer talk only about how to return the IP that was licensed but also who holds the ownership in the IP developed by the JV.

As long as the JV is in operation, the IP provider or licensor is required to provide the needed warranties, liability indemnification, and insurance. Finally, the parties should align on whether sublicensing and subcontracting are permitted or not, which brings up the last issue, the issue of compensation in the form of royalty fees. Royalty fee rules need to cover in detail the nature and extent of such financial compensation.

CHAPTER CHECKLIST

- What the process steps are to set up a successful JV
- How JV characteristics link to JV strategies
- What are the most commonly used deal structures for JVs
- How do companies best perform an integration due diligence?
- How to structure a successful JV agreement
- What are the key elements to address
  - Definition of the business
  - Completion actions
  - Directors and management
  - Funding and financing the JV
  - Restrictions and rights of shareholders
  - Business planning and accounting
  - Termination
  - Confidentiality
  - Other key JV clauses

Index

Note: Page numbers in *italics* indicate figures and tables.

Printed and bound by CPI Group (UK) Ltd, Croydon, CR0 4YY

16/04/2025

14658444-0003